From the Enemy's Point of View

MAP 1
The Araweté in South America. Location of indigenous groups most cited in text

Tapirapé = groups belonging to Tupi-Guarani linguistic family
Kayapó = groups belonging to non-Tupi families
Juruna = groups belonging to other Tupi branches
(Tupinamba) = extinct groups

Eduardo Viveiros de Castro

From the Enemy's Point of View

Humanity and Divinity in an Amazonian Society

Translated by Catherine V. Howard

The University of Chicago Press
Chicago & London

Eduardo Viveiros de Castro is professor of anthropology at the Museu Nacional do Brasil, Rio de Janeiro.

The University of Chicago Press, Chicago 60637
The University of Chicago Press, Ltd., London

Printed in the United States of America
01 00 99 98 97 96 95 94 93 92 5 4 3 2 1
ISBN (cloth): 0-226-85801-4
ISBN (paper): 0-226-85802-2

Originally published as *Araweté: os deuses canibais* (Rio de Janeiro: Jorge Zahar Editor LTDA), © 1986, Eduardo Viveiros de Castro.

Library of Congress Cataloging-in-Publication Data

Castro, Eduardo Batalha Viveiros de.
[Araweté. English]
From the enemy's point of view : humanity and divinity in an Amazonian society / Eduardo Viveiros de Castro : translated by Catherine V. Howard.
p. cm.
Translation of: Araweté.
Includes bibliographical references and index.
1. Araweté Indians. 2. Tupi Indians—Religion and mythology. 3. Indians of South America—Brazil—Religion and mythology. 4. Cannibalism—Brazil. I. Title.
F2520.1.A77C3713 1992
299'.883—dc20 91-31969
CIP

The paper used in this publication meets the minimum requirements of the American National Standard for Information Sciences—Permanence of Paper for Printed Library Materials, ANSI Z39.48-1984.

To Déborah, my wife

Car, décidément, l'étranger, la brousse, l'éxterieur nous envahissent de toutes parts. Nous sommes tous, soit des chasseurs qui renions tout, nous vouons volontairement au monde du dehors pour être pénétrés, faire notre nourriture et nous enorgueillir de certaines forces supérieures, grandes comme le sang qui bout au coeur des animaux, l'inspiration fatalement diabolique, le vert des feuilles et la folie; soit des possédés que cette même marée du dehors vient un jour déborder et qui, au prix de mille tourments qui parfois les font mourir, acquièrent le droit de signer définitivement le pacte avec l'éternel démon imaginaire du dehors et du dedans qu'est notre propre esprit.

Michel Leiris, *L'Afrique fantôme*

ἀθάνατοι θνητοί, θνητοὶ ἀθάνατοι,
ζῶντες τὸν ἐκείνων θάνατον
τὸν δὲ ἐκείνων βίον τεθνεῶντες.

Mortal immortals, immortal mortals,
living each other's death,
dying each other's life.

Heraclitus, *The Fragments*

Contents

Illustrations

Translator's Note

For references to and quotations from foreign works cited in this book, I have used previously published English translations if they exist (preserving the original spellings and syntax of early texts); in all other cases, I have given my own renditions.

A certain portion of the references cited by the author are to sixteenth- and seventeenth-century texts (concerning the major comparative case, the Tupinamba). The original dates are relevant to the context and are needed to distinguish them from contemporary ethnographies. However, since it is distracting and redundant to indicate both published and original dates every single time, I have compromised by placing the original date in brackets the first time the citation appears in each chapter, as well as in the bibliography. Some works written in this century also have their original publication date indicated when relevant, for instance, to give a sense of when they appeared in the course of certain debates or to avoid confusion over the general period covered by the ethnographic present.

For help in clarifying the meaning of certain Brazilian idioms, the archaic Portuguese of the chroniclers, and various difficult passages in the original text, I would like to thank Ana-Maria Lima, Lecturer in Portuguese at the University of Chicago, who was generous in providing advice in response to my questions.

Preface

This book is an ethnography of the Araweté, a Tupi-Guarani people of eastern Amazonia (Middle Xingu, Brazil), that intends to situate them within the South American ethnological corpus—in particular, within the panorama of the Tupi-Guarani linguistic family. Its focus is the description and interpretation of Araweté cosmology, approached from the perspective of concepts about the person, death, Divinity, and systems of shamanism and warfare. The theme of divine cannibalism, central to the Araweté definition of the human condition, will be treated as part of the complex of Tupi-Guarani ritual anthropophagy. Along this guiding thread, I will propose a vision of Araweté metaphysics that explores the place of humanity in the cosmos, its fundamental inscription within temporality, and the logic of identity and difference that governs the distinctive ontology of this group.

A considerable part of the book describes the social organization of the Araweté, tracing parallels and contrasts with other groups of the same linguistic family. Broadly, this book is an exercise in the comparative analysis of South American cosmologies; more narrowly, it concentrates on the construction of a global cosmological model for the Tupi-Guarani. Thus, coexisting in this book are an ethnography, a middle-level synthesis, and hypotheses with a broader sweep. The somewhat culturalist idea of "the Tupi-Guarani cosmology" should be understood as a provisional heuristic instrument permitting the consolidation of materials that until now have been dispersed and superficially thematized. In the near future, South American ethnology will allow less intuitive formulations than this present work. The linguistic-cultural criteria employed here should be seen as a mere scaffolding for structural models of greater empirical breadth and analytic power.

This examination of Araweté cosmology proceeds in two registers: the category of the person, as elaborated in discourse about eschatology and the gods; and the Araweté conception of society, as revealed in social and ritual practice. The consideration of certain substances, modes, and attributes of the Araweté universe—the gods, the dead, enemies, shamans, warriors, cannibalism, songs—will lead to the depiction of a native anthropology where concepts of alterity and Becoming will emerge as the defining qualities and processes of human Being. The inchoate state of the person, the paradoxical character of the society, and the "minimalist" functioning of the institutional arrangements will be examined to see how their implications challenge the representation of "primitive society" current in anthropological discourse.

This book is a modified version of my doctoral thesis, written from May to July and defended in August of 1984 at the National Museum of Rio de Janeiro. It was published (with additions) in Brazil in 1986. The modifications for this English version are aimed especially at textual clarity and fluidity, but some, enjoined upon me by time, colleagues, and a return to the Araweté in 1988, are corrections of faulty observations or interpretations. Excessively rambling passages and some of the usual apparatus of an academic thesis were deleted, as well as numerous comparative notes and a chapter summarizing the Tupi-Guarani literature.

The effort of reducing the original version prevented me from undertaking a serious updating of the comparative references. Moreover, some works written prior to 1984 receive less attention than their relevance would demand: this is especially the case for Robert Murphy's monograph on Mundurucu religion (1958). Of works that appeared later, J. C. Crocker's book (1985) on Bororo shamanism and especially Bruce Albert's thesis (1985) on the warfare-funerary system of the Yanomami discuss questions that closely concern those developed here. Within the Tupi-Guarani arena, I must mention the theses by William Balée (1984) on the Kaapor, Isabelle Combès (1986) on Tupinamba cannibalism, Regina Müller (1987) on the Asuriní, Dominique Gallois (1988) on Wayãpi cosmology, and Alan Campbell's book (1989) also on the Wayãpi. Concerning the Araweté, the articles by Balée (1988, 1989a, 1989b), covering aspects of the group's praxis that I was not prepared to deal with, represent a fundamental contribution.

Perhaps I should warn the reader that this is a traditional ethnography; the questions it pursues were imposed by the Araweté but handled according to my own concerns. I suppose that if the Araweté were to bother themselves with what I have to say in this book, my approach would strike them as simply another enemy's point of view on their society—although, as will become clear later on, even this may be a somewhat presumptuous thing to say. My theoretical leanings and orientation will be evident from the outset. I have no doubt that another ethnographer, observing the same "facts," would come away with a much different image of the Araweté. At no time did I aspire to conduct experiments with literary genres or anything of the sort. Although it will be clear that polyphony and dialogism are marked characteristics of Araweté culture, they do not pervade the fabric of my description. But I have lost no sleep over this. I do not suffer from what Sahlins once called "epistemological hypochondria" and I am convinced that the Araweté are sufficiently interesting and unknown (by myself included) as to dispense with discursive fantasies. At any rate, this book is somewhat less technical and rigorous, and somewhat more rhetorical and philosophically pretentious, than the standard monograph. Between the absences and the excesses, I can only hope that something remains—which will be, no doubt, the part that falls to the Araweté.

From the beginning of my research among the Araweté through the writing of this book, I was helped by a considerable number of people. To name all of them would fill up an entire chapter, a pleasure I must, unfortunately, forgo. I would like, however, to extend special thanks to certain professors, colleagues, and friends of mine in Brazil and elsewhere: Anthony Seeger, Bartomeu Meliá, Bruce Albert, Bruna Franchetto, Berta Ribeiro, Carlos Alberto Ricardo, Dominique Gallois, Gilberto Azanha, Gilberto Velho, Joanna Overing, Manuela Carneiro da Cunha, Marshall Sahlins, Nádia Farage, Patrick Menget, Peter Fry, Peter Gow, Peter Rivière, Roque Laraia, Steve Schwartzman, Tania S. Lima, Waud Kracke, William Balée, and Yonne Leite. I would also like to thank my students of the Graduate Program in Social Anthropology (PPGAS) at the National Museum in Rio de Janeiro, who form an enthusiastic team of promising ethnologists. The Department of Anthropology and the PPGAS of the National Museum, where I graduated and now teach, gave me all the necessary support: I thank the professors and staff for this exceptional, sine qua non situation. The National Council for Scientific and Technological Development (CNPq) supported a large part of my work through grants for graduate study and research, and the Research and Project Foundation (FINEP) followed up with further financial support.

Working with my colleague Catherine V. Howard, who translated this book, was a pleasure. We kept up a correspondence that lasted a year and a half and filled hundreds of pages. I pestered her with comments and suggestions, oftentimes impertinent, and she proposed various improvements in the text. The translation she has worked out fully satisfies me.

Iara Ferraz, fellow anthropologist and my former wife, first brought me to the Araweté. Without her I would not have begun and would not have understood many things.

I wrote this book because of Toiyi, Iwã-Mayo, Araiyi-kãñĩ-no, Iwã-kãñĩ, Marɨpã-no, Tapaya-hi, Kãñĩ-newo-hi—my dearest Araweté friends; they should know I did my best.

August 1989

Note on Orthography

All words in foreign languages are written in italics. Araweté personal names, when designating human beings, are not in italics, but names of spirits and divinities follow the norm of italicization.

The spelling of Araweté words is not phonological, since this language has not yet been described by a specialist. The approximate phonetic values of the symbols are:

VOWELS

a like the *a* in "mama"
e like the *e* in "ebb"
i like the *ee* in "meet"
ɨ high central unrounded, similar to "ooh" but without rounding (close to the vowel written "y" in classic Tupi-Guarani dictionaries)
ï similar to the *i* in the English "bit," but produced with the tip of the tongue turned downward (probably an allophone of *i*)
o a shwa sound (middle central unrounded), similar to the vowels in "abut"
The tilde (~) indicates nasalization and can occur with all vowels
A vowel is underlined to indicate that the syllable receives the stress, which otherwise falls on the last syllable

CONSONANTS

b, h, k, m, n, p, t, w approximate the sounds of English (with varying degree of aspiration)
č like the *ch* in "chair"
c like the *ts* in "mats"
d a flap similar to the *d* in "body"
đ like the voiced *th* of "that"
ñ like the *ny* in "canyon"

r a flap similar to the *r* in the Spanish or Portuguese "caro"
y̌ like the *y* in "yes," with greater palatization
An apostrophe (') indicates a light glottal stop
An asterisk (*) indicates a hypothetical or reconstructed form of a word

1 Cosmology and Society

1. The Cannibal Gods

The Araweté say that the souls of the dead, once they have arrived in the heavens, are devoured by the *Maï*, the gods, who then resuscitate them from the bones; they then become like the gods, immortal. This assertion, which draws together central cosmological themes of Araweté culture and encapsulates its concept of the person, is what the present book will attempt to understand. For the Araweté, the person is inherently in transition; human destiny is a process of "Other-becoming."

To trace out all the implications entailed by this motif, I will turn towards a comparative horizon to see how other Tupi-Guarani treat the same questions. In turn, analyzing Araweté discourse about the person will make it possible to open up a path linking the other peoples of this linguistic family, and then to formulate some hypotheses about the properties of a single Tupi-Guarani structure of the person. This method, therefore, will be recursive: inserting the Araweté facts into a system, which in turn will be built upon these facts.

This is only a first step in my broader aim to conduct an experiment. To construct the Araweté conception of the person, I will explore certain facts about their social organization and cosmology. I will then line up a series of considerations (admittedly schematic) about Tupi-Guarani cosmologies to show that the same metaphysics underlies phenomena as disparate as cannibalism, shamanism, social morphology, and forms of marriage. Here too I will be guided by the Araweté, taking the question of the person as the connecting thread.

I start with the hypothesis that there exists something in common among the different Tupi-Guarani societies beyond their linguistic identity and behind their apparent morphosociological diversity. It remains to be seen in the course of this work if such a hypothesis is acceptable. For now, I advance a few generalizations.

The Araweté, one of the formerly numerous peoples of the region between the Xingu and Tocantins rivers, do not display any striking features or anomalies that would make them stand out from the physiognomy common to the Tupi-Guarani peoples of eastern Amazonia. If they are to be distinguished in some way, it is rather for having relatively few of the institutional and ceremonial forms present in the other societies of this family. This cannot, in my opinon, be attributed merely to disorganization caused by contact with Western society, nor to pressure from enemy tribes that in recent decades have dislodged them from their former territory. Indeed, I believe that the Araweté have been much less affected by contact than have most of the other groups in the region—at least up to now.

The Araweté parsimony of social categories and institutions has as its counterpart a complex, highly developed cosmological discourse, albeit not architectonically elaborated or dogmatically invariant. The Araweté imaginary is manifested in speech and in song. Very little of what really matters is visible; the essential takes place on another stage. In a certain sense, one could say of them what has been said of the Guarani: here too "all is Word" (Meliá 1978 : 57). But the words of the Araweté seem less to echo the ascetic withdrawal of their Guarani relatives (adherents of *logos*) and more to evoke the excessive gestures of the remote sixteenth-century Tupinamba.

On the other hand, perhaps the very nature of Araweté society, both "simple" and "archaic," will allow us to discover fundamental structures of the Tupi-Guarani by revealing principles that also operate in those societies having more differentiated social and ritual institutions.[1]

One question in particular stands out about the Araweté and resonates with what has been written about other Tupi-Guarani societies. It concerns what appears to be an excess or a supplementary quality of cosmological discourse as compared to social organization. How to account for the coexistence of, on the one hand, a "loosely structured" organization (few social categories, absence of global segmentations, weak institutionalization of interpersonal relations, lack of differentiation between public and domestic spheres) with, on the other hand, an extensive taxonomy of the spiritual world (not easily reducible to homogeneous principles), an active presence of that world in daily life, and a thoroughly vertical, "Gothic" orientation of thought? What is to be done with this preponderance of discourse over institution, of the spoken word over the schematism of ritual, of the cosmological over the sociological series?

Societies such as the Araweté reveal how utterly trivial any attempts are to establish functional consistencies or formal correspondences between morphology and cosmology or between institution and representation. The ethnological literature on the Tupi-Guarani has found it difficult to avoid alternating between theoretical truisms and anecdotal descriptions, when it is not lamenting the social disintegration of the peoples studied. But neither is it enough to say that among the Araweté (and other Tupi-Guarani groups), cosmology "predominates" over social organization,[2] nor to acknowledge that cosmology is a constitutive part of the social structure and the inevitable means of access to it. Rather, it is essential to grasp the problematic sense of this cosmology and then try to account for the "fluid" character of the morphology.

Upon reflection, one is struck by a certain "something," obscure but distinct, that seems to determine Araweté society. It is as if somehow the society were submitted to a centrifugal dynamic, a turning towards the exterior, an exiting from itself towards those regions above and beyond the social, as if something crucial were occurring out there. But to achieve this, Araweté society seems to occupy itself with undoing any internal divisions and articulations, real or virtual. It presents itself as smooth, unified (but not around a center), homogeneous (but dispersed), equal in all its parts, as if it were a monad floating in a populous and fractured cosmos defined by multiplicity and open-endedness. This internal nondifferentiation, however, is put to the service of a radical difference, of an impulse leading outside itself, a passion for exteriority which, despite the apparent repetitive calmness of Araweté daily life, inscribes Becoming in the very heart of this society. Thus, its "center" is outside, its "identity" is elsewhere, and its Other is not a mirror for man, but his destiny.

The Araweté case appears to invert the traditional representation that anthropology makes of "primitive society" as a closed system, a taxonomic theater where every entity, real or conceptual, finds its place in a system of classification; where the order of the universe reflects the social order; where temporality is recognized only to be denied by myth and ritual; where what is defined as exterior to the social (nature and supernature) exists merely to counterproduce the society as a haven of interiority and self-identity. Such a vision cannot be accommodated to the Araweté by any means whatsoever. Not for the obvious reason that it cannot be accommodated to any real society (societies change, temporality being their very substance; classifications are political instruments; and between norms and practice there must be a rupture, or else social life would be impossible), but rather, because the Araweté lean in another direction. I believe that in fact many cosmologies approximate the traditional representation, and that many societies attempt to remain, in a nontrivial sense, identical with themselves and coextensive with the cosmos. To do so, they must be capable of introjecting and domesticating difference, by means of devices that put difference to the service of identity. For such societies, opposition is the precondition of composition; to divide is to prepare a synthesis; and to exclude is to create an interiority.

Against these societies without an exterior that struggle to conjure away difference and congeal Becoming (as far as this is possible), I contrast the Araweté, a society without an interior—or, to put it less bluntly, a society with a dynamic that dissolves those spatial metaphors so common in sociological discourse: interior, exterior, center, margins, boundaries, limen, etc. Here, we move into a non-Euclidean social space.

The simplicity of Araweté society masks a complexity of another order. We shall see that the Tupi-Guarani method of constructing the person follows the same non-Euclidean tendency. It has nothing to do with some mirror chamber of reflections and inversions between the Self and the Other that tends toward symmetry and stability. Rather, the Tupi-Guarani construct the person through a process of continuous topological deformation, where ego and enemy, living and dead, man and god, are interwoven, before or beyond representation, metaphorical substitution, and complementary opposition. We move into a universe where Becoming is prior to Being and unsubmissive to it.

I will attempt to demonstrate that the complex of relations between human beings and the gods is the most strategic avenue to understanding Araweté society. In such a complex, death is the productive event. It is not merely the moment when it is possible to analyze the person into its components; it is the place where the person is actualized. We will see that here, as with the Gê societies, "the dead are the others" (Carneiro da Cunha 1978), and death is where the conceptual determination of alterity takes place. But in the case of Tupi-Guarani, the difference between the living and the dead cannot be conceived as an opposition, either formal or real. Nor can it be reduced to the model of phonological contrast or to "the work of the negative." They envision a positivity in death that does not imply a vision of life as a negativity. If the Gê use the method of double negation to posit the person, the Tupi-Guarani risk a double affirmation; this *and* that, the living *and* the dead, the Self *and* the Other.[3] Araweté society is not dialectic.

The reference to the Gê is not fortuitous; they will be the exemplary contrastive case throughout this book, although not always explicitly so. If there exists such a thing as dialectical societies (Maybury-Lewis 1979), the Gê and Bororo would rank as perfect examples. In them we find the maximal development of complementary oppositions in social categories and cosmological values, oppositions that fold, refold, intersect, and echo each other in a vertiginous baroque progression. The person is constructed as a delicate synthesis between nature and culture, being and becoming, achieving its reality by articulating itself with symmetrical positions determined by ceremonial names, formal friendships, and rites of mortuary impersonation. In such societies, everything signifies: from the landscape to the body, the *socius* inscribes its principles in the universe. The Gê are justly famous for their sociological complexity and conservatism, and for being the best-studied peoples of Brazil. They were the point of departure for the work of Lévi-Strauss on native American mythologies, and they appear to be one of the strongest cases supporting structural anthropology.

None of the attributes I've just described, unfortunately, are applicable to the Tupi-Guarani. Compared to the crystalline properties of Gê societies, the Tupi-Guarani evoke images of amorphous bodies—clouds or smoke—in their weak and casual social organization, their absence of clear conceptual boundaries between cosmological arenas, their fragility in the face of contact with Western society (though more in appearance than in essence), their plasticity, and their otherworldly style of thought.

The contrast between the Gê and Tupi-Guarani forms becomes all the more evident when considering their long history of ecological competition, warfare, and cultural interchange. But this point should be qualified: we must not overlook the internal differences of each group nor assume that language and culture coincide (ignoring the intense pre-Columbian cultural dynamic). Above all, we should not ignore the innumerable other South American cosmologies that as a set form a vast system of transformations: Gê, Tupi, Tukano, Yanomami, Carib, Upper Xingu. Ever since Lévi-Strauss's *Mythologiques* (1969b, 1973, 1978, 1981), it has become increasingly evident that the sociological, linguistic, and cultural units of the continent are combinatory variants of a structure that operates with the same basic symbolic materials.

Thus, the Tupi-Guarani do not enjoy any privileged relation with the Gê, and the Gê are certainly not the only pertinent contrast. Nevertheless, the Gê are strategically valuable for comparisons made on a continental scale. They are a "pivotal element" in the history of South American ethnology (Lévi-Strauss 1963a, 1969b: 9), as testified by the special place they occupy in recent syntheses (Kaplan 1981b, 1984; Rivière 1984). Every Americanist will find it easy to confirm the basic similarities between the Araweté and other minimalist societies that serve as points of departure for such syntheses, such as the Trio (Rivère 1969) and the Piaroa (Kaplan 1975) of northern Amazonia. It is easy to understand as well why the crystalline features and terse institutional dialectic of the Gê serve as a heuristic counterpoint and define a theoretical problem.

What is notable about the differences between the Gê and the Tupi-Guarani is that they can be found within a common ground. Both utilize what Héritier (1982: 158–59) calls the "elementary symbolics of the identical and the different" with which a society arranges the parameters of its self-representation. But each of them uses the same symbolic materials to pursue a different strategy, with results that appear to diverge radically in their philosophies. This is why I view with reservation the idea that the same basic macrostructure corresponds to the same social philosophy for all South American cosmologies, a philosophy that considers identity to be an impossible security, and difference a dangerous necessity—meaning that difference is either introjected and domesticated, or banished and denied (as J. Overing Kaplan has so well formulated). We shall see that Tupi-Guarani cannibalism complicates the essential question of the differential forms of conceptualizing difference.

2. Living with the Araweté

I spent twelve months among the Araweté, divided among periods from May to July 1981; February to April, June to September, and December 1982; January 1983; and February 1988. I did not observe the activities that occur during the part of their annual cycle falling in October and November.

After short research experiences among the Yawalapíti, Kulina, and Yanomami, which were not continued for various reasons, I began to turn my attention towards Tupi-Guarani peoples. The impression I got from the literature on these groups was ambiguous. Although the material on the early Tupinamba and Guarani suggested a great complexity, the monographs on contemporary Tupi-Guarani groups were discouraging. The majority of them, characterized by the problem of "acculturation," portrayed the ethnographic present as little more than a fleeting instant between a remote past of sociocultural plenitude that was reconstructed at risk, and an imminent, inevitable future of disaggregation or disappearance. The picture that emerged was of simplified social systems, where demographic losses had led to a generalized disfunctional state, an emergency adaptation in which only fragments of the themes common to almost all South American societies persisted: bits and pieces of the great cycle of mythic twins, the couvade, the extended family, shamanism. It was impossible to know whether the impression of superficiality that these works left was due to the authors' theoretical perspectives or to the situation of the peoples studied—or if, after all, the Tupi-Guarani were not especially "interesting."

Moreover, in the 1960s and early 1970s, the Tupi-Guarani practically disappeared from the ethnological scene. What little research was undertaken and published about them was not only outside the main current of ethnographic discussions, but also failed to clearly delineate a problematic that could be contrasted with the models constructed for other South American systems. Everything led one to believe in the end that the Tupi-Guarani really *were* peoples of the past, dominated by the glorious shadow of the Tupinamba.

Since the mid-1970s, however, interest in Tupi-Guarani societies began to reemerge, as part of a general increase in field research projects. The relative maturity of Brazilian ethnology, especially since high standards of description were established for the societies of Central Brazil, made it necessary to reexamine "marginalized" social systems such as those of the Tupi-Guarani.

My choice of the Araweté took place within this context. Thanks to the books of F. Fernandes (1963 [1949], 1970 [1952]) on Tupinamba warfare and that of H. Clastres on Tupi-Guarani prophetism (1978 [1975]), I became aware of a remarkable conception of the person and of society, perceptible even in the "acculturation" monographs on the Tupi of eastern Amazonia. I decided to experiment with synthesizing the Tupi-Guarani facts based on research in the field, given that the available syntheses relied almost exclusively on historical sources or secondhand ethnographic descriptions.

The Araweté were among the groups of the Xingu-Tocantins region that the expanding frontier in southern Pará had recently overtaken with the construction of the Transamazon Highway. From their "contact" in 1976 to 1980, only one anthropologist, who worked with the Asuriní (neighbors of the Araweté), made a short visit to Ipixuna, an affluent of the middle Xingu, where the Araweté had been settled by the government's national Indian agency, FUNAI (Fundação Nacional do Índio). I knew nothing more about them.

In May 1980, I requested authorization from FUNAI to do research in the area. It was granted to me in January 1981 to begin in May of that year. The long interval between my request and the granting of permission was due to the fact that relations between the governmental organ and the anthropological community had deteriorated to an even lower level than usual.

After overcoming a long series of bureaucratic and political obstacles, I finally arrived among the Araweté on 2 May 1981. I left the area at the end of July for what I thought would be a period of only one month. But the rapid fall in the waters during the dry season meant I had to wait seven months before returning. Navigating the Ipixuna is practically impossible between September and December, since the river dries up to expose miles of bare rock. I returned in the rainy season at the end of January 1982. In March, a violent influenza epidemic fell upon the village, brought by the family of a FUNAI worker and which caused one death. I left the area in early May, responding to a request from FUNAI that I present a proposal for delimiting an Araweté area (Viveiros de Castro 1982) with a view towards its demarcation, which FUNAI has still (as of 1991) not undertaken.[4] I returned in early June, leaving the Ipixuna in late September after I came down with malaria. I returned in December, staying until February, when repeated attacks of *falciparum* malaria, resistent to medication, made it dangerous for me to continue fieldwork.[5]

My stay at Ipixuna was thus not only rather drawn out, but also intermittent. This made it more difficult for me to learn the language. The group was practically monolingual, and not even my reasonably good ear for language nor my recourse to the Tupi-Guarani literature could compensate for the lack of continuous exposure to Araweté speech. Its prosody follows a rapid rhythm, with a predominance of nasal vocalics and weak articulation. Wagley (1977:20) said that he always felt there was a "linguistic haze" between himself and the Tapirapé; I have a feeling that something thicker than that lay between myself and the Araweté. Although I managed to understand everyday speech (especially when they spoke directly to me), and although I could use metalinguistic resources to learn how to learn the language, I was not able to understand the shamanic songs without the help of glosses. For this reason, my interpretation of the songs of the gods and of warfare—central aspects of Araweté culture—is somewhat superficial.

Likewise, I was unable to obtain more than fragmentary versions of the corpus of myths. Araweté mythology operates as a kind of implicit assemblage that serves as an underlying context to the daily proliferation of shamanic songs. People rarely told myths as discursive events separated from the flow of informal conversation, nor were they willing to recite artificially prompted versions to a tape recorder. Not out of any sort of shyness: they needed no urging whatsoever from me (quite the contrary) to sing and tape-record the musical repertoire of the group. The songs of the shamans, living or dead, far from being "sacred," are popular successes, and war songs are often used as lullabies. But my attempts to record prosaic speech, whether myths or stories, always produced timid and confused reactions. As a final reservation, I should note that although the Araweté, due to their characteristic politeness and irony (or lack of comparative cases), declared that I had a reasonable command of their language, I have no doubt that they had little interest in narrating stories to me, knowing that I would only comprehend them in part, given my problems with the linguistic code or my ignorance of their context. Therefore, I had to cling to the "implicit mythology" and to rely on more general cosmological attitudes expressed in discourse and practice.

Living among the Araweté—"affable savages" like Huxley's Kaapor (1956)—was easy. What was difficult was "to do anthropology." Few human groups, I imagine, are as amenable in nature and as amusing in their sociability—as long as one has a good ability to laugh at oneself (and mine is at most fair to middling).[6] Fond of touch and physical closeness, informal to a sometimes overwhelming degree, demanding in their giving and requesting, exaggerated in their demonstrations of affection, lovers of the flesh and of the feast, free with their tongues and constant in their laughter, sarcastic and at times delirious—the Araweté, it always seemed to me, could not be adequately described using concepts such as rules and norms. Their long history of wars and flights and their demographic catastrophe upon contact were not extinguished from their memory, but these did not diminish their vital energies and essential joyfulness. Brazilians who have lived with both the Araweté and the neighboring Asuriní (very close linguistically and culturally) commonly establish a contrast between the "melancholy" and "defeatism" of the Asuriní and the "optimism" of the Araweté. This difference translates into opposite demographic politics, recessive in the case of the former, expansionist in the latter. In compensation, the Asuriní are always praised for their moderation and their artistic taste, while the Araweté are portrayed as happy and carefree barbarians, technologically poor, perhaps only recently turned sedentary (Ribeiro 1981).

A mixture of truth and superficial stereotypes underlies this contrast. But I should note that even at the end of my stay, when I knew them a bit better, the impression never left me that, with the Araweté, everything was possible. Perhaps this simply suggests how little

I actually knew them. But I cannot forget my surprise at seeing a mother-in-law delousing the head of her son-in-law (a gesture of intense affective intimacy), seeing a boy suckle at his sister's breast, hearing children joke about the dead, seeing a man take a walk through the village wearing the new clothes of his wife "just to try them on" (with nothing "symbolic" about it). My previous ethnographic experiences with the Yawalapíti, Kulina, and Yanomami had not prepared me for any of this. One of the most surprising features of Araweté life was the boldness with which women treated men (foreigners or fellow tribesmen) and the strong presence of women in collective affairs.

Little reflection is needed to perceive that this Olympian (or rather, Dionysian) indifference towards what is conventionally called "social conventions" is itself a convention, and that the prescriptions of exuberance and extroversion proscribed sentiments such as anger, envy, jealousy, or the desire to be alone. It should be added that the assertiveness and volubility of the women had as its counterpoint an extreme corporal modesty.[7]

Social conventions, however, are the privileged raw materials of social anthropology, whether we take this notion to mean ritualized behavior or rules of interaction. The Araweté indifference towards conventions, although not disagreeable to me as a lifestyle, disoriented me in its sociological indifference: the nondifferentiation of segments, categories, roles, and social attitudes. Their society seemed to me little institutionalized or little ritualized—if we understand "ritualization" as that set of procedures (gestural, graphic, spatial, verbal) that materialize the cognitive premises and basic categories of a culture.

What I call ritualization is more than a mere envelope of ideas and social differences that might exist on their own; it is in fact the very mechanism that produces these differences. The ritual apparatus that inscribes meanings in the land and in the body *is* society itself, and nothing less than that. For the Araweté, however, this apparatus seemed to produce nondifferentiation, which could not be considered the product of some kind of regression or simplification of any prior, more "differentiated" form. The Araweté ethos struck me as being articulated with some determinant global posture of their own.

This is a provisional oversimplification, of course. In later pages, I will describe the processes and categories of Araweté social organization, but for now I am speaking of tendencies and nuances. Resorting to a loose and analogical way of speaking, it is as if societies, when faced with the imperative of classifying, were able to choose between two opposite directions. One leads to a multiplying of internal differences and a generalized segmentation—a highly productive mechanism, where each opposition automatically generates a counter-opposition, intersecting the first, due to a kind of drive towards parity that seeks to deter the asymmetrical dynamism and brute difference inherent in the real (Lévi-Strauss 1977b: 181). Furthermore, this direction leads towards the emblematic exteriorization of all differences and towards the capture of discontinuities from the real, in order to impose on them a surplus value of signification.

In the opposite direction lies the dispersion of differences to the threshold of nonsignification, the circulation of a supplementarity throughout the entire social body (the parts of which are not complementary, but equivalent and redundant) and the projection of differences to the outside of society. This direction also reveals a drive to minimize oppositions, to make significations invisible by emphasizing the internal continuity of the social system. And more: an effort to reach beyond the external limits of the system to recuperate the differences that were ejected, using metonymical or metamorphic devices (processes without mediation).

This contrast might be phrased as one between "metaphoric" and "metonymic" societies, or (using a well-known opposition) between "totemic" and "sacrificial" ones (Lévi-Strauss 1963b: 15–29; 1966: 223–28). Gê groups can be recognized in the first case, being "legible" societies (Da Matta 1982: 38) while the Araweté and others would fit in the second, being "imperceptible" ones.

Before I began to reflect on all these questions, I could not avoid the dispiriting fact that the Araweté "did not have" a great many of those features that awaken the professional interest of anthropologists. Such an inventory of absences would include: no rule or form of avoidance between affines, a low structural yield to the naming system, an absence of initiation ceremonies and little emphasis on life-cycle changes, simple funeral rites with no marking of the mourning phase or its termination, a fluid division of labor, a seemingly chaotic spatial morphology, a simplified ceremonial pattern, a minimal repertoire of social roles, and an absence of any global segmentation. Added to this is a rather simple material culture, technologically and aesthetically speaking, and an agriculture rudimentary by Tupi-Guarani standards.

The violent depopulation the Araweté suffered in 1976–77 and especially the long history of forced transhumance and dislocations due to the pressure of successive waves of enemies cannot be discarded when explaining the simplicity of their social system. Nevertheless, I believe that these factors had a more significant effect on techno-economic aspects. Nothing authorizes us to postulate that in some hypothetical and remote period of "peace" and territorial isolation, Araweté society had at its disposal a more differentiated social organization. It should be noted nonetheless that the demographic reduction and the recent concentration of the tribe in a single village modified certain fundamental patterns. The status quo up to the 1960s consisted of the occupation of a vast territory by small local groups that were linked by marriage and war alliances, with mutual visiting during the feasting season (a typical morphology of the tropical forest).

In my opinion, the mechanisms of production and reproduction of Araweté society never depended on a large population. From the standpoint of the infrastructure, it is the cultivation of maize that produces village aggregations; from that of the superstructure, it is shamanism that guarantees its integration and symbolic reproduction. A garden of maize and a shaman are enough to define a village and a horizon of life. The Araweté explain their seeking contact with white people in 1976 by the fact that they could no longer plant maize in lands infested with enemies: "We were tired of eating only meat." As for shamanism, although I know of no moment in their history when they were deprived of this institution, it will become clear later on how the shaman incarnates the local group.[8]

Thus, I had to confront Araweté simplicity in all its complexity, without resorting to hypotheses about simplification by depopulation or regression. Even if there is some truth along these lines, such a hypothesis is neither necessary nor interesting. I had to find a Tupi-Guarani explanation for a Tupi-Guarani society, and not speculate about historical vicissitudes. It was necessary to look in the right direction to see what it was that interested the Araweté themselves.

I am not referring here to the topics that dominated everyday talk. These were more or less the topics that have interested humanity ever since it began: food, sex, death, and so on. Rather, I am referring to the task of discovering the idiom in which the Araweté spoke about their society. If the sociological code is not the privileged one, what is the dominant language? Where is the vantage point from which to formulate, if not an impossible totalization, then at least a meaningful description? Where do the Araweté place meaning?

From the time I first arrived among the Araweté and throughout my entire stay, I was surprised by the extreme contrast between the diurnal and nocturnal life of the village. During the day, nothing happened. Of course, there were the hunting trips, the Pantagruelesque collective meals, the interminable conversations in the family patios at nightfall, the never-ending tasks revolving around maize; but everything was done in that peculiar manner at once agitated and apathetic, erratic and monotonous, cheerful and distracted. Every night, however, in the small hours of the morning, I heard emerging from the silence a high, solitary intonation, sometimes exalted, sometimes melancholic, but always austere, solemn, and, to me, somewhat macabre. It was the shamans singing the *Maï marakã*, the music of the gods. Only during the most acute phase of the influenza epidemic and for a period after the death of a middle-aged woman did these songs cease. On certain nights, three or four shamans sang at the same time or successively, each experiencing his own vision. Sometimes only one sang, starting with a gentle humming and droning, gradually raising his voice, tracing a staccato articulation that stood out against the continuous, sibilant backdrop of an *aray* rattle, until it reached a pitch and intensity that was maintained for over an hour. It then descended back slowly into the first light of sunrise, the "hour when the earth is unveiled" (*iwi pïdawa me*), until it returned into silence. More rarely (which meant once or twice a week for each active shaman), the climax of the song brought the shaman outside his house to the patio. There he danced, bent over with his cigar and *aray* rattle, stamping his right foot on the ground, panting, singing continuously—this was the descent to earth of the divinities.

It was hard for me to believe that these solemn voices, these somber figures that I watched from the door of my house, had anything to do with those men who spent their days either laughing or whining, bantering or begging, and scorned by the employees of the government outpost. But they were the same men. Or rather, they were not, since the contrast that I perceived (which does not exist as such, as something to be "perceived," in the eyes of the Araweté) was the difference between the diurnal human world—a people struggling with the misery brought about by Western contact and a society that seemed too fragile to sustain this closeness—and the nocturnal world of the gods and the dead.

Through the shamanic songs, I was introduced to the cosmology of the Araweté (as well as to their rhythm, spending much of the night awake and sleeping a few hours in the afternoon). I began to learn the names and some of the attributes of a legion of beings, facts, and actions that were invisible in the light of day. I discovered that the "music of the gods" fulfilled multiple functions in the daily life of the group and marked the economic rhythms of the year. I came to perceive the presence of the gods, as a reality or a source of examples, in every minute routine action. Most important, it was through them that I could discern the participation of the dead in the world of the living.

Even if I seem to exaggerate, it is important to maintain this contrast between day and night, the human world and the divine world, so that the omnipresence of the other-worldly does not lend the impression that the Araweté are a mystical people. Nor does the affective tone of their life present any traits customarily associated with the notion of religiosity: reverence, psychological withdrawal, or devaluation of the "real" world. On the contrary, if anyone appreciates the good things of life, it is the Araweté. Besides, the daily contact with the gods breeds familiarity; nothing is more natural to them than the "supernatural" evoked by the nightly litanies of the shamans. Although tradition holds that the contrast between the earth and the sky was founded on a primordial separation, such a contrast is not thought of as constituting an ontological barrier. Araweté society, with all its gods, is "atheological," as H. Clastres (1978 : 32) described the early Guarani, precisely because the difference between men and gods is established in order to be overcome. Man becomes the equal of god—not dialectically, but directly. Death is where this ambiguous and complex operation takes place.

The Araweté not only took pleasure in unraveling to me the names of their innumerable races of celestial, subterranean, and forest spirits, but enjoyed no less enumerating names of their dead during conversations we entertained at night. These recitations grew as soon as they perceived that both subjects interested me. Soon they began to give me periodic "exams" to see if, through my pieces of paper, I had in fact registered their words.

With time, I came to see that the Araweté spoke a great deal about their dead, and not just to me. They spoke about what the dead said, what they did, their appearance and gestures, their qualities and quirks. And the dead spoke plenty as well. Even years after a person had passed away, he could spring up in a shamanic song or come down to earth to take part in a banquet of tortoise, fish, or honey served with fermented beverages. The songs of dead shamans and warriors were always remembered. For whatever reason, I myself was frequently compared to people who had died. The Araweté are great appreciators of individual peculiarities: the dead are remembered in detail, and the memory of the living is extensive.[9]

In the beginning, I thought that their interest in the dead, which is not veneration or fear and does not constitute anything like a cult, might be an obsessional formation linked to the trauma of the contact situation, when fully one-third of the population died within two years. The years 1976–77 are always remembered with deep sadness and anguish. But the experience of seeing entire families disappear, of losing all of one's close relatives, of having to disperse and hide in the forest—all appear to have been part of Araweté life for a long time. Their history reveals an incessant movement of fleeing and dispersing, and a state of war seems to have been the rule and the custom.

Their interest in the dead is not, however, merely a matter of familiarity with violent death. The dead populate Araweté daily discourse, history, and geography. Death is the event that literally puts society and the person into movement, as we will see.

I hasten to add that the importance of death and the dead does not imply that the Araweté "desire" death, envy the destiny of the dead, or anything of the sort. They certainly are not morbid; they lament the dead, not the living.[10] Nevertheless, the importance they attach to such events and activities, evident in the ambit of daily conversation and ceremonial life, points to the value of death as the structuring locus of Araweté cosmology. In sum, it is through the gods and the dead, those two legions that populate the cosmos, that we will best come to know the living.

During my stay, Tatoawĩ-hi, a middle-aged woman, mother of several children, died of pneumonia. Four infants died during 1982 of the same cause. The first death, occurring at the peak of the influenza epidemic, plunged everybody into profound anxiety. The only thing that prevented the village from dispersing to the forest, as customarily occurs after the death of an adult, was their general state of weakness, as well as the arrival of an employee of the government Indian Post bringing the first thirty shotguns ever used by the Araweté. Staying in the village not only intensified the presence of death in daily discourse, but also brought to the scene the *ta̲'o we,* the fearful earthly specter of the recently deceased.

□

The Araweté live in conjugal houses arranged in "residential sections," groups of houses of close relatives facing onto their own patios. There are no clearcut boundaries between the cluster of buildings of the FUNAI Indian Post and the sections of the village, but there are conceptual boundaries: the surroundings of the Post make up the "patio of the whites" (*kamarã nɨkã*) and are not identified with any section. After trying out a few different accommodations, I realized that living in any particular residential section meant becoming the property of its members. While this did not impede my visiting the houses of other sections, it inhibited their members from coming to visit me. There was an intense competition to monopolize my trade goods and myself, at least in the beginning. Also, the residential sections have boundaries that can be activated in situations such as the presence of outsiders.

Since none of the houses available to me were located in sections where I wanted to live, I decided to occupy a small abandoned house near the FUNAI Post next to the path leading to the river. There I could be visited by anyone who so wished, and many things could be told to me without fear that indiscreet neighbors would overhear. But there were also some disadvantages. My house was distant from the main cluster of village houses, so I could not hear the movements of the shamans who lived in the other extreme of the village complex.

I cannot claim that I had informants, except during the final months of 1982 when Toiyi came to my house late at night to talk with me over coffee. I developed stronger ties with certain people, either out of friendship or because some of them seemed to have special inclinations and talents for teaching me what I wanted to know. Naturally, I was able to obtain much richer explanations about events that occurred while I was among the Araweté. Had I been living in the village during the Parakanã attacks in 1983, I would know much more than the little I did learn about the posthomicide rites. I was told that the Araweté brought back the head of the Parakanã they had killed in retaliation for a previous attack by that group. However, my tiresome questions about their practice of this custom (common to various groups in the region) always received vigorous denials. The ones who did such things, they said, were the *Towa̱ho* (an archetypal enemy group) with the heads of the Araweté. It was true, someone told me on a certain occasion, that once the Araweté brought back the skull of an Asuriní, but it was just once . . .

My apprenticeship thus occurred less through interviews with isolated individuals than in group situations: in the clamor of collective meals or during conversations in the patio of a family house before bed. Usually, any of my questions of an "anthropological" nature prompted a shower of laughter and replies of "Why do you want to know that?" followed by a confusing polyphony of humorous, untrue explanations or a rapid recitation of names. On the next day, however, some charitable soul would come to help me discriminate the true from the false, to explain some fortuitous impropriety I had committed, and to elaborate on the topic. At other times, everyone would take a genuine interest in what I was investigating and would start to collaborate. That was what happened when I began to draw on the memories of one of the oldest men of the village, asking him to tell me about the people and events of his boyhood and to recount the story of the beginning of the world. Upon seeing me head for the section where Meñã-no lived, people from various parts of the village would run over to listen to the old man's stories. They would then explain them to me, asking me afterwards to play back the tape recorder so they could amuse themselves by identifying one another's voices.

On the eve of my departure, an adolescent girl jokingly told me that when the old people of the village died, the children would have to turn to me to learn the stories of their ancestors, since, after all, I was now a *pirowï'hã*, a wise old man, who knew everything about such matters. But what kind of knowledge was it that they were attributing to me?

The concept of "stories of the ancestors" (*pirowï'hã mo-erape*) refers to a miscellany of genres: etiological and cosmogonic myths, histories of past wars, deeds of the ancestors, and a long saga of titanic beings. But the concept must not be thought of as designating an impersonal knowledge, since the Araweté do not do so. I cannot imagine them saying anything like "thus spoke our ancestors" (Grenand 1982) without specifying *who* said "thus spoke the ancients." Whenever someone referred to any event he had not witnessed, he added, "thus said so-and-so." This form of citation and the prevalence of direct discourse can lead to an interminable embedding of citations within citations before finally getting to the person who spoke directly to the primary transmitter of the message. Such a style makes a curious impression on the non-native listener.[11] When the topic is something commonplace (especially malicious gossip), the impression is one of a cautious disengagement by the speaker from the veracity of the message. But when speaking of something distant in space or time (the realm of the gods, the beginning of the world, or the like), the effect is to attribute a special authority to the one who "spoke." Two traits of Araweté discursive practice are entailed by this: first, the importance of the *pirowï'hã necã he re*, "those who saw the ancestors"—that is, the elders who saw, or who heard from those who saw, the events of the past. In the second place (and most important), it is a way of giving the message the authority of a shamanic statement. All information that was imparted to me about the nonterrestrial worlds was guaranteed by the clarification, "thus spoke so-and-so [a shaman living or dead]." In a certain sense, it is the shaman more than the "ancestors"—hence, the individual more than an impersonal tradition—who is responsible for the prevailing state of the cosmology.

The shamanic songs are, properly speaking, myths in action and in transformation.[12]

Despite this importance of the words of elders and shamans, Araweté knowledge is quite democratized. Esoteric themes or prohibited subjects are apparently absent. I was astonished by the amount of cosmological knowledge that children possessed. Women, for their part, were generally more loquacious and precise than men concerning the world of the *Maï̱*. It was perfectly natural for cosmological knowledge to be so widespread, since everyone listened night after night to such knowledge being expounded and elaborated in the shamanic songs. But as I soon came to understand, no one could be less appropriate as a commentator on shamanic songs than the very ones who produced them. A shaman would act as though he were ignorant of what he sang, and he did not like to speak directly about the songs and visions of others. The discomfort such matters entailed is associated with the prevalence of cited discourse: it is easier, or more proper, to talk about what someone else said, abolishing oneself as the primary source of discourse and preventing the coincidence of the subject in the utterance (*énoncé*) and the subject who does the uttering (*énonciation*). For this reason, women (and youths who were not shamans) always showed more interest in discussing "theology" and eschatology, at least when dealing with the shamans' songs. Such a stance towards discourse, in which citation is an oblique form of assertion, but which distances the words for any center and makes them always emanate from someone else in an infinite recursivity, presents complex problems of interpretation (Sperber 1985:23). The shamans, as we will see, are not themselves the focus or the subject of their songs; they too make citations.

Meanwhile, I cannot omit my own role in the relations I established with the Araweté. Let me comment on my position at the Ipixuna Post and how this affected my methods and research results.

Having spent most of my time living near the Indian Post, I could not help being identified by the Araweté with the things happening there, the whites living there, and the processes of interaction occurring between the village and the Post. By this, I do not mean to imply that had I opted to live in some residential section or had I tried to copy the group's lifestyle (as far as I could) I would have avoided being identified as a *kamarã*, a white (a subspecies of *awĩ*, enemy). But neither does this mean that the Araweté put up barriers between themselves and the *kamarã*, protected themselves behind a façade, or impeded interchanges between themselves and "us." To the contrary: the most difficult thing for me was to resist the power of seduction or suction exercised by the group, in the sense of their trying to transform me into one of their kind. As an open and "anthropophagous" society, its radical desire for the Other led it to try at any cost to be just like the him (i.e., like us) or else to pull him (i.e., me) into itself. Of course, this openness of Araweté society is derived in part from its minimal contact with whites and from its still unclear perception of the catastrophe such contact involves; but I believe that it is also rooted more deeply in a movement essential to its mode of being.

The situation at the Ipixuna Indian Post is less a matter of an Indian Post being next to a village, than of a village being next to an Indian Post. Until November 1981, there were two Araweté villages, one next to the Post and another a short distance away on the other side of the Ipixuna River. Then the residents of the latter moved into the former in order to be closer to the source of trade goods the Post represented. But shifts had begun earlier. In 1976, the population of various villages, fleeing the Parakanã, came to the banks of the Xingu River seeking contact with whites. After a series of tragic vicissitudes, they were gathered together by FUNAI around an "Attraction Post" on the upper Ipixuna. In 1978, after renewed attacks by the Parakanã, both Indians and whites moved to the middle course of the river and formed two villages. Finally, in late 1981 and early 1982, all 136 of the Araweté gathered around the Ipixuna Indian Post (see maps in Appendix 1-A).[13]

The Araweté depend on a series of goods and services offered by the Post: kerosene, salt, matches, pots, clothes (for the men), soap, batteries, flashlights, plates, spoons, sugar, knives, machetes, axes, scissors, combs, mirrors, cooking oil, rifles, ammunition, and medicines. During the acute phase of the flu epidemic in March 1982, when the maize had barely begun to mature, they depended on imported foods as well. Until 1987, the canoes they used were made by whites or Asuriní Indians contracted by the whites. At the Post are also certain collective pieces of equipment, such as the large pan for toasting maize and manioc meal, a machine for grinding maize, and another for squeezing manioc.[14]

The degree of dependency on each of these items varies, and the Araweté, a people of simple technology and a high capacity for improvisation, know how to go without almost all of them if necessary, although the introduction of firearms has provoked important modifications in the availability of game and the techniques of obtaining it. What was alarming, however, was the rapidity—between 1981 and 1983—with which the majority of these goods were introduced and adopted. Until March 1982, the counterprestations from the Araweté were limited to some game meat and maize for the whites' food supply at the Post. Then FUNAI tried to establish a "consignment canteen," introducing firearms and considerably increasing the amount of imported goods, in turn obligating the Indians to produce artisanry to finance these imports. But Araweté material culture is sober and simple; few of their articles are able to sell well on the market (controlled by FUNAI).[15]

The dependency of the Araweté on Western medicines and types of cures (to the extent that they exist at the Post) is quite high, although without having reached a point of extinguishing traditional curing methods. They apparently never had an especially elaborated pharmacological knowledge. But I observed an excessive number of requests for medicines and an intense demand for the services of the health worker (and of all the other whites), which greatly amplified the real or imagined necessities of the Indians, thereby attaining a politico-ritual dimension. If this could be seen clearly in the case of medical care, it was due in part to the crisis provoked by the epidemic of 1982 that plunged the Indians into a deep dependency, both objective and subjective, on the whites. But I had already witnessed something similar in 1981 during a phase of good health of the group. In fact, such a complex of ritual dependency on the whiteman's goods and services manifested itself in various other arenas of life beyond that of physical ailments. This same attitude underlay the voracious and rapid adoption of a wide range of the *kamarã*'s technological and symbolic paraphernalia, and a certain enthusiastic mimicry of all that came from the whiteman's world. Everything seemed to lead to the conclusion that the Araweté were definitively in the hands of the whites, condemned to follow the rapid and pathetic path of ethnic disfiguration.

This dependency, however, was ambiguous. Their "mimicry" had something subtly aggressive about it; their hyperactive soliciting had the character of a constant test or experiment to which we whites were submitted. I came to realize that all of this was a kind of intellectual enterprise through which the Araweté, in their characteristically overstated style, were elaborating the conceptual difference between themselves and us. They seemed ready either to fling themselves into the world of the whites,[16] or to demand just as insistently that the whites turn into Araweté—which affected me even more strongly, as they wanted me to plant a garden of maize with theirs, to marry, and to never leave again. All or everything, as it were, in one direction or the other. If they could, they would have brought the entire population of the city of Altamira, maybe even all the *kamarã*, to their village on the Ipixuna.

Perhaps there is nothing striking in this, or even anything particularly different from what happens with any indigenous tribe that has been recently submitted to the methods of "attraction and pacification" used by the Brazilian state. But there are certain features specific to this case, and the system of power relations established at the Ipixuna Post is based on certain traits of the Araweté social structure.

One of the fundamental characteristics of the Araweté village is the absence of a communal patio, an area equidistant from all the houses. The unity of society is not expressed in a clear or constant manner in the ritual use of space. The limited nature of their chieftaincy does not suffice in producing this unity either. In the present conditions, with the village being an aggregation of the remnants of divers local groups, this sociomorphological noncentralization becomes even more accentuated. As a result, the Post and its personnel assume a central place in the life of the group. The FUNAI teams who were active at the Post ever since contact seem to have encouraged the Araweté to transfer decisions that affected the entire population to the whitemen's hands. The successive crises befalling the group (epidemics, enemy attacks, relocations) consolidated this tendency.

Without a public space but only individual patios belonging to each residential section or extended family, the area of the Post and its installations (some used collectively for production) have become this space. However, it does not lose its identification with the *kamarã* who are the owners and disciplinarians of this area and its resources. This means that the Araweté collective space is at the same time "communal" (a free zone without restrictions on access by any of the residential sections) *and* of the whites, who have come to exercise a preeminent power over the entire Araweté society. The patio of the whites becomes the "central patio," a politically encompassing element. This is the stuff power is made of. For if those things that the whites say "belong to all the Araweté" (the canoes, health station, toasting pan, and so on) in fact belong first and foremost, both in time and in causality, "to the head of the Post," "to FUNAI," then the Araweté, as a totality, become determined—one should say constructed—from the outside, i.e., from the whiteman's point of view. What was outside becomes a center, and the Araweté village becomes a function of the Post.

Could this objective contradiction, sensed in some way by the Araweté, explain certain curious attitudes that drove the Post employees mad, such as the Indians' "vandalism" or their "carelessness" in maintaining the equipment and installations of the Post, which, after all, "belonged" to them? Moreover, is it not this double movement of production-expropriation of an Araweté "being" by the *kamarã* that lies behind that aggressive mimicry whereby the voracious Araweté end up being the devoured?[17]

But is this just an issue with the whites? Or rather, in contrast with societies like the Gê (with their internal self-constituting dialectic), won't the Araweté and other Tupi-Guarani always need this relation with the exterior in order to constitute and move themselves? In fact, the celebrated sociological conservatism of the Gê involves an internal dialectic and an encompassing center (physical, political, ceremonial) from which the whites and the others are in principle excluded. On the other hand, it could be that the relative fragility of the Tupi-Guarani societies in the face of the impact of "civilization"—which may very well mask other forms of resistance—is rooted in this search outside for an Other, propelled by an allomorphic impetus which has nothing to do with the unhappy consciousness or anything like seeing oneself with the Master's eyes. Cannibalism, with its ambivalence, is more than a metaphor for the Tupi-Guarani.

In sum, it was from the Post and as a *kamarã* that I spoke of and with the Araweté. From this center, I situated myself in relation to them as a totality objectified by my presence (and that of the Post and the whites). My constant circulation through all the patios and residential sections (which led some people to censure my "inconstancy") only reinforced my generic and abstract exteriority in relation to them. I do not know if I had any other choice.

When we first arrived in May 1981, we were received not with surprise, but rather, curiosity.[18] They did not know many *kamarã*. Moreover, I had brought some gifts. I participated as much as I could in the routine of the group: hunting, going to the garden, working on corn, participating in the dances and nightly conversations. I accompanied a collective hunting trip that lasted a week, part of the ritual cycle of maize beer. I spent a few days in the garden camp of a certain set of families; I went on fishing excursions and in search of honey. Nevertheless, I went out of the village much less often and for less time than what is normal for an Araweté man. Availing myself of a reserve of food brought from Altamira, I could establish food exchanges with various residential sections, compensating for my laziness and ineptness as a hunter. Because I was not in the area during the months of October and November, I did not see the collective fishing trips in which they used fish poison. Nor was I able to participate in an important seasonal movement, the *awacï motiarã*, when, during the rainy season between the planting of maize and its maturation, the entire population abandons the village and camps in the forest, living off the products of hunting and gathering. Although they had done so in 1981, they did not leave for the forest in the rainy seasons of 1982 or 1983. This was probably due to the increasing effects of sedentarization and concentration induced by the Post.

In 1981, the Araweté were just learning to handle firearms. My arriving with a shiny new shotgun caused great excitement. Even after March 1982, when almost all the adults possessed their own weapons, someone was always asking to borrow mine. The Araweté's interest and curiosity about me were concentrated on two objects and one activity of mine, which in a certain way were concrete symbols of my relationship with them: my shotgun, my tape recorder, and my writing. Because of the shotgun, I was invited to hunt innumerable times; later I entrusted the weapon to the most experienced men, and the competition over my .20 shotgun practically led to lines forming at my door. The tape recorder was everybody's favorite diversion. The "music of the enemies," the nocturnal solos of the shamans, and the recordings of maize beer festivals were requested daily, and the various patios jealously competed for the recorder at night. During the dead hours of the day, someone usually came and asked to sing into the recorder. They thoroughly enjoyed hearing the singing voice reproduced,[19] but they never showed any interest in Western music. Even though they liked to see photos I brought of them and other Indians, nothing substituted for listening to the tape recorder. I discovered that the dead sang when someone once jokingly referred to a tape containing a shaman's song as "*Maïcĩ–no riro*," "Maïcĩ–no's body" or "Maïcĩ–no's container," alluding to someone who had died some time ago.

Such were the two objects, the shotgun and the tape recorder, that interested the Araweté the most: an instrument that increased the productivity of the hunt, and an ideological apparatus that reproduced the singularity of the voice. Production and reproducibility, nature and supernature, eating and singing, animals and gods. These themes will come up again throughout the pages that follow.

My incessant activity of writing produced no less curiosity, although not so much objective interest. Many would ask me for paper and pencil, and produce lines of hieroglyphs, parodying my letters; some made "designs" (*kučã*) of the deceased. Others, as soon as they realized that certain topics of conversation would unleash my graphic activity, would ironically order me to write down what they told me.

Eventually they decided that I was there "in order to write" and that I wrote "in order to know" (*to ko̱ã*). One time, while discussing with Toiyi the manner of training shamans through tobacco intoxication, I was told that they did so "in order to know/learn" about the gods. I asked about the word "to know" (*ko̱ã*) and he clarified, "It's like what you do with your writing—it is in order to know, it's the same thing." So, if the Araweté confronted the magic of my technology through the shotgun and the tape recorder, in writing they glimpsed the technology of my magic. Later on, I came to learn about a whole set of associations between graphics and the Other—the jaguar, the gods, the dead, and enemies. Through my writing, I came to be integrated into this series, after a fashion.

3. The Tupi-Guarani Landscape

The peoples of the Tupi-Guarani family (who today in Brazil number at least 33,000 people speaking 21 languages) are found dispersed over an enormous area of South America, from northern Argentina to French Guiana, from the Brazilian northeast to the Peruvian Amazon. At the time of the European invasion, they occupied almost the entire eastern coast of Brazil and the Paraguayan basin; their population was somewhere around 4,000,000 (Rodrigues 1986).

The first thing that calls the attention of anyone who examines the literature on these peoples is the association between a minimal differentiation at the linguistic level, a maximal dispersion in geographic terms, and a marked heterogeneity in social morphology. If the connection between the first two phenomena is due to the Tupi-Guarani "migratory complex" and the population dislocations caused by the European invasion, the relationship between the last two phenomena can be articulated causally, at least as a first approximation. By this view, the variability of organizational forms would be attributed to adaptations to the different ecological and cultural surroundings.

Of the various peoples who speak such closely related languages, we find groups ranging from small bands of nomadic hunters (Guajá, Siriono, Héta, Aché) up to the enormous Tupinamba villages of the sixteenth century with their sophisticated economy, and from almost amorphous social systems where no intermediary structure lies between the nuclear family and the "tribe" up to segmentary morphologies that are dualistic (Tapirapé, Parintintin) or based on clans (Suruí, Tupi-Kawahib). Equally varied are the forms of residence, village morphologies, kinship terminologies, ceremonial structures, attitudes towards war, and the importance of shamanism. The variation in all these features is strikingly similar to the likewise dispersed and "metamorphic" Caribs (Basso 1977: 19).

As a rule, attempts to account for such a situation start from an ideal origin: Tupinamba society. Tupinologists like to speculate about the fate of the Tupinamba population that moved deep into the interior starting in the first decades of the sixteenth century. Baldus and Wagley, for instance, saw the lost Tupinamba in the Tapirapé. As for the Guarani, the problem is understanding the relation among the contemporary groups, the Indians of the Jesuit missions, and those who were never missionized. The anomalous situation of the nomadic groups is explained away as a regressive process caused by geographical confinement, pressure from more powerful groups, and forced transhumance. Anthropologists usually approach the variation among the agricultural groups by considering them to be fragments of a mosaic which, if recomposed (discarding alien influences and cultural losses), would restore the true image of Tupinamba society, an image that would thereby serve as a model.

The reliance on the Tupinamba is explicable in part by their being historically anterior; in part, by the Tupinologists' tradition of using their language as a sort of Latin; and finally, by the supposition that the Tupinamba, as described by the chroniclers who encountered them on the southeast coast of Brazil (not in Maranhão where they were described a century later), were a set of "pure" societies where almost nothing could be considered an effect of the European presence. Even though this last point is problematic, it is usually taken for granted.

But we should look at things from the opposite point of view. The historical Guarani and Tupinamba societies, which were in the midst of a process of expansion when Europeans arrived, should not be considered the civilizational matrix that later degenerated into the contemporary societies, but rather, a specialized and hyperbolic development of a more flexible and generalized social structure. Therefore, it is less a matter of reconstituting routes of historical degradation than one of inserting the facts, past and present, into a neutral series where not only do the Tupinamba throw light on the Kaapor or Tapirapé or others, but the latter, for their part, illuminate the former.

Such a task still remains to be done. The first necessary step is to point out the very fact of the morphosociological variability of the Tupi-Guarani. Rather than a testament to the mutual independence of language and culture (since this is not exactly the case), such a fact indicates the eminently plastic capacity of the Tupi-Guarani matrix at this level. The Tupi-Guarani social structure reveals itself to be capable of diverse surface actualizations; it resists radically different demographic and ecological situations, being capable of absorbing morphological traits prevalent in the regions where it occurs and transferring basic functions from one institution to another. I would argue that this signifies that the social structure has a low degree of specialization, being capable of reproducing itself as much in the periphery of the city of São Paulo (such as some Guarani groups) as in the forests of the Oiapoque to the far north.

This would also signify that its privileged locus of integration, ignoring specific sociological conditions, is situated elsewhere than in the social morphology. Here it is necessary to consider a persistent feature: language. Tupi-Guarani linguistic homogeneity carries a memory—through mythology, religion, and institutional vocabulary—that has resisted five centuries of changes. What appears common to all the Tupi-Guarani groups is language and what can be stored in this medium, a "cosmology." In contrast to other South American situations where a linguistic unity corresponds to a basic morphological structure (such as the Gê), or where a geographical community unifies diverse languages under the same culture (Upper Xingu, Vaupés), what seems to be common to the Tupi-Guarani peoples is an *eidos* manifested in discourse.

It was precisely this empirical fact of close linguistic relatedness that led me to restrict the comparative horizon of this book to the Tupi-Guarani peoples, leaving aside materials on peoples of the Tupi stock but of other linguistic families. We can be certain of studying a substantive unity at the level of the linguistic family; beyond that, there appears to be no privileged basis for comparisons.

But to take refuge in linguistic homogeneity is a simplistic manner of viewing the question. In the first place, what is conveyed by their common cosmological-institutional vocabulary varies significantly from group to group in the semantic drift of key concepts and in the inflections they receive by articulation with diverse sociological conditions. In the second place, the plasticity of Tupi-Guarani social structure presupposes that such a structure can be elaborated, i.e., that it "exists." Thus, it is not possible to be rid of the question of sociological variability by simply appealing to a cosmological-discursive unity.

As a matter of fact, the Tupi-Guarani case is a privileged example of the precariousness of the functionalist distinction between "cosmology" and "social organization." This distinction is perhaps useful as a point of departure, but it must be soon abandoned in the case of societies where the principles of social organization are at the same time metaphysical principles, where every attempt at sociological reduction brings us back to cosmology, or where there is no way to privilege the sociological codification because we risk finding almost nothing—or something else: the gods, the dead, and discourse.

This issue is not simply a question of method. For that matter, as Lévi-Strauss has argued, a social structure is not an empirical resultant, but the formal cause of certain aspects of the praxis of a particular human group; moreover, it operates on multiple semantic materials. The real problem is ethnological. For some time now, Americanists have been dealing with the impropriety of applying the so-called classic models of anthropological analysis, which posit a determinant or fundamental order (kinship, economy) that reduces the symbolic dimension to the condition of a direct or inverted reflex of that order (Kaplan 1977; Seeger, Da Matta & Viveiros de Castro 1979). Against the "African" juralist problematic has been counterposed a problematic of social identity, an analysis of conceptualizations of the universe and the interrelations among their various domains, and a description of social units as aggregations of symbolically determined categories.

However, this antimorphological reaction[20] is not sufficient in itself for specifying the questions posed by Tupi-Guarani ethnology. We cannot simply proceed—whether because of theoretical choice or by following the "idealistic" penchant of South American societies—to the logical subordination of social organization to native metaphysics. These metaphysics do in fact appear to order concrete organizations according to a symbolic logic of identity and difference, same and other, human and extrahuman. But the question that concerns us here is accounting for the low degree of specialization on the sociological plane of the Tupi-Guarani structure, when that structure is articulated with an overabundance or density of discourse about cosmology: on the one hand, fluidity and variability of the social organization; on the other, conceptual insistency.

Tupi-Guarani cosmologies (in the strict sense) do not replicate homologously the sociological armatures from which they spring (as in the Gê case), nor do they possess a high degree of symbolic-taxonomic integration (as in the Tukano mode). On the contrary, the Tupi-Guarani of Amazonia are frequently described as having a vision of the supernatural world that is "not very well organized" (Wagley 1977: 174ff.) or "not having a high degree of elaboration" (Holmberg 1969: 238). In those cosmologies that are more developed, such as the Araweté, Asuriní, or Wayãpi, the luxuriant proliferation of supernatural beings evokes Borges's famous Chinese encyclopedia, it being difficult to reduce them to homogeneous principles of classification. If we turn towards the Guarani, on the other hand, we see the great importance of individual "theologies" of religious shaman-chiefs, who idiosyncratically interpret a set of basic dogmas (Schaden 1969). It is difficult to detect at first sight any "general principle" of these Tupi-Guarani cosmologies that would correspond to Gê dualism or Tukano clanic-functional hierarchy.

If, however, we search for a recurring theme in descriptions of the Tupi-Guarani, we run up against a certain word used to characterize different aspects of these societies: "ambivalence." The literature has said that the attitude of the Guarani in the face of death was ambivalent (Schaden 1969: 173); that the role of the Tapirapé shaman was the object of ambivalent evaluation (Wagley 1977: 193ff.; Baldus 1970 [1949]: 401); that a Tupinamba war prisoner exemplified ambivalence and contradiction (Huxley 1956: 254); that the natural and supernatural worlds appear ambivalent from society's point of view (Kracke 1983: 34–35); that the place of authority is essentially ambiguous (Kracke 1978: 71); and finally, that ambivalence is constitutive of the human condition or cultural state (H. Clastres 1978: 93–97).

It is tempting to associate the frequent use of the notion of ambivalence in characterizing the Tupi-Guarani with the central role of cannibalism in their cosmologies. An anthropologist of a psychoanalytic orientation would certainly do so, since ambivalence, orality, and sadistic-cannibalistic impulses form a conceptual complex in psychoanalysis. But this idea could also be linked to the constitutive ambivalence of the sacrificial system, what Hubert and Mauss (1964 [1898]: 67) called the "fundamental complexity of sacrifice which we cannot overemphasize." For Tupi-Guarani philosophy, indeed, does not seem to strive for a totemic correspondence between the natural and the social series, but rather, for an immediate transformation of one series (the social) into another (the divine). The cannibal short circuit brings forth the figure of Becoming, irreducible to a problematic of representation (as Hubert and Mauss had already perceived).

I know that ambivalence is one of those words that create more problems than they solve (in the context of cannibalism, it could even lead us to the "ambivalence of the primitive sacred"). Nevertheless, I would follow the intuition of H. Clastres about Guarani cosmology when she proposes that ambivalence, according to the Tupi-Guarani conceptualization, is nothing less than the distinctive quality of society. Culture or Society is thought of as a moment interposed between Nature and Supernature. The "active refusal" of Society, which she saw in the early Tupi-Guarani prophetism, is found in a form that is less spectacular, but still efficacious, in contemporary Amazonia. Here we are far from the Nature/Culture dialectic of the Gê cosmologies: ambiguity and ambivalence do not mark the boundary between these two domains and their processes of intercommunication, but are an intrinsic property of the social state itself. The *socius* is a margin or a boundary, an unstable and precarious space between Nature (animality) and Supernature (divinity). Perhaps for this same reason, the social morphology and the "sociological code" are plastic and fluid in these cultures. The unfolding of the cosmological series—animality and divinity—may also suggest an answer for what I have called an excess or supplementarity of cosmology (*stricto sensu*) over sociology.

Of course, the ontological triad Nature/Society/Supernature is not restricted to the Tupi-Guarani; it is found in times and places as venerable in the history of Western thought as classical Greece and the Renaissance (Detienne 1972; Panofsky 1970:24). What distinguishes the Tupi-Guarani case is the way in which it is hierarchically ordered: the focus is not on the central domain, *humanitas*, but on the other two, *feritas* and *divinitas*. Society is a space of dispersal and a time of transition, encompassed by that which is exterior to it.

2 Approaching the Araweté

1. The Country

The Araweté live in a single village next to the Ipixuna Indian Attraction Post (I.P. Ipixuna) (4°45′40″S / 52°30′15″W) on the middle Ipixuna, an eastern tributary of the Xingu River, in the state of Pará. The Ipixuna is a blackwater river with many rapids and waterfalls, flowing in a rocky bed from the southeast to the northwest from the watershed of the Bacajá-Xingu rivers. The dominant vegetation near the present village site is liana forest, where trees are rarely over 25 meters and great quantities of vines and thorny bushes made travel arduous (Pires & Prance 1985; Balée 1989b). The area is dotted with granite irruptions and small rocky hills crowned with cactus, bromeliads, and century plants. Game is abundant due to the great variety of fruit-bearing trees, especially palms. The high feline population led to the penetration of the area by fur hunters in the 1960s and the consequent "discovery" of the Araweté.

Rainfall is quite high from December to March; the remaining part of the year could be called a "dry season." Between August and November, the river becomes impassable, exposing extensive beds of flat rocks and forming stagnant pools of water favorable for fishing with ichthiotoxic vines. During the rains, which fall with greatest intensity in February, the waters of the river rise five meters or more above its lowest level. The Ipixuna is not especially rich in fish.

The Araweté numbered 136 people in February of 1983 and 168 five years later. They are the survivors of a population of hunters and agriculturalists of the terra firme forest who were dislocated by the Kayapó-Xikrin about thirty years ago from the headwaters of the Bacajá River and who migrated towards the Xingu. Since then, they have been living within an area lying between the river basins of the Bom Jardim in the south and the Piranhaquara in the north, which includes the Canafístula, Jatobá, and Ipixuna rivers. The Xingu River, which they never cross, represents the westernmost limit of their territory. The region of the Bacajá-Xingu watershed to the east has not been traversed for a long time; there lies the domain of the feared Kayapó-Xikrin. Nor do they venture beyond the Bom Jardim where a Parakanã group (the same that attacked them in 1976 and 1983) was contacted by FUNAI in 1984. On the eastern banks of the Piranhaquara begins the land of the Asuriní, another traditional enemy. The area most thoroughly exploited by the Araweté, given their present state of dependency upon the FUNAI Post, covers a band of almost sixty kilometers on each side of the Ipixuna from its mouth to its headwaters.

This area showed no sign of invasion or occupation by ranchers during the years 1981–83. After the decline of the big-cat hunters (the commerce in furs having been prohibited in 1967), the only non-Araweté to be found there were less than a dozen peasants and rubber tappers living on the banks of the Xingu. The territorial situation of the Araweté, however, is far from secure. Only in late 1987 did FUNAI decide to "interdict" (an innocuous juridical measure) an area of 985,000 hectares, after innumerable proposals were submitted by anthropologists (and certain members of the agency itself) for the creation of an Araweté reservation and the joint demarcation of the Araweté, Asuriní, Xikrin and Parakanã territories. The probability that this or any area will be effectively demarcated is low (at least for one that would be larger than a two-kilometer circle around the village), given that the question of indigenous land holdings is in the hands of the military, whose dominant ideology is "national security and integration." They consider the Indians to be a hindrance to the development and Brazilianization of Amazonia, an inferior race that must be dissolved into the regional population.

Two major threats are waiting for the Araweté in the near future: the inundation of part of their territory by the reservoirs of the Xingu Hydroelectric Dam Complex and the crossing of its southern and eastern boundaries by mining and logging companies. In fact, the first sign of the coming crisis appeared in 1986, when two clandestine loggers penetrated Parakanã and Araweté lands, opening airstrips and extracting enormous quantities of mahogany. FUNAI reacted with only slightly less sluggishness and complacency than usual, obtaining a financial compensation in 1988 earmarked for the two plundered areas (Fausto 1989). The invaders pulled out of these lands, which FUNAI recognizes halfheartedly as the Indians', but they continue to extract wood within the "corridor" along the Bacajá-Xingu watershed. It is imperative, however, that this latter area be reserved for the exclusive usufruct of the indigenous peoples of the region.

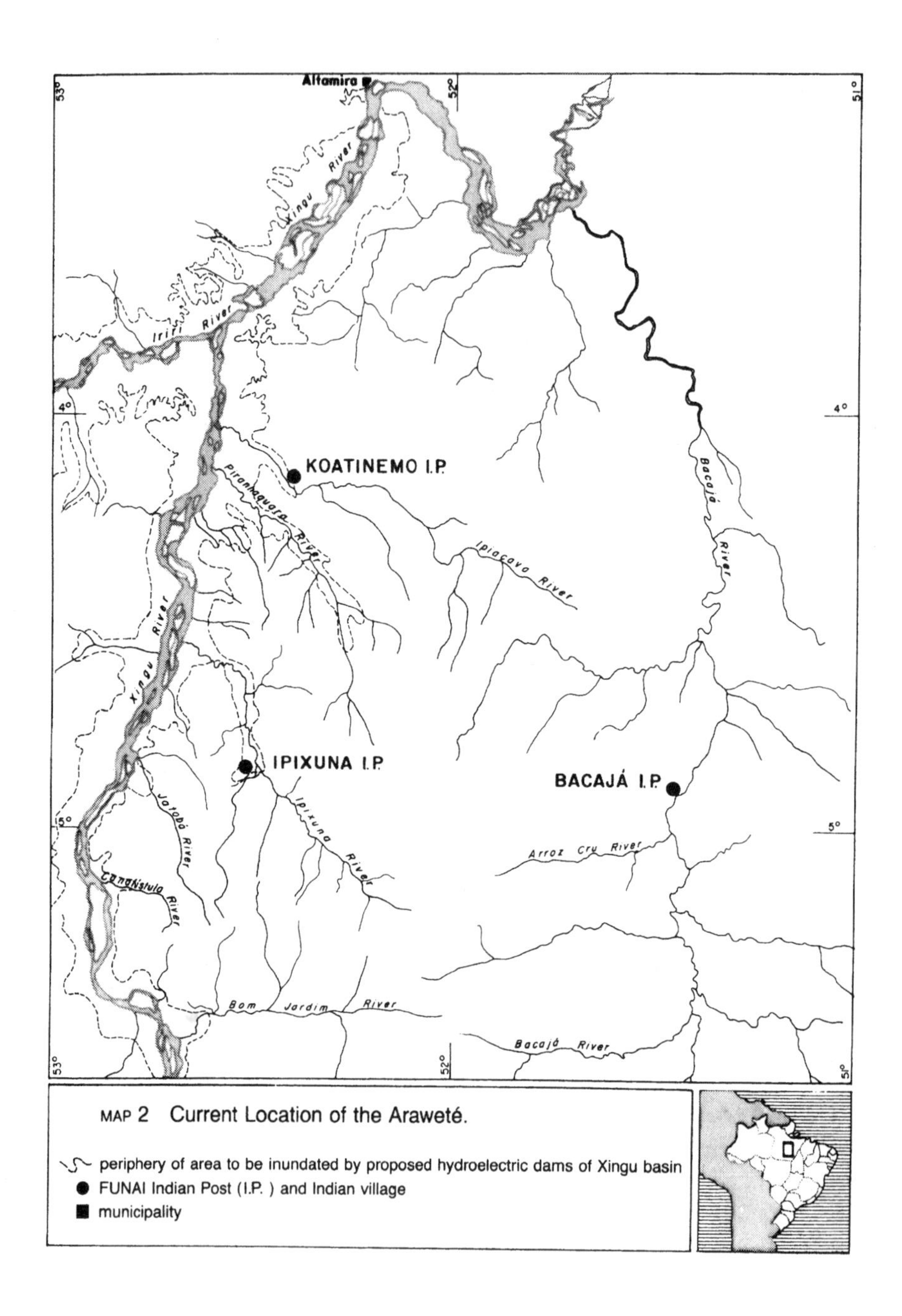

MAP 2 Current Location of the Araweté.

The two poles of influence on Araweté country are the municipal seats of Altamira, to the northwest, and São Felix do Xingu, to the south. The first city, capital of the middle Xingu, grew vertiginously with the construction of the Transamazon Highway in 1970. The regional headquarters of FUNAI are located in Altamira; to them are transported the most seriously ill Araweté, and from them come the goods and services destined for the Ipixuna Post. The second city is one of the fastest growing in Pará (and in Brazil); the municipality is a critical area of frontier expansion, the site of intense mining, colonization projects, plantations, and ranches.

To speak of the boundaries of Araweté country only makes sense from an outsider's point of view. The Araweté conception of territoriality is open; until recently, they did not have a notion of exclusive dominion over a continuous and homogeneous space. Dislodged by other groups from the area they previously occupied, they migrated to the Ipixuna River and in turn dislodged the Asuriní. Their history testifies to a constant movement of fleeing more powerful enemies. Apart from the vague notion that they are now on the edge of the earth (which is sadly true from the political perspective) and that their ancestral site was in the center of the earth, the Araweté do not appear to have a mythical geography or sacred sites. Their objective and subjective inclination was to push forward incessantly, leaving behind their dead and their enemies. The idea of reoccupying a former area seems strange to them; they avoid doing this even within the present limits of their territory.

The wars they were involved in were never conceived of as territorial disputes; the tribes that invaded their area were seen less as menaces to the group's territorial integrity than as threats to its physical survival. Similarly, when fur hunters entered the Ipixuna region during the 1960s, they were not viewed as invaders who had to be expelled, but rather, as a welcome source of iron tools, provided they manifested no hostile intentions.

Only when they were contacted and fixed in a restricted area did a closed conception of territory begin to emerge. On the one hand, establishing a single village next to the FUNAI Post broke with the traditional geopolitical pattern of several contemporaneous and dispersed villages, smaller than the present one; the dependency on the Post also diminished their radius of movement. On the other hand, contact with Western concepts of territoriality (transmitted directly or indirectly by the whites) and the situation of geographical confinement has been leading to a closed and exclusive territorial notion, consecrating a new historical situation: an "Araweté territory" still awaiting recognition by the national state (Seeger & Viveiros de Castro 1979).

The Araweté, like so many other groups, sought contact with the whites—whom they pacified (*mo-katɨ*)—not because they felt territorially hemmed in, but in order to flee the hostilities of enemy tribes that, for their part, were invading foreign territory after being dislocated by the national frontier (the reach of the whiteman being long indeed). The Parakanã attacks during the 1960s made the Araweté seek the populated banks of the Xingu. Their incessant drifting in search of lands far from enemies ended. From now on, they will also have to cohabit with their dead—if even this much be granted them.

2. The Regional Context

From the basins of the Gurupí and Pindaré rivers in the eastern extreme of Amazonia to the forests of the Tocantins-Xingu river basin stretches a region occupied since at least the seventeenth century by peoples of the Tupi-Guarani family, with a single important intrusion, the Arara of the Carib family. Its northern limits coincided with the channel of the Amazon River; to the south and southeast were various Gê groups (Kayapó, Timbira). In the Xingu region and farther to the west, in the Tapajós basin, large Tupi tribes of other linguistic families (Juruna and Shipaya, Munducucu and Kuruaya) interrupt the continuity of the Tupi-Guarani, who reappear on the Madeira River as the central Tupi (Kagwahiv, Tupi-Cawahib). Many of the groups have disappeared, known only through missionary chronicles and reports of provincial presidents.

In the Xingu-Tocantins area, where the Araweté live, the list of former occupants includes the Pacajá, Tapiraua, Kupe-rob, and Anambé, all in the forests of the western banks of the Tocantins; and the Takunyapé, near the Xingu. Of the ethnonyms still heard today, there have been reports of "Asuriní" living between the Xingu and its tributary, the Bacajá, since the end of the last century (Coudreau 1977 [1897]); the "Parakanã" appeared on the western banks of the Tocantins at the beginning of the present century (Nimuendaju 1948a: 206–7). During the 1920s, the Suruí and the Akuáwa-Asuriní began to be sighted in the region of the lower Araguaia, Itacaíunas, and Tucuruí; their definitive contact occurred only in the 1950s (Laraia & Da Matta 1967). Separated from this homogeneous bloc by Kayapó territory are the Tapirapé, far to the south in the transitional area between the forest and the central Brazilian scrublands, and the Tupi-

Guarani groups of the Upper Xingu regional system, the Kamayura and Aweti, near whom the Kayabi, a central Tupi group, recently settled.

The Tocantins-Xingu mesopotamia was also occupied by the Juruna and the Arara. The former, a canoe tribe probably coming from the Amazon channel, dominated the lower and middle Xingu in the eighteenth and nineteenth centuries. Their migratory movements, the result of conflicts with whites and the Kayapó, brought them to the upper Xingu at the beginning of the twentieth century. The Shipaya, linguistically and culturally close to the Juruna, do not appear to have ever settled on the eastern banks of the Xingu. The Arara have also been known since the nineteenth century—or at least this ethnonym was applied to Indians sighted on the Pacajá,[1] the Tocantins, and on both sides of the Xingu. However, it is doubtful that all belonged to the same group, the ancestors of the Carib-speaking Arara contacted in 1891 on the Iriri River.

Finally, another contemporary Tupi-Guarani group originating from the middle Xingu should be mentioned; the Wayãpi, who occupied the confluence of the Iriri and the Xingu in the mid-seventeenth century, then initiated a long migration northwards in the following century. Fleeing attempts to settle them in mission villages, they crossed the Amazon River and reached the upper Jari and Oiapoque rivers (Gallois 1980:55–59).

It is difficult to trace the historical origins of this group of Tupi-Guarani tribes of eastern Amazonia, which should include groups beyond the Tocantins such as the Amanayé, Kaapor, Guajá, and Tenetehara. Some writers associate them with the Tupinamba migration from Maranhão towards the mouth of the Amazon at the beginning of the seventeenth century. Grenand (1982:150–531), speaking of the Wayãpi, includes them in movements of the Tupi-Guarani who, after having failed to master the varzea in the seventeenth century, occupied the terra firme forests between the Gurupí and the Xingu. In this same era, the groups on the fertile varzea were destroyed by the Europeans, who then forced the Tupi-Guarani groups to disperse yet again to interfluvial areas. According to Grenand, the Wayãpi, Asuriní, Tenetehara, and other modern Tupi-Guarani tribes were the result of this process.

Métraux (1928:308–12), in fact, believed that these peoples (of which little was known at the time he wrote) were associated with the last great migration of the Tupi from their ancestral site of dispersal, which he located on the upper Tapajós.[2] However, casting all the current Tupi-Guarani as direct descendents of a "Tupinamba" tribe is problematic, given that peoples such as the Pacajá and Tenetehara existed contemporaneously with the Tupinamba of the coast.

The reconstruction of the Tupi-Guarani movements in the region is a task that still remains to be done. Laraia (1985) points to a recurrent theme in the oral traditions of the current peoples: the fissioning of a large ancestral group, usually after disputes over women. He notes that the Kaapor were formerly located much further west of their current territory and that they have a tradition about the migration of part of the tribe to the other side of the Tocantins. The Suruí and Akuáwa-Asuriní say they came from a region to the northwest of their current site. If we add to this the Araweté tradition of an origin from east of the Ipixuna, it is tempting to speculate on an ancestral Tupi-Guarani location in the Xingu-Tocantins interfluvial region, maybe on the headwaters of the Pacajá—perhaps even suggesting that the origin of the contemporary groups was the oft-mentioned tribe of the Pacajás, whose light skin, "bluish" eyes, and chestnut hair evoke so strongly the appearance of the Araweté (Daniel 1976 [1757–76]: 273; cf. Adalbert 1849 [1847]: 269, who gives the same description of the Takunyapé).

Two great movements, separated by two centuries, bore down upon the Xingu-Tocantins region, with profound impacts on the Tupi-Guarani. The first proceeded in a north-to-south direction, following the course of the large rivers: this was the Portuguese invasion, initiated in the beginning of the seventeenth century, shortly after the expulsion of the Dutch and British in 1623, with intense catechizing and settling of the Indians at missions (Castello Branco 1956). The missionaries were followed by military expeditions from 1650 onward (Gallois 1980: 56). The effects of this conquest were the usual: the "reduction" and "descent" (dislocation and resettlement) of different peoples to form mixed mission villages where the *Língua Geral* was imposed,[3] with conditions that often provoked the missionized populations to resist by fleeing to join their relatives who were still roaming free in the terra firme forests further from the main rivers.

In the middle of the past century, the second movement began, this time south-to-north. The expansion of the Kayapó from the plains of the Araguaia (taken over by the pastoral colonization front) towards the forests of the Xingu radically transformed the demographic situation of the Tupi-Guarani, Juruna, and Arara. In 1936, already established on the middle Xingu (near the Fresco River), the Gorotire, "in their expansion northwards, attacked and defeated the Asuriní" (Nimuendaju 1948b: 225). Also dating to this era was the fissioning of the Xikrin and the migration of part of the tribe to the Bacajá, where they collided with the Asuriní, Araweté, and Parakanã. But even the part that remained in the Tocantins basin made occasional incursions against these groups (Vidal 1977).

Finally, since the 1970s, the construction of the Transamazon Highway and the expansion of the frontier towards the Xingu region completed the process of enclosing these indigenous peoples. All the groups of the Xingu-Tocantins ended up coming under the control of the Brazilian state—in 1971, the Asuriní; in 1976, the Araweté; in 1981, the Arara; in 1984, the last of the Parakanã. Or almost all: recent information indicates the presence of unknown Indians at the headwaters of the Ipiaçava in Asuriní country . . .

□

There were no references made to the Araweté until the 1970s. The scarce descriptions of extinct groups do not warrant drawing any clear conclusions. The Takunyapé would seem at first sight to be good candidates for the status of the Araweté's ancestors: the eastern banks of the Xingu near the Great Bend (4° S / 53° W) was known in the seventeenth century as the "land of the Takonhapés," and the "river of the Takonhapés" was probably the Bacajá (Nimuendaju1948b: 222). This tribe was settled in mission villages several times, but part of it fled to the middle Curuá. In 1863, an epidemic decimated its numerous population; by the end of the century, it was thought to be extinct. A vocabulary was collected in 1919 (Nimuendaju 1932), but it does not reveal any special resemblance to contemporary Araweté. Other than a "dance of the souls" that the group on the Curuá had in common with the Shipaya, nothing more is known about this people.

The eastern side of the Xingu and the region of the Bacajá were known at the end of the nineteenth century as "the land of the Asuriní" (Müller et al. 1979: 1). This ethnonym is of Juruna origin and means "red Indians." It could have been applied to different Tupi-Guarani groups, among which are the contemporary Asuriní (called "Asuriní of the Trocará [Post]," in contrast to the Akuáwa-Asuriní, called "Asuriní of the Koatinemo [Post]," who live in the Tocantins basin). It is not improbable that some of these "Asuriní," who in the beginning of this century attacked rubber tappers on the Bacajá and warred against the Arara and Takunyapé, were the Araweté. Nimuendaju stated in 1948 that the Kayapó applied the enthnonym "Kubekamreg-ti" (which also means "red Indians") to the "Asuriní." More recent information, however, indicates that the Xikrin of the Bacajá call the Araweté "Kube-kamrek-ti," while the Asuriní of the Koatinemo are called by another ethnonym, "Krã-akâro" (Müller et al. 1979:34). The descriptive label "red Indians" perhaps applies more properly to the Indians of the Ipixuna than to those of the Ipiaçava, since the Araweté use red annatto paint more abundantly than the Asuriní. Possible inconsistencies made by Coudreau (1977[1897]:37, 48), such as when he asserts that the Bacajá is the habitat of "most of the tribe" of the Asuriní and that the Ipixuna is the site of their "main village," may be due to a confusion between two distinct groups. If so, it could be that the "Asuriní" of the Bacajá were the Araweté who managed to reach the Ipixuna only around 1960, dislodging from there the contemporary Asuriní.

3. The People

The Araweté do not denominate themselves by any descriptive ethnonym, using instead the form *bïde*, "human beings," "we," "people." The word "Araweté" is an invention of the FUNAI expeditionist J. E. Carvalho (1977), who derived this pseudoform from **awa ete*, "true humans." Arnaud (1978) consolidated the use of this designation. The expression **awa ete* does not exist in the language of the group; rather, it is the Asuriní who designate themselves by this term, while calling the Araweté the *Ararawa*, macaw people. The neighboring Parakanã call them the *Orowïjara* (perhaps surubim [catfish] people [C. Fausto, pers. comm., 1989]).

The Araweté language belongs to the Tupi-Guarani family, but it is quite idiosyncratic. It could be included in the northeastern group (which Nimuendaju called the "*He* group," according to the form of the first person singular), but such a classification is considered illegitimate in modern scholarship. Their language has still not been studied by any specialist; the criteria used for establishing subgroups within the Tupi-Guarani family (Lemle 1971; Rodrigues 1985) do not permit its unequivocal classification. The most that can be said is that it is an eastern Amazonian Tupi-Guarani language, displaying variations that are not shared with any other language.

The Araweté are aware of their obvious linguistic relatedness to the Asuriní and the Parakanã. The language (*ñe'e*) they speak is the "correct (able) mouth" (*yɨrɨ kara katɨ*), in opposition to the "hampered (or mixed) mouth" (*yɨrɨ parawï*) of whitemen and other enemies. The other Tupi-Guarani are thus closer to true human beings; although this does not modify their current definition as enemies (*awĩ*), it can sometimes lead to their reclassification as *bïde pe*, "ex-Araweté," or *ɨre anĩ neme pa re,* "descendants of our deceased siblings/relatives," referring to a tradition about an early fissioning of the group.

□

The Araweté have a material culture that is comparatively simple within the spectrum of Tupi-Guarani groups. Their dearth of objects is perhaps surpassed only by the nomadic Guajá, Siriono, and Héta, with whom they have been compared. Berta Ribeiro, who spent two months in 1981 on the Ipixuna and wrote preliminary but excellent accounts of Araweté material culture, especially of their weaving techniques, describes them as having "rustic" equipment, a "low agricultural technology," and "little artistic sense" (1981; 1983; 1985). Even putting aside the author's value judgments, one cannot avoid acknowledging the parsimony of the Araweté in their ergological and artisanal techniques and the casual character of the visual or visible aspects of their culture: body painting, architecture, cuisine, and etiquette. Such simplicity can be explained in part by the constant state of alarm and flight from enemies they have endured in recent decades, and in part by the trauma of contact. But this austerity is a given of Araweté culture that appears consistent with their more general orientation.

The very simplicity of the material culture thwarts attempts to associate the Araweté with any specific Tupi-Guarani group (Ribeiro 1983:22). Furthermore, certain unexpectedly complex items are unique to them, such as their shaman rattle (made of woven itiriti[4] strips and covered with cotton) and their lovely female clothing. The absolute predominance of the cultivation of maize over that of manioc also distinguishes them from the rest of the Amazonian Tupi-Guarani.

The people are attractive, of modest height (men average 1.6 meters; women, 1.5), generally light-skinned, with hair and eye color between pitch black and light chestnut; although very strong, they do not have obvious musculature, and the women tend to be plump. The variety of physical types is nevertheless great. Men have sparse whiskers and usually let them grow into goatees; they go about nude and only depilate their eyebrows. Traditionally (before using pants), they tied the prepuce with string. Women wear an outfit of four tubular pieces (girdle, skirt, sling-blouse, and head covering), used as a complete set after puberty, woven of cotton and tinted with red annatto dye.[5] All women wear earrings made of tiny macaw feathers arranged in a flower shape that hangs from strings of black soapberry seeds (*čĩñã*), the same kind of seed used in their necklaces. Men use similar earrings with shorter pendants, and some wear wristbands of crocheted cotton, which, used since infancy, sometimes cut deep grooves in the flesh. Their haircut features straight bangs across the forehead to the top of the ears, while in back it hangs to the base of the neck for men and down to the shoulders for women.

The basic dye and coloring of the Araweté is the bright red of annatto (made from the pulp surrounding the seeds of the *Bixa orellana* tree), with which they coat their hair and smear their entire bodies. On the face, however, they trace only the *yiriã* pattern: a horizontal line at the top of the eyebrows, one along the nose, and a line from each ear to the corners of the mouth. This pattern is also used for festive decoration (there being only one type of ceremonial body ornamentation for any category of person); in this case, it is traced in perfumed resin and covered with the minuscule feathers of the *moneme*, an iridescent blue cotinga. Harpy eagle down is glued to the hair and on the back and chest in a rectangular pattern.

Genipap dye[6] is rarely seen in the village; it is associated with the forest, warfare, and the dead. On hunting and gathering expeditions, men and women often blacken themselves with genipap. But they do not make delicate designs on the body; their appearance usually has a blotchy and incomplete look, even at festivals, since they leave body ornamentation to the last minute. In contrast, the gods and the souls of the dead have a splendid appearance, elegantly painted (with genipap, since they do not use annatto) and seductively perfumed.

During the nocturnal dances and the ceremony of strong maize beer, men wear a diadem of macaw feathers, a symbol of masculine and warlike values. One of the epithets for the male community in the context of beer festivals is "masters of the diadem" (*yiakã ñã*).[7]

□

Agriculture is the basis of Araweté subsistence. The two main products of their gardens are maize (four varieties), consumed from March to November, and bitter manioc (three varieties) for the complementary season. Other important cultigens are sweet potatoes, yams, and sweet manioc. Also planted in the gardens or in the village are cotton, tobacco, sisal, papaya, banana, pineapple, calabashtree, soapberry, and annatto.[8] Maize (*awaci*) clearly predominates over manioc (*madïda*) in both thought and practice. Manioc is only consumed when the stock of maize is exhausted and the green maize has not yet been harvested, i.e., in the rainy season. The garden (*ka*), opened annually by slash-and-burn techniques, is a garden of maize (*awacï dɨpã*, support [ground] of maize), interspersed with manioc, yams, potatoes, etc., planted with greater or lesser density.[9] Maize is consumed in various forms depending on the season: roasted ears, green maize porridge, flour made from untoasted maize, toasted cornmeal, and two kinds of maize beer—a weaker type (of low fermentation) and a stronger type (of medium fermentation). Cornmeal, made of ripe maize that is toasted and ground, is the basic form of meal in the diet, being consumed for nine months of the year. *Kã̠'ɨ̃'da*, the stronger maize beer made by saliva-induced fermentation, is the focus of their most important ceremony, enacted several times a year during the dry season.

Manioc, grated on paxiúba roots, squeezed manually, then dried in the sun or smoked on wooden racks, is consumed as tapioca bread or as toasted meal made from freshly harvested roots (a different technique of soaking manioc roots for several days to soften and decompose was introduced by white people). Although the Araweté appreciate the products made from this plant, they say they consume them in the rainy season because there is no more maize or because the green maize is not yet ready—clearly indicating the subordinate role of manioc. Sweet potatoes, yams, and sweet manioc are consumed boiled or roasted. While maize is obligatorily planted by all domestic units in quantities sufficient to last through the dry season and for ceremonial purposes, the other products vary greatly in the quantity planted from year to year and from house to house. A large portion of the potatoes, yams, and bitter and sweet manioc is harvested in gardens planted up to two years earlier (*ka pe*). Tools used in opening the gardens are fire, machetes, and iron axes;[10] digging sticks are used in planting. Gardens cover an average of 1.5 hectares; the size of each varies according to the production unit involved, whether a single house or a residential section. They are cluttered with incompletely burned trunks and branches; apparently not much care is taken in making bonfires. Bitter manioc, sweet manioc, cotton, tobacco, and bananas are planted in separate sections on the periphery of the plots of maize. Potatoes and yams are dispersed through the maize fields in clumps growing at regular intervals.

□

Hunting is the focus of intense cultural investment. The accusation of "laziness" (*čiranahi*), frequently levelled in marital separations, refers only to women's domestic work and men's agricultural chores. In the heavens, no one gardens, since the plants grow on their own, but everyone hunts. The gods are hunters, not agriculturalists.

The Araweté hunt a variety of animals larger than those usually pursued by other Tupi-Guarani groups, and they appear to have fewer food prohibitions, either general or specific. The following are in approximate order of nutritional importance: land tortoises, armadillos, curassows, guans, agoutis, collared peccaries, white-lipped peccaries, howler monkeys, capuchin monkeys, pacas, deer, tinamous (three species),[11] macaws, toucans, trumpeter birds, and tapirs. Toucans, macaws, harpy eagles, smaller hawks, curassows, oropendolas, and two types of cotingas are sought for their feathers to make arrows and adornments. Scarlet and canindé macaws and parrots are captured alive and raised in the village as pets (*temimã*) (in 1982, the village had 54 tame macaws). The harpy eagle (*kanoho*), if captured alive, is kept in a cage.

Tortoises and armadillos are not so much hunted as "collected," given that they do not require weapons (the generic verb for "hunting" is simply *ɨatã,* to go for a walk; for tortoises and armadillos, the verb *kati,* to fetch, is used). Tortoises are available in any season of the year, even though they are associated with life in the forest and with the rainy season when *ara̱ho* (sapodilla fruits) are ripe. These fruits fatten them and enlarge their livers, the favorite dish of the Araweté. Tortoises can be kept as a food reserve for difficult days, and they are the object of ceremonial hunts. Armadillos are an important food at the beginning of the dry season, when they are at their fattest.

In the village, game from the hunt is eaten boiled, and the broth is used to make a mush or soup of maize. Roasting is used for parts of certain animals, such as armadillo tails and the fatty lining of their shells, and for a few birds, such as the trumpeter bird. Aside from these, roasting is viewed as a selfish form of food preparation, since it limits the number of mouths that can be fed. Alimentary generosity is an essential value in Araweté society. Their ceremonies are little more than great collective meals; to eat alone is the mark of a stingy person (*hakataĩ*). In the forest during the men's expeditions that are mounted to bring back a large quantity of game, smoking is used as the method of preparation, or more precisely, the method of treatment, since smoked meats are usually boiled back in the village before being consumed. At the hunting camps, game is eaten roasted. When excursions include women and children, pots are always brought for boiling the meat.

Cleaning and preparing the meat are male tasks, although women can help, which is in line with the characteristic fluidity of the Araweté division of labor. But the association between men and meat extends from its acquisition and preparation up through its consumption. During collective meals, it is always the men who crowd around the pot or serving vessel containing the meat; it is they who divide up the pieces, eat first, and then hand over the rest to their wives (who divide them up among their children). Perhaps that is why the hunter's wife jealously calculates the quantity of meat her husband brings back and tries to contain his impulses towards generosity when he invites other houses to share in the meal.

The weapons used for hunting are a short wide bow made of bow wood (*Tabebuia serratifolia*), admirably fashioned, and arrows with points of lanceolate bamboo (which can be as long as 70 cm), howler monkey legbone, or fire-hardened wood. The first type, used for large game and warfare, bears harpy eagle feathers; the other two, curassow feathers. Men sometimes go out into the forest without their bows, searching for tortoises or armadillos (in general, a hunter goes out with a particular prey in mind). Their capacity for improvising weapons in the forest is notable—which does not prevent many who brought only a machete from seeing their lack of foresight punished by the sudden appearance of a herd of peccaries.

Although the Araweté claim that the introduction of firearms in 1982 increased their capacity to obtain game, their use led to the flight or exhaustion of the animal population near the village as early as 1983, obliging them to cover a wider range of territory. The shotguns made it necessary for the bands of hunters to break up into smaller units during the ceremonial hunts for beer festivals—due as much to the noise of the gunshots as to the risk of accidents. With the adoption of flashlights, the paca, an animal stalked at night, became an important source of food.

Fishing is divided into two periods: the season of "beating (killing) the fish" (*pïdã nopĩ me*), when poison vines are used (October-November); and the months of daily fishing outings using bow and arrow or hook and line. To fish with poison vine, the village fragments into smaller groups that camp next to deep pockets in the waters of the Ipixuna and the nearly dry streams. Both men and women participate in such trips. The fish are prepared by smoking. The paradigm for this kind of fishing is the trairão (*pïda oho*, "large fish"). The daily fishing trips increase in frequency as the water level of the rivers drops. Boys and girls between five and fifteen years old are the most assiduous fishers; the products of their efforts contribute substantially to the village food supply. Women fish almost as much as men.

Although fish is a highly valued food, it is less so than game, and fishing is a secondary activity for adult men. Besides fishing with poison vines, men participate in collective fishing with the *hara*, a manual fusiform fishtrap made of splints of babassu palm, used in ponds during the dry season.

Most elderly people do not know how to swim. Water for drinking and cooking is drawn by the women from water holes dug on the sandy banks of the rivers and streams or in groves of assai palms. The Araweté say river water is hot; they greatly appreciate the milky coloring of the water from the water holes, which they compare with colostrum,[12] within a complex of associations among water, milk, maize beer, semen, and fish poison (i.e., water made turbid by the sap of the poison vine).[13]

Gathering is an important activity. Its main products are:[14] honey (*e*), which the Araweté classify into at least forty-five categories, edible or not, from bees and wasps; assai palmfruits, consumed with honey during a particular ceremony; bacaba palmfruits; Brazil nuts, an important food during the dry season; babassu nuts, eaten and used as a binder with annatto and as a lubricant for the wood of bows; cupuaçu fruits; various fruits of lesser importance in the diet such as cacao, hog plum, ingá, various species of the sapote family; river turtle eggs, the objective of family excursions in September (although the small number of beaches on the Ipixuna hampers this activity); and palm grubs, eaten toasted.[15] Gathering is pursued by both sexes, usually by couples (except for honey and assai, which are sought on collective expeditions).

Other resources important to the Araweté way of life should be mentioned: leaves and splices of babassu for houses, mats, and basketry; the spathes of babassu, cokerite, and assai palms, used as bowls and serving vessels; two types of bamboo for arrow points and shafts; splices of taquarinha and other plants for sieves and shaman rattles; wild gourds for dance maracas; special types of wood for pestles, axe handles, bows, arrow points, house supports and beams, and chisel sharpeners; digging sticks; fibers and vines; and clay for the simple Araweté ceramics.

The sexual division of labor is summarized in table 1. The first thing that should be noted is the relatively high fluidity of the division of labor. Tasks exclusively associated with men are those that involve the use of weapons or great physical strength (e.g., felling trees); those with women, weaving and ceramics. No interdiction exists, however, against the handling of bows and arrows by women or against the occasional participation of men in female tasks. It is not uncommon to see men carrying water, spinning, boiling potatoes, husking and toasting corn, etc., along with their wives or if the latter are busy with something else.[16] For their part, women do not avoid the task of felling trees for firewood, assisting in the construction of houses, capturing tortoises, and so on. Tobacco is a masculine plant important in shamanism, but women prepare the cigarettes for their husbands, hold the cigars of shamans in trance, and also smoke. In the range of tasks performed during planting, the division by sex is not rigid either. Men or women can open furrows for receiving seeds, and both can plant maize. Only manioc is planted exclusively by men. As for the rest of the tasks, the two sexes *oyo pitiwã,* cooperate, substituting for each other in the same activities.

Similarly, the average work load is equitably distributed between the sexes (see Ribeiro 1985:363–64); perhaps if weighed on the scales, the balance would favor women, contrary to what is customarily said about the "burden of the Indian woman" (cf. similar observations about the Kayabi in Grünberg n.d. [1970]:109). Araweté women, in short, show a great deal of assertiveness, independence, and extroversion. The relative lack of differentiation in the sexual division of work has repercussions in the political sphere, kinship relations, and other contexts.

Nevertheless, there are some significant oppositions. The forest (hunting) is a masculine domain, and the garden, with maize as its focal cultigen, a feminine domain. The garden is cleared "by the husbands for their wives, who in exchange make them cotton hammocks." Although both sexes dedicate themselves to agriculture, maize and its processing are associated with women in both practice and discourse: they pass the greater part of their time between cotton and maize, spinning and grinding. In the garden, manioc is under the care of men, who plant it; manioc is a "man's affair" (*kɨme'e apa*). It is opposed to maize and subordinated to it, just as man is to woman in the garden.

The typical and ideal meal consists of meat and maize. Meat is never eaten without some type of flour (*ɗepe*) of either maize, manioc, or even the mesocarp of the babassu coconut, the last resource in the final months of the rainy-season excursions, when manioc flour is used up. But maize is the model of vegetable foods, which complete the carnivorous meal—or rather, the other way around. Toasted cornmeal (*awacï mepi*) accompanies other foods besides meat (papaya, banana, nuts); it can be eaten alone when nothing else is left. On the other hand, the exhaustion of the supply of cornmeal carried by men on hunts is the signal for their return to the village. Meat is not eaten

TABLE I Sexual division of labor

Men	Women
Activities	
Select new garden sites, clear trees, burn brush	Assist in burning
Plant manioc, sweet manioc, tobacco, bananas, sisal	Plant maize, potatoes, cotton, annatto, papayas, pineapples, flatsedge, yams
Assist in harvesting (except cotton and annatto)	Harvest all plants (except tobacco and sisal), carry maize and potatoes to village
Construct platforms and containers for storing ears of maize for planting, transport seeds to new gardens	Separate and shell maize for plantings, prepare seedlings and cuttings for planting
Hunt all animals, prepare fish poison, fish with poison, arrows, hooks, and fishtraps	Assist in locating tortoises, fish with poison and hooks
Carry, skin, pluck, and clean game animals	Assist in plucking game birds, clean fish, open tortoises
Gather assai and bacaba palmfruits, gather honey by felling tree or erecting platform	Make receptacles in forest for honey, carry honey to village
Collect Brazil nuts and other fruits	Collect Brazil nuts and other fruits
Cut thatching and wood for houses	Fetch clay for ceramics
Cook game	Assist in cooking game
Assist in grinding maize and grating manioc	Shell, grind, and toast maize; cook other vegetables; grate, press manioc; and dry manioc meal
Assist in grinding and cooking maize beverages, homogenize fermenting beer	Prepare and cook maize beverage and masticate maize for fermentation
Cut and carry large firewood, make fires	Cut and carry smaller firewood, make fires, supply firewood during men's collective hunts, fetch water
Construct and maintain houses	Weave mats to use as doors on traditional houses, prepare babassu leaves for roofs, keep houses clean
Dry and prepare tobacco and sisal	Husk, beat, and spin cotton; prepare annatto dye
Bury the dead	Paint and decorate the dead

TABLE 1 (*continued*)

Men	Women
	Artifacts constructed*
Bows (male use)	Female clothing
Arrows (male use)	Cotton headbands
Chisels and sharpeners (male use)	Cotton thread
Feather ornaments	Hammocks
Necklaces and earrings (perforate soapberry seeds)	Fire fans
Combs	Burden baskets
Maracas	Small baskets for cornmeal
Storage boxes for feathers	Mats for sitting and for front and back walls of traditional house
Sieves	Gourd bowls
Manioc grater (cut sections of paxiúba root)	Ceramics (4 types)
Final decoration of shaman rattle with cotton string, feathers (male use)	Woven portion of shaman rattle (male use)
Mortar and pestle	
Wooden spoons	
Spindles (female use)	
Awls	
Looms (female use)	
Digging sticks	
Bowls, vessels (gather and prepare palm spathes)	
Sisal twine	
Fishtraps	

*Except where indicated, artifacts are used by both sexes.

without maize, the mark of civilization. The Araweté say they sought out the gardens of whites on the banks of the Xingu because enemy attacks left them without maize and they were tired of eating just meat—which meant living like a savage.[17]

Nevertheless, meat is the most valued food from the point of view of taste and nutrition. A meal without meat induces discomfort and psychological depression. If a meal without maize is unfit, one without meat is insubstantial. One can be hungry (*ho'imã*) in the midst of an abundance of maize, potatoes, and other vegetable foods.[18] Although the Araweté may be considered somewhat careless and improvident agriculturalists, they are excellent hunters and live in an area of plentiful game. Except during the months when a violent flu struck the village, no one failed to eat meat at least once a day throughout my time there. Food reciprocity and the reserve supplies of tortoises guaranteed this situation during difficult days.

Of the edible parts of animals, the fat (*čewe*) is the most esteemed. The first thing a hunter does after killing his prey is to make a slice in the chest and observe the quantity of fat; when someone brings back a wild pig or deer to the village, the men crowd noisily around the animal exclaiming, "*Č͟ãne, čewe hetĩ!*", "Look how fat it is!" The fat from the throat of the male howler monkey is especially appreciated, since it makes anyone who eats it a good singer. The fat from the neck of the white-lipped peccary is also a delicacy; its bone marrow is coveted by women. But the greatest preference falls to the liver and eggs of tortoises. It could be said that if maize is the paradigm of vegetable foods, the fatty liver of the tortoise is the quintessence of meat. This pair, maize/tortoise, is central in Araweté life.[19]

4. History

Before moving to the region of the Ipixuna, the Araweté lived at the headwaters of the Bacajá River. At the end of the 1950s, repeated attacks by the Kayapó made them seek out the banks of the Bom Jardim, Jatobá, and finally, to the north, the Ipixuna, where they came into conflict with the Asuriní and expulsed them. They always point towards the east and the southeast as the direction of their ancestral villages. This is where the center of the earth (*iwi pite*) lies, today the domain of enemies. A somewhat obscure tradition says that before reaching the headwaters of the Bacajá, they crossed two large rivers, broad like the Xingu, in the east. I do not have data that would confirm if they were the Pacajá and Tocantins rivers.

The movement towards the Ipixuna, however, was not uniform. Part of the tribe arrived at its headwaters twenty-five years ago, leaving relatives in several villages further south on the Bom Jardim, Canafístula, and Jatobá rivers. This part of the tribe assaulted the Asuriní villages established on the Ipixuna much earlier (see Müller et al. 1979, for the history of the Asuriní movements). Another bloc, also composed of various villages, settled in the region of the Piranhaquara to the north and maintained tenuous contacts with the other group for ten years. At the end of the 1960s, this bloc divided in half in the face of new Kayapó attacks; one part went to join the group on the Ipixuna, which had abandoned the southern villages and gathered on former Asuriní territory; the other part, the larger, crossed the Ipixuna on its lower course and moved into the region of the Bom Jardim to the south. Two new blocs were thus formed, separated for another ten years. A Parakanã assault caused the southern bloc to flee towards the group on the Ipixuna, where villages were attacked by the same enemy, but both parts of the tribe only succeeded in meeting up again on the banks of the Xingu, south of the mouth of the Ipixuna, where they decided to take refuge. A synthesis of these movements is shown in map 3.

Many indications suggest that the Araweté did not make a direct, single relocation from the Bacajá headwaters to the Ipixuna region. The middle and lower courses of the Bacajá and its affluents are recognized and named as the locale of earlier villages. The earliest identifiable movement of the tribe was probably from the middle to the upper Bacajá, and from there to the region of the Xingu. My historical data are unfortunately vague, which reveals as much about the difficulties of obtaining this type of information as it does a certain lack of interest by the Araweté in detailing for me their trajectory through time and space.

The number of villages built by the Araweté from approximately 1945 to 1976 is surprisingly high: about sixty villages for the tribe as a whole during these thirty years (data on these villages are presented in Appendix 1-B). On occasion, six or seven villages coexisted; the average was four. My estimate is that the total population did not surpass three hundred people during this period. The average population in each village was therefore about sixty-five individuals in periods of relative peace. Attacks by the Kayapó caused successive divisions of the tribe into blocs that were geographically semi-isolated; on the other hand, they also prompted some fusions of certain villages. In addition, these attacks diminished the average length of time that a village was occupied.[20] Finally, the main factor in the decision to move the village was death. I was told that a village was abandoned as soon as a death occurred there. Another village would be erected nearby so that the gardens could still be used while others were being planted in a more distant site.

The manner of naming villages (*tã, tã pe*) reflects the importance of death. There are four basic forms of names:

1. Name of a vegetable species or a notable tree, followed respectively by *-ti* (a collective) or by *-(r)ɨpã,* "ground" or "support." For example: *Orokoyi'i ti,* "place where mbocayá palms trees abound"; *Ia'i rɨpã,* "place (support) of the Brazil-nut tree."
2. Verb phrase that describes an action, followed by the locatives *-he*

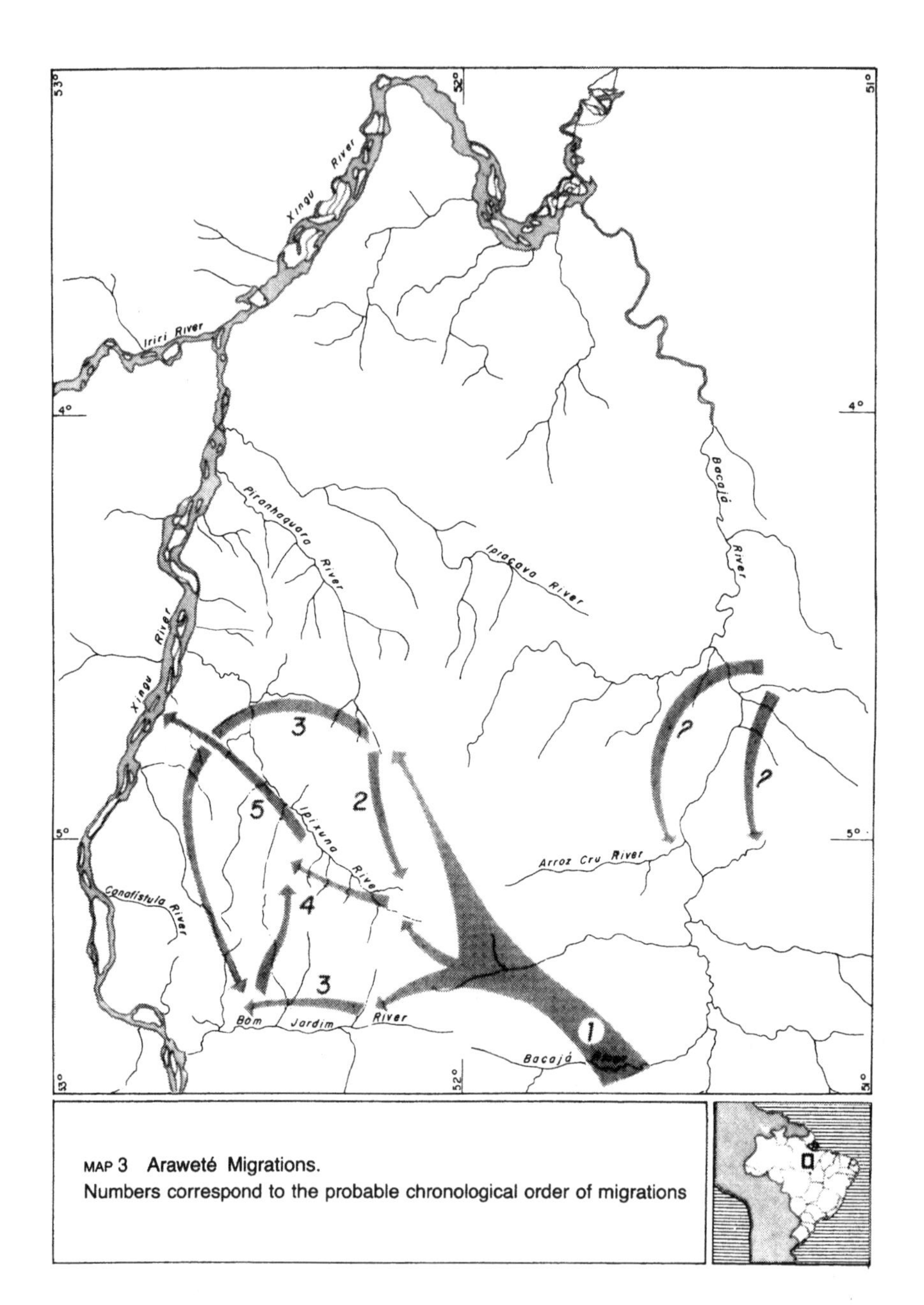

MAP 3 Araweté Migrations.
Numbers correspond to the probable chronological order of migrations

or *-pi*. For example: *Tiwawĩ-no iwã-iwã he*, "where Tiwawï-no was shot [with an arrow]," or *Pïdã ihi pi*, "place of the fishing line" (where a line left by white hunters was found).

3. Descriptive names of topographic peculiarities or historic associations: *Itã pɨkɨ*, "long rock," *Awĩ ka pe*, "enemies' clearing."
4. Name of a person, followed by the form *-rɨpã*. In this case, the village is named after a person who died there: *Todïnã-hi rɨpã*, "the grounds of Todïnã-hi."

Villages can be referred to by more than one name, but one of them tends to be used much more. Of the 62 villages about which I was able to obtain good information, 37 are usually named by form 4, 16 by form 1, and only 9 by forms 2 and 3. Apparently, only the villages that were abandoned for reasons other than death keep names of the first three types. No village has alternative designations using the names of more than one deceased person. But the statement often made to me that only one death was needed for a village to be abandoned has little verisimilitude: were this true, the villages would number as many as the dead. I will return to this later; in any case, death is obviously important in this necronymical geography, where past villages are not so much places where certain people were born, but rather, places where others died. Earlier villages are the grounds of the dead and must be left behind.[21] Grenand's observation (1982: 237) applies perfectly to the Araweté: "The relation that the Wayãpi maintain with their dead profoundly determines their territorial mobility."

Other toponyms are constructed according to the same semantic principles, such that it is not always possible to differentiate by their form common placenames (river, waterfall, hill) from those that designate villages. Nevertheless, the names of the dead are much less frequently used for such toponyms, and seem to apply only by extension to landscape features or areas that lie near a village. The most common usage in this case is form 2.[22] Other marks used in toponymy are hunting camps struck during expeditions to supply large feasts (I was honored with such a toponym, *Yɨado reyɨpã*, "Eduardo's camp") and concentrations of fruit-bearing trees. In the area surrounding a village, toponyms often refer to places where children were born (mothers seek out the nearby forest to give birth). Garden clearings are also called by the names of the people who opened gardens there.

Araweté geography is thus impregnated with memory, particularly that of people's deaths. But it conforms to the trajectory of the living as they move through space. Neither in their current territory nor in the memory of the oldest persons do sites appear to be endowed with mythological value. This does not mean that the most archaic history is not stamped on the world. For example, the large patches of wild banana trees (the fruits of which the Araweté consider nonedible) are the former "gardens" of the *Maï* who ate this plant before learning about maize. The rocky hillocks are fragments of those suspended by the gods to form the celestial dome, and they display scars of the cataclysm. The rocks in the Ipixuna rapids (showing ancient signs of stone tool sharpening) still have the imprints left by the feet and bodies of the *Maï*, vestiges of the time when rocks were soft (*itã time me*)—the primordial world. No particular hill or rapids, however, is singled out by a name; the signs of the gods are everywhere.

□

The conflicts with enemy peoples are deeply inscribed in Araweté memory and were responsible for their migrations. The expansion of the Kayapó was especially lethal. Of the 477 persons who died in the last six generations (counting the children of 1982) whose names I was able to obtain, 167 (35 percent) were killed or captured by enemies, and of this total, 114 (74 percent) occurred at the hands of the Kayapó,[23] who attacked them at the headwaters of the Bacajá, Bom Jardim, and Ipixuna. Some women they had captured managed to escape, bringing back various personal names still used today. The Asuriní, for their part, suffered many more losses at the hands of the Araweté than vice versa. The familiarity of the latter with the former's culture can be explained in part by the Araweté occupation of Asuriní villages abandoned in haste. But tradition identifies them as an ancient group, the *Todï*, from whom sweet potatoes were obtained. There are tales about captives being taken from one another in a long series of retaliations, accompanied by reciprocal anthropophagy. This was the time of the ancients (*pirowï'hã*) when the Araweté used, in addition to the bow, the *irapẽ* club (which can still be seen, transformed into a miniature ritual ornament, among present-day Asuriní [Müller 1987]). Various personal names are derived from the *Todï*.

The Parakanã are the most recent enemies of the Araweté and have had the upper hand in their attacks. Some elders assert that they are the former *Iriwi pepa ñã*, "Masters of vulture feathers" (with which they feather their arrows).

An important group that combated the Araweté in the Bacajá region about eighty years ago are the *Towaho*. This term may be a form of the Tupi-Guarani *towaja, enemy, plus the suffix *-(o)ho*, large. I was told how they wore their hair long over the neck and parted it in the middle; their bows were very long and made of *Tabebuia* wood.

They used to carry off the heads of their enemies as trophies; the Araweté also claim (in a typical fantasy) that they cut off the women's vaginal lips to eat them. The *Towaho* are conspicuous in the cosmology; war songs use many images taken from accounts of warfare against them, and one type of celestial spirits is called *Towaho peye*, "Shaman of the *Towaho*."[24]

A considerable legion of enemies, more or less imaginary, existed in the early days: the *Iapï'ï wï*, the *Kɨpe iwawi* (who carried beehives on their backs), the *Ayɨrɨ awï*, "parrot enemies," the *Ãñirã awï*, "bats," (who sleep hanging upside-down), the *Tato awï*, "armadillos," and many others, in a quasi-totemic proliferation in which natural species or other criteria differentiate the types of people who populate the earth. The "totemic operator" of the Araweté is utilized not to classify groups in the interior of society, but species of enemies in the cosmos. This is an essential conception: human beings proper (*bïde*) are a species within a multiplicity of other species of human beings, who form just as many other societies, more or less different from Araweté society. This open seriality of the various species of people is reflected in the composition of celestial populations.

Finally, a persistent though vague tradition speaks of a fission of a large Tupi-Guarani group—or rather, an Araweté one, given that they think of themselves as the only group that has maintained a continuous identity over time. This fission generated diverse peoples: the *Todï*, the *Ireiere wï*, the *Irãñi'i oho*, and others. Some are said to be inoffensive (*marï ï me'e*); others *odï moawï*, turned into enemies. The era of this separation is not clear; it is sometimes confounded with the originating event, the separation of men and gods. On both occasions, the reason for the fission was a conflict between husband and wife, which led the man's relatives to leave forever. On the other hand, the historical memory registers various disputes *about* women, with wives being captured between villages and lasting hostilities arising between them. The *Ama'ï wï* were one of these groups, separating about half a century ago. In any case, the Araweté conceive of themselves as being the fruit of a speciation that began from an initial state in which they were confused with the "future others" (*amïte rï*) or "ex-Araweté" (*bïde pe*). In this sense, the difference between "us" and "enemies" is not diachronically clear. The conceptual boundaries of the group are thus fluid, even if synchronically it is quite obvious who its enemies are. Such a lack of definition in the contours of collective identity has innumerable implications; being Araweté, in a certain sense, is an open question—for them.

The Araweté were divided into two large blocs, which, after being separated by the Kayapó and united by the Parakanã, sought contact with whitemen at more or less the same time. These blocs, without mutual interaction for ten years, were nonetheless linked by kinship, and began to intermarry again in 1977–78. The identification of a person with one or another original bloc is always present in people's memories and can be activated in situations of interpersonal conflict. Each bloc defines itself as "we" (exclusive: *ire*) and specifies the pronoun by the expression *X wĩ*, "those with X," where X is the name of one or more important persons, alive or dead, normally the "owners" of early villages in each bloc. The names of former villages are never used as identification.

Each bloc, moreover, defines the other as *iwi amĩte pa re:* "children (ex-inhabitants) of another country." This sets up a distinction between the *tã dĩ*, nearby villages—those that belonged to the same bloc as the speaker's—and the villages "on the other side of the earth" (*iwi rowãñã ti hã*) or "of another land" (*iwi amĩte*).[25] But this is as far as the matter goes. The different origins of the inhabitants of the present village are not spatially marked, do not imply political or cultural differences, and do not form the basis of any type of collective action. In short, affiliation to former villages does not have significant repercussions on morphology or social practice. The sentiment of belonging to a village is notably vague from the sociological point of view, which reflects the historical variability in the composition of the villages and their rapid abandonment. Possibly in the past the situation was more marked. But my general impression was that the kindred predominates over the village as a category of identification.[26]

Contact with whites occurred long before the 1970s. At least fifty years ago, a group of whites massacred thirteen Araweté in the Bacajá area. Epidemics that probably originated from the whites also raged among the Araweté while they still lived on that river. In addition, the custom of obtaining iron axes from abandoned clearings suggests a long-standing ecological symbiosis, even if marginal.

But adults assert that they only managed to really see whites for the first time when they arrived on the Ipixuna; in other words, that was where they had their first peaceful interactions with them. Present on the Ipixuna in great numbers in the 1960s and 1970s, hunters were encouraged by their bosses to give presents to the Indians; this did not prevent some armed conflicts from occurring, with deaths on both sides.

In 1970, FUNAI was alerted of a visit made by some Araweté to the banks of the Xingu (brought by a friendly fur hunter); faced with repeated reports of Indians in the region, the agency began the work of "attraction" between the Ipiaçava and the Bom Jardim. The Asuriní were discovered in 1971; that same year, the Araweté had brief encounters with the FUNAI expeditionists, but did not permit visits to their village. In 1974, FUNAI constructed a Post and opened gardens on the upper course of the Ipixuna, 100 kilometers from its source, near an abandoned Araweté village. But it was only in 1976 that contact with them was successful. At the beginning of the year, the Parakanã attacked villages on the upper Ipixuna and the Bom Jardim, causing residents to flee to the Jatobá. One part of the group sought the banks of the Xingu, where they camped in a peasant's garden. The attraction team encountered them in May 1976 in a terrible state of health. The expeditionists then convinced the Indians to move to the Attraction Post. They made the trip by land, a trek lasting twenty-two days; the majority were too weak to walk and at least thirty died on the trail or were abandoned. At the end of the year, a Parakanã attack on a village that still existed on the Jatobá impelled the members to join the group that had moved to the Post. They remained there until 1978, when the Indians and expeditionists decided to move to the middle course of the Ipixuna, due to a new Parakanã attack attempted at the end of 1977. They built two villages, which by early 1982 came together to form a single one, next to the new Post—and there they are to this day.[27]

I would estimate the population to have been 200 people immediately before the enemy attacks and the move to the Xingu. The number of deaths caused by epidemics and malnutrition was higher than the losses due to war. Between May and December of 1976 when they were settled in the FUNAI village, 60 people died. The first census in March 1977 registered 120 Araweté. In 1979, the population rose to 133, indicating a rapid demographic recuperation. In 1980, an epidemic interrupted the upward impetus; in February 1983 the Araweté numbered 136. The population under twenty-five years old was 55 percent of the total, with 32.7 percent in the age bracket of zero to nine years old, indicating a good birth rate. The sex ratio was reasonably balanced; the difference in favor of women (72) over men (64) was due to the higher rate of female births and survival (see population data in Appendix 2-A).

From October 1977 (the first birth record) to February 1983, there were 38 births, a rate that was sufficient to compensate for the epidemics and a relatively high incidence of miscarriages. Infant mortality was high: each adult woman had on the average fewer than half of her children living.

□

Upon my return to Ipixuna in February 1988, the Araweté numbered 168. Three women (among them the eldest of the group, over eighty years old) and 4 children had died; on the other hand, 35 children had been born, considerably elevating the high spirits and noise of the village. The growth rate of the group continues to advance steadily.

This census, however, gives us a difference of four people: 136 − 7 + 35 = 164. From where did the additional four come?

In September 1987, the Kayapó-Xikrin of the village of Cateté, hundreds of kilometers to the southwest of the Ipixuna on the other side of the Carajás Range, attacked a small group of unknown Indians, killing a man and a boy and capturing two women and another boy. A FUNAI doctor passing through recognized the fair complexion and light eyes of the Araweté and the characteristic earrings worn by the women. It was soon learned that an elderly man had remained hidden in the forest. Notified by radio, the Araweté sent emissaries to rescue these lost relatives, without the least idea of who they might be. The negotiations were complicated; the Xikrin demanded from FUNAI a quantity of items in compensation, but eventually everything was worked out. The Araweté then went out to search for the old man. At first he resisted their calls and shot arrows at them. Finally, however, he recognized the emissaries and approached. He and the freed captives were then brought to the Ipixuna to join the rest of the Araweté.

In the village, the mystery was cleared up. They were the survivors of Iwarawï's (the old man's) group, which had split off thirty years ago at the headwaters of the Bacajá when Iwarawï was still a youth. During a Kayapó attack, he escaped into the forest with an adolescent girl (his sister, MZD) and two little boys (his nephews, ZS). They were given up as dead or captured. In fact, they had gotten lost from the rest of the group, which had gone in the opposite direction towards the waters of the Ipixuna. Iwarawï and his sister had two daughters, who married the two boys, and all lived together for thirty years as a miniature Araweté society. A hard life, always on the run from enemies: without even time to wait for cotton to grow, the women substituted their customary outfit with small bark skirts; having to move their camping spot with each maize harvest, they depended most of the time on babassu flour.

That February, Iwarawï was sent to Altamira to treat a severe case of pneumonia that he caught soon after contact. The two women had married: Mitãñã-kãñĩ-hi and her son went to live with a recent widower; Pïdĩ-hi, wife and mother of the two killed in the Xikrin attack, was given to an unmarried cousin. Although surrounded by close relatives in the village, these survivors did not have an easy time. They were constantly held under the sarcastic lights of collective attention; they were obliged to sing and recount their life innumerable times to anyone who ordered them to do so. Their demeanor was considered bizarre; they were laughed at for their timid and bewildered air, their difficulty in employing traditional techniques, and their lack of familiarity with clothes. In a sense, the women were viewed as everybody's wives, not unlike war captives. But a youth mused to me that when their father returned from Altamira, things would change: Iwarawï was feared as a great killer of enemies. They showed me his weapons. His wide bow, riddled with shot from Kayapó guns—he had used it as a shield—had killed both whites and Indians during those thirty years. The arrows were strange, crooked, dirty and poorly feathered, a caricature of Araweté arms. Examining them, an elder of the village declared that Iwarawï was becoming less and less an Araweté and was starting to "become an enemy." Moreover, all had a strange accent and used words that they alone comprehended.

The story of Iwarawï is not uncommon: for instance, it echoes Wagley's account of Kamaira (1977:40–53). How many other small bands of fugitives still wander in the forests of the Xingu-Tocantins, lost survivors of so many once numerous peoples?

Iwarawï died by drowning in the mouth of the Ipixuna River in August of 1988.

3 The Forsaken Ones

1. The Separation

"We are in the middle," say the Araweté about humankind. The initiating event in their cosmogony was the differentiation between the layers or supports (*hɨpã*)[1] which today compose the universe. Besides our earth, there is a subterranean world and two celestial tiers. The assertion "we are in the middle" (*bïde ipite re*) summarizes a conception of the terrestrial world as being surrounded by the *Maï dɨpã*, the supports of the divinities, defined as other lands or skies (*iwi amɨ̃te, iwã amɨ̃te*) that separated from our layer during the inaugural cataclysm.

Humans are defined as those who were left behind, the forsaken ones (*heñã mi re*). Before that, humankind and the future gods (*Maï dĩ*) lived together on the earth, a world without work or death, but also without fire or cultivated plants. Then, as a result of being insulted by his wife *Tadïde*, the god *Aranãmĩ* decided to leave, exasperated with humans.[2] Accompanied by his nephew (*yi'i*, ZS) *Hehede'a*, he took up a shaman rattle and started to sing and smoke. As he sang, he caused the stone ground on which they stood to rise upwards, forming a firmament. With them went a multitude of *Maï* and beings of other categories. Others rose even higher, constituting a second tier; they were the *Iwã pïdĩ pa*, inhabitants of the red heaven. The material used for the celestial supports were large *itape*, granite formations similar to those found in the forests of the Ipixuna. The heavens are made of stone—as are the houses, pots, bows, and axes of the gods. Stone is as malleable to them as clay is to us.

The ascent of the heavens unleashed a catastrophe. Deprived of its stone foundation, the earth dissolved (*ikɨe*) under the waters of a flood that, according to some versions, was caused by a river or, according to others, by heavy rains. *Pako ačo* and *Yičire ačo*, the monstrous piranha and alligator, devoured the humans. Only two men and a woman (no one could tell me their names) saved themselves by climbing a bacaba palm. They were the *tema ipi,* the "origin of the creeping vines"—the ancestors of current humankind.[3] After the flood, there followed an era when mythic heroes rehardened the terrestrial crust. The current landscape is therefore the mold or the negative of the disengagement of the celestial surface and the ensuing deluge.

Other beings (also *Maï̱*) fled from the monsters of the flood by sinking in the waters and consolidating the lower world. They were the *Tarayo* and *Motïnã ãčo,* who ever since have lived on the islands of a great river. The subterranean world has an aquatic connotation. It does not, however, play an especially significant role in the cosmology. Of all the nonterrestrial layers, the most important is the first above us, its underside being the visible sky. Its name is *Maï̱ pi,* the place of the divinities.

Our earth is conceptualized as a disk that rises progressively at its edges until being intercepted by the sky, which is a dome that curves down toward earth. At the far edges of the world (*iwi yeče pã we,* "where the earth enters," or *iwã neyi pã we,* "where the sky descends"), all the different cosmic tiers communicate with each other. Each of the layers of the universe has its own stars and moon, which shine from the lower part of the layers immediately above. The stars are *iwitaha̱'ï,* a species of luminescent caterpillar found in swiddens.[4] The moon (*yahi*) that we see is a masculine being. His occasional red halo is the blood of women with whom he has copulated and thus caused to menstruate. The visible sun (*karahi*), on the other hand, is the same that shines in all layers of the universe. It is a piece of the Rainbow snake, cut up by the gods. When it is night on the earth, the sun is traveling across the lower world (*iwi kati*) from west to east, bringing day upon its arrival. However, the Araweté also assert that during the night the same sun illuminates the upper worlds. Such a topical inconsistency does not worry them; they insist on the singularity of the sun, which contrasts with the multiplicity of moons. Not only does each tier have its own moon, but each lunar cycle brings forth another (*amɨ̃te*) moon as well, which wanes as it is carved up with an axe by the female spirit *Maraiama.*[5] Time is counted in terms of lunar cycles; shorter periods are indicated by the position of the moon at nightfall.

The concept of a single sun that shines at night in the lower and upper worlds expresses a global opposition between the human world and the worlds of the *Maï̱:* when it is day here, it is night there, and vice versa.[6] A similar inversion explains why shamanic songs are always nocturnal.

However, representing the universe as composed of superimposed layers proves inadequate, even if it finds support in Araweté modes of speech. For example, the different races of *Maï̲ pi* gods live at varying distances from the earth in terms of both the horizontal axis and the vertical, although they inhabit the "same" tier.

No one showed much interest in explaining to me the origin of the sun and the moon. Some told me the *Maï̲* put them in the sky; others said they were created (*mara*) by the twins *Ñã-Maï̲* and *Miko ra'i*. The pygmy owl (*orokoro̲'ã*) is generally considered to be the creator of the night, that is, of the periodicity of light and darkness. Before that, there had been only day, so the world of long ago was terribly hot.[7] The pygmy owl also seems to have been the donor of celestial fire to the *Maï̲*. Cooking fire was revealed to the gods by a human, *Pïïpï* (which is also the name of an unidentified red bird).

Rain is the water exuded from the body of a large celestial hawk, the *Tamĩ howĩ'hã*. Another animal, this time terrestrial, that is associated with the rain is the small *tarayo* lizard, which must not be killed by humans lest he provoke a deluge similar to the primordial one.[8] The end of the rains and beginning of the dry season are attributed to brown tinamous, which dry the rivers, and to cicadas, the song of which announces the time for clearing new gardens in September–October.

Thunder (*o'i pepo*) is the sound made by the bow of *Maï̲ oho* (the "great *Maï̲*") when he shoots his arrows, lightning bolts (*tatã ipe*). Other versions say that flashes of lightning are the bodies of the gods, which glitter, or that they are caused by the gods' shaman rattles. Others say that the lightning bolts are hung inside the celestial stone house, where they get hit when the gods' children bump their heads against them as they play, making them light up here on earth.

Such variations indicate less a lack of interest in these meteorological phenomena than a proliferation of different versions in shamanic discourse. Meteorological phenomena in general are interpreted as indices of processes to which the dead are being submitted in the sky. Thunder is linked to the cooking of their souls and their rejuvenating bath; lightning bolts are indirectly associated with the apocalyptic theme of the splitting of the sky;[9] and even high winds represent some divine will, which is interpreted according to circumstances. Lightning is moreover a metaphor for ejaculation, and vice versa; the scrotum is called *tatã ipe riro*, sac of lightning bolts, which "*Maï̲ oho*'s semen" is one of the tropes for lightning.

So, although the Araweté certainly do not worship meteorological phenomena—as chroniclers thought the Tupi did—there is no doubt that the celestial population (especially the god who causes thunder and lighting) is central in their cosmology. The original separation between the *Maï* and mankind is the precondition and the reason for shamanism.

The universe is crossed by innumerable paths that lead to other cosmic layers and, within each one, to the villages of the various races of divinities. But there is one main road, the *kɨrepe* (cf. *hepe,* trail), which follows the sun's path. By this route, shamans ascend to the heavens, and gods and souls descend to stroll (*ɨpoho*) and participate in ceremonial banquets. The *kɨrepe* is a broad path, shaded and perfumed, that extends from the zenith to the east, or alternatively, rises from the village here on earth up to an indefinite point in the easterly sky. Upon reaching the world of the *Maï,* it passes through a sort of portal, the dangerous Rainbow snake. This path was opened by the mythic hero Irayo-ro. The gods close it on certain occasions, such as during an epidemic or the period immediately following a death.

The western part of this road, which extends from the village to an indefinite point in the western sky, is the route followed by the souls of the recently deceased. It is a narrow and dark path—one of the reasons for lighting fires on top of graves. This path is called *Mo'iročo kati,* "*Mo'iročo*'s way," named after one of the two Masters of White-lipped Peccaries, who inhabits the western edge of the earth. Another Rainbow snake resides in this western extreme.

As soon as the souls of the dead reach the heavens, they are greeted by *Iriwɨ morodï tã,* the Master of Vultures. This divinity is said to be very close to the earth ("just up there," say the Araweté, pointing with their lips to the western sky). The *Maï hete,* the "real gods," into which the dead will be transformed, inhabit the zenith in the center of the upper world; but they also inhabit the "middle" of the skies, that is, an intermediate distance from humankind along the vertical axis, in between the gods who are the closest and the farthest away.

The following system of equivalences summarizes the values analyzed up to this point:

Sky	Earth
East	West
High	Low
Center/Middle	Edge
Zenith	Nadir
Stone	Water
Gods	Dead

Such a system represents my reconstruction, not an explicit framework of Araweté cosmology, which is as little articulated as possible around polar oppositions.

To lend the above schema some solidity, it should be compared to other Tupi-Guarani materials, especially to the widespread association of the underworld with the terrestrial portion of the soul of a deceased person. This association is not found among the Araweté, however, except in the weakened form of a "lower" location of the earth-sky path in the west taken by the celestial soul of the deceased (while the terrestrial specter moves along the horizontal axis with no reference to the cardinal points).

Some further remarks are necessary. In the first place, the association between "West" and "Edge" is based on the Araweté idea that they now inhabit the brink or edge (*heme̱'i*) of the earth, relative to the center of the world in the East, their ancestral site. In the second place, the notion of *-pite,* "center," has a connotation that is both radial and serial. That is, *-pite* is opposed to *heme̱'i,* "periphery," and also belongs to the triad *tenotã, ipite, tačipe:* "in the front, the first"; "in the middle"; "behind, the last" (a system used, for example, to designate the birth order of a group of siblings). This semantic ambivalence (which I also see at work in the central/intermediate situation of the *Ma̱ï hete*) appears to be correlated with the insignificance of a radial concept of the "center" in village morphology.

The separation of the cosmic layers is referred to as the time of the dispersal (*ohĩ-ohĩ me*) or time of the division (*ɨwa̱wa me*). This refers as much to the separation of men and gods as to the dispersal of the different human tribes on earth. In apparent contradiction to the version that says the flood spared only the ancestors of the Araweté, it is also asserted that the ascent of the skies generated a sociological speciation. An obscure passage of the myth narrates how the *awĩ* (enemies), thought of as either Kayapó or whites, attempted to shoot *Aranãmĩ* and his companions as they rose with the sky; this aggression is then cast as the *cause* of the prior event, the ascension of the gods. I should emphasize my ignorance about the events of this era of dispersal, due in part to linguistic difficulties. But the Araweté always told me that they did not know exactly what happened during that time. "We are children" (*ɨre ta'i đoho*), "We have existed for only a short time" (*ɨre deme ɨka*), hence we cannot know what occurred in that era.

The oft-repeated idea that we are children, advanced even by mature men to my questions about ancient times, may be more than simple irony or the result of disinterest. It evokes some sort of conception that the living are by definition children, that is, incomplete beings. The notion, therefore, does not refer merely to the past (we have been on earth only a short time, we know nothing about its origins), but also to the future. The gods, despite their vitality and capacity for rejuvenation, are described as having long white beards and are sometimes called *tamõy*, grandfathers (alternatively, by affinal terms). The gods are also much taller than humans. Some people emphasized to me that our teeth will grow out again in the sky; adult dentition, thus, is as transitory as the milk teeth of children. And one of the processes to which souls are submitted in the sky is "stretching" (*ipiha*)—they are made to grow. The celestial gods and souls are thus considered adults in comparison to the living.

Paradoxically, the era of dispersal was not so distant. Beyond the second generation above the eldest men begins a time that merges into this mythic phase of dispersal. The grandparents and great-grandparents of Aya-ro, an aged man of eighty years, are referred to as *iwi ɨkɨe me he re*, "belonging to the time when the earth dissolved," that is, people who witnessed the ascent of the skies. The period between this era and that of ancestors who are genealogically identifiable is filled with numerous heroic feats and replete with personalities who, although human, rose to the heavens without dying. They wandered on the edge of the earth and interacted with the tribes living there, such as the *Towãyñiwãy* (people with pierced lips and masters of perfumed resins), the *Araṟĩñã*, and so on. These rhapsodic accounts tell how numerous cultural items were obtained then, such as the rattle, glass beads, and annatto. To this same heroic period belongs the above-mentioned dispersal of a Tupi-Guarani proto-group.

Thus, in the formation of the present cosmos, two original separations were essential: that of heaven and earth, with the abandonment of mankind, and the dispersal of the latter. This creates the differences between men and gods, and Araweté and enemies, the central problems of Araweté philosophy.

Like other Tupi-Guarani peoples, the Araweté say a day will come when the earth will end. The sky, heavy with so many dead, will burst open and collapse upon the earth, annihilating the living and restoring the world's original nondifferentiation. The gods and the dead will return to live in our tier. This event is highly feared. The expression *iwã ɨhana*, "the sky is splitting," is the most severe oral interdiction in Araweté culture; one should not even think about it, much less speak about it.[10]

2. Who's Who in the Cosmos

The various cosmic domains are the habitats of different categories of beings. The terrestrial layer is first and foremost the berth of humanity (*bïde ɨpã*), while the others are the homes of the gods (*Maï dɨpã*), but spirits exist in all of them, just as do animals and plants. I will now offer translations of certain concepts and justify the use of interpretive terms such as "gods" and "divinities."

The Araweté language does not offer simple equivalents of categories such as "humanity," "animality," "spirituality."[11] Their generic monolexemic concepts have significations that depend on context and levels of contrast, and they may be dissolved into specific names that cannot be subsumed within more general categories. On the other hand, a certain number of descriptive oppositions can be reconstructed: between beings that were "created" and those that were "simply existent"; between "the forsaken ones" and "those that left"; between those that are "really existent" and those that "inhabit a fabricated environment"; between those "to be eaten" and those "that eat us." Some of these oppositions partially coincide in extension.

But first, let us explore the monolexemic categories and see how the Araweté conceptualize the general forms of being in the universe.

Bïde is the first of these categories. Its principal meaning is "human being," "people."[12] In its most extensive usage, it designates every anthropomorphic being, including the various races of spirits. This level of contrast is rarely activated; *bïde* in this sense is not opposed to any single general term that would correspond to "nonanthropomorphic animate being."

There is no way to distinguish unequivocally between humans and what we would call spirits, a notion that covers very heterogeneous beings. The form *bïde herĩ*, "similar to humans," can be used to specify that the beings under discussion are not exactly *bïde*, granted one knows on what level of contrast this latter term is being used.[13]

What characterizes all the beings that we would call spirits is that they possess a shamanic power or quality, *ɨpeye hã*. Actually, since *ɨpeye hã* is inherent in such beings, it may be better to invert the definition and say that shamans (*peye*) are endowed with a spiritual potency. Thus, it would be less a matter of defining all spirits as shamanic than of defining some humans as "spiritual."[14]

In its minimal extension, the notion of *bïde* means "Araweté": it is the auto-denomination of the Indians who live on the Ipixuna. On this level, it contrasts with *awĩ*, enemy or stranger: the Kayapó, *kamarã*, Asuriní, and sundry other species of humans who people the earth.

The opposition *bïde/awĩ* is the strong form of a central opposition: *bïde*, "we," "us people," and *amɨ̃te*, "other," "the others." *Amɨ̃te* is not a category of person, but a position, one of alterity in relation to the unmarked pole, an "other" versus a "same." Thus, *bïde* and *amïte* can be opposed in all contexts of contrast in which the first term enters: an anthropomorphic being versus anything else; humans versus spirits; Araweté versus other tribes. It is equally possible to construct the form *bïde amïte* to designate the ambiguous status of the early "Araweté" who fled at the time of the ancestral fissioning.[15]

Beings defined as *amïte* in contrast to *bïde* have as their paradigmatic focus the position of enemy, *awĩ*. Like *bïde, awĩ* is not a substantive essence, but a position or quality: humans, jaguars, spirits, and divinities are *awĩ* in contrast to *bïde* as humans, Araweté, or gods. The Araweté themselves are *awĩ* from the point of view of peccaries, howler monkeys, and Asurinĩ.[16]

The concept of *bïde,* beyond its substantive signification (human being or Araweté), is therefore endowed with a kind of logical overdetermination, due to its contrast with purely positional notions. *Bïde,* in the final analysis, connotes a position: the position of Subject, in a linguistic, logical, and metaphysical sense. In its radical or "transcendental" sense, it contrasts with the maximal determination of the Other: *awĩ,* the Enemy. But this Self/Other opposition, although basic, is not stable. Such a conceptual dualism does not exhaust the philosophy of the person. It still remains to be determined in a positive sense what *bïde* is—in other words, what the person is.

To do so, it is necessary to examine the concept of *M̲a̲ï,* which I translate as "gods," "divinities," or "Divinity."[17] Its most inclusive or indeterminate meaning can be glossed as "transcendental cause"—an abstract but not impersonal agency. The "*M̲a̲ï*-effect" is distinguished from the natural effects or these produced by chance (which are cosmologically insignificant) and from those produced by human agency. Thus, high winds may be interpreted as "*iwito te,*" "just the wind," or they may be met with the comment, "*M̲a̲ï,*" without this implying anything more than an indeterminate manifestation of a *M̲a̲ï*-cause.

As a transcendental agency, the notion of *M̲a̲ï* can include (although only in a rare and inexact extension of its sense) the effects or manifestations or terrestrial spirits. This might be explained by considering the concept of *M̲a̲ï* as the "subjective" counterpart of the shamanic potency (*ipeye hã*) characteristic of all spirits—a force that is concrete (and localized in the *aray* rattle) but impersonal.

The most common use of the term, however, is as a designation for nonterrestrial beings, "those who went away" (*iha me'e pe*) from here in the primordial separation. They are thus distinguished from humans and terrestrial spirits, all referred to as *iwi pa,* inhabitants of the earth. It is in this sense of the term that the Araweté speak of "seeing

Maï" (*Maï deča*) and hearing the "music of the gods" (*Maï marakã*) in the trances and songs of shamans.

More specifically, *Maï* designates the divinities of the celestial tiers, above all the inhabitants of the first heaven, the *Maï pi*. When one speaks in generic way of *Maï*, one looks upwards.

In its maximal determination, *Maï* are the *Maï hete*, the "gods par excellence" or "real gods," and their specifications: *Maï oho*, the Master of Thunder, and his *Maï* "children," "wives," and "grandparents."[18] These divinities live in the same cosmic tier as the other celestial races, but do not occupy the same logical plane. This species does not have a proper name, since it refers to "the very *Maï* themselves," *Maï* in its proper sense. Nevertheless, they have a concrete and distinct existence. The village of the *Maï hete*, as mentioned earlier, lies in a central and medial position in the sky.

The *Maï hete* do indeed occupy a central place in the cosmology. They are the ones who devour the souls of the dead and the ones into whom these souls will be transformed. They epitomize the generic attributes of all gods. They are beings similar to the Araweté, but taller and stronger, with long white beards, a glistening appearance, and elaborate bodily decoration. They are fond of perfumes and own many pet birds; they are imbued with abundant sexuality, expertise in singing, and absolute shamanic potency (capable of elevating the sky, resuscitating the dead, and dispensing with agricultural toil). Above all, they know the science of perpetual rejuvenation: the *Maï* are immortal.[19]

The notion of *Maï hete* is thus correlated with the concept of *bïde* in its maximal determination. These gods are the celestial equivalent of true human beings, the Araweté. The other divinities, *Maï amĩte*, are scattered throughout the sky in their own villages at variable distances from that of the *Maï hete*. The distinction the Araweté make between *tã dĩ* and *tã amĩte* villages, i.e., those close to Ego's and those located in "another land," applies to the celestial ones too. Certain gods live close to the *Maï hete*; others live far away, at the "end of the sky" or in "another sky."

Finally, there are certain inhabitants of the heavens whose definition as *Maï* is problematic, such as the *Iaracĩ* cannibals. Another important class of beings is called *Awĩ peye*, "shamans of the enemies," who represent attributes of the Araweté's enemies in the sky. I will discuss these species at greater length later on.

Everything, in sum, would seem to suggest that the general concept of Divinity, *Maï*, corresponds to the general concept of the Human, *Bïde*, and that the real gods, *Maï hete*, correspond to real humans, *bïde* (Araweté). Accordingly, the heavens would mirror the earth—or rather, the latter would be a residual image of celestial perfection. But things are not as simple as this.

In the first place, no direct correspondence exists between the races of humankind and the species of celestial gods (or the species of gods found in the lower world and in the second heaven). It is only the form of the relation among the different divinities that resembles the Araweté vision of the earth. Moreover, only the Araweté have a place in the sky after death; deceased enemies are *not* transformed in to *Awĩ peye.* The various divine races do not correspond to either personifications or hypostases of species of animals, plants, or the like, in the manner of those "Masters" we encounter in other South American cosmologies. Rather, they form an essentially heterogeneous set.

In the second place, different kinds of humans and humanlike beings live in the sky: the souls of the dead, a number of ancestral heroes who rose to the heavens without dying, and the gods. The Araweté distinguish between *ire rema ipi,* "our ancestors," and entities described as *bïde kire,* literally, "pieces of humanity," fractions of the human species who are not related to the Araweté but who ascended to the skies in the primordial separation. Among these *bïde kire* are precisely the *Mai̱ hete,* who accordingly are not conceived of as ancestors, creators, or parents of humankind.

In the third place, *Mai̱* is a category tinged with temporality. It is said of all the *bïde* who inhabit nonterrestrial worlds that "they made themselves into gods" (*o̱dï moMai̱*) or "they transformed themselves into gods" (*o̱dï Mai̱ mõ*).[20] One of the ways of referring to the original cataclysm is a curious tautology, *e'e me Mai̱ o̱dï moMai̱,* "when the gods divinized themselves," which suggests that Divinity is not a substance but a movement. To be divinized is to be separated from humans, to leave the earth. The gods, therefore, were once humans—just as humans, after death, will be transformed into *Mai̱.*

A detailed account of the celestial races follows in the next section. For now, it is time to introduce a third population of beings that complicates the opposition *Mai̱*/humans: the terrestrial spirits, who are also legion. They are not subsumed under any general category, being "inhabitants of the earth" like ourselves. They include *Iaradï* and *Mo'iročo,* father and son, Masters of White-lipped Peccaries, who live at the ends of the earth, one in the East, the other in the West. They keep the pigs inside large stone houses. When lightning flashes on the horizon, it is a sign that the masters of the pigs are releasing their pets. Another terrestrial spirit is *Ayaraetã,* who wanders through the forest during the season of honey gathering. There is also the feared

Iwikatihã, Lord of the River or Master of Water, who steals women and carries off the souls of children. A series of spirits are called "Masters" (*ñã*) of plant species or notable landscape features such as rocks or clearings. Then there is *Iwi yari,* "Grandmother Earth," a necrophagous subterranean spirit. And finally, there is the large family of the *Ãñĩ* and their relatives, *Koropï, Karo̱ã, Yɨrɨpaɗï.*

The *Ãñĩ* are spirits of the forest, ferocious, cannibalistic, kidnappers of women, and assassins of men. They live in the hollows of trees, walk around without ornaments, and have an ugly style of singing and unmistakable stench. They can infiltrate the village at night, where they are detected and killed by the shamans with the *Ma̱ï hete*'s assistance. The *Ãñĩ* are not "masters of animals" or "masters of the forest." However, various animal species call them by affinal terms. They are defined as *ɨka hete me'e,* an expression that translates as "really existent" and connotes savagery or deculturated existence; it implies that the *Ãñĩ* do not live in villages as do humans, the *Ma̱ï,* and even certain animals. Men call them "our big grandfathers" (*ɨre ramõy oho*) and are reciprocally called "grandsons" (*hããmõnõ*), suggesting distance as well as a kind of primeval quality of the *Ãñĩ.*[21]

The *Ãñĩ* are conceived above all as enemies (*awĩ*), savage and brutish. They do not distinguish people from beasts; they view humans as if the latter were wild pigs.[22] Finally, they have a particular relationship to the dead. The terrestrial specter of the deceased is said to accompany the *Ãñĩ,* to be a thing of the Ãñĩ (just as the celestial aspect of the human soul is said to be a thing of the gods, *Ma̱ï ɗapa*). The *Ãñĩ* are, moreover, necrophagous, banqueting on the flesh of the dead and making flutes out of their tibias.

All terrestrial spirits, with the exception of the distant and benign Masters of Peccaries, are dangerous: some so for all humans (especially females), others mainly for small children or the parents of newborns. The principal danger they pose is shooting or capturing people or carrying off their life principle (*ĩ*), causing the victims to languish and die. People who have been killed or kidnapped by these spirits do not have access to the sky, and thus "truly die" (*ɨmanɨ̃ nete*). All these spirits (except the Masters of Peccaries) are classified as *yokã mi,* "to be killed": they can and should be killed by shamans.

Nevertheless, the malignity of the *Ãñĩ* and their congeners does not mean the Araweté regard them with respect (except for the Master of Water, whose name must never be pronounced near his domain). Humans are afraid of these beings, but hold them in contempt. They bear quite different attitudes towards the *Ma̱ĩ,* who have an impressive appearance and induce fear-respect (*čiye*) in the shaman, who trembles upon seeing them. The *Maï* are *ipoïhi:* extraordinary, splendid, but also dreadful, weird—in a word, awesome.[23]

Although the term *Ãñĩ* designates a particular species of beings, the variety of spirits of the forest is simplified by the expression *Ãñĩ herĩ*, "similar to the *Ãñĩ*." This suggests that the *Ãñĩ* as a species are to terrestrial spirits at large what the *Maï hete* are to the celestial gods. Indeed, a series of oppositions can be established between the *Maï* and the terrestrial spirits epitomized by the *Ãñĩ*. A similar dual classification would correspond, on the plane of the human person, to the two "souls" liberated after death, the benign celestial soul and the malignant terrestrial specter. If the *Maï* could be seen as correlates of the Araweté, the *Ãñĩ* would be the hypostasis of the Enemy. Accordingly, we would have:

Maï	***Ãñĩ***
Sky	Earth
Village	Forest
Perfume, beauty	Stench, ugliness
Immortality	Mortality, lethalness
Celestial soul	Terrestrial specter
(Super-)Culture	Nature (Pre-Culture)
Human	Animal
Araweté	Enemy

This system, although pertinent in *grosso modo*, omits some irreducible oppositions and ambivalent factors. In the first place, the opposition sky/earth does not exhaust the cosmology. *Iwikatihã*, the Master of Water, whose name connotes his belonging to a lower world, is never confounded with the *Ãñĩ* class of beings; he is not a savage, since he has houses and gardens on the river bottoms and wears elaborate ornamentation. Nor do the Masters of Peccaries or *Ayaraetã*, the hypostasis of honey, fit into any simple classification.

But the fact that such a binary machine only precariously divides up the Araweté cosmology is not the major problem. The real problem lies in the fundamentally ambiguous status of the celestial divinities, especially the *Maï hete*.

The *Maï hete* are more perfect than humans, without a doubt: they manifest a superabundance of being and a splendid vitality that makes terrestrial beings seem like pale copies. Their abode in the *Maï pi* is called *teka katɨ we*, the "place of good existence"—the Araweté Land without Evil.[24] There, everything is redolent of permanence (objects are stone, rejuvenation is perpetual), abundance (food is never lacking, maize beer is drunk all day long), beauty (*Maï* men and women are models of beauty, and macaws and cotingas abound, providing feathers for earrings and diadems), great size (in the *Maï pi* everything is much larger, from maize to Brazil-nut trees), and ease (the forest has no vines, there are no mosquitos, axes cut by themselves, maize plants itself).

But the *Maï hete* are *not* culture heroes who extricated humanity from a bestial state (as attributed by other Tupi-Guarani peoples to the *Maíra*). On the contrary, they manifest a fundamental primitivity. They knew nothing about fire or cultivated plants until humans (*tema ipi*, Araweté ancestors) or other mythical beings revealed such things to them. Ignorant of maize, they used to eat the fruits of wild banana trees growing spontaneously in the forest, said to be "something planted by the *Maï*" (*Maï remï-tĩ we*) or "the former maize of the gods" (*Maï awacï pe*). A strange epithet recalls the savage nature of the *Maï: me'e wi a re*, "eaters of raw flesh," an expression that also describes jaguars.[25]

Thus, the inimitable shamanic power of the gods, which relieves them of agricultural toil and of death, is paradoxically associated with a cultural primitivity. Less than and more than humans, the gods are consequently super-natural and extra-cultural; they evoke the archaic background of a bestial humanity, but point towards a blissful future—an eternal life in the Land without Evil.

Strange gods indeed. The *Maï*'s physical aspect and body ornamentation are hyperboles of the Araweté ideal model. However, they abhor annatto, emblem of the living. They paint themselves only with the black dye of genipap in delicate and complex designs. Notably, body designs that are made with genipap juice are considered the emblem of the spotted jaguar (the "owner" of genipap); they are also the body-painting style used by enemies (Kayapó and Asuriní) and by the dead, who are decorated in this way as soon as they arrive in the sky. The Araweté only use genipap on hunting and war expeditions, and always apply it on continuous areas of the body, never in lines or geometric patterns. The appearance of the gods is thus a mixture of the figure of the Araweté (wearing diadems of macaw feathers, harpy eagle down, and cotinga earrings) and of the figure of enemies.

Finally, when I would ask if the *Maï hete* were *bïde* or "like *bïde*," the first answer I would receive was always in the affirmative. After all, the *Maï* are anthropomorphic and live like the Araweté (or as the latter would like to live). But soon after, my interlocutors would muse that no, actually the *Maï hete* are like *awĩ*, since they paint themselves with genipap, are ferocious (*ñarã*), and above all are cannibals, killing and devouring the souls who have recently arrived in heaven.

It is true that, in contrast to the numerous other races of celestial and terrestrial cannibals, the *Maï̲ hete,* after having eaten the dead, recompose and resuscitate them, thereby transforming them into beings akin to themselves. As such, this is an initiatory and regenerative cannibalism, as opposed to the savage and destructive cannibalism of the rest of the spirits.[26] But this does not prevent the *Maï̲ hete* from being anything less than *pɨrɨ o,* cannibals, and *bïde yokã hã,* killers of people. Nor does their having fire nowadays (and eating the dead cooked) prevent them from being "eaters of raw flesh." Nor does their being beautiful mean they are not fearful or do not resemble enemies. Strange gods: primitives, enemies, cannibals, but ideal. Indeed, *gods who are strangers:* for what the *Maï̲* incarnate is the essential ambiguity of the Other. The *Maï̲* are the Enemy—but the *Maï̲* are the Araweté. This is the problem—and divine cannibalism is the solution, as we will see later. For now, we may say that the exterior of society is not an immobile mirror where man gazes at himself peacefully, constituting his identity as interiority. Heaven is neither a reflection nor an inversion of the earth; it is something other than an "image."

□

The difference between men and animals is not clear either; I cannot find a simple manner of characterizing the place of "Nature" in Araweté cosmology. As mentioned earlier, there is no taxon for "animal"; there are a few generic terms, such as "fish," "bird," and a number of metonyms for other species according to their habitat, food habits, function for man (*ɗo pi,* "for eating," *temimã nĩ,*" "potential pets"), and relation to shamanism and food taboos.

The distinctions within the domain of animals are essentially the same that apply for other categories of beings. *Maï̲,* humans, and spirits have always existed, they were not created; the same is true for certain animals, such as the tortoise (said to be very old, *i̲mĩ*) and certain species of fish and insects. All these beings simply exist, *ɨka te.* The majority of animals, however, were created, *mara mi re.* The verb *mara* translates literally as "to place, to put, to present," in both a locative sense (to put something in some place) and a metaphysical one. Creation is a positing of being; it is distinct from fabrication (*moñĩ* or *apa*), an act conceptualized as the gradual elaboration of a raw material. Cultural objects are "fabricated," but songs, for example, are "placed" or "put forth." *Mara* is, properly speaking, to posit as existent, to actualize.[27]

Created animals used to be humans long ago. During a great maize beer festival, *Ñã-Ma̲ï* ("Jaguar-God," brother of *Miko ra'i*, "Opposum's Son"), seeking revenge for the death of his mother at the claws of the monstrous jaguar *Ñã nowĩ'hã*, transformed all the human guests into the animals of today: harpy eagles, vultures, jaguars, giant river otters, howler monkeys, capuchin monkeys, saki monkeys, agoutis, collared peccaries, tapirs, curassows, toucans, deer, guans, pacas, and anteaters. *Ñã-Ma̲ï* transformed or "created" them with the help of his *aray* (shaman rattle) and tobacco. Then he transformed cultural objects of vegetal origin into various fishes: the serving vessel made of cokerite palm spathes turned into the trairão; the *tupe* mat turned into the matrinxã; the fire fan, pestle, and so on turned into other species of fish. *Miko ra'i*, for his part, transformed the smoke of a bonfire into mosquitos and other insect pests.

The mythic cycle of the twins "Jaguar/Opposum," so widespread among the Tupi-Guarani, is in the Araweté case exclusively associated with the creation of animals. The cycle unfolded during the epoch following the separation of the sky and earth by *Aranãmĩ*. After transforming the animals, *Ñã-Ma̲ï* ascended to the heavens, taking with him the majority of each species he had created, leaving behind some of each; thus, terrestrial animals were, like humans, those forsaken (*heñã mi re*).[28]

The divinity *Ñã-Ma̲ï* has a son (in some versions, a brother), *Tiwa̲wĩ*, who is the shaman responsible for resurrecting the cannibal victims of the *Ma̲ï hete*, which transforms the human dead into *Ma̲ï*. This function is at times shared with his father/brother. These gods are thus associated with retrogressive or progressive transformations of human material (which is apparently the primordial substance of living entities): from the human to the animal, and from the human to the divine, involving, in other words, transformations into the hunted or the hunter.

The closest idea to what we would call "animality" or "nature" is the form *ɨka hete me'e*, "those that are really existent" (*ɨka* means to be or to exist). This expression has various connotations. First, it refers to beings that are not *hɨkãy pa*, inhabitants of enclosed or encircled areas (*-ɨkãy* being a root that designates altered, delimited spaces, such as a house, village, or pen). It includes certain enemy tribes who are nomadic. Another fundamental characteristic of "really existent" entities is their being bereft of gardens and fire; even the *Ma̲ï hete* can be jokingly referred to as examples of *ɨka hete me'e* beings.[29] On the other hand, some animals are not *ɨka hete me'e*. Vultures, fish, and peccaries are *hɨkãy pa* entities, since they are pets of certain spirits and therefore live in pens or villages; they are domesticated and cannot be eaten by their owners.

Similarly, in the sky exist *ɨka hete me'e* animals, those that are hunted and eaten by the gods,[30] and those that are not, being the gods' pets. Such pets often appear in shamanic songs, frequently serving to characterize a "modulation" of a general concept of *Maï̱*. These animals are identified by the suffix *-ačo*, great, or *-yo*, yellow (meaning eternal or perfect).[31] They should be distinguished from the entities that have the name of an animal followed by the expression *-o̱dɨ̈ moMaï̱* ("divinized"), which indicates fully anthropomorphic gods. They are also distinct from *ho̱wɨ̈'hã* animals, "great" or "monstrous" ones, which are either beings from mythical times, of animal form and human behavior, or else animal manifestations of the *Maï̱*, such as *Ñã no̱wɨ̃̈'hã*, which is a "God turned jaguar" (and not a "jaguar turned God").

When applied to animals, the notion of *ɨka hete me'e* thus designates the untamed, that which one eats, as opposed to that which one raises and cares for. But it is also opposed to a more general notion, that of beings and things "of the divinities" (*Maï̱ apa*), a category that includes not just the pets of the gods, but everything that has a relationship to Divinity.[32]

Here, *ɨka hete me'e* connotes less a nonpossessed mode of existence than an indeterminate or insignificant mode. "Really existent" signifies an absence of transcendence, that is, an existence pure and simple, so to speak. The expression thus conjoins two senses that are not wholly equivalent: absence of culture and absence of transcendence. Humans are the *Maï̱ apa* beings par excellence, since they have a dual condition: they possess not only culture, but something more. They are "things of the gods" or "matters of divinity," not because the *Maï̱ hete* are their owners, but because they bear a celestial destiny. Men are not brutes because they are other than themselves—they are not simply and really existent.

In sum, we see an insistent theme in Araweté cosmology: the division of the cosmos between that which left (*ɨha*) and that which remained (*opitã*) or merely exists (*ɨka te*)—that which was abandoned. The human race is the most notable species of these forsaken beings. The most notable because, despite having stayed behind, their destiny is to leave; contrary to the rest of the beings who *ɨka*, exist, humans are said to be *ɨha me'e rĩ*, "those who will go." This is, in the final analysis, the distinguishing mark of the human within the world; temporality constitutes its essence. Animals have a spirit (*ha̱'o we*) and a vital principle (*ĩ*), but they will not "leave." Beings of the earth belong to the earth; those of the sky belong to the sky. Only humans are between the earth and the sky, the past and the future; only they will not "really die."

The abandonment of humanity was less a matter of its fall than it was an ascent of the gods. Left behind, men are, properly speaking, the absence of divinity. Many cosmologies of the continent conceptualize Culture and the human condition as a conquest over an original Nature or animality, and as a stable state defined as a positivity that negates Nature (defined as anti- and ante-Culture). In contrast, the Araweté conceptualize the human in terms of separation from Supernature, as the abandonment of a superhuman, extracultural condition. Contrary to cosmologies such as those of the Gê, which posit Culture as that which animals no longer have, the Araweté cosmology defines men as no longer being what the gods are. The problem humans face, therefore, is not how to distinguish themselves from the animal, but how to transform themselves into the divine. The Other of humanity is not animality, but divinity. Actually, it is men who are the Others of the gods, their forsaken remains. Made of time, existing in the interval between the no-longer and the not-yet, men turn towards the latter: the cosmogony prepares an eschatology.

3. Gods and Spirits

The manner and extent to which the dozens of supernatural entities are involved in human life is highly variable. For example, among the *Ma̱ï* beings are well-defined species with determinate functions in co̱llective religious life, but also entities that are fortuitous modifications of a "*Ma̱ï*-substance" that emerge in a single shamanic vision. Some *Ma̱ï* are characters in etiological myths in which they are thought of as individuals, but on other occasions, the same names designate a race or family of beings. An extensive series of gods has names of animals (mostly birds). Some gods are conspicuous, while others have never come down to earth, little more being known about them other than their names.

When elaborating the characteristics of a divinity, the Araweté invariably cite passages from shamans' songs. All celestial and subterranean beings can be identified by their songs. Certain refrains and themes are associated with particular gods and are repeated from shaman to shaman with slight variations. The form of communication between the gods and the living is essentially by song: the gods are singing as they descend to earth, while the shamans sing as they go up to the sky to meet them. The presence of the *Ma̱ï* in daily life is astonishing: for each and every purpose, they are cited as models of action, paradigms of body ornamentation, standards for interpreting events, and sources of news; shamanic songs easily become popular successes.

Among the *Maï*, as among terrestrial spirits, certain beings are Masters (*Ñã*) of animal and plant species and natural domains. But, with the possible exception of *Me'e Ñã*, the "Jaguar-Thing" (a *Maï* who keeps jaguars as his intimates and agents of intimidation), the celestial spirits are not Masters of important things, or at least this is not the form in which they are present in Araweté life.[33]

On the other hand, only among the celestial gods do we find a category of beings that contrasts clearly with the *ñã* beings. They are the *'ã*, "eaters" of certain types of food that must be brought to earth by shamans on occasions when these products are ceremonially consumed. Each kind of food belonging to the class defined as "food of the gods" (*Maï demï-do*), which coincides with "shamanizable" foods (*ipeyo pi*), is associated with specific divinities. Only the *Maï hete* and the dead may eat everything. Both these "eater" spirits and those who come to earth simply to "stroll" may surge forth in shamanic songs at any time, but those of the first category customarily appear most during the season when their preferred foods are abundant.

All Araweté collective ceremonies are organized in the form of a banquet of the gods and the dead, followed by a meal for humans; the gods partake of the food *ɨpeye hã iwe*, "in the shamanic mode," leaving its substance intact. Thus, the feast is not actually a matter of commensality, but rather, involves a divine prelibation of the productive force of the community; it exhibits, in other words, a sacrificial structure. The foods of the gods are invariably those resulting from acts of production and consumption by the village as a whole. The notion refers less to the specific types of food as such than to the collective form of producing and consuming them. These foods of the gods are: mild and strong maize beer, fish, honey, assai palmfruits, tortoises, howler monkeys, and sweet potato porridge. The gods also come to eat tapir and deer, which, due to the quantity of meat they provide, are consumed by more than one residential section. The only game animals that are not the object of such prelibation, even when slaughtered in quantity, are white-lipped peccaries—a food belonging to humans (there are no pigs in the sky) and a meat on which no restriction weighs.[34]

Inasmuch as these eater-gods are not masters of the species of food consumed, they lack direct powers of sanction against humanity (for instance, by preventing these products from being obtained or by producing illness if the food were not brought to them for consumption). As far as I know, only *Me'e Ñã*, "Jaguar-Thing," and his partner *Moropïcï*, the Master of Snakes, both of which eat tortoises, may become enraged and release their pets against humans who are negligent in inviting them to banquets of tortoise meat. But even here, this is not the reason for their being summoned. The system of food offerings to the *Maï* does not suggest an intention to propitiate or any similar motive. The gods come because men like them to come: they like to hear the gods' songs. True, some nocturnal songs of the shamans are interpreted as manifesting the anger of the *Maï* when feasts of some food or other in season are lacking; they threaten to eat the shaman. But such threats are common and are not restricted to this context; the gods are "eaters" par excellence. I was also told that if banquets are not offered to the gods, they close the *kɨrepe*, the path to the heavens, impeding shamanic communication. The danger, therefore, is that of cutting off relations between heaven and earth, not that of prejudicing the relations between humans and food sources.[35]

It should be noted that, apart from the case of fishing with vine poison (which involves work teams broader than one residential section), none of the foods of the gods technically requires the economic coordination of the whole village. The gods and the dead impose such a unification by positing themselves as the recipients of a global offering from the community of the living. Such collective banquets mark the Araweté annual cycle in a form similar to that observed among the Guarani, where "not infrequently the economic activities appear as simply a pretext for the performance of ceremonies for contact with the supernatural . . . the annual economic cycle is . . . basically and primarily a cycle of the religious life" (Schaden 1969:49–50).

□

Apart from a division among celestial, terrestrial, and aquatic beings, it is not easy to determine taxonomic criteria for the spiritual population. The quality of information I obtained on each type of being varies a great deal. Moreover, the list is open: shamans constantly create new modifications of Divinity.[36] I will enumerate the supernatural beings in a somewhat arbitrary fashion, lingering on these I know best—which no doubt reflects their importance at the time I lived with the Araweté.

As far as I can tell, all the spirit names denote categories of beings, not individuals. However, in the following list I often refer to these beings in the singular, not the plural (for instance, the "Master of Assai Palms"), in much the same way that we sometimes characterize a type through its token (as in "the jaguar is a carnivorous animal"). Actually, the ontological question of whether spirit names refer to unique or multiple incarnations of a particular category is quite foreign to the Araweté (their language, moreover, does not inflect nouns according to number). More interesting to them is the question of whether the particular spirit category is comprised of beings who live gregariously or alone. Throughout the book, I tend to use singular forms either for solitary kinds of spirits or as a shorthand way of speaking about a spirit type, while I tend to use the plural form for broad classes of spirits or for kinds of beings that the Araweté appear to conceive of as living in groups.

i. Celestial beings *(iwã hã)*
a. The *Ma̱ï*

Ma̱ï hete and their manifestations, designated by kinship terms ("*Ma̱ï*'s sons," "daughters," etc.), are associated with thunder and lightning. Their favorite pets are swallows (*taperã*) and oropendola orioles (*yapɨ*).

Aranãmĩ, who raised up the firmament, is also called *hɨwã oho*, "large forehead," because his use of a macaw diadem exposes his forehead, and *kɨpe oho*, "large back," because he walks bent over. He is not a cannibal. He comes to earth to eat xupé honey (*iwaho*) and tortoise. Holding up the celestial disk, he was the last to follow in the ascent of the skies.[37] He lives with the *Ma̱ï hete* and has two wives. *Heheḏe̱'a*, his nephew, also raised up the skies. He is associated with the swallow-tailed kite (*tape*).[38]

Marairã, his wife *Mo'irewo* ("perfumed beads"), and daughter *Mãñato* are consumers of honey, tortoise, and strong beer.

Awerɨkã, Master of Bacaba Trees, was one of the last to ascend in the time of the deluge, having taken refuge inside a blind in a bacaba palm. He is evoked in an incantation that brings on the wind and makes gardens burn well. He is called "our father-in-law."

An important triad is *Ñã-Ma̱ï*, "Jaguar Divinity" ("it's just a name," I was told; he has nothing to do with jaguars), his brother *Miko ra'i*, "Opossum's Son" (idem), and *Tiwa̱wï*, called the maker of our bones because he reassembles them and resuscitates us after we have been devoured by the *Ma̱ï hete*.

A spirit called *Yičire ačo*, "large alligator" (who bears no special relation with the animal), is the chief drinker of strong beer. He is described as *hemiyika me'e,* provided with many wives, and as a licentious spirit.

Iapidacī is the main consumer of xupé honey.

Moropïcï is the Master of Snakes, which he carries tangled up in his hair. A drinker of strong beer, when intoxicated he releases the snakes to prowl about the village during the feast. He also comes to eat tortoise, after which he gathers up his pets and brings them back to the sky. This Medusa lives apart from the *Maï hete* along with his friend (*apĩhi-pihã*) *Me'e Ñã,* Jaguar-Thing, the main eater of tortoise among the divinities. Another name for the latter being is *Maï čiye hã,* the gods' tool of fear. He is associated with other celestial jaguars, such as Grandmother Jaguar and Monstrous Jaguar. If a shaman dreams of any of these big cats, it indicates the desire of the Jaguar-Thing to eat tortoise and so foreshadows a ceremonial hunt. The Master of Snakes and his feline partner are called *bïde rati,* "our fathers-in-law," by humans.

Maï paracïpe is the main consumer of howler monkeys. He is the master of stone hills in the sky.

Haka odï mo-Maï, "Heron-turned-Divinity," comes to eat fish killed by fish poison.

Iriwɨ morodï tã, Master of Vultures, makes his earrings and diadems out of king vulture feathers. He partakes of deer and tapir and greets the souls of the dead. His domains close off the *Maï pi,* that is, they lie at the lowest level of the sky, as do villages of other "bird" gods, such as *Kanoho odï mo-Maï,* "Harpy-eagle-turned-Divinity," *Iwadï ti pehã,* "those-living-with-blue-macaws," and the *Ara'ï ti pehã,* "those-living-with-blue-headed-parrots." The latter live in hills in the sky and come to eat tortoise. Close to the terrestrial tier is *Da'ï ñã,* the Master of Small Birds, who inhabits the level at the top of the tallest trees. Nearby too are the domains of *Orokoro'ã mo-Maï,* "Pygmy-Owl-turned-Divinity," whose song is associated with the arrival of enemies.

Among the most dangerous cannibal gods are the *Ayɨrɨ ti pehã,* "those-living-with-parrots," the *Teredetã* and the *Iwã pïdï pa,* "inhabitants-of-the-red-sky," who live apart in other heavens.

The *Ita oho pehã,* "those-living-close-to-boulders," are gods associated with the *Towaho* enemies, their dance companions (*anãwe*). They come to drink strong beer. They have no buttocks.[39]

Ayirime or *Tato-Maï* is "Armadillo God." Eating armadillo snouts is said to inspire dreams in which this divinity makes us sing.

There are four species of female divinities who shamanically cause the celestial maize to plant and harvest itself. They do not usually come to stroll about on earth. They are *Tapïdokã kãñĩ,* "wasp-woman," *Mamãñã-yo kãñĩ,* "bumblebee-woman," *Kawawa-yo kãñĩ,* "*kawawa*-wasp-woman" and *Moiyiawadïdo.*

Another series of divinities is associated with natural phenomena or living species and rarely come to earth. They include *Iwito yari,* Grandmother Wind; *Madïde toti,* "*Madïde*'s uncle," Master of Lightning; the *Topĩ* and their daughters, who are masters of babassu flower buds and associated with lightning (in some way that I did not understand); *Payikã,* whose name is the same as that of the *Anadenanthera peregrina* tree, the pods of which are psychoactive; and *Nata'i čiri oho pihã,* "he-who-lives-by-the-large-babassu-buds," master of capuchin monkeys.

Tepere and his son *Moia'iwoti* are gods who do not eat any food but who merely come to earth for strolls. *Tepere*'s pet is the laughing falcon. A myth recounts how he died, was buried, and rose from the grave; his song tells of the worms that devoured him. He is responsible for the presence of loose rocks in the Ipixuna rapids (which get exposed during the dry season), formed when he blasted or burned (*hapi*) them.

Various other gods have names formed by that of an animal followed by *terekĩ,* "carrier," such as *Tukãhãyi rerekĩ,* the carrier of the tocandeira ant, one of the occupants of the *Maï*'s canoe when it descends to earth to fetch the dying. Another common way of forming the names of the *Maï* is by using the name of an animal followed by *peye,* shaman. Many of these gods are individual creations of shamans. For example, the *Mamãñã-yo peye,* shaman of the eternal bumblebee,[40] appeared at a tortoise feast I attended in 1983 and was said to have emerged for the first time in the song of a deceased shaman some years ago. "*Ɨpapã-papã te kɨ, peye,*" someone told me, "They sure give a lot of names, these shamans!"

Finally, there are certain spirits who, although celestial, are not properly called *Maï*:

b. Those who live in the *Maï pi* (*Maï pi hã*)

The *Awĩ peye,* "shamans of the enemies": the most important are the *Towaho peye,* who come to eat sweet potato porridge, and the *Kamarã peye,* "shamans of the whites," whose song mentions machetes, mirrors, and axes. The latter are "the ones who brought the metal axe to the gods."

The most dangerous cannibals of the cosmos are called *Iaracĩ,*

Kapewa, or *Ipĩ'ã oho* ("Big Liver"). This race lives on the banks of a celestial river that runs above the Xingu. They eat the livers and brains of victims, human or divine. They are *Maï yokã hã*, killers of gods. Their name must not be pronounced out loud, except by those who have already killed an enemy. They eat the fruits of assai palm (the usual manner of naming them is "eaters of assai"); they come down to earth when this fruit is ripe. When a shaman sings the sinister song of *Iaracĩ*, talking of human livers and of the big pots in which they will be cooked, the whole village rushes immediately to the forest to spend several days collecting assai and xupé honey. Upon returning, humans hold a great banquet of assai sweetened with honey. A shaman brings the *Iaracĩ* to eat first. This spiritual feast may not be witnessed by anyone; only after the cannibal's ascent can people come out of their houses and eat. Feasts of assai sweetened with other types of honey are eaten by different beings, such as the *Maï hete* and the *Awĩ peye*. The *Iaracĩ*, like all the other celestial cannibals, cannot be killed by shamans.

ii. Gods of the underworld (*Iwi kati*)

The *Tarayo* are those who live on islands in the subterranean river (mentioned at the beginning of this chapter). They are frequently invoked in combats against the *Ãñĩ*. The other subterranean race, the *Motïnã ãčo*, is one I know little about.

iii. Terrestrial spirits (*Iwi pa*)

The *Ãñĩ* are the epitome of terrestrial spirits. Various other forest spirits are classified along with the *Ãñĩ*, especially three called *toti*, "maternal uncle" (a position that connotes familiarity and sexual partnership) by the *Ãñĩ*.

Koropï is a hunter and cannibal who lives in the hollows of Brazil-nut trees.

Karoã, Master of the Hills (*iwiti ñã*), has large plantations of bamboo. He is also ferocious and cannibalistic.

Yiripadï, Master of Calabash Trees, carries their fruits strung together on his back. As Master of Assai Palms, he punishes anyone who cuts them down (the Araweté do not eat assai palm hearts).[41]

These spirits habitually attack hunting camps and must be killed by shamans. Besides them, there is a series of owners of trees and landscape features:

Iwirã ñã, Master of Trees, is apparently the one who plants the forest trees that do not have specific spirits as owners.

Yɨara'i ñã, Master of Mumbaca Palms, is a spirit who trembles and smells bad. Pregnant women must not have sexual relations near a mumbaca palm tree or else their children will suffer convulsions (*hadi*).

Iwiaho ñã or *Kopi'ï ñã* is Master of Termite Nests.

Itõ'õ ñã is master of a certain type of soil, the sludge that gets parched after the waters recede in areas of the forest that were flooded.

Ĩhã ñã is Master of *Ĩhã* (a large, red, and ferocious species of ants).

Itã ñã is Master of Stones. Like all the spirits described above (with the exception of *Yɨara'i ñã*, dangerous for pregnant women), these are dangerous for the fathers of newborns; they pierce their feet with arrows if they venture out of the village.[42]

Hɨkaroho ñã is Master of Clearings, and *Orokoyi'i ñã*, Master of Mbocayá Palms.

The eight spirit types above form a special group. They are entities defined vaguely as *me'e ñã*, owners of things, who are seen by shaman apprentices. Men often gather together for collective smoking sessions. When "killed by the tobacco," those who are not yet shamans see these entities rather than the *Maï*; this prepares them for the superior experience of viewing the *Maï*. The owners of things are dangerous, but not as much as the *Ãñĩ* and their uncles, who often ambush men and capture women, and who can only be confronted by shamans.

The terrestrial spirits are savages. None of them sing or paint themselves. They always carry heavy, wide-blade arrows. Nevertheless, it is said that the *Ãñĩ* and their uncles have large plantations of manioc, not of maize. This marks them with a masculine nature, reinforcing their definition as kidnappers of women.

The same spirits who threaten the fathers of newborns play an important positive role. The *Iwirã ñã*, *Ĩhã ñã*, and *Itõ'õ ñã* blow on the face of a killer to revive him when he enters a temporary state of death after his deed. They thus associate themselves with the spirit of the dead enemy, who urges the killer to get up and dance.[43]

Also inhabiting the earth are the *Iwi yari*, Grandmother Earth, a race of fat old spirits who eat human corpses, which thereby links these spirits to the necrophagy of the *Ãñĩ*.

The *Ayaraetã:* these beings are not owners but hypostases of honey, particularly xupé honey (*iwaho*), the most abundant kind in the region.[44] They "come along with honey" and are called the fathers of xupé (*iwaho rɨ*), just as bees in general are called fathers of honey, (*e rɨ*). They have not a single hair on their bodies (undoubtedly because the bees cut it all off) and begin to wander through the forest starting in the middle of the dry season.

An *Ayaraetã* is an "eater of honey," but by nature different from the *Maï* who descend to earth for this reason. He is dangerous and must be killed by the shamans; his manifestation prompts a general flight to the forest to collect honey. If people stay in the village, the *Ayaraetã* captures their souls and keeps them inside his great *aray* rattle, where they remain eternally eating honey.

The *Ayaraetã* are male beings who often appear to women in dreams, saying in a soft voice, "Here is my semen, take it; here is my bowl filled with honey." Various deaths are attributed to *Ayaraetã* who have extracted a person's soul (*ĩ*); such thefts, typical of these mellifluous beings and the Master of Water, must be confronted by the shamans, who recapture and return the *ĩ* to their owners through an operation called *imone.*

iv. The Master of Water

This is a well-known figure in Lowland South American cosmologies. In Araweté he receives various names: *Iwikatihã*, "He-of-Underneath"; *I pa*, "Water-Dweller"; *Maï ɗamirã pe*, "Former Pestle of the Gods" (possibly referring to the myth of the creation of fish); *Pïda oho ñã*, "Master of Trairão Fish." The *Iwikatihã* race lives at the bottom of rivers. Although cannibals and very dangerous, these spirits are not savages like the *Ãñĩ* and their kind. They live in villages and have many cultivated plants (especially tubers). Their pets are the gypsy birds that fly loudly over the roofs of their houses on the riverbanks, like macaws do in Araweté villages. *Iwikatihã* controls fish in general; during fish poisoning expeditions, a song is sung that aims at convincing him to liberate his "stock." His name must never be pronounced while fishing or swimming.

Menstruating women should not bathe in flowing waters, or else the Master of Water will provoke floods, as well as shoot spindles and combs (typical female objects) into the body of the guilty person, causing death. He habitually copulates with pregnant women while they sleep; this mixture of different semen produces monsters, if it does not first kill the woman. Another way he attacks is by kidnapping the body and soul of any woman who goes to bathe alone.

Iwikatihã also captures the souls of small children when, during their baths, they escape from their mothers' hands and plunge their heads underwater. One of the most common activities of the shamans is returning infants' souls to their proper place.

Araweté men call this spirit, semijocularly, "our brother-in-law" (*ɨre rado'i*), due to his predilection for their wives. In contrast to the *Ãñĩ* and similar beings, he is the object of great respect. Nevertheless, he can be killed, he does not sing, and he does not come to earth to partake of human foods: he is not a *Maï̲*. His role in Araweté cosmology is lesser than that of his analogs among the Tenetehara (*ywan:* Wagley & Galvão 1949: 102–4), Kayabi (*karuat:* Grünberg n.d. [1970] 156), Wayãpi (*moyo,* anaconda: Campbell 1982: 276–77; 1989), and of other cultures (Roe 1982; S. Hugh-Jones 1979: 127; Menget 1977: 173). He does, however, maintain the same complex of associations: hypersexuality, pathogenic power, and aversion to the smell of blood.

4. Tupi-Guarani Cosmologies

A stratified conception of the cosmos is common among the Tupi-Guarani, but the values attributed to each layer are variable. Thus, the Kaapor distinguish three layers: the celestial world inhabited by the souls of the dead and associated with the creator hero *Mair;* the terrestrial human world; and the lower world, linked to the specters of decomposed bodies, to jaguars, and to femininity (Huxley 1956: 169, 214–16, 232–33). The subterranean world is especially important, since from it originated the bodily ornaments that distinguish the Kaapor. The celestial world, conversely, is little elaborated; sometimes it blends with the far ends of the earth (a "burnt world"), while at other times it is associated with the east and an island (Huxley 1956: 200, 214–16). The Kayabi distinguish the same three worlds; in the celestial one (*ɨwak*) towards the east lives the immortal part of the souls of the dead (Grünberg n.d. [1970]: 166).

The Wayãpi also differentiate three layers (or four, if we distinguish the lower sky, domain of the bicephalous Vulture, from the upper sky [Gallois 1984]), but the terrestrial world receives more elaboration, involving contrasts between village and forest, land and water. The celestial world, where the souls of the dead go, is the domain of *Ianejar,* master of the human race—an entity who is relatively distant (and should remain so). The underworld is inhabited by giant sloths and has as its master the kinkajou;[45] it has little importance in Wayãpi cosmology (Grenand 1982: 42; Gallois 1985). But when the firmament falls, humans will go to the subterranean world and transform themselves into *añã* (terrestrial specters of the recent dead); the celestial souls will then occupy the place of the living (Gallois 1984, 1988).

The Parintintin distinguish two skies, like the Araweté, but for the former, the second sky is the most important, being the domain of the "celestial people," a powerful race that caused their abode to ascend and abandoned mankind on the earth (Kracke 1983: 18). The subterranean domain is the abode of the *añang*, spirits of the dead, but they are also said to be living in villages in the forest. The terrestrial domain is associated with the hero *Mbahira*, who is opposed to the celestial people.[46]

The Tapirapé data are ambiguous. Baldus (1970 [1949]: 357ff.) mentions a representation of the cosmos with two skies and a lower world, but he emphasizes that the horizontal axis predominates over the vertical. Wagley (1977: 169) believes that the version of the cosmology with a lower world and a single upper world is due to missionary influence—although he also reports that shamans travel to the skies, encounter celestial jaguars, and the like.

Among the Tapirapé, the East/West axis apparently assumes some of the functions of the Sky/Earth axis found among other Tupi-Guarani. Thus, the opposition between the destinies of the souls of shamans and those of common people is expressed in horizontal space: the souls of the latter wander ceaselessly in the forest (with no precise localization), while those of the former go to the village of *Maratawa*, located west of the village of the living (Wagley 1977: 169). But Baldus (1970: 358) cites another work of Wagley (1940) that states that the village of *Maratawa* is placed to the East, counterposed to a village in the West that is the destination of the souls of shamans executed for being sorcerers; there the souls stay until they have recuperated from their wounds and then go on to *Maratawa*. Hence, there is a progression: forest → western village → eastern village, which reflects a system of recursive oppositions: (Forest: Village) :: (Commoners: Shamans) :: (Dead: Living) :: (Humans: Gods) :: (West: East). The opposition "Humans: Gods" is justified by the fact that *Maratawa* is the place of mythic heroes and eternal life, and is at times confounded with a celestial place (Wagley 1977: 178ff.).[47]

The Tenetehara situation resembles that of the Tapirapé. The nonterrestrial domains are weakly elaborated in favor of oppositions on the horizontal axis: village/forest, woods/rivers. The subterranean world is only mentioned as being the domain of the jaguars that taught humans the Feast of Honey (Wagley & Galvão 1949: 143–44). The "village of supernaturals," home of *Maíra* and other creator heroes and the souls of those who died a "good death" (i.e., those who were not killed by or executed as sorcerers), is distant from mankind and does not have a precise localization.

The Tupinamba materials are not very informative with respect to the architecture of the cosmos. There are strong indications of a celestial world (the *Guajupia*), paradise of the souls of the valorous dead. Some chroniclers situate it in the West ("beyond the high mountains," meaning the Andes). But I would argue that this is the direction of the ascent of the souls to the sky, as among the Araweté. Montaigne, who had a good informant (a French sailor who was left among the Indians to become an interpreter), reports that worthy souls resided in the eastern sky; the "damned," in the western (1943 [1580]: 83). Since the souls of cowards, according to other sources, stayed with the forest-dwelling, necrophagous spirits on earth, here too is found the same equivalence of (East: West) :: (Sky: Earth) :: (Village: Forest).

The Aché conceive of a primeval subterranean world from which humanity emerged and a celestial prairie or forest, the domain of Thunder and destination of a part of the deceased's person. Both domains play little part in daily life (and the Aché do not have shamans [P. Clastres 1972: 16–17, 303]).

Among the Guarani is found the most detailed elaboration of the celestial domain and of vertical oppositions. I did not find, however, any reference in the literature to a subterranean world. On the other hand, the Guarani cosmologies include seven or more paradises (Cadogan 1959: 28ff.), intermediate skies functioning as limbo (Nimuendaju 1978: 60ff.), divine regions arranged according to the cardinal points, and so on.

It is not my intention to discuss at length the complex Guarani pantheons. Suffice it to say that the general opposition that predominates is between the celestial domains and the forest, with the human domain (village) in an intermediate position. The East/West axis echoes the significance seen elsewhere. The apocalypse will begin in the West: for this reason, Guarani migrations move towards the East (Nimuendaju 1978: 87–88). The Land without Evil is located either in the East or at the zenith (Schaden 1969: 207). To reach it, it is necessary to become lightweight by dancing and then ascending.

□

The data above suggest some general propositions. The vertical axis is the dominant dimension of the Tupi-Guarani "proto-cosmology." The separation gods/mankind entails the differentiation of the universe into layers. The most complete elaboration of this axis involves an underworld, a human level, and two or more celestial worlds. The opposition sky/earth surface is the canonical form of this vertical polarization; the underworld is little marked and is frequently projected onto a horizontal axis of cosmological oppositions. The second celestial tier appears redundant in cosmologies such as that of the Araweté; it is, like the underworld, a sort of frame for the central duality, sky/earth.

However, the actual weight of the sky/earth opposition varies among the Tupi-Guarani cultures. The greater the presence of the gods and celestial souls of the dead in the culture's ritual life, the greater the weight of this opposition. Consequently, the opposition sky/earth can be transformed into, or articulated with, horizontal oppositions.

When a horizontal transfer of the sky/earth axis occurs, it corresponds to the opposition east/west. In such cases, the relationship between the human world and the animal world (represented by the Masters of Animals) prevails over the relationship between humanity and the "vertical," humanlike gods (such as the *Ma̱ï hete*).

The celestial portion of the person is associated with these divinities and with immortality. The earthly and corruptible portion of the person is associated with the subterranean world. In its pristine form or when transported to the horizontal axis (when it coincides with the forest, in opposition to the village), this lower world is associated with pre- and antisocial values: primitivity, animality, beings of the *Ãñĩ* sort.

This model of Tupi-Guarani cosmology contains three domains: (1) gods, divinized souls, sky; (2) living humans, earth surface, village; (3) animals, specters of the dead, forest (or subterranean world). These domains correspond to ontological categories that can be glossed as (1) Supernature, (2) Society, and (3) Nature. These three levels of being may be qualified respectively as metacultural, cultural, and infracultural, and are associated with the future, the present, and cultural, and are associated with the future, the present, and the past.

Such a structure is complex, exhibiting hierarchical oppositions. The two modalities of the extrasocial (supernature and nature) are opposed globally to the central term of the triad (society), and encompass it hierarchically. In turn, one of these two forms of the extrasocial will be emphasized to the detriment of the other, and the set they form will thereby contain a secondary encompassment. Each Tupi-Guarani cosmology will vary according to the relative weight conferred on the forms of the extrasocial. The invariant of the Tupi-Guarani cosmological structure is the metaphysical encompassment of the domain of the social by the macrodomain of the extrasocial. The interior of the *socius* and its values are subordinated to exteriority.

□

Throughout this book, I will offer evidence that supports the propositions advanced above. For now, I return to the spiritual population of the Araweté for final comments.

There are many things I cannot explain. The relationship between the "eater" divinities and their foods is rarely clear. While it seems clear why the heron divinity eats fish (the diet of his eponymous bird), I do not know why *Aranãmĩ* eats honey and tortoise but not, say, howler monkeys or some other food. Yet again, besides some relatively stable associations, the entire system appears to depend not only on economic circumstances, but also on what I would hazard to call the oneiric caprices of the shamans. Thus, for example, one night in January 1983 a shaman brought to earth a *ɨrɨwã-yo rerekĩ*, a *Ma̲ï* whose emblem is the *ɨrɨwã* bird. Since this occurred at a time of ceremonial tortoise hunts, the song referred to the expedition that would take place the next day. Granted that my ethnographic knowledge may be lacking, I can only say that there is no obvious association between the *ɨrɨwã* and tortoises. Several examples of this sort occurred.

I also do not know how to explain why certain gods descend to earth more often than others, or why some are "eaters" and others not. This is the same type of problem I encountered in attempting to document the reasons why a particular deceased person was chosen as an eponym for an abandoned village. The same problem will come up again later when I discuss why certain deceased souls, but not others, return to earth in shamanic songs.

In sum, the current Araweté cosmology appears *to me* as a contingent summary of the versions created by the shamans and remembered by the community. Apart from a few stable general principles that I can identify—among which is precisely the inventive power of the shamans—I am at a loss to push it further.[48]

Another question remains. How to explain the heteroclite proliferation of the supernatural population? Why, within the *Ma̲ï* category, does one find such disparate entities, in both their conceptualization and their mode of existence? Beyond the limited considerations reviewed above—such as how the multiplicity of the celestial series replicates the variety of races in the terrestrial series, with the *Ma̲ï hete* and the Araweté in the central positions—a great deal remains to be accounted for. In the first place, it is not possible to take the *Maï*-beings as celestial doubles of all that exists in the visible world, either as "owners" or as "spiritual hypostases." The notion of *Maï* does not attain the abstraction encountered, for example, in the Kamayura and Kayabi concepts of *mama'e* (Lins 1985) or in the Wayãpi *ijar*. In the second place, although the creation of a large portion of this pantheon falls to the shamans, the *Maï* are neither their spirit "familiars" nor associated with specific shamans.

The number of gods with names of animals should be interpreted not as an anthropomorphization or spiritualization of such animal species, but rather, as animal modifications or animalizations of the concept of Divinity. I am suggesting that, perhaps contrary to the etymologies, it is not a case of, for example, a harpy eagle turned divinity, but of Divinity conceived as a harpy eagle, a "harpy eagle mode" of Divinity. The position of the *Maï hete* as the celestial counterpart of the *bïde* justifies such an interpretation. The *Maï hete* are the human modification of the Divinity-substance; they are, so to speak, "humans-turned-divinity"; the divinization of man is the humanization of the god. And, if indeed the gods with names of animals are "humans" (*bïde*) and not animals, it is because divinization (*odï moMaï*) is, *in general*, a humanization.

This is not the place to analyze the semantic slippages that occur between certain concepts about the spiritual world from one Tupi-Guarani cosmology to another. But some notions, which usually have an abstract or generic nature, are endowed with a concrete and specific nature in the Araweté case. This occurs, for instance, with the term *Ãñĩ*, which designates a well-defined race of beings. Among the Tapirapé, Parintintin, and Kayabi, their cognates designate the spirits of the forest in general; among the Wayãpi, the term connotes the spiritual force of shamans and the Masters of nature, as well as the specters of the dead. Nevertheless, in all these languages (and in those where the concept has a range comparable to the Araweté case: the Kaapor, Asuriní, Guarani), the reference that remains constant is the association of this concept to the specters of the dead and to the position of the enemy.[49]

On the other hand, the notion of *Maï* has been developed in such a way that it comes to partially fulfill the role of a causal operator, which in other cosmologies falls to notions such as *karowara*, *mama'e*, etc. The Tupi-Guarani cognates of the form **Mahira* tend to signify something like culture heroes or creators, although there are important variations. Thus, for example, the Kayabi *Ma'it* are the souls of deceased shamans, resident in the sky, who descend to help living shamans. This calls to mind the Tapirapé Thunder, with whom the souls of shamans go to live (Grünberg n.d. [1970]; 157–58; Wagley 1977 : 200). Among the Araweté, the *Maï hete* are associated as much with thunder as with the souls of the dead (shamans or otherwise). The *Maíra* of the Tenetehara, Kaapor, and Asuriní are beings distant from humans, associated with mythic times.

If the Araweté *Maï* have kept some of the associations present in the *Maíra* of the other groups,[50] they have also been endowed with supplementary attributes. Only among the Araweté do we find the system of the descent of the *Maï* to come eat, the central ritual of their religious life. This transforms the role of shamanism: in contrast to what occurs among the rest of the Tupi-Guarani of Amazonia, curing is not the main activity of the shaman. The *Maï* do not interfere in a decisive way in therapy; they are not assistants or familiars of the shamans, although they help in capturing the *Ãñĩ*. To the contrary, shamans often have to release the living from the hold of the *Maï*, for they capture souls that wander in the sky during dreams. Thus, the Araweté shaman is less a curer than a singer. He presents greater affinities to the Guarani *Pái* than to his Amazonian congeners (Nimuendaju 1978 : 92ff.; Schaden 1969 : 119ff.).

The *Maï* assert their presence in Araweté life much more than do their counterparts among other Tupi-Guarani. The motif common in other cosmologies, which situates the *Maíra* apart from humans, beyond shamanic contact, and accessible only to the dead, is not found here. The *Maï* are indeed those who abandoned us,[51] but they return frequently. This is a consequence of the strong presence of the celestial souls of the dead in Araweté life, greater than what is usual among other Amazonian Tupi-Guarani groups (here again we are closer to the Tupinamba and the contemporary Guarani). Such an emphasis keeps the cosmology oriented along a vertical axis and diminishes the importance of the terrestrial and aquatic spirits, the Masters of nature. The relationship of humans with their "own" kind—that is, with the *Maï* and celestial souls—prevails over the relationship of Society with Nature. Although their pantheon includes the usual cast of characters of Amazon cosmologies (such as spirits of the forest, masters of animals, Lord of the Waters), Araweté cosmology subordinates them to the diversified and rich celestial population.

Comparative data allowed us to establish a system of oppositions between the gods or celestial heroes and the spirits of the forest for all

Tupi-Guarani cosmologies. But such a structure, although pertinent, conceals something essential in the Araweté case: the constitutive ambivalence of the *Maï hete* from the point of view of human society.

The ambivalent evaluation of the precultural state of humanity is common among the Tupi-Guarani. Before the separation of gods and mankind, there was neither fire nor cultivated plants, but also no death or work. The Araweté project such a state into the future as well. That is, they identify the *Maï hete,* symbol of this past-future (the constitutive nonpresence of the human condition) with the maximum of ambiguity: splendid cannibals, enemy Araweté, savage gods.

The ambiguous status of the *Maï* can be synthesized in their double characterization as "singers" and "eaters" par excellence. They thus establish two poles of orality: speaking and eating, which in the case of the *Maï hete* assume their maximum values: song and cannibalism.

These singer-eater gods are distinguished clearly from the spirits of the terrestrial level. All of the latter (with the exception of the Masters of Peccaries, said to be "almost gods") are dangerous, cannibalistic, and kidnappers of women. They are unequivocally enemies; men can and should kill them. In confronting the celestial gods, on the other hand, men want to (and must) establish exchange relations, both verbal and alimentary. Nonetheless, they do not cease being cannibals or cease threatening to steal the souls of the living; like all inhabitants of the realms outside society, they covet humans. But contrary to the case of terrestrial spirits, the desire between gods and men is reciprocal.

The gods are given that curious epithet, "eaters of raw flesh," an oblique manner of calling them jaguars. Thus, if the *Ãñĩ* are associated with the rotten, the *Maï hete* connote not the cooked, but the raw. If, as Lévi-Strauss would have it, the rotten is a natural transformation of food, and the cooked a cultural transformation, then its brute state, pure potentiality, is the raw—the perfect metaphor of divine ambivalence.

What do these contradictory determinations of the gods signify? If we note that, of all the Tupi-Guarani, the Araweté are the only ones who do not conceive of the *Maï* or their equivalents as paternal figures—masters, creators, or cultural heroes of humanity—but identify them as both separate from, but close to, humans, a hypothesis emerges: *the gods are affines.* The game played out between heaven and earth is alliance.

The cannibalism of the *Maï hete* constitutes the core assertion of Araweté cosmology. It is as if here the Tupinamba cannibal complex had undergone a translation into an axis both vertical and diachronic. The operation resembles that noted by H. Clastres about the theme of the Land without Evil when turning from the Tupinamba migrations to the shamanic self-discipline of the contemporary Guarani (1978: 109ff.). The *Maï* are, in a certain sense, divinized Tupinamba.

4 The Frame of Life

1. The Year

If I asked any Araweté why they would leave their villages to camp in the forest during the rainy season, when it became so disagreeable to walk through the forest (an opinion they shared), the response was invariably, "Why, there's no maize during the rains, and tortoises live in the woods . . ."

Despite its tone of ironic annoyance, the explanation is not all that obvious; after all, tortoises live in the forest all year round, and the Araweté don't. What it indicates are the values associated with the rhythms of life. One lives in a village because of maize. Their social morphology knows two phases, concentration and dispersal, which depend on the economy of maize. Maize concentrates; it is practically the only force that does so. Many other forces work towards dispersal.

In the first rains of November–December, people plant their gardens ("the maize"). As each family finishes planting and stocking up on manioc meal, they start abandoning the village for the forest, where they will stay until the maize is ready for harvesting about three or four months later. The men hunt, stock tortoises, gather honey; the women collect Brazil nuts, babassu palmfruits, larvae, and fruits, and toast the last reserves of the old maize they brought. This phase of dispersal (*ohĩ*) is called *awacï mo-tiarã*, "making the maize mature." They say that if they do not go to the forest, the maize will not grow. In February–March, after several trips to inspect the gardens, someone finally brings some maize silk to the camp to show how mature the plants are. They then perform the last tortoise *peyo* (shamanic rite, or "shamanry") and the first *pɨrahẽ* dance, then return to the village. It is the "time of the green maize" (*awacï či me*), the beginning of the year.

The weeks of the green maize are marked by the making of nonfermented maize porridge (*kãyi*) and, soon after, mild maize beer (*ka̲'ĩ hẽ'ẽ*), a thinner type of porridge of low fermentation. Then the first maize shamanry is performed, which summons the gods to come drink the beer; this rite is called the *kã'ĩ peyo*, said to be the counterpart (*pepi kã*) of the tortoise shamanry performed in the forest before heading back.

The return to the village is gradual and uncoordinated, like all collective movements of the Araweté. Only when all the families are back is the first *peyo* of mild beer held, to be followed by others. For every feast, the maize is harvested collectively from the garden of a single family, but processed by each residential unit of the village. This manifestation of the unity of the local group opens (*ïpïdawa*) the season of maize beer.[1] This is also the time when women process great quantities of annatto paint, which, lavished liberally on bodies and garments, spreading thence to hammocks, utensils, and so on, casts a reddish tinge over the entire village. From April on, the rains diminish and the phase of village life stabilizes, filled with the incessant chores of processing mature maize, which furnishes *mepi*, toasted cornmeal, the basis of their diet in the dry season.

The season of strong beer, called *kã'ĩ'da me* (after the name of the drink), extends from June to October. It is the height of the dry season. The nights are animated by the *pɨrahẽ* dances, which intensify during the weeks when the beer is being prepared. These dances are said to "make the beer heat up" (*kã'ĩ mo-akɨ*). This beverage is produced by a family or residential section with maize from their own garden. Different sections sponsor various drinking parties during the dry season. The festival of strong beer is a great *pɨrahẽ* in which the men, served by the host family, dance and sing, drinking until dawn.

In the final phase of fermentation (a process lasting about twenty days) the men go out on a collective hunt. They return a week later on the day of the feast, bringing a large quantity of smoked meat so as to relieve them of the need to hunt for several days. On the eve of the hunters' arrival, a session is held for the descent of the gods and the dead to partake of the beer. Although this spiritual prelibation follows the general style of food shamanry, it is not called a *peyo*, a "blowing" or "gusting" (referring to the movement of the shaman's rattle), but rather, a *ɗokã*, a "serving" of the beer. The festivals of strong beer used to bring together more than one village; they are still the culminating moment of sociability and the occasion when the group experiences its greatest physical density.

In July and August, the frequency and duration of the movements of dispersal begin to augment. Families move to the gardens, even if located near the village, and camp there for a fortnight or more. This is the season of "detaching the maize" (*awacï mo'ï*), the time when the rest of the maize is harvested and stored in huge baskets placed on platforms along the periphery of the gardens. Food supplies are drawn from these baskets until the end of the dry season, when the remaining baskets are carried to the new planting site, where the ears of maize are shelled for seeds (the shelling may also take place in the village).[2] More than one conjugal family gathers in the camp during this period, either because the garden belongs to a multifamily residential section or because the owners of nearby gardens decide to camp together. During this time of picking the maize, the men go out every day to hunt while the women harvest the ears and make cornmeal. The women also spend time weaving, since this is the time of picking cotton as well.

Such periods in the garden are considered very pleasant; after five or six months of living together in the village, the Araweté get restless and bored. In the garden camps, everyone feels more relaxed and able to speak freely without fear of neighbors' ridicule.

During the peak of the dry season, rarely a week passes without a group of men deciding to mount a hunting expedition, when they spend one to five days away from the village. Starting in August, families often take excursions to look for tortoise eggs, to fish and hunt, and to capture macaws. Except during the months from March to July, there are very few occasions when all the family groups spend the night in the village at the same time.[3]

In September, the season of maize beer begins to give way to the period of assai and honey. The village disperses to gather these products, prompted by the arrival of the spirits *Iaracï* and *Ayaraetã*. Even before these spirits appear in shamanic visions, families begin to spend the day in the forest, individually (in the case of assai) or in groups (for honey). October to November, with the waters at the lowest level, is the time for fishing with poison, which also causes the village to split up into smaller groups. All these products present opportunities for *peyo* feasts, being the food of the *Maï*.[4]

However, the dispersal caused by these gathering and fishing activities is yet again counterbalanced by the requirements of maize. In September, the felling of trees for new gardens begins; at the end of October, the burning; with the first rains of November and December, the planting. In the case of more distant gardens, the period of planting may bring families to camp for a few days in the garden. While felling trees, however, the men go out and come back on the same day. Garden burning is accomplished in one or two days, often being left to the women and children to do; other people may be asked to do the burning if the owners want to go on a trip at the time. To guarantee a good burning, howler monkeys should be hunted and shamanized, for this has the power of delaying the rains.[5]

In December and January, the season for the rites of tortoise shamanry begins. Since the Araweté did not disperse while the maize was maturing during the years that I was with them, this *peyo* was performed several times in the village. But like the shamanry of honey, it is characteristic of life in the forest. The tortoises offered in the village are boiled, but the "true" *peyo* of tortoise is held in the forest over smoked animals.

At the end of the year, the exhaustion of the supplies of maize leads to the harvesting and processing of manioc for meal used in the forest.

Such is the Araweté annual cycle: an oscillation between the village and the forest, agriculture and hunting-gathering, the dry season and the rainy; or, as they would put it, between corn and tortoise. Life in the village falls under the aegis of maize and its most elaborate product, strong beer, while life in the forest falls under the aegis of tortoise and honey.

In the village, interaction between different domestic groups is episodic and weak, except during ceremonies. In the forest, the families that camp together interact in a much more intense fashion, if only because the shelters in the campsite do not have walls. In the village, the most conspicuous unit is the couple, the conjugal family, which occupies an individual house. The forest, on the contrary, is the place and time to consummate a central institution of the Araweté: the *apĩhi-pihã* relationship, the exchange of spouses as lovers, or "friends." Thus, the village is the domain of the greatest extension of contacts at a much lower intensity, with the conjugal unit being relatively closed, while the forest is the domain of a narrower extension but greater intensity of relations, with the couple being open.

It can be said that in the context of village life, women predominate over men, to the extent that the village is a function of the maize and maize is "women's business." If, as stated earlier, manioc is planted by men and consumed during the rains in the forest (a masculine domain) we have:

VILLAGE
(Female > Male) :: (Agriculture > Hunting) :: (Maize > Manioc)

In the context of the forest, the principal opposition lies between hunting and gathering, or between the two most important products of these activities: meat and honey. Men hunt and women gather; but honey is gathered by the men "for the women" (*kãñĩ ne*), who are the first to consume it, whereas meat is consumed first by the men.

TABLE 2 Annual cycle

	Jan	Feb	Mar	Apr	May	Jun	Jul	Aug	Sept	Oct	Nov	Dec.
Precipitation	heavy rains			light rains, rivers recede			dry, occasional storms		rivers at lowest level		first rains	
Domain, movements	--FOREST--]		[-----------------------------------VILLAGE -----------------------------------]								[------FOREST------	
	dispersal ---->		concentration -------->			short cycles of dispersal, increasing -------->					dispersal	
Economic activities								CLEAR GARDENS		BURNING	PLANTING	
	hunting, gathering		harvest new maize	[----------------- process mature maize -----------------]						process manioc		hunting, gathering

				stock maize supplies	collect honey, assai	
				harvest cotton		fish poisoning
Foods	tortoises, honey, Brazil nuts, bacaba, cupuaçu	maize porridge	[------------ *mepi* cornmeal	------------]		manioc meal
	manioc meal	mild beer	[-------- sweet potatoes, yams	--------]		
	tortoises	armadillos	armadillos, curassows, wild pigs, tortoises, fish			tortoises, howler monkeys, fish
				[------ strong beer ------]		
Ceremonial activities	-------- *PEYO*	--------]		[-------- *ĐOKÃ* --------]		[----- *PEYO* -----
				hunting expeditions for strong beer		
		(*pɨrahẽ*)	[------------ *PƗRAHẼ*	------------]		dispersal for honey and assai, fishing

Honey and manioc are linked by a double inversion: the former is obtained by men and consumed preferentially by women; the latter is planted by men and processed preferentially by women. Honey is associated with female sexuality by a series of metaphors, but it is also the sperm of the *Ayaraetã* spirit; its position is ambiguous. The system in the forest is thus more complex:

FOREST
(Male > Female) :: (Hunting > Gathering) :: (Meat + Honey > Honey + Manioc)

where now the encompassing element is the male, not the female.[6]

Hence, we have a set of opposed values:

FOREST	VILLAGE
Rainy season	Dry season
Hunting and gathering	Agriculture
Tortoises	Green maize
Manioc	Maize
Honey	Beer
Raw, smoked	Boiled, fermented
Black (genipap)	Red (annatto)
Shamanry	Dancing
Dispersal	Concentration
Intimacy	Distance
Quartet (*apĩhi-pihã*)	Couple
Men	Women

As with the other systems outlined earlier, this one has a limited value. It "flattens" recursive figures, such as the male/female oppositions just mentioned, and one particular situation transcends it: the festival of strong beer. This ritual is the culminating point of village life, but it dramatizes both forest and village values: its focus is the men, it is preceded by a hunt and followed by the consumption of smoked meat, the lines of dancers conform to *apĩhi-pihã* relationships, the physical concentration leads to affective intimacy, and the dance is preceded by a shamanic rite of the descent of the gods. In contrast to the strong beer festivals are the oppositions cited above, valid only for everyday life.

2. The Village

The establishment of a new settlement shows that even the layout of an Araweté village is a function of maize. If every garden was once forest, every village was once a garden. When a group decides to move to another place, it first opens up a maize garden and settles in the middle of it. Little by little, the plantations retreat until there remains only the village, the form of which reflects everything from topographic contingencies to the order in which families arrived. There is, thus, no village plan, no preconceived spatial inscription of society. But clearly there is a spatial effect from a certain conception of sociability.

The first impression given by an Araweté village (of which I saw two) is one of chaos. The houses are very close to one another and do not obey any principle of alignment; the backyards of some are the front patios of others, and twisted paths cross the agglomeration, moving between thickets of fruit trees, fallen trunks, and holes (where clay for the houses has been dug up). Tortoise shells and maize debris are scattered all over; the underbrush grows freely wherever it can, so the borders between the village space and the surrounding scrub are not very clear.

In 1982–83, the Araweté population occupied a village of forty-five houses (of which thirteen belonged to the former inhabitants of the village on the Ipixuna's eastern bank, who moved in at the end of 1981). The village is built on some high ground on the river's western bank; the structures of the FUNAI Post lie on a lower level towards the river. The terrain is relatively flat, and great puddles form during the rains of the wet season, making circulation between the houses difficult.

Only three of the houses were constructed in the traditional style;[7] they were being progressively substituted by houses similar to those of regional colonists, made of wattle and daub with a rectangular floor plan and roofed with leaves of babassu palm. Some principles of the traditional houses were maintained, such as the absence of windows and the small size of the doorway. Many of the new houses had partitioned rooms, used as sleeping quarters or pens for tortoises.

The inhabitants of a house form a monogamous conjugal family: a couple and their children up to ten or twelve years old. After this age, a boy constructs a small house next door, identical to that of his parents, and sleeps there alone, although continuing to use the family hearth. The girls sleep in the parental house until shortly before puberty, when they must leave it and marry; parents will die if their daughter has her first menses while still living with them.

It is difficult to define which member of a couple owns the house. The man constructs it, the woman cleans and maintains it. Although certain customs—such as that of boys building their houses, or temporary spouse exchanges, when the woman moves to the house of her new partner—appear to indicate a masculine identification of the house, the immediate postmarital residence is ideally uxorilocal; the husband builds his house in the wife's section. Separation, frequent among couples without children, results in the husband abandoning the uxorilocal house.

As part of its property, each residence possesses a yard or patio, *hɨkã*, an area more or less cleared of brush in front or to the side of the doorway. There various implements are kept (mortars, griddles, kettles) and activities take place on fine days, such as toasting maize, making arrows, weaving, and cooking. The yard is the place where conversations and meals are held and where visitors are received (rarely does anyone except the wife's sisters or the *apĩhi-pihã* enter the houses of other people). At night the doors are closed and small openings are blocked up, so that the spirits, especially the specters of the dead, do not enter.

Although each conjugal house has its own yard or patio, groups of houses tend to share a common space; that is, different conjugal patios form a continuous area, which is the basic frame of daily socializing. The village is a constellation of these larger patios or sets of patios. Sections of the village sharing the same patio have the extended uxorilocal family as their structural core. But the actual arrangements are highly varied, the borders of each section are fluid, and the degree of inclusion of different houses in the same *hɨkã* depends on the context and person classifying them. Some houses do not attach their patio to any other, and some extended families, although acting as a unit in other situations, are dispersed throughout the village. The residential sections are interwoven, with some houses serving as the transition between contiguous sections since they shelter couples that belong to two localized groups of siblings. Since intermarriage of fraternal groups is common, a residential section may be compactly interconnected with another, even united with it.

The residential sections can be divided into two types: those occupied by families of two generations of married members and those formed of groups of actual or classificatory siblings. The first type forms units that are socially and spatially more integrated and face onto a single common patio; the second is composed of neighboring or contiguous patios. These two types represent two moments in the developmental cycle of the domestic group: although residence tends to be uxorilocal, over the long run a gradual movement occurs involving the spatial recomposition of groups of siblings who bring their spouses along (unless the serial intermarriage of groups of siblings forms this situation from the very beginning or shortly thereafter).

These two types of residential section are generally embedded in each other, forming broader sectors of the village: groups of nearby houses, occupied by a group of siblings, containing subunits formed by the houses of these siblings and the houses of their married children. Map 4 shows the distribution of these broader residential sectors in the Araweté village as of January 1983 (the situation was essentially the same in February 1988). Appendix 2-B presents data on the genealogical composition of the residential sectors; Appendix 1 shows more detailed maps of the two villages I studied.

In the residential sections and sectors of contiguous siblings' patios, one house is focal, either because of its spatial position or because it belongs to the head couple of an extended family; the section is named after the occupants of this house, there being a slight tendency to use the women as reference points. A patio, section, or residential sector is a polythetic unit, a "fuzzy sector," that results from the more or less redundant overlapping of various attributes: kinship ties, spatial proximity, frequency of interdomestic commensality, and economic cooperation. A common patio or section is thus a sort of small sociological nebula without clear-cut boundaries. This is yet another expression of Araweté social organization, founded on the bilateral extended kindred; postmarital residence depends on the political weight of the relatives involved and does not suffice in itself to produce significant matrilateral sections. Araweté social units—with the exception of the conjugal family—are essentially contextual.

There is a reasonable degree of correspondence between the residential situation and the agricultural one. The sections formed of extended families open a single garden, identified by the name of the oldest couple. In the sections composed of married siblings without adult children, each house opens its own garden, but these are generally adjacent, separated only by a few trees left standing. This difference is homologous to the two types of residential arrangements: the sections of extended families share a single patio, while those formed by groups of siblings juxtapose their own patios. Finally, some houses, whether their patios are isolated or not, open small gardens apart from others; these are extended families in embryo.

The Araweté village is pluricentric: a public and central space is conspicuously absent. The village looks like an aggregate of small villages, juxtaposed but isolated nuclei of houses turned inwards. The gravitational field of each patio prevents the formation of a *locus communis* that would be socially equidistant from all the houses.

There exists, it is true, a "central" place in the village: the area that comprises the patios of houses 13 and 14 and the clearing in front of

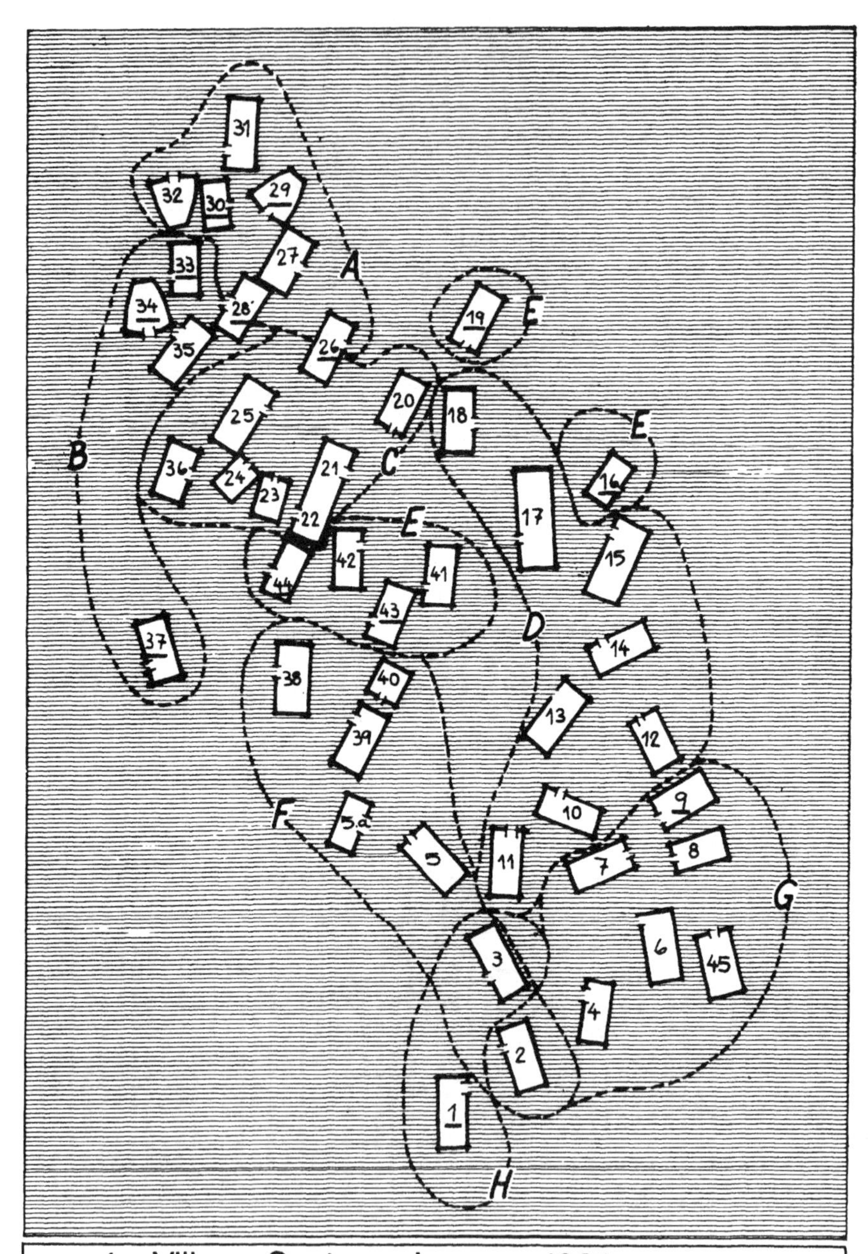

MAP 4 Village Sectors. January 1983

them. There the spaces between the houses are larger, and through it runs a path for traffic between the river and more distant houses, and between the more compact blocs to the east and west. In this "middle of the village" (*tã pite*) the feasts of mild beer and of tortoise are held. There are two reasons for choosing this area: it is a larger space with enough room for the pots of food to be lined up; and it lies along the path of the sun, sloping in such a way that no house blocks the horizon of the rising sun (the morning rays mark the path of the descent of the celestial guests).

This geographical middle, however, does not qualify as a social center. Notably, the festival of strong beer, the most important one in the eyes of the Araweté, is always held in the patio of the family that offers the drink; hence, only when houses 13 and 14 sponsor the festival does it happen to coincide with the medial area. The most dangerous food offering, that of assai with honey for *Iaracï*, is held in the patio of the shaman in charge.[8]

So even if the ceremonial organization actually unites the local group, it does not succeed in constituting a center instilled with religious values. Nor are the everyday shamanic rites exercised in a public space. The temple of the shaman is his house; there he dreams and sings at night, going out to his patio when the gods descend. If he must return someone's soul, he goes to the patio of the patient or to the river (when the thief is the Master of Water). Among the Araweté, not only are the ceremonial houses of the Guarani, Asuriní, and Tapirapé absent, but also missing is the "tocaia" complex (small shelters of straw where shamans receive the spirits—a tropical version of the Algonquin "shaking tent"), which is present in almost all the other Amazonian Tupi-Guarani groups.

All this reiterates the basic observation that the village is a derived form: a result, not a cause. Economically, it is a function of maize; sociologically, it is a juxtaposition of lesser units, not their organizing center. It is the product of a temporary equilibrium between the centripetal and centrifugal forces of the various patios, through which their tendency towards closure is compensated by the continuous differentiation spawned by the developmental cycle of the domestic group. A metonymical morphology, one might say, if compared to the metaphorical ordering of the villages of Central Brazil or the longhouses of the Northwest Amazon, where the domestic units gravitate around a unifying center. Among the Araweté, the domestic group is the subordinating element; the village is the subordinated whole. Such subordination of the whole to the parts (at times I imagined the Araweté case to be one where the whole was *less* than the sum of its parts . . .) is a structure we will encounter in other Amazonian societies.[9]

I was not able to observe the composition of the groups that made excursions in the rainy season. But in reconstituting them in conversations with the Araweté, I found the situation to be the following: (1) the village normally fragments into three or four groups, one of them considerably larger (that of the *tenotã mõ,* "leader," to be discussed shortly); (2) the residential section tends to remain cohesive and to link up with nearby sections; (3) a young couple may, however, join another section, the one of the couple with whom they have a spouse-sharing relationship; these couples tend to form camp subunits; and (4) families circulate among different camps during the season.

3. A Day in the Dry Season

The Araweté wake up late; except for a few men who go out before sunrise to hunt curassow, it is only around seven o'clock that the village begins to show signs of movement. Families have something to eat in their yards, then people either go to visit the Post, stroll through neighboring sections to find out what others plan to do, or stay home to work. During the dry season, the women start work early on cotton, removing the seeds and beating the cottonballs, spinning and weaving the thread. Family members then plan their day. The husband goes out to hunt, generally with two or three companions; if not, he goes with his wife to help her toast maize in the big griddle at the Post or accompanies her to the garden to fetch maize and potatoes, taking the opportunity to hunt in the surroundings. At midday the village is empty. Those who have gone to the garden and already returned retreat into their houses and sleep.

The intense heat of the afternoon begins to abate around four o'clock; the village comes to life again. The women pound maize, collect firewood, and fetch water in expectation of the hunters' return. The men who stayed in the village help with the chores of the maize or work on making or repairing their weapons.

Between five and seven o'clock, as it is growing dark, the hunters filter back. Alone or in groups, they enter the village hurriedly and silently, ignoring the comments prompted by their load as they pass through the sections. They stop only when they arrive in the yard in front of their houses. Then they go to bathe while the women build up the fires for the evening meal. When the day's hunt has been abundant, everybody gets caught up in the excitement. Those who are not busy cooking stroll through the patios, observing what is being prepared in each one. The children run about, dance and play through the village; the macaws let out deafening shrieks and their owners start to gather them up.

At nightfall, people begin to make their "gastronomic rounds" from patio to patio to consume that day's products. When there is a lot of meat, these rounds can last until ten o'clock or later, each family successively inviting others. The host gives sharp and prolonged shouts, summoning the residents of other sections to come eat wild pig, curassow, or armadillo prepared by his household. The families come over and gather in the host's patio, sometimes bringing their children (depending on their estimate of the amount of available food).[10] Each couple that arrives brings a basket with toasted cornmeal. Some meals consist of certain types of game preceded by the consumption of cornmeal mush (*namo pi re*). In such cases, the guests who have just arrived pour part of the cornmeal they brought into a serving vessel and mix it with the hosts' cornmeal and stew broth. The mush is stirred by one of the male guests (rarely by the host); when ready, the men crowd around the serving vessel, each grabbing what he can and returning to join his wife, with whom he shares mouthfuls of the dish. Everyone sits on mats on the ground near the meat, chattering, laughing, making a general commotion. Then the meat is cut up and the pieces put in the serving vessel; once again the men run up to it and come back to share what they captured with their families. The style of grabbing portions is, to say the least, informal: they literally advance on the food.[11] The host family never competes for its share in the dispute; the members are served by the man who divided up the pieces of meat, and then eat along with everyone else.

Smaller game (tortoises and curassows) is consumed in the reverse order. Instead of initially consuming the mush made of toasted and ground maize, people eat *iyi*, a thick porridge made of maize that is ground and boiled right away in the water where the meat is being cooked. The *iyi* maize comes from the hosts. After the meat is distributed and consumed, the porridge is put in two pots, one for the men, the other for the women, who sit and leisurely eat in separate circles. The meals of *iyi* involve fewer people than the repasts of armadillo, wild pig, paca, or fish that are accompanied by cornmeal mush.

The quantity and identity of the guests are determined in subtle ways, involving an estimate of how much food the host has, who has invited him on former occasions, how much food is available in the village as a whole, the actual or desired prestige of the host, and so on. The forms of commensality are, as everywhere, precise but complex indicators of the state of social relations in a community. Nevertheless, it is possible to speak in a general way of concentric circles of commensality and sociability. The house is the place of sharing between spouses, who remain there when food is scarce in the village, when the husband brings back little game, or when they want to enjoy some choice morsels in peace. Preparing food in the patio, on the other hand, is a way of "signaling" to the rest of the residents of the section, and always involves an invitation to one or more members of this circle. This is the most common level of commensality: each family eats successively from the pots of the other families in the same section. On those occasions when several houses kill game (which usually happens on the days of collective expeditions), the wider gastronomic round takes place. This may at times involve everybody, but in unequal ways: one family may be invited to several other patios, while another is invited to only a few or only those within its own section. The quantity of invitations that one receives is a sure index of prestige.

Finally, food consumption that involves a preliminary offering to the gods and the dead, supported by a collective effort to obtain or process the food, marks situations of maximum commensality. In these feasts, practically everyone eats in all the patios or from all the family pots. This total integration of the village, characteristically occurring through serial visiting to different patios, is what defines them as ceremonies.

Currently, the yards at the Post are used for the distribution of raw meat of large game animals such as deer, tapir, and pig. In former villages, this used to be done on the banks of the river; the Post, as noted earlier, has assumed or created the function of a common public place. The hunter, on such occasions, never presides over the distribution of the meat; this is done instead by the man of the highest prestige who shows up. It is an exclusively male activity and maintains the tumultuous style of the collective meals. It is not uncommon for the hunter to receive no portion; on the other hand, he will be invited to eat at all the patios that receive meat.[12] Another form of distribution takes place in the forest: if a man in a group of hunters has had no luck, the more fortunate divide their quarry with him. In such cases too, the donors will be invited to eat.

When a family makes an excursion into the forest, it may ask another to prepare cornmeal to be used immediately upon its return. In exchange for this service (done by women), those who went on the expedition hand over part of the game they bring back. The family that travels thus assumes the masculine position, as the provider of meat; the one that stayed behind, the feminine position, as the processor of maize—a central opposition in the ceremony of strong beer, as we will see later.

I did not observe other forms of alimentary reciprocity (outside of the context of maize beer festivals). The Araweté do not elaborate structures of food exchange in order to mark social positions and relations. Here, as in other domains, the ideology of mutuality (the other face of which is competition) prevails over the fact of reciprocity (and the requirement of cooperation). The typical form of repetition—eating the same thing from house to house—prevails over any metaphorical complementarity.

Nevertheless, if a man decides to invite someone from outside his house, certain relatives are always invited to eat: his parents, wife's parents, married children (and their spouses). In the case of youths who live uxorilocally, the father-in-law is the first person invited. Spatial contiguity is important: between an actual brother who lives on the other side of the village, and an uncle or classificatory sibling who lives nearby, the tendency is for the latter to be invited more frequently.

□

After the evening meal, the village begins to quiet down. Families return to their patios, where they lie on mats and talk. Around midnight, almost everybody is inside their houses, unless a *pirahẽ* dance is taking place in some patio.

The *pirahẽ* is the only form of dance performed by the Araweté. A compact mass of men arranged in rows moves slowly in counterclockwise circles, singing. In the middle of the center row is the singer (*marakay*), who carries a dance rattle (*maraka̲'i*) to mark the rhythm. Directly behind him is the *marakay memo'o hã*, the "singer's teacher," usually an elderly man, who proposes the songs' themes, corrects the words, and prevents the rhythm from faltering. The relative position of the dancers is rigorously respected; the medial and internal positions of the group are considered the most noble. After a set of songs, the dancers disperse, sitting on mats around the patio together with their wives. After a few minutes, the singer stands up along with the "teacher"; the group then reforms in the same order. Each row is composed of men with their arms intertwined, lined right up against the row ahead. In the front rows are the younger men. The women may come join the dancers; each passes her arm under that of her partner, holding on to his shoulder and leaning her head on it. Female dancers always form on the outside of the bloc, and none of them will get between two men. A woman dances with her husband or with her *apĩno* (her sexual partner in the forest), in which case her husband must be dancing with the wife of this man on the other end of the same row.

The occasions for a *pirahẽ* are varied, as is the degree of participation in these dances. They are loosely organized, similar in their tone and processual form to all Araweté collective movements. Despite having a formal beginning marked by the singer rising to his feet, a dance takes some time to catch on: people arrive little by little, the number of dancers varies greatly during the session (although the nucleus usually remains constant, those who leave returning to the same position), and well before the singer closes the dance, several people have already retired. Each *pirahẽ* has only one singer per night.[13]

A *pirahẽ* can be organized simply for diversion by a group of youths, but it is usually part of the cycle of dances held to "make the beer heat up" as it is being prepared for an oncoming festival; the dance will reach its climax on the night of the feast. It is also held to commemorate the death of a jaguar or an enemy, and also appears to have had other functions.[14] Its model, however, is always the same one: the *pirahẽ* is a war dance. Every participant should carry his weapons, at least an arrow, held vertically against his chest, and almost all the chants are of the "music of the enemies" genre, songs referring to war and death. The paradigm of the singer is the homicidal warrior. His definition as "he who makes the others rise up with him" (*wĩ nero-poĩ hã*) is suggestive; it is the same epithet of the Wayãpi war chief, "he who makes us stand up" (Grenand 1982:222). To rise to dance is to rise for war.[15]

In the moments of greatest enthusiasm in the *pirahẽ* (on the night of the maize beer and, I suppose, when an enemy is killed) the hypnotic rhythm of the songs, the close physical proximity, the smells, the darkness—all this generates a "collective effervescence," creating a unitary rhythmic crowd that is at the same time a war pack (as Canetti [1981] would say). Araweté dance, more than a stylized representation of society, is its transformation into a unified mass around a singer-killer, who is in charge of the "symbolic," a living metaphor of a *Maï̱*. If, as we will see, the death of a group member disperses the living, the death of an enemy reunites and unifies them.

Except for the maize beer dance, a *pirahẽ* never goes beyond two o'clock in the morning. From this time until the first light of dawn extends the domain of the shamans and their solitary chants. Night is the time of and for the gods and the dead, who take the place of the living in the deserted patios. Early in the morning they disappear, unless it is a day for a *peyo*, when the inhabitants of the sky are brought with the dawn (which is afternoon in their world) to stay on earth until the sun is high (nighttime up there).

4. Difficulty at the Beginning

I have already mentioned the "disordered" and "gradual" character of Araweté collective movements, the dynamic equivalent of their spatial multicentrism. It remains to be seen what such disorder expresses and how it is circumvented.

Whether initiating an action that unlooses a coordinated movement or joining a process already begun and thereby recognizing it as such, the Araweté find creating or sanctioning a discontinuity in the smooth flow of daily life paralyzing. One might say they are extremely reluctant to begin together, as if they felt shy about inaugurations; certain minute attitudes suggest a kind of embarrassment in acting *like* someone else, as if this implied they were doing something *because* another is. It suggests a kind of deliberate disregard of signs that something is happening and that this demands a choice: to follow or refuse to follow. A kind of ostensible inertia, so to speak, a perpetual hesitation before commencing, the fruit of an obstinate individualism that is sensitive about any imposition (even if only through example) of the "general will" and that is no less cautious about imposing one's own—all tokens of the ineffable tone of Araweté group life, their way of interpreting the Nietzschean maxim about the vileness of beginnings.

Indeed, what this manifests is a desire to hide or deny the fact that there is, after all, collective consonance. It involves something other than a "horror of authority" or a refusal to acknowledge a place for power within the social body. Rather, it concerns some sort of a resistance against legitimating this body, organizing it, moving it harmoniously. It does not involve the establishment of a maximum of similarity among all, an *isonomia* founded in a superior *meson* (Vernant 1983: 185–229), but rather, the creation of the maximum of difference: to defer and to differ, delay and divert the individual response in the face of social stimuli that demand it. The Araweté indifference to intrasocietal ritual cues, an indifference to "conventions," is the effect of an interminable multiplication of nontotalizable differences.

For this reason, I had difficulty in determining the initial moment of any collective action; everything was left to the last minute, no one would start anything. I had the impression that the problem for the

Araweté was not the one so often imputed to "primitive societies," to wit, how to find a space for individuality, constricted as it supposedly is by a theatrical world of obligations and roles. Rather, the problem was how to make, from these proudly inert monads that knew no common measure, something resembling a society.[16]

This is precisely where the notion of *tenotã mõ*, "leader," comes into play. It designates a position that is both omnipresent and discrete, difficult and indispensable. Without a leader, there is no collective action; without him, there is no village.

Tenotã mõ means "he who goes in front," "he who begins." This word designates the initial term of a spatial or temporal series: the firstborn among a group of siblings, the father in relation to the son, the man who heads a single-file line along a forest path, the family that leaves the village first for excursions during the rainy season. The position of *tenotã mõ* is followed by those who are *ipite re*, in-between, and *tačipe*, those who are behind or last. The Araweté leader is therefore he who begins, not he who commands; he who goes in front, not he who stays at the center.

Every collective undertaking presumes a *tenotã mõ*. Nothing begins if there is no one in particular who begins. Between the *tenotã mõ*'s reluctant beginning and the others' dilatory following, an interval is always interposed, vague but nonetheless essential. The inaugurating action is answered as if it were a pole of contagion, not an exhortative opening; nevertheless, it is awaited.

Pure contagion—that is, the propagation of an unconcerted activity, when everyone does the same thing on his own—is the routine form of Araweté economic activity. One fine day, for example, two neighbors get together and start to prepare annatto—not because any ceremony is in sight, or for any seasonal reason, but merely because they decide to do so. Within a few hours, all the women in the village can be seen doing the same thing. Or suppose a man wanders by someone else's patio and sees him making arrows; he decides to do the same thing, so in a little while, there they are, each man seated in his patio making arrows. This form of propagation should be distinguished from those activities for which the cue to take action is given by nature. But even there, emulation is important: after an extended period of time in the village, a certain group of families decides to go on an excursion; in the space of a few days, various other groups leave, each going their own way. It is as if all of a sudden, everybody discovered that they could not tolerate the village tedium any longer. At other times, the "contagion" is no more than the desire for sociability: seeing a small group of women go to toast maize in the griddle at the Post, various others head over there too. If somebody walks by on the path to the water holes, she is certain to attract others from the patios she crosses.

This form of "collective" action presents an interesting solution to the problem of beginning, since each person does the same thing at the same time, but for himself: a curious mixture of submission to custom and maintenance of autonomy.[17] It exhibits a tendency towards an extrinsic repetition of activities, which ties in nicely with the above-mentioned autonomy of the village patios.

Certain fundamental activities, however, cannot take place without a *tenotã mõ*. Even if the form of work is simple cooperation, they presume a formal start. The main types are: collective hunts, whether ceremonial or not; the harvesting and processing of maize, assai, or other food for *peyo* feasts; *pɨrahẽ* dances; war expeditions; and the choosing of sites for multifamily gardens and new villages.[18]

A *tenotã mõ* is someone who decides (*odɨ̈cã*) when and where to go do something, and the one who goes in front to do it. Whoever proposes an undertaking to another is its *tenotã mõ*; whoever asks "Shall we go?" has to go in front, or else nothing happens.

Since diverse occasions have diverse *tenotã mõ*, the function of leadership (which at times implies no more than the burden of beginning) circulates among all the adults. The leader of an undertaking can be the one who got the idea to do it, or the one who knows how to carry it out. Such a position may fall to more than one individual for the same task. The village may break up into various groups, each one with its *tenotã mõ*. To the leader falls the task of summoning others and taking the initial movement; little by little, the rest follow.

Such a position is thought of as somewhat uncomfortable. A *tenotã mõ* is someone who does not have "fear-shame" (*čiye*) about taking the risk of summoning others. He needs to know how to interpret the prevailing mood in the village before actually beginning, or else no one will follow him. The actual process of making decisions is discreet: in seemingly distracted conversations in the nightly patios, declarations to no one in particular about what one plans to do tomorrow, confidential agreements among friends—all of which end up generating a leader for a task.

But beyond this form of determining temporary and limited positions of *tenotã mõ*, the whole village recognized one man, or rather, one couple, Yɨrĩñato-ro and Arado-hi, as *ire renotã mõ*, "our leaders," a fixed and general position.

Yɨrĩñato-ro was a man of about forty-five years, married to a widow ten years older. They had two married young daughters who lived in the same section, along with another "daughter," a "son-in-law," and a married "brother." This section opened a single garden, the largest of the village, since it could count on the largest number of men (five) to clear it. Three other houses shared the same patio but did not work in the same garden. This was the liveliest patio of the village; not only did it always have a lot of game (Yiríñato-ro and his sons-in-law were excellent hunters and the first to learn how to use shotguns), but the head couple was the most frequent host of the collective banquets as well. Yiríñato-ro was a shaman respected for the beauty and originality of his songs; he was the one who usually performed the shamanry of assai with xupé honey, the most dangerous one (but he "did not know" how to summon the gods for the feast of strong beer). He was a good singer in the *pirahẽ*, although he had not yet achieved killer status. Finally, he had always been adroit in dealing with whitemen.

Yiríñato-ro did not have a strong group of siblings behind him (though his wife offered access to an important kin group). But he was perhaps the only person of the village to systematically address everyone by kinship terms instead of their personal names, the usual form. Despite his age, his generational situation made him the "brother" or "brother-in-law" of the older men, and the "father" or "father-in-law" of various adults. He did not make orations and did not exercise visible authority over his peers, but young people showed him respect. He belonged to an implicit class of "important men": leaders of extended families, shamans, generous hosts.

As soon as the head of the FUNAI Post discovered that he was the "chief" of the Araweté, however, his position began evolving towards one of real power, especially over the redistribution of ammunition for the recently-introduced firearms. FUNAI also began to use him as an overseer for work projects, such as opening up a landing strip; he did this halfheartedly, as did everybody else. It was only in these two contexts that I heard veiled accusations against him and his wife.

As the *tenotã mõ*, it fell to Yiríñato-ro to open the seasons for gathering honey, fishing with vine poison, and dispersing to the forest to "ripen the maize." Every time I asked if and when they were going to do such activities, people always answered, "It's up to the *tenotã mõ*," "Let's wait for Yiríñato-ro to decide." This did not mean waiting for an order, but for a "stimulus," a movement that would place the activity within the collective horizon of choice. It was not a matter of waiting for him to begin, but of leaving everything as it was until he began; *then* each person would decide for himself what to do.

In fact, the first large excursion for honey gathering took place on the day that Yiríñato-ro went out, followed by a third of the village (his section and the couples linked to him or his sons-in-law by *apĩhi-pihã* ties). Four other smaller groups went in different directions, each one led by a *tenotã mõ* who had staked out a beehive. Before this day, several families had already gone out to fetch honey, but only on the day that Yɨrĩñato-ro went out did nearly all of the families go. The hunting groups of which he was the *tenotã mõ* tended to muster more men than when others were in this position; moreover, he was the leader of hunting parties more frequently than the rest. Everything indicated that the initial movement for the dispersal of the rainy season was his traditional responsibility. Nevertheless, in the winter of 1983, when neither he nor the majority of the village undertook excursions, a sizeable group of families went out to the forest and stayed there a month. But, people told me, had he gone, then "everyone" would have too.

Actually, the range of activities in which Yɨrĩñato-ro formally acted as *tenotã mõ* of the village as a whole was minimal. I only discovered he was the *tenotã mõ* when I learned the word and the general aspects of its function; I never suspected such eminence on his part.[19]

The head couple belonged to the southern Araweté group, the one that had recently arrived at the Ipixuna. About twenty-five years ago, Yɨrĩñato-ro left the northern group, which was settled on the Ipixuna, and went to live uxorilocally with his present wife. He thus had connections with both blocs. At the same time, his residential section in the current village of Ipixuna was highly centripetal, not belonging to any sector of contiguous patios formed by siblings (it was a sector unto itself—see map 4, sector III). Such a situation placed him in a strategically privileged position: his section would not be capable of constituting itself as an independent unit were any serious impetus towards fissioning to take place, and hence it could function, even if only weakly, as a pole of agglutination.

The words and actions of Yɨrĩñato-ro, despite his position as *tenotã mõ* and his prestige as a shaman, had limited weight. His initiatives did indeed muster more people and were capable of drawing a larger number of houses out of their inertia, but this appeared to be due not simply to the formal position of headman but also to the assiduousness with which he and his wife established *apĩhi-pihã* ties with different residential sections and to his astute matrimonial policies regarding his daughters. Except as a member of the class of respected men, Yɨrĩñato-ro had nothing to say on decisions such as the organization of the festival of strong beer (which would involve a long discussion among all the sections of the village without mediation); nor was it his responsibility to open the season of mild beer, which would unite the village after the rainy season. Why, then, was he called "our leader"?

Yiriñato-ro and his wife were the *tã ñã*, "owners of the village," meaning the present village by the Post. The *tã ñã* or *tã nipã ñã* ("masters of the village grounds") are the couple or couples who first opened a maize garden at the site of a new village, around which other gardens and other houses began to aggregate. The *tã ñã* is thus the founder of a village, and this makes him a *tenotã mõ*.[20]

The model here is that of a garden opened by an extended family in which a hierarchy of functions exists. The gardens are identified with a titular head, the eldest man or couple. This man selects an area to be cleared and cuts down the brush. Then the *iwirã mo-pẽ hã*, "tree cutters," begin the heavy work (with some assistance from the elderly man); as a rule, they are the sons or sons-in-law of the titular couple. Such participation, followed by the multifamily planting, guarantees to all the conjugal units the shared right to appropriate the maize.[21]

The *tã ñã* is the "owner of the village" insofar as it was erected in a space that he opened or marked out and his extended family cleared. Then again, the position of *iwirã mo-pẽ hã* corresponds to that of *tã nipã nã hã* (a term I do not know how to translate literally), which designates the men who actually cleared the tree cover for the village grounds and who can function as "substitutes" or "auxiliaries" of the owner. This distinction was not operative in the case of the village by the FUNAI Post.

Every village is thus a former garden (*ka pe*) of a certain family, or, at times, of more than one family, since some villages had more than one *tã ñã*. In these cases, the site was not opened in the usual "vertical" manner (based on an extended family), but rather, "horizontally," involving autonomous families (of brothers or brothers-in-law) that opened contiguous gardens.

Thus, not only the village but also its leadership is a function of maize. The notion of the *tenotã mõ* of a village is no more than the temporal unfolding of the movement of starting a new village. Although called the "owner of the village," the name does not signify that its bearer has at his disposal any right over the village grounds, nor does it determine where other families will build their houses or make their gardens, nor does it mean he is responsible for "communal" spaces or for coordinating public works. While in some villages (such as that of the Post) the *tã ñã* was the *tenotã mõ* of the collective expeditions and the dispersal during the rains, in others this function fell to one of his brothers, sons or sons-in-law, or to one of the *tã nipã nã hã*.

I do not know what criteria underlie the determination of a man or couple as a *tã ñã*. Of the twenty-six former villages about which I could gather information, all were opened by the heads of extended families (father/father-in-law and sons/sons-in-law) *or* by one of the brothers of a group of siblings who moved together—in other words, the two types of residential section present in the current village discussed earlier. These twenty-six villages corresponded to seventeen *tã ñã*, all of whom were either prestigious shamans (twelve) or killers (seven).

The autonomy of Araweté residential sections is so great that it is difficult to discover "factions" in the village, unless they are seen as coinciding with the sectors indicated in the village map (see map 4). But these fluid units apparently compete for nothing; they are not political groups turned inward towards society, but rather, units of dispersal—potential villages.

The current situation of the Araweté, notably the fact that the village by the Post is a fusion of survivors of sundry groups and has a much larger population than traditional local groups did, certainly accounts for this autonomy of the residential sections and the consequent minimization of the position of the chief. The authority of a traditional "owner of the village" was probably greater precisely because the local group was smaller. What is nowadays the marked autonomy of the residential section would have been in the past the autonomy of the local group, at the time closer to its sociological matrix: the uxorilocal extended family, or more properly (since, as in most of Amazonia, uxorilocal residence is not a mechanical rule, but obeys the proviso of *ceteris paribus*), the extended family that manages to attract sons-in-law and to retain sons at the same time.

The prominence of the *tã ñã* appears in fact to have been greater in the past. After mentioning the names of the old villages, the Araweté would usually specify their "owners": a village was, for example, "Moko-ro *apa*," "of Moko-ro," and its residents were designated generically as "Moko-ro *wĩ*," "Moko-ro's people." As we saw, however, the villages are not named after those who founded them, but after those who brought them to a close, the dead who caused them to be abandoned (or, prior to a death, according to landscape features).

The former autonomy of local groups, which today is expressed in the centripetal thrust of the residential sections, did not imply a fixed and stable composition of its inhabitants. As mentioned earlier, village populations varied greatly and the sentiment of belonging to each one was apparently not strong. The system of temporary uxorilocality gave rise to a constant movement between villages, as did the deaths of relatives and enemy attacks. Thus, precisely because the degree of cohesiveness in the social structure is low, the position of leadership emerges as a pole of agglutination. Its force of attraction varies according to a series of factors, from the phase of the development cycle of the local group (i.e., of the different domestic groups), to the personality of the leader. In any case, the emergent tendency is one in which leadership of the extended family subordinates the position of village leadership, just as the domestic group logically subordinates the village. If the Araweté village is rarely something more than a juxtaposition of self-centered residential groups, rarely is the master of the village more than a head of his own domestic group, which, by assuming the serial position of "the first"—*tenotã mõ*—is capable of ordering the rest of the sections by contagion.[22]

□

The model of village leadership does not appear to have ever been patterned after the leadership of war expeditions. If the *tã ñã* is associated with any other role, it is that of the shaman. The signs for the dispersal of the village—honey gathering, fishing, "ripening the maize," hunting to furnish a *peyo*—are intimately associated with shamanic visions.[23]

As the season of a given economic-ceremonial activity approaches, the shamans' songs begin to mention it, expressing the gods' desire to eat the associated kind of food (or at least that is how the often ambiguous words of the songs are interpreted). Many times, after the village mood had thus been readied, a night would come when Yɨrĩñato-ro would sing a vision that would be taken as a cue for the enterprise to take place the next day or soon afterwards. This indirectly sanctioned the prior shamans' songs (after all, the ones who sing are the gods, not the shamans) and at the same time rendered the song of the "owner of the village" a kind of conclusion.[24] In short, everything suggests that the celebrated "chiefly discourses," the "plaza speeches" (which say no more than what everyone already knows, but sanction the existence of the community by compelling its members to be aware of it), are, in the Araweté case, transferred to the shamanic song. It is the words of the gods, expressed by the shamans, that create the conditions for collective action.

Thus, the focal point from which the words extend and concern everyone is not an isonomic, equidistant pole towards which the domestic units converge. Distant, to be sure: the Araweté plaza is not of this world, and the voices that animate it are the words of others—the

A village sector, 1983

Arariñã, 1988

Relaxing in a patio, 1983

All photos by the author

Villagers, 1982

Yiriñato-ro, the *tenotã mõ*, 1982

Iapï'ï-hi, 1982

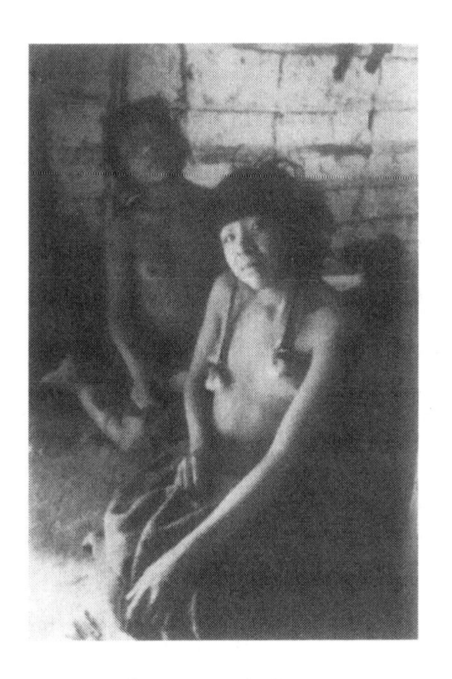

Kɨrere and Kãñĩ-ti, 1982

Mitã-hi cooking strong beer, 1982

A family on the morning after a night's festival, 1982

Festival of mild beer, 1982

Pĩnãhã and Mirã-no, two *apĩhi-pihã,* 1982

Resting during a *pɨrahẽ* festival, 1981

Gathering honey, 1982

Return from a ceremonial hunt to a beer festival, 1981

Kãñĩ-paye-ro at a hunting camp, 1981

Fishing with *hara* in a lake, 1982

Extracting an armadillo from its burrow, 1981

The extracted armadillo, 1981

Weaving, 1983

Planting maize, 1983

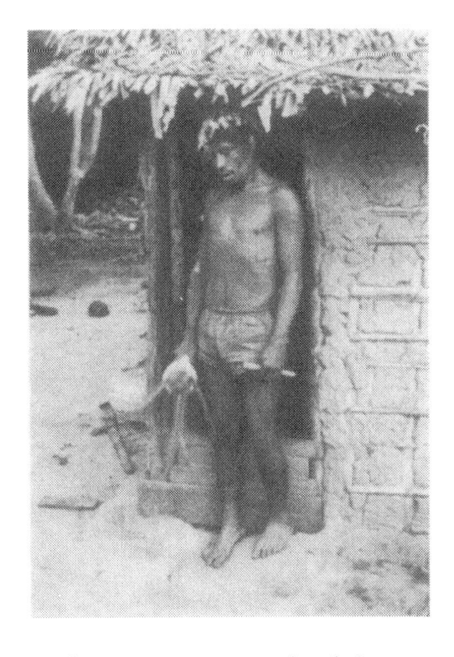

The shaman Kãñĩ-paye-ro headed for the patio for a tortoise festival, 1982

Bringing the celestial guests for a tortoise festival, 1982

A shaman and his wife, 1982

End of a festival, 1982

voices of the gods, albeit through the mouths of the shamans. Every residential section has at least one shaman, and when he sings, this man is expressing the position of his section. However, he is not speaking on its behalf: it is the gods who speak, and on their own behalf. In this way, the basic decisions of Araweté collective life receive their impetus from the outside; the burden of beginnings is transferred to the gods. *No one* decides, to be precise: it is always an other who begins—which gives him the final say-so. What awakens men from their lethargy and autism, the forces capable of moving them in concert, are these celestial voices that fill the vastness of the night.

For various reasons, war leadership does not serve as the model for the position of headman of the local group. It is true that the *moropĩ'nã*, "killer," is a focal symbol of the community—the songs and dances of the maize beer festivals demonstrate this. The *tenotã mõ* of the war expeditions are always *moropĩ'nã*. The warrior-singer is the exemplary case of the figure of the leader, "he who makes everyone rise up with him," the first to stand up. He contrasts with the shaman in several ways. Each night may bring with it various independent shamanic solos, simultaneous or consecutive, by each shaman in his own house. A *peyo* or *ɗokã* may be performed by more than one shaman at the same time. But the singer of the *pɨrahẽ*, a war song, is a singular figure, one who promotes the unison of all the men. Shamans, in other words, juxtapose themselves and represent the residential sections, while the killer unifies and promotes nondifferentiation. His melody is taken up by the voice of all.

Nevertheless, the killer does not possess the astuteness of the shaman, who is capable of assuming the political function of interpreting the will of his residential group and adjusting it to the general will, all the while eluding identification with any enunciative role. A shaman represents the others: the gods and the dead. The killer *is* an other: a dead enemy and a *Maï*. This makes him dangerous. If the shaman is a "mediator," the killer is a "mediated." But this will wait for another chapter.

□

At the foundation of Araweté leadership is thus the role of the head of an extended family and the possibility of occupying, both domestically and globally, the position of father and father-in-law of younger men. Given the ideal model of uxorilocality, the "father-in-law function" is logically anterior and superior to the "father function": the village headman is a generalized father-in-law. The absence of structural mediations between the level of the extended family and that of the village causes the leadership of the first to constitute the other; the village is formed around a family and its head, who is conceived as the founder and the foundation of the local group. Situations like that of the contemporary Araweté, whose village unites various equipotent extended families, leads to the weakening of the role of chief, transforming it into a residual place occupied by an "employee" assigned the difficult but indispensable task of beginning, of moving the *disjecta membra* of the social body.

But if the concrete basis of leadership is the position of the father-in-law,[25] its symbolic representation brings to the forefront two other attributes: that of the shaman and that of the warrior. On the concrete level, what is set up is a structure of *authority* in which the control over women (or mediation through the feminine sphere) is the essential lever (Turner 1979); while on the symbolic level, what is emphasized is not life (reproduction), but the relation with death. Here, authority is founded on *alterity,* in the relation with the "others": gods, the dead, and enemies. A common characteristic of Tupi-Guarani ideologies (and perhaps a widespread trait of "bride-service societies" [Collier & Rosaldo 1981]) is that the symbolic attributes of the positions linked to alterity encompass hierarchically the material dimensions of authority. What we have here is a triadic structure analogous to that proposed for Tupi-Guarani cosmologies (see chap. 3, sect. 4): the internal (sociological) aspect of leadership is subordinated to those aspects pointing towards the extrasocial. Indeed, it is the *same* structure: the encompassment of the interior by the exterior, of society (the "father-in-law function") by that which surrounds and transcends it (the shaman and his gods, the warrior and his enemies).

Finally, note that the three positions—father-in-law (head of the extended family), shaman, and warrior—correspond to the three spheres of activity for which Araweté society requires a *tenotã mõ:* choosing the site of gardens and villages, alimentary shamanism, and war and dance.[26]

5 Nurture and Supernature

1. Mild Beer

The categories of "owner," "leader," "shaman," and "singer" make up the repertoire of roles in Araweté ritual organization, which consists of the *peyo* of foods and mild beer, consumed by the gods and the dead, and the *đokã* of strong beer, the occasion for a war dance. Although the shamanry of mild beer is identical to the *peyo* of other foods, the ceremonial system can be divided into a ritual complex of maize and one of meats and honeys, for the products prepared from cooked maize follow a certain sequence.

Starting with the harvesting of new maize, there is a progression in which the terms occupy increasingly longer periods in the annual cycle: from solid to liquid, from hot to cold, from rapid to slow, from less fermented and more substantial to more fermented and less substantial, from the informal to the ceremonial, from "endo-consumption" to "exo-consumption":

1. *Kãyi* ("maize soup"): a thick porridge of green maize, ground and immediately boiled. It is nonfermented and eaten hot, and considered to be very nutritious. It is eaten privately or within the residential section (not being the object of any ceremony).
2. *Ka̰'ĩ hẽ'ẽ* (literally, "sweet beer," i.e., mild beer): a thin gruel of maize (green or semi-dried), prepared on the eve of consumption. It involves more thorough grinding than the *kãyi,* but some whole grains are left to be chewed by women. It uses a greater quantity of water than *kãyi,* yielding more potfuls. This beer should be mixed before being drunk so that the mash (part of which is eaten beforehand) becomes suspended. A drink of low fermentation, it may be prepared informally for consumption by a residential section, but is never consumed without inviting someone else; it may also be produced by the whole village for a *peyo* ceremony. It is drunk cold by both sexes.
3. *Ka̰'ĩ'da* (literally, "sour beer," i.e., strong beer): a drink of higher

fermentation made from dry maize. The maize is ground, boiled, and masticated for several days in great quantity. The mashed granules are separated from the soup and eaten collectively during the phase of preparing the drink. The fermented beer, then, is pure liquid (*ti*). It is not considered a food, since drinking the beverage causes hunger, and it is normally vomited. This beer is processed only for ceremonial occasions, each time by a single family, who does not drink any of it but instead serves it (*ɖokã*). During the festival, women drink little of this beverage—it is "men's affair," even though it has been chewed by the women. It is drunk cold.

□

When everyone has returned to the village after the dispersal of the rainy season, one conjugal family announces that it will conduct a *dawoči*, a collective harvest of maize from its garden, in order to make mild beer. The couple thus becomes the *tenotã mõ*, leader or sponsor, and *awacï ñã*, "owner of the maize," for this festival. One morning, the male sponsor (who may be any of the men who opened a multifamily garden, even a son-in-law of the titular head of the garden) calls out to all the villagers, inviting them to the garden. Upon arrival, the family of the owner is the first to harvest an ear. Then everyone else begins the work, divided into conjugal units.

Once back in the village, each family begins to husk and prepare the maize. A small portion of the grains is toasted and ground, producing about two liters of *mepi* (toasted cornmeal)[1]; the rest will be used to make the beer. The entire day is spent in the tasks of grinding, boiling, and chewing the maize, continuing after dark. By the end of the evening, each woman goes to the patio of the owners of the maize and hands over to the wife half the flour or cornmeal she has produced, keeping the other half for her own family's consumption. The owners of the maize also make cornmeal and beer, producing more of the latter than the rest of the households do. By the end of the day, the owners of the maize will have received about twenty liters of cornmeal.

Meanwhile, the male owner of the maize must seek out a shaman for the *peyo* of the beer the following day. Independently of the invitation, one or more shamans may show up when the *peyo* is held, since it is the gods who are in command of their own descent. The essential rule is that the owner of the maize cannot be the shaman.

The next day, shortly before dawn, the owner-sponsor brings his pots to the "central" patio mentioned earlier (chap. 4, sect. 2). For a couple of hours, the muffled sound of solo singing has been emanating from inside the shaman's house. Little by little, responding to the summons shouted by the sponsor, the men arrive drowsily and deposit their pots in a line in front of and behind those of the owner of the maize, whose pots consequently occupy the middle position. This line must be adjusted precisely along the first sunbeams. The families gather around the pots and estimate their number,[2] but they stay at a certain distance away from them, leaning against the walls of the houses surrounding the patio. Nobody is decorated; many do not even show up.

Then the shaman emerges from his house, erect, head bent, singing with his eyes closed, smoking his cigar, and holding an *aray* rattle. He slowly follows the path leading to the patio, accompanied closely by his wife, who often relights his cigar. In certain places along the path, he stops and crouches, singing. Arriving at the patio, he executes a circle (counterclockwise) with rapid steps around the line of pots, half-crouching, stamping the ground forcefully with his right foot. This is the *opiwani* movement, indicating that the gods are arriving on earth. His entire trajectory from the house to the patio is described in the song and corresponds to the path from the sky to the earth along which he brings the celestial guests. Having led the line of spirits into the village (the patio), he then goes to the end as soon as they enter, and the guests take the lead.

During this rhythmic encircling of the pots, the shaman may be accompanied by his wife and an *apĩhi,* sexual partner. This position, besides being honorific, is also a protection against a dangerous principle infusing the food or drink, which is being dispersed by the shaman: this principle is *ipeye we,* "shamanic stuff."

After the circuit, the shaman begins a series of movements around the pots, shaking the rattle from up to down into the palm of his left hand, turning towards the beer. This gesture is the *peyo,* properly speaking: it indicates the contact of the gods with the food or drink resting on the ground. At certain moments, the shaman inverts the direction of his strokes, shaking the rattle away from the beer: this is the dispersion of the malignity of the drink.

At a certain point in the *peyo,* still singing except for short pauses to smoke, the shaman turns his back on the pots and crouches: the gods and the dead are drinking. Now almost no one is left in the patio; the only constant presence is the shaman's wife, who watches out for him. The majority of the villagers have gone to paint and decorate themselves. This moment of the feast does not belong to humans, so it is not appropriate to be near the pots. The gods are present, tripping over themselves around the beer, shoving the shaman, drinking, singing, and enjoying themselves.

But a few people stay, mostly mothers with infants. The shaman may come perform the *peyo* over them, which has protective or restorative functions, such as returning a soul or closing the body of a child. The women, who are the object of the operation or simply carry children who are, maintain a distracted air, but from time to time they repeat in spoken form the phrases sung by the shaman: this is called *Maï moyitã,* "calming the gods." This spoken repetition, frequent in contexts in which a shaman acts upon something, is peculiar to women; for instance, the shaman's wife will utter such repetitions during his nightly solos inside their house. Sometimes they make brief commentaries on what is being sung, especially if a deceased soul enters upon the scene, when they speak about his presence. It struck me as a calm exchange of impressions among the women about some news brought by the shaman. The men, if any are present, speak little.

Present or not in the patio, everyone displays an aloofness broken only by the spoken repetitions, uttered in a strangely neutral tone. Otherwise, people carry on conversations, laugh, and even ask the shaman's wife for a puff of her husband's cigar before she returns it to him relit. But everybody is perfectly attentive to the songs, judging their aesthetic merits and pondering their theological-social contents. Each is remembered for a long time.

The shaman then begins his return home in the same style that he left it; the *opiwani* movements intensify and his song becomes louder, interpolated with the stamping of his foot and the grunting produced by the brusque expulsion of air from his lungs. Once inside his house, the song gradually diminishes until extinguished.

By this time, about eight or nine o'clock in the morning, all are painted with annatto, wearing their best earrings, and befeathered with harpy eagle down, while the women are also wearing their soapberry seed necklaces. The owner of the maize returns to the central patio, opens his pot, and shouts for everyone to come. The sponsor's beer is quickly emptied; as always, the men elbow each other and fill their gourd bowls with the beverage, returning to drink it with their wives, who keep their distance. Pot by pot, the beer is consumed in the patio. At each one, the owner of the pot repeats the invitation to the others. Except for the feast sponsor, each man invites only a portion of those standing around to come drink the beer made by his wife; in general, the circles of daily commensality are maintained.

The owner of the maize, who invited all to drink, is obligatorily invited to drink by all.

In contrast to the long *peyo*, the drinking of beer by humans does not last more than an hour. The feast is now over. The owner of the maize then convokes all the men for a collective hunt; he leads the expedition of "digesting the beer" (*kã̱'ĩ mo-yawẽ*). Ideally, when they return, the *tenotã mõ* should have killed a lot of game so that he can offer a feast in which the cornmeal he received is used for the *namo pi re* mush. Actually, his family may pass several days without having to make cornmeal, eating from what they received as "payment" (*pepi kã*) for the beer.

The feast of mild beer contrasts systematically with that of strong beer. In the opinion of the Araweté, the first is not as good as the second since it has no dancing.

2. Strong Beer

When a couple decides to make beer of higher alcoholic content, they notify the whole village and ask for all the pots from everybody's houses. Then begins the tedious work. Husband and wife grind the maize and boil it; the wife chews and strains the gruel. They must maintain sexual abstinence throughout this period, lest the beer not ferment.[3] The husband goes out less frequently to hunt, but goes every day to his garden to fetch maize. The full pots are gradually lined up inside their house along the walls. The abundance of metal pots received by the Araweté after FUNAI established the "consignment canteen" led to an increase in the quantity of beer produced. At one of the feasts, I calculated that about 300 liters of beverage were consumed.

Nobody outside the family should look at the fermenting beer, or else the process will come to a halt. During the nights, people dance in the patio of the host to "make the beer heat up"—a reference not just to the daily cooking of the gruel, but also to the process of fermentation, which liberates a considerable quantity of heat and is described as a boiling (*ipipo*) because of the froth. The mornings are marked by the collective consumption of *hati pe*, the sour pulp of the beer separated from the liquid.

Meanwhile, the male "owner of the beer" (*kã̱'ĩ ñã*, the title applied to the sponsor couple, contrasting with the "owner of the maize," which designates the sponsor couple of the mild beer feast) invites a man to be the singer for the festival. This *marakay* (singer) will also be the *tenotã mõ* of the ritual hunt that precedes the beer feast. When all the gruel has been processed and is fermenting, the owner advises the *marakay* that it is time to go out on the expedition of *ka̱'ĩ mo-ra,* "making the beer sour." He stipulates the duration of the hunt according to the degree of the beer's fermentation. On a certain morning, the couple that is the sponsor of the feast goes to the singer's house, bringing two gourd bowls with some half-fermented drink. The man serves the singer; the woman serves his wife.

After being served, the singer gets ready to leave. He goes from patio to patio summoning the men of the village. The scene is particularly discreet. Those asked hardly answer and do not look at the *tenotã mõ*—just as he did not look at the owner of the beer when told how long to stay in the forest. Gradually they leave to follow him to the forest, after he has already left the village with his close relatives.

While the men are gone, the singer's wife becomes the *tenotã mõ* of the village, which is now reduced to the female community and the male owner of the beer. He is the only one who cannot go hunting, since he must perform the operation of *ka̱'ĩ moyo pepi,* mixing the beer, i.e., homogenizing the degree of fermentation among all the pots, mixing the more sour with the less, removing the froth, and making sure that no potfuls "rot" (*itoyo*) by an excess of acidity. This operation should not be viewed by anyone. This contrasts with the simultaneous masticating and mixing of mild beer, both done by the wife, without visual restrictions.

Led out to the forest by the *tenotã mõ,* the men camp together or divide up into two campsites.[4] As the days pass, the camps move closer and closer to the village. Then one afternoon, when the beer is ready, the owner of the beer goes to "bring the news" to the hunters that they can return. Just as the shaman of the mild beer leads the gods into the village, so the owner of the strong beer leads the line of hunters as they return from the forest; as they draw near to the village, however, he takes a shortcut and enters his house unobtrusively, allowing the hunters to take the lead.

Before the men return from the forest, the village belongs to the women, who dedicate themselves to toasting maize and collecting firewood for the meat that will be brought. Every night they dance in the patio of the beer to "heat it up," led by the wife of the leader of the hunt. Such dances are a simulacrum of the male dances—disorganized and infused with a puerile and jocular tone—and suffer from a basic absence: there are no female songs. All Araweté music comes from the gods or dead enemies, and the only ones who can be the "authors" of this music are shamans and warriors. Women may sing the songs of warfare or shamanism, and certainly like to do so, but they cannot utter them for the first time. Thus, as they dance in the absence of the men, they simply mimic the dances and repeat the songs of others. If by chance some man has remained in the village, he is called on to be the singer or the "song teacher" for the female dancers. But they never ask the man who by definition stays in the village, the owner of the beer: neither he nor his wife dances, sings, or drinks beer.

Besides the owner of the beer, another man may stay in the village to serve the beer (*kã̱'ɨ̃ ɗokã*) to the gods, or a few hunters may return early to do so.[5] This ceremony ideally takes place in the sponsor's patio on the eve of the hunters' arrival; this is the first time the pots are taken out of his house.

The session over the soured beer takes place at night between two and four o'clock in the morning. The shaman's approach is conducted exactly like that of the *peyo* of mild beer. But the pots are not consecrated as a group; they are brought out one by one from the house by the female owner of the beer and placed on her husband's lap as he sits on a mortar used as a bench. After being emptied by the gods and the dead, the pot is returned to the house and substituted with another. The owner of the strong beer, like that of the mild, cannot be the shaman who brings the gods; his role here is to hold the pots of drink while the celestial visitors are served by the shaman. The owner of the beer and the shaman are described by the same name, *kã̱'ɨ̃ ɗokã hã*, servers of the beer: the first serves the hunters; the second, the gods and the dead. The shaman is a double of the owner of the beer; he goes "to bring the news" to the visitors from the celestial *Ma̱ï pi*.

The shaman's performance differs from that of the various alimentary *peyo*, since it concerns an alcoholic drink. His song is more violent and his movements imitate the staggering and jolting of the inebriated gods. The boundary between the citational narration of the speech of others (the dominant style in the *peyo*) and an "incorporation" of the divinity in these scenes becomes difficult to trace, given that the voice of the shaman harbors the satiated groans and thunderous coughing of his guests.

A complex superimposition is in effect, which partially explains this situation. A food *peyo* portrays a collective meal that, like the human meal that follows it, does not actually involve songs, except in the sense that the gods only speak by singing their *Ma̱ï marakã*. But the *ɗokã* is a mystical beer feast and therefore involves an invisible *pɨrahẽ*, that is, a war dance and song, held in the patio of the beer. Nevertheless, the form of the shamanic songs for strong beer is identical to the rest of the *Ma̱ï marakã*, not to war songs. The difference from the other kinds of *peyo* lies in the theme and cast of characters:

the songs speak of beer and not of tortoises, honey, etc., and different gods descend. Despite the more violent tone, the strokes of the rattle are the same as those of other *peyo* (what is dispersed here is the *dačĩ nahi we,* a "headache" that is in the beer). In short, the shaman stages a divine beer festival and fuses in his own person the positions of both server and served, owner and guest. But he does not reproduce a *pɨrahẽ,* he describes one; he does not sing the alleged songs of this invisible beer festival. Thus, by means of a metalinguistic embedding, the fundamental difference is preserved between the music of the gods and the music of the enemies.

This *ɗokã* is attended by the women, who afterwards will tell their husbands about it when they come to drink the beverage. The soured beer, when drunk by the men, will be referred to as *Mai̱ dem̱ï-ɗo pe,* the "ex-food of the gods." This is the same expression that designates the celestial dead, ex-food of the *Mai̱* and future eaters of human food.

If no man has stayed behind for the shamanry rite, it can be postponed until the night of the beer festival, a time considered dangerous, since the gods get infuriated with the light of the fires and knock the shamans down with their invisible lightning bolts. In any case, the gods *should* come to drink the beer,[6] especially *Yičire ačo,* a lascivious divinity who is the *tenotã mõ* of the retinue and who always comes accompanied by a female soul. The *marakay* singers of the mystical beer feasts I attended were all souls of men killed in war and/or killers; I do not know if this is the rule, but it happened four times (consistent, of course, with the equation singer = warrior).

A few hours before the feast, the men return from the hunt. Near the village, they stop to let the stragglers catch up and await nightfall. Then everyone bathes and sets about making *terewo,* spiral trumpets made of sheaths of babassu leaflets. When ready, the men follow the path, blowing on the *terewo,* which make a hollow sound that can be heard far away. The women hurry to bathe and beautify themselves and to light the fires. The men arrive in the same order that they left, but now all are present at the same time, the *marakay* in the front. As soon as they enter the village, they disperse, silently and resolutely, and head for their patios. The meat they have brought is placed on grills or wooden racks prepared in advance. Soon the voice of the owner of the beer is heard summoning everybody—first the *marakay*—to taste (*haĩ*) the drink. Night falls. Families go to their patios to decorate themselves. This is the occasion when the Araweté ornament themselves the most, especially the singer, with his *yɨakã* diadem, his head covered with down, his face decorated with the *yɨrɨã* pattern using tiny cotinga feathers and perfumed resin: he is *Mai̱ herĩ,* "like a god." The owner of the beer, in contrast, does not paint or decorate himself.

Around nine o'clock, the *marakay* stands up in his patio and begins to summon the others. First he calls his *marakay rehã*, those who will dance by his side (a position that was agreed upon in the forest), of whom some are his *apĩhi-pihã*, partners in spouse-swapping. Next he calls the *memo'o hã*, the song teacher.

After the singer arrives in the patio of the feast and, along with his family, occupies the place closest to the door of the host's house, other families come over and settle down on mats around the patio. Gradually the dance begins, constantly interrupted by the owner of the beer, his wife, and children, who shove bowlfuls of drink in the men's mouths, serving each line in its entirety. It is a point of honor to drink the entire bowlful (half a liter) at one go. The dancers are forcefully served, standing still while the owners of the beer circle around them giving them drink. This is exactly the inverse of the usual manner of commensality, where the men throw themselves at the vessel of food (or mild beer), grabbing what they can and dispersing to share the morsels with their family under the detached gaze of the host.

The pots are quickly emptied and pile up in a corner. In contrast to mild beer, everybody drinks from all the pots, except for the *kã'ĩ ñã*, the family sponsoring the festival, who does not drink. Furthermore, people say that near relatives of the couple should consume very little of the drink, especially if they share the same patio and plant in the same garden. This norm indicates two principles: (1) formulated in terms of genealogical proximity, it coincides with the *ikoako* circle, those abstaining from food because of a relative's illness; it also suggests that drinking beer chewed by a sister, daughter, or mother is a type of oral incest; (2) formulated in terms of social proximity (same residential section, same garden), it defines strong beer as an "exo-beverage." In the feasts of foods and mild beer, the first to be invited are those who live the closest, with commensality expanding to circles of decreasing density. In the feast of strong beer, by contrast, the singer (the focal figure and main one served) may never come from the same section as the owner of the drink; the only ones who do not drink are those who always eat together with the sponsors.

The current concentration of all the Araweté in a single village weakens an opposition that used to be fundamental in beer festivals: the singer was always supposed to come from *another* village than that of the owner of the beer. More than one village convened for this ceremony (ideally, all those that comprised a bloc, the *tã dĩ*); the men of the guest villages formed the main nucleus of the dancers, interspersed with some *apĩhi-pihã* of the host village. The *kã'ĩ ñã*, sponsor of the beer feast, thus incarnated the host village, while the *marakay*, singer, incarnated the guest villages. The co-residents of the sponsor were in an intermediate position (nowadays occupied by the sponsor's relatives), drinking less beer than the guests. However, the sponsor's co-residents would also go out to hunt; as today, only the owner of the beer stayed behind for the fermentation. The singer would be the leader of the hunt mounted from his village; in the host's village, the leader would be the owner of the village (*tã ñã*) or the singer of the next beer feast offered in reciprocation by the other village. The main opposition, nowadays as in the past, is between the house offering the beer and the rest of society. The invariable pole is the domestic group, and its complement is of an historically variable extension: village, territorial bloc, or tribe. Indeed, in 1981, when there were still two villages and I attended a beer festival in each one, they respected the principle of the exteriority of the singers and their function as leaders of the hunts in their respective villages.[7]

Let us return to the feast. As the night progresses, the dancers become drunker and a few women become emboldened to dance. The men vomit the beer that is so implacably served them. The sound of the singer's rattle and those of the shamans (who may be found in parallel arenas closing the bodies of children so their parents can drink without danger) mix together with the groans, shouts, and songs of all and sundry. Some people begin to weep despairingly, the eldest crying out the names of their dead children; others simply babble phrases incoherently. When one is drunk (*ka'o*), I was told, ears of maize swirl in front of one's eyes. For some, the beer festival finally ends with the *heti*, a sort of furious trance in which the victim begins to howl and thrash about, running the risk of wounding others with his weapons; he is seized and carried over to his wife, as rigid as a corpse. This type of manifestation usually attacks recently married youths.

The beer feast ends with the first light of dawn; few are still on their feet. The singer is the last to retire from the patio. If any pots of beer are left over, the festival continues the next day. As evening approaches, the men gather inside the house of the owner of the beer and form rows along the walls, with the *marakay* in the middle of the main row. There they stand singing and drinking until sunset. Only then do they shift to the patio, where they maintain the same formation, immobile and without dancing, singing until the last drop. Exhausted (not everyone can endure this second round), they disperse; the festival is over.

During the beer ritual, no one eats anything—a disjunction that has already been noted for the Tupinamba.[8] The next day, the women (led by the singer's wife) go visit the female sponsor and hand over part of the smoked meat brought back by their husbands. This is called the *kã'ĩ pepi kã*, the payment for the beer. As in the case of cornmeal given for mild beer, the owners of the beer will invite the villagers to eat from this meat they receive. The "payment" is thus partially neutralized, since those who gave game end up partaking of it in the patio of the owners of the drink.

□

That is the ritual complex of maize. There are no set sponsors or singers for festivals; the circulation of sponsorship does not follow any pre-established order; and the relationship between the central ritual roles, owner and singer, have no other specification than that they belong to different residential sections (formerly, villages).[9] The feasts do not appear to convey special prestige to the sponsors, much less material advantages. The oppositions underlying the strong beer ritual are condensed in the attributes of the singer and the owner of the beer, as described in table 3.

This chart reveals some of the symbolic values of strong beer rituals. The owner of the beer occupies a feminine position; devoted to maize, he does not hunt, dance, or drink. On the other hand, his role is a synthesis of two masculine states: that of the father in couvade, and of the male working to form a child. As the former, he cannot have sexual relations or leave the village; as the latter, he "heats up" the beer, cooking it and watching over its fermentation, just as a man "heats up" the fetus with frequent contributions of semen (*hadĩ mo-akɨ*, "making-hot the child"), a gradual process indispensable for healthy gestation.[10] The owners of the beer are like the "owners of children" (a term that describes the parents of newborns), who should be attentive to what happens with their "products" (*hemï-mõñĩ*).

I hasten to add that the Araweté never draw explicit parallels between the fermentation of beer and gestation. Nonetheless, a series of associations link these processes. In the first place, both fermentation and gestation occur by means of a woman, and both are transformations (*herɨwã*) of a prime material: male semen, the substance of the child, is "transformed" in the maternal uterus, and maize cooked with water is transformed into beer in the woman's mouth (and in the pots). Similarly, a menstruating woman cannot chew the beer, and a miscarriage "aborts" the fermentation.

TABLE 3 Roles of *marakay* and *kã̱'ɨ ñã* in ritual of strong beer

Marakay (singer)	*Kã̱ɨ ñã* (owner of beer)
Hunter, leader of men, brings them to forest	Cook, stays with women, "brings the news" and brings back men
Dancer, "he who arises," served beer, gives meat	Does not dance, serves beer, receives meat
Ornaments, rattle, weapons	No ornaments, instrument is gourd bowl for serving beer
Marakã mẽ hã: "giver of song"	*Kã̱'ɨ mẽ hã:* "giver of beer"
Apĩhi-pihã as dance unit	Married couple as production unit
Men, village, strangers	Women, house, villagers
Ma̱ï as model	Double of shaman ("server")
Killer	Feeder

But there are a few inversions and dislocations. In the case of conception, the man is the dominant figure; his semen is the exclusive substance of the child, while the woman is only a *hiro,* a vessel (a pot?). In the case of beer, the man is an auxiliary of the woman, either because maize is a feminine product or because the fecundating saliva comes from the woman, while the man watches over the fermentation in the pots. On the other hand, if in conception the semen forms the child, in fermentation what is transformed is an equivalent of semen. The parents of a small child cannot have sexual relations or drink strong beer: the child would become filled with paternal sperm (even if expended on some woman other than its mother) and the beer they consume, causing it to gag and die of suffocation.

Another association of semen and beer appears: semen goes from men to women, but beer goes from women (who masticate it but hardly drink at all) to men. The beer feast is the only occasion when women (or the couple occupying the feminine position) serve men. Full of beer, the dancers swell up (*ɨwo*) and say their bellies have become as large as those of pregnant women. As a process of artificial insemination, the beer operates as a kind of *female semen,* the counterpart and equivalent of male semen. (Would this be why women asked us for bowlfuls of semen? See note 5.) Perhaps it is to mark this seminal nature of beer that the presence of a man is required in the process of production, although he is placed in a feminine position: a "feminine" inseminator of the men, one who gives maize and receives game. Sperm, a woman told me, is "sour like beer."

The proper fermentation of the drink excludes the expending of semen by its owner: fermentation excludes fecundation, so that equally hot processes are not added together, and especially so that male sperm does not infect (*mo-wã*, "pass on to") the artificial female semen, beer. Otherwise, men would be truly self-inseminating, a disastrous situation: beer polluted by the owner's semen would rot (the accumulation of hot processes being inverted into rottenness), and the dancers' bellies would burst, a sort of fatal male childbirth.[11] The beer festival, moreover, has a strong erotic tinge. The Araweté say that the days after the festival are witness to intense sexual activity, for the drink causes hunger and sexual desire. It thus prepares the way for a literal insemination of women by men.

Because of its stupefying effects, beer is also compared to fish poison (*cïma*). It is a "killer of people," just as fish poison is a "killer of fish": "During the beer feast, we become like fish drunk with poison." A happy comparison, since fish poison is not actually poisonous, but narcotic; the fish, if not captured while stunned, may revive and escape. This character of beer as an attenuated poison has a proverbial expression: "Manioc juice can truly kill us, but that of maize cannot."

Another association of beer is with maternal milk, which is said to be "the beer of children." This is why parents of nursing infants should have them undergo the operation of closing their bodies, or else the beer—the milk drunk by adults, as it were—will pass to the child. The equation beer = milk, moreover, evokes the nurturant position of women in relation to men during the ceremony. Mothers often premasticate the food they give their babies (and pet birds)—just as they do with beer.

Sterile semen, gentle poison, sour milk—beer is an overdetermined drink. It is an "anti-food," as Lévi-Strauss would say: instead of nourishing, it causes hunger; swallowed, it must be vomited; a female semen, it is introduced into men through the oral tract. It forms a system with tobacco, also an anti-food, used in collective sessions of intoxication in which everyone vomits (and used in the beer festival to "help one to vomit"). But in contrast to beer, tobacco takes away hunger; instead of making us swell up, it makes us "diaphanous" (*mo-kɨyaho*), makes us "smooth" (*mo-kawo*) inside, and makes us "lightweight" (*mo-wewe*)—effects that are essential for contact with the supernatural. Tobacco is also a "killer of people": novice shamans and women usually faint and have convulsions from an excess of tobacco; in other words, they "die" (*imanɨ̃*).

Tobacco and beer have their sonoral equivalents: tobacco and the *aray* rattle are emblems of the shaman, instruments of contact with the gods; beer and the *maraka'i* rattle are such instruments for the singer. But the dance rattle is a passive instrument, merely accompanying the singing, and is not creative like the *aray.* It should now be clear why it was during a beer festival that humans were transformed into animals by the *Ñã-Maï* by means of tobacco plus the *aray* (see chap. 3, sect. 2). The *tobacco* of a god transforms *men,* drunk on *beer,* into *animals:*

Beer : Men → Animals :: Tobacco : Men → Gods

These modes of transformation are passive and active, respectively: the first, regressive (culture → nature); the second, progressive (culture → supernature). Recall that tobacco, besides putting shamans in contact with the gods, was originally used by the latter to ascend to the skies during the primordial separation. Finally, the regressive power of beer can be observed in the treatment that dancers undergo as they are passively served a drink masticated by women, as if they were children. Regarding the inverse direction, recall that the gods may be considered adults in relation to the living (see chap. 3, sect. 1).

□

The Araweté would tell me that they did not dance when a *peyo* of mild beer was held "because we are not going hunting." In fact, they do go hunting, but only *after* the mild beer is consumed, "in order to digest it," while they go hunting *before* a strong beer festival "in order to ferment it."[12]

The two types of beer rituals are organized along a series of contrasts, as seen in table 4.

Mild beer is the analogue of other ceremonial meals (*peyo*); strong beer occupies a singular position.

When the Araweté say that in the *peyo* of mild beer, they do not dance or sing "because we will not go hunting," in contrast to the *kã'ĩ 'da,* they are making an implicit association between the ceremonial hunts for a feast and a war expedition. The singer for the strong beer festival, leader of the hunt, has the symbolic attributes of a killer. One of the epithets conferred on enemies is *kã'ĩ 'da rãhĩ,* "seasoning for the beer"—that which gives it flavor, what enlivens it. Note that the first thing said by the Tupinamba after they captured Hans Staden was that they would kill him *"Kawewi Pepicke"* (in Araweté, *kã'ĩ pepi kã,* "in return for beer"); that is, that he would be devoured after a beer feast prepared by the women (Staden 1928 [1557]: 64). This clearly suggests a cannibalistic "origin" for the Araweté *kã'ĩ'da.*

TABLE 4 *Kã'ɨ hẽ'ẽ* and *kã'ɨ 'da* rituals

Kã'ɨ hẽ'ẽ (mild beer ritual)	*Kã'ɨ 'da* (strong beer ritual)
Consumption minimally deferred	Consumption maximally deferred
Rapid hunt after festival, to digest beer	Prolonged hunt before festival, to ferment beer
Beer exchanged for cornmeal (given before beer consumed)	Beer exchanged for meat (given after beer consumed)
Owner is main guest	Owner does not drink, but serves
Owner is *tenotã mõ* of hunt	Owner is not *tenotã mõ* of hunt
Pots in communal patio, feast likewise	Pots inside owner's house, feast in his patio
Global *peyo* of pots arranged in line, placed on ground	Serial *ɗokã* serving of pots, in "high" position (owner's lap)
Morning (dawn)	Night (evening)
Men take beer and drink with wives	Women serve and take care of men, hardly drink
Juxtaposition of conjugal houses	Host's house contrasts with village
Focus on shaman	Focus on singer

The *pepi kã* of the feast are the animals brought back by the hunters and given to the owner of the beer. The *pɨrahẽ* is a dance around the singer-killer, just as the Tupinamba *poracé* was a dance around the war prisoner.

Given the orgiastic climate, the pan-village gathering, and the association of beer and war songs, the Araweté beer festival resembles the famous precannibalistic drinking parties of the Tupinamba and shows numerous analogies with the war ceremonies of other Tupi-Guarani peoples, such as the Parintintin "dance of heads" and the Kayabi *yawotsi* (Kracke 1978: 45; Grünberg n.d. [1970]: 169ff.). Hunting and warfare are strictly associated in Araweté thought: in relation to animals, the Araweté are *awĩ*, enemies. The exception is the jaguar, for he is the *awĩ* and we are his *hemïnã* (prey); hence, a dance is held over the death of a jaguar as over the death of an enemy (a classic Tupinamba theme). The festival of strong beer, in short, is a war ceremony. The ambivalent character of this drink reflects, I would argue, the ambiguous status of its focus—the killer.

3. Meat and Honey

The shamanizing and consumption of products derived from maize occur exclusively during the phase of living in the village; all other products can be shamanized either in the village or in the forest. Strong beer, the culminating term of the maize series, enters into a system with other foods and forms of consumption. As a drink that is masculine but prepared by women, insubstantial and sour, it is opposed to honey, also a liquid (*ti*), obtained by men but offered first to women, very substantial (*čewe:* see chap. 2, note 19) and eaten raw. Besides, honey can serve as seasoning (*ãhĩ*) for drinks such as assai, while strong beer needs seasoning—dead enemies. Finally, if the beer is sour like semen, honey is sweet like a vagina. Eating honey makes us flaccid (*mo-time*), as does sexual intercourse. Xupé honey makes our stomachs growl, the same symptom provoked by incestuous copulation. The sexual symbolism of honey is multiple and ambivalent. From the point of view of women, honey is the semen of the spirit *Ayaraetã*, which, if tasted in a dream, causes their souls to be imprisoned in the spirit's rattle, where it stays eternally, eating honey and being "eaten" by the spirit.[13] From the male point of view, honey acts like a vagina, and like it, is "fat." Although women are the first to taste the honey (if a man comes across a beehive in the forest, he brings back the honey for his wife), men also overindulge in it—while in contrast women rarely taste the strong beer.

The mellifluous character of the female sexual organ is evidenced in a crude manner in the custom of using the names of species of honey as metaphors of the "flavor" of each vagina in the village and as synecdoches for each woman.[14] What could be called "vulvonyms" enter into the construction of jocular male teknonyms; for example, a certain eminent and somewhat overbearing man was called (behind his back) *Ačiči e pihã*, "the husband of 'howler-monkey honey.'"

If strong beer is singular, honey species are multiple. The majority are named after animals, but many synonyms and metaphors are also used. Just as they can identify various women, some types of honey are called by the personal names of women. In these cases, the criterion seems to be the preference these women demonstrated (the majority of them are deceased) for particular species of honey. Some types of honey are poisonous and emetic, such as "*Ãñĩ* honey"; others make one's hair fall out, such as "leaf-cutter ant honey"; others make one's hair stick up, such as "coatimundi honey"; others make the fetus stir about in its mother's womb and awaken male fecundity, such as "fire honey."

Collective expeditions to gather honey always involve both sexes; the hives of xupé bees unite the greatest number of people. Men cut down the tree where the hive is found or they erect scaffolding from which to detach it from the trunk. In the latter case, they first burn the phallic entryway (*hakãy*, penis) of the hive to stupefy the bees. During honey-gathering expeditions, no one may smoke. Honey has arrows, which wound the mouth of anyone who smokes.[15]

Once the tree or the beehive has been knocked down, the men quickly remove the honeycombs and bring them to their wives, who keep a prudent distance. Honey is eaten *in situ*, pure and raw. But part of it can also be saved for a *peyo*, either pure or mixed with assai. The assai fruits are soaked in hot water, the pulp is removed from the pits, and the mass is thickened and sweetened with honey.

I was unable to attend the shamanry of honey and assai performed in 1982. But the descriptions I collected permit a schematic reconstitution. The shaman who brings the "eater-of-assai" (*Iaracï*) gives the signal for the village to disperse. Upon their return three to five days later, each house prepares the assai-honey mixture. In the evening, the pots are brought to the patio of the shaman (in the 1982 rite, Yiriñato-ro). At dawn, with everyone shut inside their houses, the shaman and his wife (who dances with him for protection) go out to their patio. He disperses the arrows of the honey and brings first the eater-of-assai and then other gods who eat honey. The next morning, he invites everybody to come drink some of the mixture; as in the case of mild beer, the owner of each pot calls others to drink. The shaman's pot is the first and he will drink from all the others; he is thus the *tenotã mõ* of this ceremony. Other versions I heard stated that the pots are placed in the same patio as mild beer is (the central one), not that of the shaman, who is nevertheless always the *tenotã mõ*. The shamanic songs of this ceremony are similar to those of other visitations by the gods and the dead.

I was able to attend several tortoise shamanic rites during the rainy season of 1982–83. After singing for several nights about the desire of the gods to come eat this food (especially *Me'e Ñã*, the "Jaguar-Thing"), the shamans or leaders of the residential sections decide that the time has come for the collective hunts *i-peyo pi*, "for the *peyo*." Each expedition, lasting from two to seven days, is led by a *tenotã mõ*, who will be the shaman of the ceremony (or who will recruit a shaman, ideally from his own residential section).

The return from the hunt is not marked by the pomp (or what passes for it among the Araweté) of the return for strong beer feasts. On the night of the return, the tortoises are opened, the shells roasted, and the meat boiled. The meat adhering to the shell is eaten according to the system of the nocturnal "gastronomic round" described earlier. The pots containing the meat, liver, and eggs are set aside. The following morning at dawn, the *tenotã mõ* or (if he is the shaman) one of his relatives places his pots in the patio used for mild beer and summons the others to do likewise. The *peyo* that follows is virtually identical in form to that for mild beer. The only difference is that people stay even farther away from the pots; the "shamanic stuff" (*ipeye we*) of tortoises is more dangerous than that of beer. *Me'e Ñã*, who eats the liver and eggs, leaving the flesh for the other gods who follow, is a violent and ferocious being who must be pacified (*mo-apapi*) by the shaman. The latter embraces him as he descends, enticing him to eat the tortoises. In his song, the Jaguar-Thing and the other gods refer to humans by the depreciating epithet *yaacï dadĩ a re*, "eaters of tiny tortoises."

After the *peyo*, the pots are carried away to be reheated on the domestic fires. By this time, everybody is decorated in the same way as for a feast of mild beer. Special importance is given to feathering the head with harpy eagle down, which protects against the "jaguarization" of the cosmos unleashed by the presence of the *Me'e Ñã*.[16] Then begin the calls to come eat. Each house invites others following a gastronomic circuit; the *tenotã mõ* should be both the one who invites the most people and the one who is the most invited (although his tortoises are not necessarily the first to be eaten). As always, the men are the ones who divide up and "capture" the morsels of meat and bring them over to their wives.

The authentic *peyo* of tortoise is held in the forest, with smoked tortoises arranged on a wooden rack. Like honey, tortoises contain invisible darts that must be dispersed by the shaman. But only smoked ones carry such a danger, which resides in the shells; boiled ones have simply "shamanic stuff," less malignant. Everybody but the shaman takes care to stand safely behind the backs of the tortoises aligned on the rack, since the arrows fly from the animals' heads.[17]

The ritual expeditions to hunt howler monkeys and to fish with poison vines obey the same schema. The *tenotã mõ* is the shaman or one of his close relatives; the animals should be smoked and placed on a rack. After the *peyo*, the chunks of meat are brought home and boiled over the domestic fires. People then go from patio to patio to eat (or, in the forest, from fire to fire).

The alimentary danger from howler monkeys and fish and from the two other animals that must be shamanized (tapir and deer) is different from others. All these animals liberate not only *ipeye we*, but also spirits (*ha̱'o we*) that must be killed by the shaman before the meat can be consumed by humans and gods. The technique is the same as the one used to kill terrestrial spirits and treat bites from venomous animals (see chap. 8, sect. 2).

The Araweté have not performed *peyo* rituals for tapir and deer in a long time. They say this is because such animals are shared with the employees of the FUNAI Post (who are always present at their distribution) and are no longer smoked as in earlier times. Smoking thus seems to be the form that is at the same time the most dangerous and the most appropriate to the preparation of meats, tortoise included. Nowadays, deer is eaten boiled without problems, but tapir provokes a certain fearfulness. Tapirs are killed "for the whites"; only after the latter clean and butcher the meat do a few men accede to the insistent offers of the Post employees and take pieces home to cook; the majority prefer to ignore what is happening or watch reticently.

The *peyo* of deer and tapir were considered very dangerous. The spirits of these animals flashed with light, set fire to the earth (*iwi meni-meni*), and could burn nonshamans. Two men of the village who had bald spots on their heads were said to have suffered such an accident, *hapi*, the burning of hair by the light of the spirits of tapir and deer.[18]

I do not know where or how the *peyo* of tapir and of deer were performed. Only these animals produce *hapi*; the spirits of howler monkeys and fish, if not killed, merely cause abdominal pains.

4. The Alimentary Forms of the Religious Life

The relationship between the two facets of Araweté alimentary shamanism, the leading of the celestial guests to prelibate the human meal and the dispersion of the pathogenic principles of the foods, is not completely clear to me. Honeys, tortoises, howler monkeys, fish, mild beer—all these can be consumed privately without the necessity of shamanically neutralizing the arrows, shamanic stuff, or headaches contained in them. Such forces seem to be inherently active only on occasions when foods are produced and consumed *collectively*, which in turn entails the arrival of the gods and the dead to eat. For this reason, strong beer, although less dangerous than meats and honeys from the point of view of its substantive malignity, is always shamanized. I never witnessed nor heard of an operation of dispersing pathogenic principles that was not followed by the arrival of the gods, other than minor interventions performed over individual patients who complained of pains after having *privately* consumed one of these foods (an infrequent occurrence). The general impression I had was that the dispersion of the arrows and other ceremonial precautions were aimed at rendering the product safe for humans *and* for the gods; it was not something occasioned *by* the gods who, being eaters and not "owners" of the foods, do not appear to possess any special power over such foods. Reasons of a sociotheological order seem more pertinent than bromatological theories in accounting for Araweté shamanism; its two facets, in my view, are at best only extrinsically connected. What is at issue here is a sacrificial complex of commensality, rather than an operation of neutralizing the dangers of nature, so common elsewhere in Lowland South America.[19] It is possible, however, that I let myself be swayed by the Araweté emphasis on their relations with the *Maï* and that I neglected the metaphysical interactions between the human and the animal worlds. That I did not witness the shamanry for game other than the village *peyo* of tortoise also may have impeded me from perceiving other aspects. At any rate, what seems to me to be fundamental is that the *Maï* accrue to themselves values that in most cosmologies of the continent are localized in animals and their hypostases. In the Araweté case, supernature encompasses nature as the form par excellence of the extrasocial.

□

The alimentary and culinary system of the Araweté ceremonial cycle can be simplified in a triangle: beer (fermented), meat (smoked), honey (raw). To it a fourth term, in a certain respect central, must be added: tobacco (burned), the shamanic instrument of consecrating these foods and the delight of the gods. To this system should be counterposed the mode of boiling, belonging to daily consumption.

If the fermented is feminine and the smoked masculine, then honey, strongly sexualized, is a hermaphroditic fluid: seminal for women, vaginal for men. It would be nice if we could characterize it as a male vaginal fluid (or as male menstrual blood?), maintaining the symmetry with beer and female semen, but in contrast to the latter pair, I do not find sufficient grounds to warrant it.[20]

Reading the feast of strong beer as an oral insemination of men by women brings to mind the well-known complex of male menstruation, which in Amazonia is found among the Tukano groups (S. Hugh-Jones 1979) and perhaps in the Upper Xingu (Bastos 1978: 176). Such a configuration is usually interpreted as a symbolic prestidigitation in which men capture the natural reproductive power of women and sublimate it into mystical creativity (C. Hugh-Jones 1979: 153ff.). This does not appear to me to be the case in the Araweté beer ritual. The insemination of men by women suggests precisely the attribution of certain fecundating powers to women, thus inverting the official theory, which posits men as the sole proprietors of genetic substance, sperm. What appears to take place is a certain neutralization of, or compensation for, the differences of gender. The central role of fermented drinks in South American conceptions about gender largely remains to be explored; I suspect that the idea of beer as female semen would find echoes in other societies (see, for example, C. Hugh-Jones 1979: 186ff.).

□

The ceremonial organization activates the role of "owner" (*ñã*) only in the festivals involving maize products. Similarly, only in these cases does an alimentary exchange (cornmeal, meat) occur, but it tends to be neutralized by the offering of banquets in which the sponsor returns the products received. In all the other collective meals that follow the arrival of gods, a nondifferentiation of the community takes place in which everybody produces and consumes the same thing. In these cases, the role of the *tenotã mõ* tends to be confounded with that of the shaman (*peye*), while in the two maize feats, the *peye* is a double or equivalent of the sponsor, but they cannot be one and the same person. Moreover, at the mild beer feast, the sponsor is the *tenotã mõ* of the hunt that follows the festival, while for the strong beer, the sponsor and the *tenotã mõ* are polar opposites.

There is thus a triadic permutation, which perhaps explains why the festival of mild beer, a feast of maize, is identical in its form to the feasts for game and honey: it effects the seasonal mediation between the ceremonies of the forest and that of strong beer, as described in table 5.

Although I lack facts to confirm it, I suspect that the feast of assai with xupé honey, the prelude to the rainy season dispersal, would make the seasonal mediation complementary: dry → rainy, and village → forest. It would inaugurate the phase of dispersal (closed by the festival of mild beer) and the period when the figure of the shaman is dominant (while during the strong beer festival, the focus is the singer). The occasional placement of the drinking vessels in the patio of the shaman for the arrival of *Iaracï* would transform him into a kind of sponsor of the ceremony, merging the three positions: *peye* = *tenotã mõ* = *ñã*. The drink can be considered a compromise between the raw and the fermented: the palmfruits softened in hot water and mixed with honey quickly acquire an acidic taste. Mild beer and assai with xupé honey would thus mediate between the two great ceremonial periods: rainy and dry, forest and village, tortoise + honey and strong beer, shamanic rites and war dances.

TABLE 5 Global ceremonial organization

Forest --> Village		
Peyo of meat and honey	*Peyo* of mild beer	*Đokã* of strong beer
Collective production and consumption	Collective production and consumption, product of family garden	Family production, collective consumption
Smoked and raw	Weakly fermented	Fermented
peye = *tenotã mõ*	*peye* ≠ (*ñã* = *tenotã mõ*)	(*peye* + *ñã*) ≠ *tenotã mõ*

The festival of strong beer is the most complex, involving separate representatives of the three functions, sponsor, singer, shaman: the first associated with women and agriculture; the second with hunting and warfare; the third with the gods and the dead. The main opposition is between the sponsor of the beer and the singer-warrior. In the other feasts, the main opposition is between humans and the celestial guests: the first appear as a kind of generalized sponsor of the food to be prelibated by the gods and the dead, and are represented by the shaman. The unifying point in the festival of strong beer is the singer; in the other feasts, the shaman.

What stands out most clearly about this structure is that Araweté ceremonies are oriented towards the outside. They do not reflect or elaborate differences internal to the society of the living: they do not initiate anyone, do not oppose social segments, do not consecrate statuses. There are no fixed festival owners, shamans, or singers. The essential difference is between the *bïde*, as a nondifferentiated totality, and exterior others; what defines and unites the living is their difference from enemies, gods, and the dead.

The prototype of the singer in the beer festival is a killer; around him society is unified. But the killer is something other than a subject incarnating the collectivity: he has an essential affinity (in both senses) with his dead enemy. The one who actually sings in the *pirahẽ* is this enemy, as we will see. During the beer festival, then, the host incarnates the position of *bïde*, while the invited men and their leader are unified in a process of "enemy-becoming." At the same time, this killer-enemy is "like a *Maï*."

In the other ceremonies, where war is not a theme, the shaman represents the human community as it confronts the gods and the dead; he is the *tenotã mõ* of the living. But the shaman is not a subject either, nor an image of interiority. In his capacity to self-divide by separating his body from his soul, he has an affinity with the dead. His place in the *peyo* is ambiguous; a representative of the living, he "represents" the visitors from the Beyond. From his human mouth ("from that which will rot," as the Araweté put it), those who speak are still the others: the gods and the dead.

Shamans and warriors, images of the others, are at the same time focal points of the *socius.* This is the Araweté paradox: their "ideals of the person" reflect what they cannot be, by definition—enemies, gods, the dead—but whom nevertheless they will become.

That such ideals are masculine reveals another characteristic of this cosmology: the space of the Same, of society, is feminine, facing the masculine world of the Other. Note the feminine position of the beer sponsor, and the dancers' "enemy-becoming," as men who come from outside (the forest, another village). As "food of the gods"—another epithet the Araweté use when talking about the human condition—the living are to the gods as women are to men. In contrast to other cosmologies where women are conceived of ambiguously between Culture and Nature, "we" and the enemy, here it is men who incarnate and actualize the mediation between the self and other, while women epitomize the interior of the *socius.* This is already suggested in the predilection of all spirits of the cosmos for women.

The Araweté ceremonial system, in summary, expresses and produces a nondifferentiation of the social body—which extends from the metonymic juxtaposition of its parts in daily life to its metaphoric unification through ambivalent figures in ritual—and places at center stage a single fundamental opposition: between inside and outside, the *socius* and its exterior. This exterior prevails; humans nourish the others.

6 Familiar Terms

1. The Mixture

Araweté social organization, like that of so many Amazonian societies, is founded on the ego-centered bilateral kindred and features a Dravidian-type kinship terminology. As among many Tupi-Guarani groups, marriage can occur between adjacent generations (MB/ZD, FZ/BS) and between alternate ones. Also present is another institution that is widespread on the continent, "formal friendship," a system of ritualized bonds between nonrelatives, distinct from those of marriage alliance. Among the Araweté, this friendship (*apïhi-pihã*) has as its symbol the sharing of spouses. One of its consequences is the blurring of the simple dichotomy of relative/nonrelative and the shifting of affinity to a symbolically reduced position. The overall significance of friendship can be summarized in a phrase: the Araweté subordinate complementarity to redundancy, reciprocity to mutuality.

If they cannot avoid the social imperative of matrimonial exchange, they dilute it by a variety of artifices, of which the most ingenious is this: rather than something that has been exchanged, a spouse is something to be shared. The result is expressed in an ethnogenealogical dogma: "We are all mixed." In fact, it is difficult to find someone who has only one recognized genitor. Seminal collaboration (and its terminological consequences) is the rule. Since the different genitors of an individual are not necessarily "brothers" (friends, by definition, are not siblings), the result is a mixture of semens and of categories. The "patrilinearity" latent in the theory of conception gets neutralized, the options of classification multiply, and even the minimal principle of the kindred is obscured. Not even two actual brothers necessarily have the same terminological field, due to the differential collaboration of genitors. Casuistry reigns as a result of conflicting versions about the number and identity of someone's genitors, the high number of successive marriages (leaving variable marks in the terminology), the temporary or definitive exchanges of spouses, and the ad hoc conversion of "siblings" into "ex-siblings" (and thence into spouses). In addition, the depopulation after contact led to a profound rearrangement of the conjugal situation; the number of technically incestuous marriages, however, has always been fairly high, despite the surprisingly low number of prohibited positions in the terminology. Finally, added to all this is the global torsion of a system with frequent oblique marriages, constituting an "elementary" system of kinship that would require a complex description because of its complicated functioning.

Personal names are used in daily communication more than kinship terms. Let us begin with this.

2. Names

Personal names are freely used. Only two restrictions apply: an adult's name from childhood should not be used in his or her presence, since this produces "fear-shame" (*čiye*) and angers (*mo-irã*) the person; and one does not say his or her own name in contexts where the subject in the utterance (*énoncé*) would be the subject who does the uttering (*énonciation*). On the other hand, the childhood names of various adults are embedded in the teknonyms of their parents, where they suffer no restriction on being mentioned, except by the "eponym," who avoids naming them. However, this avoidance is not as strict as that of auto-denomination. Also, a person can say his own name if he is citing someone else's discourse. The typical case is the shamanic song, where gods and the dead sometimes refer to the shaman by name, who thereby "names himself" (*o̲ɗï nɨẽ*).

Each person receives only one name (*eray*) in childhood and will carry it (*hereka*) until his or her first child is born. This rule is obligatory for women. Men may be denominated teknonymically after marriage. The form used is "X-*pihã*," partner of X (wife's name).[1] When the first child is born, the couple throws out (*heti*) their childhood names and switches (*herɨwã*) to teknonyms: Y-*ro* and Y-*hi*, father and mother of Y (child's name). The parents can be renamed with each child that is born. In practice, only one or two teknonyms (in some cases, three) tend to be employed for the rest of their lives, and usually the name of the firstborn is the one they keep. The first child is considered the name-giver (*heray here*) of the parents. He is given a name more quickly than subsequent children are; the choice of his name is the object of great care, and in naming the child, thought is always given to the name the parents will carry. In a certain sense, the ones who are actually being named are the parents. Teknonyms are more proper names than those of childhood; once they are obtained, the latter become "painful to hear."

In this respect, the birth of a child is even more important for women than for men, since men can leave behind their childhood names upon marriage, while women can do so only when they bear a child. In a system that is conceptually uxorilocal, marriage transforms a man into someone who "is together" (*-pihã*) with a woman; on the other hand, it is only the birth of the first child that confers on a woman an autonomous existence vis-à-vis her own mother.[2]

Even after a man obtains a "father of Y" teknonym through (social) paternity, he may continue to be called "partner of X," or rather, "partner of the mother of Y," since this is now his wife's name. For example, after his marriage with Morehã, Payikã was called Morehã-pihã (or sometimes still Payikã). When Heweye was born, Morehã became Heweye-hi; Payikã became Heweye-ro, or sometimes Heweye-hi-pihã.

The teknonym through one's wife tends to be used most among men, while the form "father of Y" tends to be used by women and children. In the context of the village, these forms vary freely; some men are more often referred to as "father of Y," others as "partner of X." However, in the exclusively male ambience of hunting camps, the *pihã* form is systematically used, even for youths who, because they have not yet had children, may still be called by their childhood names in the village. Similarly, when a man summons the others for a collective hunt, he uses the *pihã* form; to call them to a meal, he alternates freely between the forms. The *pihã* form is thus a "formal" mode of address among men. Underscoring the matrimonial bond, it suggests that the relations among men exist through women—and not merely with reference to affinity, since brothers also address each other in this way, and so does a father to his son.[3] It is as if what defined a man for another were his condition of being connected to a woman. Note, finally, that the *pihã* form does not reflect an actual residential situation: a youth who brings his wife to reside in his section is similarly named through her. "Residence" with a woman is an abstract situation, which appears to express the axial value of the feminine position in the organization of social life. After a man dies, the *pihã* form disappears; the personal name that persists is the one expressing his status as father of Y. (On the other hand, some living men are designated half-jokingly by their current wives as "Y-*pihere*," "ex-husband of Y," someone deceased.)

I am not suggesting that paternity is not fundamental for men to attain adult status. So important is it that in various cases, men took definitive names based on children who were conceived by others, or in whose conception their collaboration was minor. These cases involved men who had not yet had children and, marrying widows who were pregnant or nursing, "picked up" (*hopi*) the children or "made them grow" (*mo-hi*). Also common is the formation of male teknonyms derived from female teknonyms referring to long-dead children whom the present husband never knew. Finally, successive marriages can lead to the differential accumulation of teknonyms; for example, Tayopi-ro (a man) is also known as Taranĩ-no, but Tayopi-hi and Taranĩ-hi are successive wives he had, through whom he conceived Tayopi and Taranĩ. Thus, naming situations are complex and do not permit genealogical connections to be deduced from teknonymy.

The naming of children is not the object of any ceremony, and name-givers are not predetermined according to kinship position or other criteria. The majority of name-givers[4] are older people who have close kinship connections with one of the parents. Eminent women are often consulted and choose the names. The parents can choose of their own accord the names of their children, although rarely that of the firstborn; being young, they yield to the decisions of their elders, particularly their own parents. Only one rule is invariably respected: there cannot be two people with the same name. This applies to the childhood names of living adults, which are not conferred upon children. A name must be either a brand-new one or that of a deceased person.[5]

After death, an individual is mentioned by his or her name followed by the suffix *-reme* (or *-ami*), attached also to kinship terms. In the shamanic songs that bring the dead to earth, the latter are systematically named *without* these suffixes: they connote absence or distance and can be affixed to the names of people who have not been seen for a long time. The childhood names of the dead are freely mentioned, although out of the range of hearing of close relatives. However, the persistence of teknonyms is the norm, in daily conversation as well as in the shamanic songs.

The Araweté naming system depends on three basic criteria. A child can be named "after a deceased member of the group" (*pɨrowĩ'hã ne*), "after an enemy" (*awĩ ne*), or "after a divinity" (*Maï de*). A small number of names are conferred using another criterion, names invented (*mara te*, "simply created") according to the whims of the name-giver. The three basic *criteria* of *naming* must not be confused with the semantic *classes* into which *names* are grouped. Such a distinction is necessary because the majority of names belong to the "enemy" and "divinity" semantic series, without this implying that they were conferred according to the criteria *awĩ ne* and *Maï de.*

The first criterion means that the child is named in order to put back into circulation the name of someone who died long ago. The child is thought of as substituting (*hekowïnã*) or bringing back (*hereka yipe*) a name once in use. The notion of *pirowï'hã* in this context signifies simply "ancient people," or more exactly, deceased. The exact kinship relation between the eponym (*ipihã*, "the first") and the person named is not important; the eponym may well be a child who died without leaving descendents. For this reason *pirowï'hã* cannot be translated as "ancestor" when considering naming criteria.

There may be more than one deceased person who bore the name, but the choice is made with a particular person in mind. What is being replaced is, strictly speaking, a triad, the child and its parents; many times the specific aim is to bring the names X-*ro* and X-*hi* back into existence, whose former bearers are present in the collective memory more vividly than a child who died young.

Such a process of onomastic replacement does not appear to have any intention other than an affective or commemorative one. There is no concept of a reincarnation of souls via names, nor of a transmission of a fixed structural relation between social positions.[6] Name-givers choose the names of people whom they knew personally and esteemed or who were dear to their own parents. Sometimes a couple will reutilize names of children who died when very young, or the grandparents may suggest the names of the child's FB and MZ. I have no examples of names passed from MB and FZ to ZS and BD, which suggests an attempt to avoid cross-transmission. There are no generational criteria. The most common explanation the Araweté gave for choosing a name was, "Because so-and-so wished to name him/her that."

Although the form of naming someone "after a deceased" depends on the inclinations of the name-giver, there appears to be some sort of order. One name can draw in another, and the subsequent children of a couple tend to be named after the siblings of the eponym of the first-born. Names tend to circulate within groups of siblings of the same sex. A reasonable (though indeterminate) period of time must pass before a name is reutilized, except in the case of children of the same couple, when the child who died had barely used the name. Finally, the name-givers often attempt to reproduce in the name-receivers the terminological relation they maintained with the eponym: they avoid, in short, giving the name of their parallel relatives to their cross ones and vice versa. It is customary for a man to give the name of a terminological "child" to the child of a woman with whom he had sexual relations, the name of a deceased wife or cross-cousin to a "granddaughter" (a marriageable category), etc. This does not lead to a systematic reproduction of the terminological kinship relations; onomastics do not interact with kinship terminology, in the manner of the Gê and Panoans (Láve 1979; Ladeira 1982; Erikson 1990, 1992; McCallum 1989). Nor does it establish any special relationship between the name-giver and the name-receiver; the only relationship is negative, in the sense that the namer can never give his or her own name to the child, since both are still alive.

The only thing I can affirm, in the final analysis, is that names circulate within kindred groups. The right that a person has to give a certain name to a child—and the right of his/her parents to bear it as a teknonym—is a question that is at times controversial, and depends on the contextual definition of the limits of the kindred. (Here the clearest parallels are with the Txicão case [Menget 1977: 253].)

In examining the genealogies, I could not find any significant regularities (see Appendixes 2-A and 2-B). Granted the possibility of technical incompetence, I consider individual whims to account for the choice of personal names "after a deceased," within the limits indicated above. In addition, some names appear four or more times in the genealogies, others only one time, and this occurs apparently on a random basis.

Names conferred according to the criterion *pɨro̱wĩ̈'hã ne* belong to varied semantic classes. Some of them are untranslatable, but the majority have a meaning: names of mythical ancestors (which may or may not have a meaning), animals (especially birds), plants, objects, verbs ("extinguished," "to open wide"), qualities ("red," "unique"), and even kinship terms or age grades ("my grandmother," "little girl," "deceased father"), besides the names of enemies and divinities. These last two semantic classes together form 70 percent of the onomastic repertoire, which, as stated above, should not be confused with the three criteria of naming.

Thus, from a sample of 219 names with criteria of attribution about which I was certain, 94 were conferred after a deceased person; 82 after an enemy; 43 after a divinity—43 percent, 37 percent, and 20 percent, respectively. Of the 94 names given in memory of the dead, however, 34 were defined as names of enemies or divinities, and the rest belonged to other semantic classes.[7] Of the 109 names or teknonymic roots that were being used in 1982, the proportion was the same: 52 names after deceased persons, 33 after enemies, 22 after gods; of the names following the first criterion, 16 belonged to the enemy and divine classes.

Names given "after an enemy" form a less heterogeneous set from a semantic point of view, but they are still quite varied: personal names or ethnonyms of mythical or historical enemies (many brought in by women who had been captives of the Kayapó), foreign words that people know have nothing to do with anthroponyms, and metaphors extracted from songs commemorating the death of an enemy. These include various names and expressions in Portuguese made unrecognizable in Araweté pronunciation. Personal names, therefore, are not necessarily derived from the personal names of enemies; they simply evoke this exterior universe. Incorporating the historical experience of the group, this is the semantic class most open to innovation.

Names given after divinities, *Maï̲ ɨde*, reflect the plethoric Araweté pantheon. Practically all the names of celestial and subterranean gods—generic (*Maï̲*), specific (*Ayɨrɨ-ti-pehã*), or "individual" (*Aranami̲*)—can be used as personal names. Names of terrestrial spirits are not used, with the exception of the Master of Peccaries (e.g., "*Yaraɨdi*-woman") and the Water-Dweller (but only his euphemistic epithets), nor is the unmentionable name of *Iaracī̈* used. In the class of names of divinities are included ad hoc shamanic creations, descriptive forms that evoke the sky ("Eternal-painted-woman"), and untranslatable terms that are summarily explained as "*Maï̲*," the meaning of which I do not know.

There were only two names in 1982 that were "simply created": Na̲'i, having no translation, and Kãñī̈-bïɨdï, "Woman-liar." This criterion means that the name was invented without the help of shamanic visions or inspiration drawn from enemies, the principal sources of naming for the two previous criteria.

All the criteria of naming (with the exception of "invented" names) can originate in shamanic visions. When the name-giver is a shaman, he has usually been inspired in his nocturnal songs to propose the name (which does not mean he dreams and sings expressly for this purpose). But any person can take advantage of the songs of others. I observed, however, that the vast majority of names "after a divinity" were conferred by shamans and also belonged to the divine semantic class. Names "after an enemy" are preferentially conferred by killers, as I was able to confirm in my most recent visit.

Between February 1983 and February 1988, the Araweté bore thirty-five children and killed one enemy. This death yielded a great many names, suggesting a kind of repressed demand. Fifteen of the children were named by the killer (one of the most important men of the village, but who had not previously killed an enemy). Fourteen names were inspired by dreams he had in which the recently deceased Parakanã taught him war songs and personal names, and one was given "after the Kayapó" (since his wife had been captured by this tribe decades earlier). Among these names, there were some that belonged to the *class* of names of divinities; as in the case of names after the dead, it is necessary to distinguish between class and criterion. The other twenty children were named in the following way: three after enemies (Asuriní), given by those who had killed people of this tribe; sixteen after deceased members of the group; and only one after a divinity (for the daughter of a shaman who named her). Two of the names given "after a deceased member" were also related to the death of the Parakanã. They involved names of men killed by this tribe, suggesting that in this case there had been a fusion of two criteria.

It can be seen that the proportion of *pirowī'hã ne* names (after deceased members) stayed close to normal, while the names "after an enemy" suffocated those "after a divinity." While this can be explained in part by the eminence the killer already enjoyed (he certainly wanted to leave the maximum of onomastic marks of his deed), it suggests an opposition between names given after the dead, on the one hand, and names given after enemies and divinities, on the other. Of the nine firstborn children, eight were given *pirowī'hã ne* names, making up half of the names given according to this criterion. A clear tendency is thus manifested: the firstborn are preferentially named after the dead, while names given after enemies and gods divide up the space left over, which corresponds to about half of the onomastic field (even if it makes up 70 percent of the repertoire).[8]

This equal partitioning of the field between two criteria (the dead vs. gods + enemies) seems to indicate a "dual articulation" of onomastic reproduction: the restoration of traditional names plus a supplement drawn from the outside. Note, however, that this supplement of names, which express historical events (shamanic visions, encounters with enemies), is ultimately integrated into the traditional repertoire when the first bearers of the names die (many names given *pirowī'hã ne* are of the divine or enemy class). Also, the majority of names of the dead are conferred by name-givers who personally knew the eponym, which gives them an equally historical nature. *Pirowī'hã* names are not "structural" names taken from a fixed repertoire of personae.[9]

If the names given after enemies and divinities are linked to the positions of killer and shaman, one may ask to what *pirowī'hã ne* names correspond. This is where women enter into the scene.

Although women can confer names according to the other criteria, they show a clear preference for the names of deceased members of the group. The typical case of naming a firstborn involves the woman's parents (particularly her mother) as name-givers. When men give names under this criterion, they do so as *fathers-in-law.* Even when this is not the case, *pɨrowĩ'hã ne* naming involves someone who is the leader of an extended family, since it is characteristic of older and eminent people. Preferred by women, or activated by a man in his status as married leader of a residential section, i.e., as a father-in-law (of the child's father or mother), it contrasts with forms of naming according to "masculine" criteria, after enemies or gods.

We thus encounter again the triads that concluded the two previous chapters: father-in-law/warrior/shaman, and sponsor of beer festival/singer/shaman. The first position defines men through their connection with the feminine world, while the other two are symbols of masculinity. We have also said that women incarnate the interior of the *socius,* in opposition to the centrifugal value of masculinity; now we see that their typical form of naming is equally "interior," restoring the names and memory of cherished dead people, insofar as the dead can be considered as relatively less foreign than enemies and gods.

But in contrast to the hierarchical global structure proposed earlier, the naming system seems to exhibit a prevalence of interiority over exteriority. *Pɨrowĩhã ne* names, preferred for firstborn children, are the basis of the teknonyms *of the parents,* the majority of whom are thus called by teknonyms derived from the names of the dead.[10] The dead prevail over enemies and gods as criteria of naming. To what can we attribute this inversion of the structure characterizing the cosmology?

The first thing to observe is the low sociological and cosmological yield of Araweté personal names, in contrast with the number of names given to each person in other Tupi-Guarani societies. Except upon marriage and the birth of children, no other occasion exists when names are changed—not puberty, dreams, or homicide, as is the case elsewhere. Names do not incarnate the spiritual essence of the person, as among the Guarani, where naming intrinsically depends on shamanism; nor do they consecrate the status of killer, as among the Tupinamba. Adult names simply indicate the status of husband, father, or mother. Shamanism and warfare are present in the naming system, but in a relatively subordinated form. The dominant value is marriage and procreation. Shamanism and warfare are subordinated to the feminine world of reproduction, just as the names of gods and enemies are subordinated to *pɨro̲wi̇̃'hã* names, and just as the relation with death and exteriority is subordinated to life and interiority. This hierarchical inversion betrays the *subordination of the naming system itself,* its secondary value in the cosmological structure.

The triad dead/gods/enemies is therefore ordered according to hierarchical oppositions and inversions. Later we will see how shamanism and warfare redistribute the values of each apex of the triangle: the analysis of the music of the gods and enemies will again bring up the contrast between *pɨro̲wi̇̃'hã,* enemies, and divinities.

□

The Araweté naming system bears further marks of exteriority. If the dead are insiders in relation to the gods and enemies, they are outsiders in relation to the living. The contrast between the first criterion of naming and the other two is attenuated once we consider that, in the final analysis, all the names themselves evoke beings that are exterior to the world of the living. Names are always the names of others: one does not use, through speech or transmission, one's own name, childhood names evoke those who are absent (the dead, gods, enemies), and adult names are teknonyms.

Even though its "coefficient of alterity" is attenuated due to the hierarchical inversion, the naming system suggests something that will become clear in the analysis of death: Araweté cosmology is one of those that situate meaning on the outside, in opposition to those with names and identities coming from within. The former cosmologies are, shall we say, open systems, in which names come from gods, dead enemies, consumed animals, while the latter are closed systems, in which names connote ritual roles and may be the property of corporate groups, with transmission among the living and name recycling being the norm. Such a contrast—perhaps a universal metaphysical choice[11]—should be understood as organizing a *continuum,* which in the Amazonian context extends from the naming systems of the Tupinamba, Txicão, and Yanomami, on one end, to the systems of the Timbira, Kayapó, Tukanoans, and Panoans, on the other.

The Tupinamba naming system revolved around warfare and the ritual execution of captives. A man dropped his childhood name only after having killed an enemy, an occurrence that was thus equivalent to the birth of a child for the Araweté; and only after obtaining a name in this way could he marry (have legitimate children) and drink beer (Cardim 1906 [1584]:420; Monteiro 1949 [1610]:409; Thevet 1953 [1575]:134)—another inversion of the Araweté case, where only after marrying does a man change his name, and where single youths may not participate in the beer festival commemorating the death of an enemy. The accumulation of names "on the heads of adversaries," in the vigorous formula of Cardim (1906:431), was an essential motive of war; there were men with more than a hundred names (Monteiro 1949:409; Staden 1928 [1557]:148).

On the subject of a killer's naming rite, Soares de Souza observed:

> It is a custom among the Tupinamba that anyone who kills an adversary hastens to take a new name, but he does not reveal it until the proper time, for which he orders large amounts of wine [i.e., beer] to be prepared. When it is ready for the festival, they paint themselves the evening before with genipap and begin singing, continuing all through the night. After they have sung a good deal, everybody in the village comes up to the killer and asks him to tell them the name he has taken; they must ask him insistently until he tells them and, as soon as he does, they compose songs based on the death of the one who was killed and on the praises of the one who killed him (1971 [1587]:323).

The strong singularizing value of a name is indicated by the fact that the killer should formally utter his own name for the first time, "naming himself," as it were. The public declaration of the name and its consecration by song belong to the "oral" complex. The beer festival, in which only killers could take part, was the context for reciting deeds of bravery, proclaimed with a verbal arrogance that exasperated the Europeans (Thevet 1953:92; Anchieta 1933 [1554–94]: 129). Lip plugs were insignia that authorized public speech, being as numerous as the enemies one had killed, according to Monteiro (1949:409). The verbal symbolism of the lip plugs among the contemporary Gê has been analyzed by Turner (1969, 1980) and Seeger (1975).

Concerning the origin of these names, Fernandes (1970 [1952]:311–12) was perhaps correct in surmising that they were left up to the free choice of the killer. But two passages of Anchieta (1554, 1560, in Leite 1956–58, 2:115; 3:259) suggest that the name that was taken was the *name of the victim.*[12] Finally, there was the custom of *giving one's own name* to an esteemed friend (Evreux 1929 [1615]:244). Friendship—in this context, certainly a case of ritual friendship—also involved the vocatives "my wife," "my teeth," "my arm," and sharing from the same plate (Vale [1562], in Leite 1956–58, 3:478–79). A meticulous inversion of enmity: eating the other became eating with the other; obtaining a name for oneself "on" a part of the other (his head—it was the crushing of the skull that authorized the renaming) became the giving of one's name to the other, called by vocatives that designated parts of ego.

Guarani onomastics revolve around the divine origin of the soul-name and the complex personology of these societies; in some cases (Apapokuva, Kayová), it is linked to celestial beings or to the reincarnation of the dead. Personal names, although belonging to classes (according to divinities and the celestial regions from which they come), are marks of individual singularity: consider the link between names and "prayers" among the Ñandeva, where "there are no two persons with the same prayer" (Schaden 1969:158).

If Tupinamba names originated with enemies, and those of the Guarani with gods or the dead who are reincarnated, the naming systems of other Tupi-Guarani groups privilege the animal world. Thus, the Aché name children according to an animal that the mother consumed during pregnancy and sensed was the one that would give its "nature" (*bikwa*) to the child. Such a transmission of substance is transformed into a reincarnation of the deceased's soul when the flesh consumed is that of a dead member of the group—in which case no transmission of name occurs (P. Clastres 1972:338–39). Among the Siriono, as soon as a pregnant woman enters into labor, the father has to go hunting: the animal he kills determines the child's name (Holmberg 1969:195–96). This is reminiscent of Sanumá and Bororo facts (Ramos & Peirano 1973). The Wayãpi generally bear animal names, conferred according to the psychical and physionomical resemblances between the animal and the child (Grenand 1980:41). For the Ñandeva-Guarani, such resemblances evoke the exact opposite of the soul-name: the *atsygua*, the terrestrial soul, which is linked to the corporal appetites and generates the specter (Nimuendaju 1978 [1914]:55). The Parintintin, who believe in the occasional incarnation of divinities in children, name them accordingly. The shaman who dreams of the conception is held to be the "associate genitor." He thus fulfills a function analogous to the Aché hunter, who kills game for the pregnant mother to eat (Kracke 1978:25; P. Clastres 1972:252).

This overview suggests that, by and large, the typical Tupi-Guarani naming system relies on the extrasocial as its source or criterion (gods, enemies, animals, the dead), that its emphasis is less on classification than on individualization, less on the conservation of a closed repertoire than on the acquisition and accumulation of names, less on the transmission intended by such conservation than on singular and nontransmissable renaming, less on synchronic sets than on diachronic series, less on mythical references than on history, less on continuity with the past than on openness to the future, less, finally, on the articulation of complementary identities inside the *socius* than on the capture of supplementary distinctions from the outside.

The Tupi-Guarani system reveals certain similarities with that of the Txicão, for whom the capture of enemies, privileged as a source of names for children because they brought in a memory from outside, was traditionally the objective of revenge warfare. Its aim was not simply to acquire a substitute for the dead member of the group, but also to obtain supplementary "identities" (Menget 1977). The Yanomami system presents other characteristics, notably its enormous onomastic consumption caused by the banishment of the names of the dead (and their constituent lexical roots) from the language. As an absolute mark of individualization, the name disappears along with its bearer. The refusal to name oneself is also linked to this: to say one's own name is to evoke one's own death, since only death completely individualizes the individual (Lizot 1973; Clastres & Lizot 1978:114–16). Every death is thought of as a cannibal act; the soul is devoured by a spirit or an enemy (Lizot 1985:3). Thus, names are created in order to avoid using the names of the dead who were eaten by enemies (among the Tupinamba, names were obtained by killing enemies who were afterwards eaten). Enemies create names because they abolish names; *aboli bibelot d'inanité sonore,* the name gains its full meaning only in its nonutterance.[13]

A thorough comparison with the Gê naming systems is not possible here. They are complex and present considerable differences among themselves (Da Matta 1982:67–71, 77–82; Lopes da Silva 1980). But it can be said that, for the northern Gê at least, they are based on the mutual exclusion of bonds by filiation and bonds by naming; potential naming relations affect the use of kinship terms, while the marriage system is linked to the "endonymical" exchange of names between brother and sister. The circulation of names is guided by a principle of conserving the repertoire, little open to innovation and referring mainly to mythology. Transmission among the living is essential, being the basis of a whole set of ceremonial relations, rights, and obligations; the names, although bearing individualizing aspects, are above all classificatory instruments (see Lave 1979; Seeger 1981:136–46; Melatti 1979:48; Carneiro da Cunha 1978: 77ff.; Verswijver 1983–84; and especially Ladeira 1982 and Lea 1986). It is as if what the Tupi-Guarani and the groups of the Guianas do at the level of matrimonial exchange, the Gê do in terms of naming exchange: endogamy versus endonymy. The same can be said of the Tukano, who are exogamous and patrilocal but have a matrimonial ideology and a naming rule aimed at repeating the masculine and feminine names of the sib in every other generation (C. Hugh-Jones 1979:133–34, 161–65). Thus, while exogamy for the Gê and Tukano seems to be compensated by endonymy, the endogamy characteristic of the Tupi-Guarani matrimonial philosophy (the Tupi-Guarani are a *locus classicus* of avuncular marriage) is compensated by an exonymy that is a true *heteronymy* (contrasting with the homonymy among the Gê), a function of the fundamental *heteronomy* of their cosmology. Let us recall, finally, that certain Panoan groups, whose naming system represents a fusion of Gê and Tukano traits, manifest nevertheless an essential dependency on the exterior for the production of "identities" (Erikson 1986, 1991). This demonstrates that the naming system is not necessarily a good path for apprehending the global orientation of any Amerindian cosmology: consider the Jivaro, whose metaphysics is of the same type as that of the Tupinamba, but for whom the killer's accumulation of names is replaced by his accumulation of a certain type of power capable of conferring immortality on him (Harner 1962; 1973).

3. Relatives

The Araweté social domain has as one of its major axes the difference between relatives (people who share a logical, and in some ways substantial, identity) and nonrelatives (a category of exclusion). This dichotomy does not correspond to any sociocentric segmentation. Typologically, the relationship system is a variant of the "Dravidian" system, but it also presents a complete series of separate affinal terms. It is therefore not a two-section terminology like that of the Wayãpi, Parintintin, or Kaapor, since the genealogical identity that is possible between, for example, MB and WF, FZH and MB, does not translate into terminological identity. The reach of its "Dravidian" calculus is very limited: the terms tend to be applied only a short distance, leaving an ample sphere of the society in the category of "nonrelatives." Also, actual affinity is strongly differentiated from potential affinity, a trait characteristic of the Amazonian "Dravidian group" systems.

The generic term for "relative" is *anĩ*, which in its focal signification denotes ego's same-sex siblings; relatives are *dĩ* (others of the same kind), people similar to ego. The term for "nonrelative" is *tiwã*, of which the closest genealogical determination is ego's same-sex cross-cousins; *tiwã* are *amĩte* (others of a different kind), dissimilar people.

Tiwã is an ambiguous term, comparable semantically and pragmatically to the Carib *pito* (Rivière 1969: 81). It carries an aggressive connotation and is usually not employed as a vocative for another Araweté. It indicates the absence of a kinship relation, a vacuum that needs to be filled. A *tiwã* is a possibility of relationship: a *potential* affine or friend. *Tiwã* address each other only by their personal names. *Tiwã* is the vocative used by the Araweté to address whites whose names they do not know; it is also a term of reciprocal address between a killer and the spirit of a dead enemy. Applied to non-Araweté, it particularizes the negative generic "relationship" that exists between *bïde* (Araweté) and *awĩ* (enemy). To call someone by the vocative *awĩ* is unthinkable, since *awĩ* are things "to be killed" (*yokã mi*), beings with whom one does not speak; to call an enemy *tiwã* is thus to create a modicum of relationship that recognizes the humanity (*bïde*) of the other. A *tiwã* is someone on the borderline between, on the one side, the absolute and generic alterity of enemies, and on the other, the identity of "similars"—siblings—or the specific and qualified difference of affines. *Tiwã* is, properly speaking, the other, the nonself in a position of subject: mediating between the general and the particular, the foreign and the same, enemy and sibling, it extracts an enemy from generality or stamps a *bïde* with potentiality.[14]

Let us turn to the main relationship terms (of reference) and their spectrum of application. Except when indicated, the terms are used by speakers of both sexes and appear in the nonpossessed form (possible for all terms).

+2 *Generation* (and above):

(1) *Tamõy*—FF, MF; any man called *papãy* (vocative "F") or *he ramõy* by ego's parents.

(2) *Đari*—FM, MM; any woman called *mãy* (vocative "M") or *he yari* by ego's parents.

+1 *Generation:*

(3) *To*—F

(3A) *To dɨ̃*—FB; any man whom ego's father calls *he reči'i* or *he či'i* (vocative "eB," "yB").

(3b) *To amɨ̃*—MH; any man whom ego's mother calls *herekɨ̃ dɨ̃* ("ZH") or *apĩno* ("lover"), or whom ego's father calls *apĩhi-pihã* ("friend").

The vocative for the three forms above is *papãy*.

(4) *Toti*—MB; any man whom ego's mother calls *he čiwi* or *či'i'ɨ̃* (vocative "B," "yB"), or whom ego's father calls *tado'i* ("WB").

(5) *Hi*—M.

(5a) *Hi dɨ̃*—MZ, etc.

(5b) *Hi amɨ̃*—FW, *apĩhi* ("lover") or *haiyĩhi* ("BW") of ego's father.

The vocative for the three forms above is *mãy*.

(6) *Đade*—FZ; any woman whom ego's father calls *he reni* (vocative "Z") or whom ego's mother calls *tado'i* ("HZ").

(7) *Hati*—WF, HF; any man called "father" by a spouse, an *apĩhi* (man speaking) or an *apĩno* (woman speaking).

(8) *Hačo*—WM, HM, etc.

0 Generation:

(9) *Anĩ*—B (FS, MS), FBS, MZS, and in principle any alter whom ego's relatives in category 3 (a, b) and 5 (a, b) call "son" (for a man speaking); Z (FD, MD), FBD, MZD, and in principle any alter whom ego's relatives in 3 and 5 call "daughter" (for a woman speaking).

(9a) *Heči'i*—eB, eFBS, eMZS, etc. (for a man speaking); eZ, eFBD, eMZD, etc. (for a woman speaking).

(9b) *Či'i*—yB, yFBS, yMZS, etc. (for a man speaking); yZ, yFBD, yMZD, etc. (for a woman speaking).

(10) *Heni*—Z (FB, MD), FBD, MZD, and in principle any woman whom ego's relatives in 3 and 5 call "daughter" (for a man speaking).

(11) *Čiwi*—B (FS, MS), FBS, MZS, etc. (for a woman speaking).

(12) *Temiyika*—W. Vocatives: *mitɨ̃ parã* (lit., "striped curassow," a female Natterer's curassow) and *tayĩ-hi* (if ego's wife already has a child).

(13) *Terekɨ̃*—H. Vocative: *ta̱dĩ-no* (if he already has a child).

(14) *Hado'i*—WB, ZH, men called "brothers" by ego's wife, and husbands of "sisters" (for a man speaking); HZ, BW, women called "sister" by ego's husband, and wives of "brothers" (for a woman speaking). The possessed and vocative forms are differentiated: *he rado'i* ("my *-ado'i*") designates sibling's spouse, while *tado'i* (the absolute form of *hado'i*) designates spouse's sibling. In the case of sister exchange, the term of address that prevails is the possessed form.

(15) *Hayĩ-hi*—BW, WZ, etc. (for a man speaking).

(16) *Hayĩ-hi pihã*—WZH, B (for a man speaking). The use of this term for reference and as a vocative for ego's married brothers is more common than the terms of category 9. It expresses

the potential marriage alliance of sets of same-sex siblings (WZH = B) and the equivalence of two brothers in relation to the same women, which translates into the levirate and, more generally, into the potential sexual access to brothers' wives.

(17) *Herekĩ dĩ*—ZH, HB (for a woman speaking). It is not used as a vocative. It also indicates the equivalence of men relative to two sisters and the possibility of the sororate.

−1 Generation:

(18) *Ta'i*—S, BS, any man whom 9 calls *ta'i* (for a man speaking). Vocatives: *api, hadi*.

(19) *Haiyi*—D, BD, etc. (for a man speaking). Same vocative as 18.

(20) *Memi*—S, D, ZS, ZD, etc. (for a woman speaking). Same vocative as 18.

(21) *Yi'i*—ZS, any man whom 10 calls *memi* (for a man speaking). The descriptive form *he reni pa re,* "son (lit., 'ex-inhabitant') of my sister," is frequently used.

(22) *Đipe*—ZD, etc. (for a man speaking). Same descriptive form as 21.

(23) *Pe'ĩ*—BS, BD, any alter whom 11 calls "child" (for a woman speaking).

(24) *Haiyimẽ*—DH; husband of any "daughter" of ego (for a man speaking).

(25) *Ta'i tati*—SW, etc. (for a man speaking).

(26) *Memi rerekĩ*—DH, etc. (for a woman speaking).

(27) *Memi tati*—SW, etc. (for a woman speaking).

−2 Generation (and subsequent ones):

(28) *Hããmõnõ*—SS, SD, DS, DD, etc. (for a man speaking). The descriptive forms *ta'i apa pe,* "of a son," and *haiyi pa re,* "child of a daughter," are also used. The vocative *he rããmõnõ* tends to be reserved for actual children's actual children. Classificatory grandchildren are marriageable: for a man, this means especially the classificatory daughters of his actual daughters, or the actual daughters of his classificatory daughters.

(29) *Hemïdađïđo*—SS, SD, DS, DD, etc. (for a woman speaking); same descriptive terms as 28.

Generationally unmarked terms:

(30) *Tiwã*—typically, MBC and FZC, and any alter whom ego's father calls "ZC" or ego's mother calls "BC." It is little used, even for reference, for cross-cousins, who are normally designated by descriptive forms ("mother's brother's child," "fa-

ther's sister's child"). The rest of the genealogical positions not included above are classified as *tiwã:* MBW, FZH, BWF, ZWF, etc.; WBW, HZH, HBW, BWB, etc.; ZSW (man speaking), BSW (woman speaking), etc. It also applies to any person whom both of ego's parents classify as *tiwã.* Note that the immediate affines of ego—WF, WM, WB, etc.—are *not* classified as *tiwã.* All *tiwã* of the opposite sex are potential sexual partners and possible spouses.

(31) *Apĩhi*—denotes for a male ego any woman in a marriageable position, or with whom ego had, has, could have, or wants to have a sexual relation. This includes classificatory grandmothers (*đari*), FZ, MBD, FZD, ZD, classificatory granddaughters, and all *tiwã.* More precisely, *apĩhi* is the wife of an *apĩhi-pihã,* that is, a woman who is ritually shared. The wife of a brother (*hayĩ-hi*) should not be called by this term.

(32) *Apĩno*—the equivalent of 31 for a female ego. The terminological positions included are: classificatory grandfathers, MB, FZS, MBS, BS, classificatory grandsons, and *tiwã.* The ZH and HB should not be called by this term. *Apĩno* is the husband of an *apĩhi-pihã.*

(33) *Apĩhi-pihã*—a reciprocal term designating same-sex non-*anĩ* who ritually share spouses. It is much more frequently used among men than among women; the form of the term, with the suffix *-pihã* ("partner of"—see sect. 1), suggests that its origin is masculine: it is the only case in which women refer to each other as X-*pihã.*

□

The Araweté relationship terminology, besides having the same lexical repertoire, has the characteristic traits of Tupi-Guarani terminologies. In the first place, many terms are analytic: the entire set of affinal terms in G−1 has a descriptive formation (*-mẽ* and *-rerekĩ* are forms for "husband," *-tati* for "wife"); the terms with *-dĩ* and *-amĩ* are derivations of the focal term of the class "father," "mother," or "husband"; the vocatives for 12–13 and the terms in 15–16 and 31–33 derive from forms for "child" followed by the suffixes for "father" and "mother." Further traits include the proliferation of descriptive circumlocutions, the presence of relationship terms that are not strictly kinship terms (*tiwã, apĩhi-pihã*), and a certain instability or opacity in the designation of cross-cousins (who, in other terminologies of this family, are either assimilated to adjacent generations, receive affinal terms or periphrases of a sexual nature,[15] or are assimilated to parallel cousins). On the other hand, the Araweté terminology shows a remarkable restriction of its genealogical and categorical scope: not only do positions such as MBW and FZH escape the terminological grid, but there is also a very limited extension of the calculus "anyone an X calls Y, I call Z" (the usual form of justifying the usage of terms). Outside the restricted circle of close relatives, the "suction" exercised by the *tiwã* category augments rapidly, as expressed in the ample categorical latitude of marriageable positions: anyone who is not a "sister," "mother," or "daughter" to a man or a "brother," "father," or "son" to a woman is a possible spouse. The presence of so many *tiwã* in a society of 168 people is explained in part by the long separation between the southern and northern groups of Araweté before contact; the *tiwã* were in general described as *iwi rowã̱nã ti hã*, "people of the other side of the earth," i.e., of another bloc of villages. But the salience of this category strikes me as transcending historical contingency. The essential fact is that the Araweté do *not* consider all the members of the group "relatives" to whom kinship terms must be applied.

All kinship terms, with the exception of those for F, M, S, and D, can be followed by nominal markers of the past or the future. The former are systematically used (the latter being, rather, joking forms). They designate relationships voided by the death of a linking relative, by divorce, or by the transformation of a "consanguine" into an "affine," and they are often used as forms of address. The last case is especially interesting. When a marriage takes place between people who classify each other by any pair of terms in the list above (except terms 30–33), the kinship position of the spouse is redefined as "ex-*X*," for example, *toti pe*, ex-MB, *đipe pe*, ex-ZD, etc. This is obviously the case when ex-siblings marry: they would never refer to each other by the "ex-terms" that are used (with a certain sarcasm) by other people to refer to them. The abandonment of the forms for MB, ZD, FZ, etc., is not an imperative (although a woman does not refer to her husband as *he toti*, "my MB," she recognizes the existence of this relationship), and it does not necessarily affect other relationships. Thus, a ZS who is at the same time a WB continues to be called "ZS" and to call the MB (ZH) *he toti*. A sister turned mother-in-law can be called either "Z," *heni*, or "WM," *hačo*; she would never be called "ex-sister." A man can call a ZS who is his DH either "nephew" or "son-in-law," and will be called either "uncle" or "father-in-law," although the tendency in this case is to use affinal terms.

Thus, at the same time that diverse categories of relatives are defined as potentially marriageable, there seems to be a certain repulsion between consanguinity and affinity—as if marriage cancels out previous bonds (at least between spouses). This is related to a distinction the Araweté make between proper and improper positions for marriage *within* the same category. A *toti hete*, "actual MB," must not marry his ZD, nor should a FZ marry her BS, nor a MF, his DD. Marriage is appropriate only with distant relatives, specified as *dĩ* when it concerns consanguineal laterality or as *amĩ* when the calculation is made through a relationship of marriage (see the difference between the terms 3a and 3b). When a MB has married his ZD, it is said that the two "became others (*amĩte*)" or "became *tiwã*," an expression that also describes the retrospective regulation of all incestuous unions.[16] Such a distinction according to distance does *not* apply to cross-cousins, who, being the primary *tiwã* within the kindred, are eminently marriageable.

This suggests that the preferential marriage is between ambilateral cross-cousins, and that unions between relatives of terminologically different generations are merely permitted. It further suggests that the terminology, despite the distinction of degrees of distance within marriageable categories, is of a prescriptive type: every spouse is a *tiwã* or becomes one (although I do not find it especially adequate to speak of "prescriptive terminology" in cases where separate terms of affinity exist). In fact, marriage between first-degree cross-cousins is rare; marriages with second- or third-degree cousins and oblique unions between classificatory relatives predominate. But there is a tendency to mask oblique terminological relations when they are distant: a FFBD is not classified as a "FZ" by her husband, but simply as *tiwã*.

I cannot estimate the relative frequencies of the different types of union, since each adult marries at least four times during his or her lifetime, since there are various paths of connection between spouses, and since the majority of marriages are considered to be between *tiwã*. Of the 44 couples present at the end of 1982, 27 stood in *tiwã* relationships (in which the connections were untraceable or the wife was a FZDD, FMBD, MMBD, etc.), 4 were unions with classificatory ZD, 1 with an actual ZD, 3 with classificatory DD (FBDD, MZSDD), 1 with a FZD, 2 with MBD, 3 with classificatory FZ, 2 stood in a relation of "ex-siblings," and 1 was criticized in private as being incestuous, since the man united with his *to amĩ nemiyika pe*, "ex-wife of his other father (MH)," therefore a *hi amĩ*, a "mother." The recent demographic losses precipitated a general recomposition of marriages. The genealogies (see Appendix 2-B) show great variety in the forms of marriage: sister exchange, serial marriage of sibling groups, the sororate, levirate, matrimonial succession (by divorce or death) by MB and ZS, and not a few improper unions (FBD, MZD, etc.).

But the verbally expressed ideal defines ambilateral cross-cousins as the spouses par excellence. Marriage with a MBD is called an "*ɨrɨwã* marriage," named after a mythical bird who married the daughter of a bushmaster snake, his MB; marriage with a FZD is called a "harpy eagle marriage" after another myth. Often adults decide the future spouses of their children, pairing them with their cross-cousins. From 1983 to 1988, I observed that only a small number of these couplings took place. The major conflict that arose in the village after contact was one that occurred in 1987, due to a matrimonial confusion between MBS and FZD: the youth's father and the girl's brother (MB and ZS) shot arrows at each other, to the great delight and scandal of everyone.

Another form of matrimonial arrangement is one in which a MB or a FZ reserves a youngster as a future spouse by asking a sibling for his or her child. These marriages (and those with first-degree cross-cousins) are seen as a way of keeping close relatives together, or more precisely, as the result of an affective link between brother and sister. Children of cross-sex siblings are desirable, either for oneself or for one's children: in this way, it is said, "we will not disperse." Finally, alliances between kindreds tend to be repeated, generating highly intricate endogamous networks. Araweté matrimonial ideology does not appear to be ordered by a notion of alliance, but cross-consanguinity: it is not the brother-in-law, but rather the sister who cedes a daughter to ego or his son (and vice versa). This does not mean that the idea of exchange is absent. Marriages between children of siblings are defined as *pepi kã*, "counterparts": a ZD whom ego marries is the *pepi kã* of his sister, a BS reserved as a spouse is the counterpart of a ceded brother, and so on. Such marriages are described as *oyo pepi-pepi*, "to exchange repeatedly." Thus, what is intended is an ideal of endogamy within the kindred. The concept is frankly that of a short cycle of reciprocity: for a sibling whom I cede, I want a spouse for my son or daughter.[17]

For this reason, I never came to understand the impropriety of unions between actual MB and ZD (frequently appearing in the genealogies). I can say only that a common phenomenon in Dravidian systems is the prohibition or disfavor of unions between overly close representatives of prescribed or permitted categories. In some Tupi-

Guarani groups, this is expressed by the "Hawaiian" neutralization in ego's generation (the famous "bifurcating generation type" of Dole [1969], otherwise called the "Tupi system," identified originally by Rivers in western Polynesia) and by the correlative rule of marriage between distant "sisters."[18]

The Araweté say that a sexual union with a close relative in one of these categories (MB, FZ, ZD, etc.) makes our stomachs growl, as do relations with a sibling; this is not, however, taken very seriously, and besides, the sexual joking between MB and ZD, FZ and BS, is very much enjoyed. Actually, there appears to be a certain indecision over whether these positions should be cognitively and attitudinally defined as relatives or as *tiwã*. In the final analysis, the age difference, social proximity, and behavior of interested parties are the deciding factors for the direction that these oblique relations will take. Note, for example, that a MB can become a ZH, a WF, even a DH. When none of these changes occur, it is still possible for MB and ZS to be *apĩhi-pihã;* the wife of a maternal uncle is a common sexual partner for a ZS, and the wife of a nephew for a MB. Oblique positions are therefore overdetermined; the idea that matrimonial relations should only be established with distant relatives in these categories may be an attempt to neutralize their intrinsic ambiguity. On the other hand, *apĩhi-pihã* relations between close MB/ZS and FZ/BD are commonplace—but this excludes precisely the relation of affinity.

I do not know a specific word for "incest." One term, *a̲wïde,* which I do not know how to translate, qualifies unions that are not especially proper. This refers to marriages between distant classificatory siblings and to close oblique unions.[19] Less adequate than marriages with *tiwã, a̲wïde* marriages are not exactly incestuous. Incest (described as "eating" a mother, sister, etc.) is a very dangerous thing: it brings about rectal protrusion, causes the couple to waste away and die of *ha'iwã* (a sanction for all cosmic infractions), and leads to enemy attacks on the village. Villages of incestuous people, it is said, used to end up so riddled with enemies' arrows that vultures were not even able to peck at the cadavers.

□

The tone of Araweté interpersonal relations is quite relaxed, and kinship positions are attitudinally little differentiated. A single relationship is cited as involving fear-shame (*čiye*) by definition, that between brother and sister. (I say "by definition" because other situations involve temporary and extrinsic fear-shame; for example, every youth who goes to reside uxorilocally feels constrained around his parents-in-law, but this rapidly dissipates.) This does not signify avoidance: siblings of the opposite sex visit each other frequently, show great reciprocal esteem, and are a person's main support. A woman will turn to her brother more often than to her husband in a fight with outsiders; when a conjugal quarrel breaks out, it is always the opposite-sex siblings who rush to console the spouses. This solidarity is respectful; the sexual joking so appreciated by the Araweté never has a sibling of the opposite sex as its object.

An enemy attack on a village that has become soft (*tɨme*) and unprepared punishes another grave breach of social norms besides incest: physical or verbal hostility between brother and sister. We can thus see that symmetrical infractions of the proper distance between brother and sister—too much or too little love—affect the survival of the entire group, suggesting the centrality of this relationship in Araweté social life.

Siblings of the same sex are equally close and are the most common work partners. They enjoy great liberty with each other, although it never reaches the joking camaraderie of *apĩhi-pihã*. Sisters in particular are extremely close. A same-sex sibling is *he dĩ*, "my equal." Nevertheless, birth order, which is marked in the terminology, generates a difference that is expressed in the authority of the elder siblings over the younger. Although not very marked, this ordering is recognized by the Araweté: siblings "follow one another" (*pirɨ*)—in the mother's womb, in the levirate, and in the sororate.

Conjugal relations are notably free but ambivalent. Public bodily contact, including the erotic, is allowed, and when things are going well, couples are very affectionate. On the other hand, scenes of jealousy and beatings frequently occur. The husbands of young women are very jealous and closely watch over their wives. When a union is consolidated with the birth of children, the women are the ones who begin to display jealousy, especially if they are older than the husband. Physical violence is common among young couples, and in general women are more aggressive. Outside the conjugal relation (and the rare corporal punishments meted out to small children), there is no other possibility of violent interaction that would not involve dangerous weapons. For this reason, marriage is overloaded, serving as a channel for exogenous tensions. *Inter alia*, this accounts for the high conjugal instability.

Wide age differences between spouses are a common feature of Tupi-Guarani societies and may be associated with oblique alliance (Fernandes 1963 [1949]: 154). It is also found among the Araweté, but confined to secondary and temporary unions, when older men sexually initiate pre-pubescent girls, or when older women choose youths for whom no wife is available. Long-lasting oblique unions occur between persons of the same chronological generation. In 1981–83, a peculiar demographic situation caused there to be nine couples in the village (among them the most eminent) characterized by an age difference of ten or more years of the wives over the husbands (as opposed to three couples in which the husband was ten or even twenty years older). This situation was due to the high mortality of the men through warfare.

Between affines of the same sex and generation, relations are little marked. There is no avoidance of any kind nor any special solidarity. "Siblings-in-law are like siblings": they go out hunting together, they may be good friends, or they may ignore each other. As part of the expression of the bonds of solidarity between brother and sister, they are among those most often invited to a person's patio. Nevertheless, the custom of opposite-sex siblings going to console spouses in conjugal fights is a translation of the tension, latent but unmistakeable, between same-sex affines, which I never saw go beyond short but vehement admonitions when beatings occurred—when, in other words, the WB and the HZ assert their sibling rights against their respective affines. Two brothers-in-law or sisters-in-law may have sexual relations with a third person (yet another sign of the general nontransitivity of the Amazonian "Dravidian" calculus), but they may not enter into *apĩhi-pihã* relations while they are linked as affines: spouse-sharing and affinity exclude each other.

Between affines of the opposite sex and same generation, relations are free; sexual joking is expected, although only indulged in when the linking sibling/spouse is absent. The relationship between two same-sex siblings with regard to their respective spouses is conceived to be one of potential succession, not simultaneity. Sexual relations between, for example, a man and his brother's wife are semiclandestine, at the most, tacitly tolerated by the brother. If they should become conspicuous, one of the parties involved will propose a definitive exchange of spouses, which frequently occurs. This diachronic relation of equivalency between same-sex siblings—and the "zero sum" of their eventual spouse exchange—is opposed to the synchronic sharing of spouses between *apĩhi-pihã*.

Between consecutive generations, the array of attitudes is varied, depending on the particular phase of the life cycle and the residential situation involved. There is little emphasis on authority structures based on generational difference. A community of substance is thought to exist between parents and children, and their relations are affectively intense. There is a vague idea that sons are "a father's thing," and girls, "a mother's thing," which is simply a translation of gender identity and its economic consequences, since the theory of conception is patrilateral and the kinship organization cognatic. But this "parallelism" is compatible with the conjugal right of the MB and FZ over the SD and BS, and may be yet another expression of the B/Z tie.

□

Araweté social life exhibits a strong matrifocal tendency, which governs residential solutions. The mother-child tie, especially the mother-daughter one, is more intense than the father-child tie. It is difficult to characterize the postmarital situation with precision. There is some disagreement over the norm. Young men say that virilocality is the proper residence form; but older people assert that traditionally youths took up residence in the section or village of their wives, and that only after the birth of the first child could they return to their village of origin (if they managed to convince the wife). I lean towards the testimony of the older people, although they, as much as the youths, are certainly expressing the norms in the manner that most favors them. Uxorilocality is indeed a basic conceptual *principle* for the Araweté. Characteristically, they explained it by psychological arguments: mothers, they said, do not want to be separated from their daughters, and besides, mothers-in-law and daughters-in-law never get along well, especially if they live in the same residential section. They never mentioned the wife's father, not even in relation to "bride service" or the likes—even though the most typical feature of marriage is the work the son-in-law does in the gardens of his wife's parents. Whatever solution is adopted, uxorilocal or virilocal, it is always conceptually a *matrilocal* residence: the in-marrying spouse is defined as living *hačo pi,* "with his/her mother-in-law," and the stationary spouse as living *ohi pi,* "with his/her mother."

The actual situation depends on various factors, notably the political weight of the kindreds involved, the number and sex-ratio of their offspring, past alliances, and so on. These days, they say, the residential solution does not matter much, since now everyone lives in a single village. The factor that continues to be determinant is the allocation of labor power. Uxorilocality is an essentially agricultural situation: the son-in-law comes to work with the father-in-law, or rather, in the mother-in-law's garden of maize. For this reason, the head couple of an extended family will only allow the departure of a daughter if it succeeds in retaining a son (by attracting a daughter-in-law) or in having another daughter immediately married uxorilocally in order to replace the "lost" son-in-law. The good administration of a family consists in arranging marriages that maintain the maximum number of children of both sexes in their residential and productive natal unit. Since this is more or less what everybody tries to do, the system veers towards uxorilocality (at the same time a result and a principle, it is less than and more than a mechanical rule); it is nonetheless always sensitive to the least shift of *ceteris paribus* conditions, which allows some to retain married sons and attract siblings, siblings-in-law, and other satellite relatives.[20]

No avoidance rules exist between affines of adjacent generations, although a certain reserve prevails, as does an obligatory commensality. Conflicts between a father-in-law and son-in-law are rare, but they do occur if the latter is negligent in agricultural work (especially in the phase of felling trees). In virilocal marriages, relations towards the older couple are generally tense; in the only two cases in which the virilocalized wives had living mothers, conflicts frequently arose between the mother-in-law and daughter-in-law—actually between the mothers of the spouses.

The relations between MB, FZ, and their nephews and nieces do not have a stable nature, as mentioned earlier: the same holds for those between alternate generations. Close relatives in all these categories are assimilated to unmarriageable kin; distant ones, to potential affines.

When I would ask if a youth, when moving to another village upon marriage, did not feel intimidated and nostalgic for home, I was always told yes, but that, besides having relatives in the wife's village, soon *apĩhi-pihã* bonds would be created between the newlywed and his *tiwã* located there.

4. Eluding Affinity

Marriage is not the object of any ceremony, and the accelerated matrimonial circulation of young people makes it a mundane affair. Nevertheless, every time a union becomes public when someone changes domicile, a subtle commotion arises in the village. Other couples immediately begin to visit the newlyweds, whose patio is the most joyful and noisy at night; there people joke, men embrace each other, women whisper and laugh. Within a few days, the new husband and another man can been seen in frequent association, and so can their wives. The two couples begin to go out together to the forest and to paint and decorate each other in the new couple's patio.

A marriage seems to expose the couple to collective desire, especially the woman. As soon as a girl becomes a wife, she begins to be considered extremely interesting by the men who up to then had ignored her. Even a matrimonial recomposition has such an effect: the new couples become the center of attention. Marriage, instead of removing the spouses from the potential sexual field of others, places them prominently within it: nothing is more desirable than a neighbor's new wife. Marriage, therefore, is literally a collective affair, interesting more people than just the couple and their immediate kindreds. It leads to the creation of multiple relationships that go well beyond affinity and affect the whole community.

It was curious to observe the generalized envy that a new marriage awakened. It not only spread throughout the village, which set about experimenting with liaisons among all the single people (see chap. 4, note 17), but also prompted a flow of covetous discourse about the couple and plans for clandestine adventures with the young wife. Such a perturbation would stabilize when one couple in particular won the competition and became the *apĩhi-pihã* of the new couple.

The characteristic mark of the *apĩhi-pihã* relationship is joyfulness, *tori*. The conviviality of *apĩhi-pihã* (friends of the same sex) consists of a joking camaraderie, with no aggressive connotation. They *oyo mo-ori*, "reciprocally make each other joyful": they are constantly embracing each other, are assiduous companions in the forest, and freely use each other's possessions. When the village men go out on collective hunts, female *apĩhi-pihã* go to sleep in the same house. In the dance formation for beer festivals, this is the focal bond between men. Friends of the opposite sex (the *apĩhi* and *apĩno*) are called *tori pã*, "joy makers."

The glue of this relation is sexual mutuality. *Apĩhi-pihã* exchange spouses temporarily according to two methods: *oyo iwi* ("to live together"), when the men go at night to the house of their *apĩhi*, occupy their friends' hammocks, and in the morning return to their wives; and *oyo pepi* ("to exchange"), when the women go to reside for a few days in the houses of their *apĩno*. In both cases, however, the quartet is always seen together in the patio of one of the couples. The interchanged couples often go out after tortoises, taking different directions; at night they reconvene to eat what they have brought back. This sexual mutuality, thus, is an alternation, not a system of "group sex."

The privileged arena for consummating the relation is the forest, especially during the period of dispersal in the rainy season, when pairs or series (nontransitive) of couples thus linked camp out together. (In the beginning of the honey season in September 1982, the minimal harvesting units almost always involved groups of *apĩhi-pihã.*) In the forest, the interchanged couples go out to hunt and gather honey, and reunite by dusk: "Daytime is for the *apĩhi*, nighttime for the wife." The expressions "to take hunting," "to take honey gathering," and "to take out to the forest" immediately bring to mind *apĩhi/apĩno* links. To find out if a man was really the *apĩno* of a woman (instead of just an occasional lover), the decisive criterion was this: "Yes, since he took her out to the forest on thus-and-such an occasion." The relationship is oriented in a particular way: the man takes the woman to the forest, a masculine domain. The forest, tortoises, and honey are symbols of the Araweté "honeymoon," an event that does not occur between husband and wife, but between *apĩhi* and *apĩno;* it does not involve one, but two couples.

Jealousy is by definition excluded from this relationship; on the contrary, it is the only situation of sexual extraconjugality that involves its opposite, the benevolent cession of a spouse to a friend. Even between brothers, who have potential access to each other's spouses, a margin for repressed jealousy and disequilibrium exists: a man may visit his brother's wife without his knowing, wanting, or reciprocating it. By contrast, the *apĩhi-pihã* relation presupposes publicity and simultaneity: it is a ritual relation of mutuality.

The symbolic complex of the *apĩhi-pihã* relationship is absolutely central in the Araweté world view. To have friends is a sign of maturity, assertiveness, generosity, vitality, prestige. The *apĩhi* is "Woman," pure sexual positivity, without the burden of domestic familiarity. The *apĩhi-pihã* is, in a certain sense, more than a brother; he represents a conquest over the territory of the *tiwã*, nonrelatives, establishing an identity where there had only been difference and indifference—he is a friend.

The frequent economic association between quartets of *apĩhi-pihã* involves not agriculture work for men (although the women may go together to the garden to harvest maize, grind it, etc.), but hunting: agricultural cooperation presupposes belonging to the same extended family or residential section, which cannot occur between *apĩhi-pihã*. In any case, the province par excellence for friendship is the forest in the rainy season, the period when the maize is "hidden" (*ti'ĩ*, also used to describe a new moon). That friendship is a "compensation" for uxorilocality is clear: for a newly-married youth, a friend is the opposite of a father-in-law in whose garden he must work. During festivals, *apĩno* and *apĩhi* pairs paint, adorn, and perfume each other. When a quartet is seen profusely decorated, with many ornaments, their heads coated with white eagle down, their bodies shiny with annatto, laughing and embracing each other, there is no doubt: they are *apĩhi-pihã*. Hunting, dancing, sex, painting, perfume—the world of the *apĩhi-pihã* is an ideal world. In the sky, the relation between the gods and the souls of the dead is always represented as sexual friendship. The dead in the sky marry the *Maï*, have children, live as we do here; but the shamanic songs always portray scenes of souls accompanied by their celestial *apĩno* or *apĩhi*, as befits festive occasions. One of the euphemisms for somebody's death alludes to this heavenly character of friendship: "*Iha kɨ otori pã katɨ we*," "He left to go join his 'joy-maker.'"

Thus, the impression one gets is that a marriage is less a means of obtaining a spouse than of gaining access to a couple capable of duplicating and idealizing the conjugal relationship and its affinal obligations. An *apĩhi-pihã* is an *anti-affine*, a sort of antidote to affinity, sought as soon as a marriage begins: an ideal synthesis of the "other self" (the *anĩ*) and the "self's other" (the *tiwã*). A quartet of friends is said to be "inter-eating" (*oyo o*), sexually speaking—however, this comes precariously close to the symbolics of incest as a cannibalistic negation of affinal exchange.[21] For youths in an uxorilocal situation, to establish relations of friendship is to remain *entre soi*, even when among others.

□

A couple can have more than one *apĩhi-pihã* couple, and there is no adult in the village who does not call at least a half dozen others by friendship terms. But these relations are actualized consecutively; rarely does a couple have more than one other as an active partner at any given moment because of the dedication required of friendship. The relationships are not transitive: the friends of my friends are not necessarily my friends. Two actual brothers, who cannot call each other by friendship terms or share spouses, usually have couples as friends in common. Friendship thus constitutes a dyadic and local relation, discontinuously linking the couples of the village in a network that is superimposed on the kinship network: a system of "restricted sharing," so to speak, which duplicates and ideologically subordinates the restricted exchange that the Araweté practice in the matrimonial plane.

Remarriages due to widowhood or divorce prompt the need to decide about renovating friendship bonds. If a member of a quarter dies, it is considered desirable to renew relations with the surviving and remarried member, leading to an *oyo iwi* ("living together") temporary exchange. Not uncommonly, temporary exchanges of spouses end up becoming definitive. Then it is said that the men have, in the proper sense of the term, exchanged (*oyo pepi*) wives. A definitive exchange undoes the *apĩhi-pihã* relationship, which loses its sense.[22]

Friendship terminology, beyond the period when sexual sharing is active, tends to be used more often among and by men. Men take the initiative in the relationship (although women can suggest or resist the arrangement). Friendship relations can be deactivated due to conflict, matrimonial recomposition, or disinterest, and can be renewed later on. The breakup of a friendship usually leads to a cancellation of the terminology, or else the terms are maintained out of courtesy among the men; if the relationship is merely going through a latent period, the terms and the general tone of the interpersonal relations remain in effect. "*Apĩhi-pihã*" is the typical friendly vocative, which the Araweté employ for strangers when they stop calling them simply *tiwã*. It serves as a concept for all extrinsic, "nonfamily resemblances." I remember a man calling another the "*apĩhi-pihã* of so-and-so" because, while building a house, he was seen carrying supports as slender as so-and-so did a short time earlier. They were not relatives, they were not building the same house: their similarity of tastes was therefore an "*apĩhi-pihã* phenomenon." Characteristically, it is this term that substitutes the classic Amerindian "brother-in-law" (and our "brother") as a generic vocative: it is the *model* for all social relations.

Active relations of friendship are much more common among couples who are young and childless—precisely those who are in an uxorilocal situation and dependent upon their affines. The only four cases of active friendship involving older couples in 1982–83 centered on the remarriage of a widower (who reactivated one relationship and established a new one) and on the couple who were the "owners of the village," who linked themselves successively to two others (both in the same terminological relationship with the man: the husbands were his "sister's sons"; the women (actual sisters) were his wife's "brother's daughters"). These last two cases indicate that friendship is an important political instrument: the leader of the village, in establishing relations with couples situated in residential sections distant from his own, extracted them from there and incorporated them into his patio and honey-season excursion group. The initiative in both cases came from the leader couple. The difference in age, social and terminological position, and the advantage of the initiative did not, however, translate into any asymmetry in the behavior of the quartets—friendship relations are symmetrical by definition and in practice—but the political uses to which such relationships are put are certainly not innocent.

In the four cases above, the first friendship relations did not last more than a month, being immediately substituted by the second ones. The couples who were "spurned" (*heti mi re,* thrown away) soon looked for two others with whom to initiate relations. The establishment or cancellation of one of these relationships thus affects the village as a whole, and, as in the case of a marriage, an entire machinery is set in motion after the first impetus: triggering both contagion and an impulse towards equilibrium, the bonds of friendship are incessantly woven and undone.[23]

□

Although the friendship relation involves two couples and is centered on the sexual access to the friend's spouse, the bonds between the same-sex partners are the fundamental ones; they are the ones that preferably persist after someone is widowed or divorced and that need to be renewed. A friend of the opposite sex is above all a means to produce an *apĩhi-pihã,* particularly for men. If a brother-in-law is someone whom one cannot avoid obtaining when securing a wife, a friend is someone whom one wants to obtain when having relations with an *apĩhi.*

Apĩhi-pihã are by definition recruited among the *tiwã:* that is, those who link themselves in this way are transformed into *tiwã.* The limits of this prescriptive retroaction are the same that we saw operating in marriage: actual siblings cannot be friends. The Araweté always corrected me when I referred to two brothers as *apĩhi-pihã* after confirming that they had exchanged (definitively and domestically) wives: "*Tiwã* are the ones we call *apĩhi-pihã; anĩ* are the ones we call *hayĩhi-pihã*" (term 16 of the vocabulary). This distinction is important, since a *tiwã* is the opposite of a *anĩ,* but when one of the former is transformed into a friend, he has something in common with a brother, access to one's spouse.

Recruited on the periphery of ego's kindred, friends come from the same place where affines are found. A friend is a nonaffinal *tiwã*—in truth, an "anti-brother-in-law," since, if what links brothers-in-law is the inaccessibility of their respective sisters, then what defines friendship is the mutual sexual accessibility of spouses. But a friend is different from a brother: the equivalence of two brothers relative to the same women is anterior to the latter's existence, access to them being a consequence of the fraternal bond. In the case of friends, it is the conjugal bond that is anterior: friendship is a consequence of prior conjugality (there are no unmarried friends). The equivalence of friends is constructed out of marriage—like the difference between brothers-in-law. A cross-cousin, a maternal uncle, a distant brother, or a nonrelative can become, through the same route of marriage, either an affine or a friend.

Bonds of friendship are established, as a general rule, between persons who are on the outer limits of the field of kinship: friends are consanguines of affines, or affines of affines: a ZHB, a WMZDH, for example (note that the WZH is a *hayĩhi-pihã*, as are brothers, not friends). When close relatives in the categories of MB, FZ, etc., become friends, they "turn into *tiwã*," as occurs in marriage. Thus, starting from the generic ground of pure negative difference (nonkinship), two particular relations are constructed, symmetrical and inverse: from the *tiwã* emerge affines and anti-affines, brothers-in-law through an interposed and forbidden sister and friends through a mediating and shared spouse.

Friendship relations impinge upon the kinship terminology. A person calls the parents of his opposite-sex friend "mother-in-law" and "father-in-law" and calls this friend's siblings "brothers-in-law" or "sisters-in-law"—a usage which has none of the social implications of affinity arising from marriage. No terminological changes occur regarding relatives of the same-sex friend; this bond, the most important, is strictly individual. In subsequent generations, terminological options emerge. The children of the female friends of ego's fathers can be addressed as siblings, since the father's friends are *hi amĩ*, "other mothers"; the same terms can be used for the children of the mother's male friends.[24] On the other hand, the same-sex bonds do not by themselves produce changes in any generation: the father's *apĩhi-pihã*, if not at the same time the mother's *apĩno*, will *not* be called "father," or vice versa. The difference is derived from the fact of sexual relations: I use the term "father-in-law" for the father of the person with whom I had sexual relations, "father" for the one who had relations with my mother, and so on. If this blockage of the calculation of terminological extension did not exist, everybody of my generation would rapidly turn into "brother" and "sister," creating serious problems for marriage.

In addition, this form of classificatory kinship permits all sorts of manipulations, and many marriages of "ex-siblings" occur between people linked by these bonds. But when the male friend of one's mother is considered an associate genitor of ego, his children by other unions are considered actual siblings and marriage is forbidden. Such considerations extend a fortiori to the establishment of friendship bonds between children of friends.

□

The atom of Araweté kinship thus appears more complex than the classical model, since "antiparticles" and a principle of uncertainty have to be incorporated in it. From the point of view of the system of attitudes, there are two central relationships: between brother and sister and between same-sex friends. The first is characterized by solidarity and respect, and is the fulcrum of affinity and reciprocity; the second is characterized by liberty and camaraderie, and is the focus of mutuality and anti-affinity. The relations between brothers-in-law and between same-sex siblings are little marked, but they strike me as hiding latent antagonisms. Note the support of an opposite-sex sibling in conjugal quarrels, and the veiled competition and jealousy that unite and oppose brothers in relation to the same women. The husband/wife relationship is opposed to the brother/sister one in that the former freely manifests *both* aspects proscribed in the latter: sex and hostility. On the other hand, the relationship between opposite-sex friends is ideally positive (and positively ideal): *apĩno* and *apĩhi* do not fight, or if so, they automatically abandon the relationship. Finally, the "joyfulness" of relations between male and female friends is opposed to the "fear-shame" (respect) between brother and sister. Figure 1 schematizes the system of Araweté sociability. The vertical line consists of a generic and given opposition (nonrelative versus relative) while the horizontal consists of a particular and constructed opposition (brother-in-law versus friend). In the face of the instability of the *tiwã* category, only two solutions are possible: to transform nonrelatives into affines or into anti-affines. In the first case, the solution stays close to the point of origin: a brother-in-law is a domesticated *tiwã*, neutralized by reciprocity, who becomes a relative, "almost a brother." In the second, the solution goes beyond destiny: a

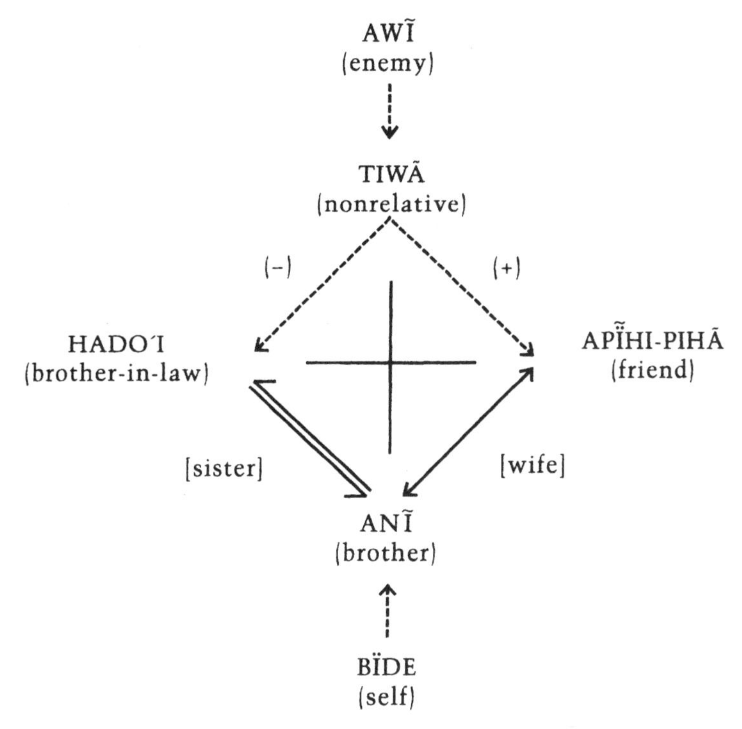

FIGURE 1. Schema of social relations

friend is more than a brother. He is a synchronal, a nonambivalent equivalent; neither brother-in-law nor brother, he is actually an included third party.

If a sister is the means of obtaining a wife, a wife is the means of obtaining a friend. If sister exchange equalizes brothers-in-law, the sharing of wives totalizes friends. The operation of friendship is of course logically posterior to marriage, but it is more fundamental to an understanding of Araweté sociability, given that it is the paradigm of all social relations. Here we can see analogies that link Araweté friendship to what would appear to be its exact opposite, the Tupinamba war captive. On the one hand, the war captive may have ritually incarnated the essence of affinity—the better to be eaten—but on the other hand, he was an anti-affine. Tupinamba warfare, as H. Clastres has noted (1972:81), was pursued in order to capture not wives, but "brothers-in-law." Instead of doing bride-service, the prisoner was the one who was served, nourished by those who would kill and eat him. Even though he was given a wife and food, it was not meant to obtain anything more than himself. Both affine and anti-affine were anchored in the captive, positions that the Araweté separate: the ambivalence of *tiwã* is pure potency, which soon bifurcates into brother-in-law and friend. And, whereas a captive was immediately transformed into a brother-in-law by the cession of one of the group's women, among the Araweté the young brother-in-law who has recently arrived in the wife's village is avidly transformed into a friend, that is, into someone with whom one "inter-eats."

It is characteristic of the Araweté that, instead of avoiding brothers-in-law (or eating them), they have opted to turn to frequenting friends. All aspects of their social philosophy seem to converge on this discreet refusal of affinity: the redundancy of alliances, closure of kindreds, oblique marriages, and at the same time the dispersion of reciprocity, nontransivity of the terminology, and proliferation of friendship bonds. A mixture, indeed—of generations, genitors, friends: "We are all mixed."

It is not accidental, after all, that anti-affinity is defined as heavenly bliss (the expression *iwã tori,* "celestial joyfulness," appears recurrently in shamans' songs and refers to friendship). It is properly an attribute of the gods, who keep to themselves, calling to mind the impossible world of living *entre soi,* which Lévi-Strauss evoked at the end of *The Elementary Structures of Kinship.*[25] But it is precisely in relation to this celestial world that affinity will reappear: disguised on earth, it seems to be so only in order to better characterize the gods as affines of humanity. Rejected, alliance ends up being exalted, placed in the beyond, the site of meaning.

□

The direct parallels of the *apĩhi-pihã* system in Tupi-Guarani societies are few. The only direct analogue that I was able to find is the Parintintin custom of important men temporarily exchanging wives "as a form of expressing friendship" (Kracke 1978:14), an echo of Tupinamba practices. Araweté friendship itself is probably of the same type as the *atuasaba* relationship mentioned by the chroniclers (see note 14). The traditional formal friendship of the Tapirapé, *anchiwawa* (= *tiwã?*), entailed avoidance and functioned as a channel of economic redistribution; its recruitment was based on the same criteria used by the Araweté, distant kinship or nonkinship (Wagley 1977:73–75). The Wayãpi institution of *yepe* ("the chosen") is close to the Araweté case: exterior friendship, as Grenand calls it (1982: 138–41), it focuses on nonrelatives, creating dyadic and exclusive bonds; the interpretation given by Gallois (1988:28) is even more directly evocative of *apĩhi-pihã*. The meta-kinship aspects of the *apĩhi-pihã* system also raise interesting questions for understanding the Carib complex of *pito* and *pawana* (Rivière 1969:227; Howard 1992).

If we compare it to the formal friendship of some of the Gê (Timbira and Suya), Araweté friendship appears to fuse a central opposition found among the former, formal friend versus companion, which connotes other oppositions, such as avoidance versus liberty, inheritance versus choice, affinity versus consanguinity, and "structure" versus "communitas" (Da Matta 1982:87–99; Seeger 1981:142–45; Carneiro da Cunha 1978:74–94; Melatti 1979:73–76). Araweté friendship is, like Gê formal friendship, an "anti-affinity," but in the contrary sense: the potential affinity that previously links Gê friends (being distant relatives, recruited from the opposite moiety, etc.) is converted into verbal and sexual avoidance and the interdiction of matrimonial exchange between friends, whereas, in the Araweté case, a potential affine becomes a wife-sharer, which an actual affine cannot be. Like companionship, *apĩhi-pihã* friendship connotes freedom of choice, synchronic equivalence, intimacy, and the exchange of wives, but its paradigmatic value in Araweté society makes it closer to formal friendship than to companionship, with this significant inversion: the central Gê institution, formal friendship, is based on a double metaphorical negation (the person is constituted in opposition to his "antonym," the formal friend [Carneiro da Cunha 1978:74–94]); whereas the central Araweté institution is founded on a double affirmation of a metonymical redundancy—complementarity versus supplementarity.

Araweté friendship can also be compared to the Upper Xingu system (Basso 1973:102–6); Viveiros de Castro 1977:193ff.). There are some common aspects, such as free choice, the contrast with kinship, and extraconjugal sexuality, but with an important difference: in the Upper Xingu, there is a disjunction between friends of the same and opposite sex. It is not a matter of a relationship between couples nor of sexual mutuality. To the contrary, many times a same-sex friend is a sibling of one's lover, a benevolent "pseudo-brother-in-law" who may play the role of Cupid. Also, their system of sexual friendship is semiclandestine. Although it too expresses the search for bonds with others without the burden of alliance, it is less central in Upper Xingu society than its Araweté equivalent: for the former, friendship is a mechanism of compensation, while for the latter, it is the dominant ideology.

The Araweté system of anti-affinity may help us to understand the paradox of an endogamous desire associated with the "passion for the other" manifested in their cosmology, which distinguishes it so clearly from the Guiana cosmologies (at least in Rivière's version [1984: 70–71]). This paradox is suggestive of another, this time Tupinamba: a system in which avuncular marriage predominates, but coexists with the ceding of women to war captives and a general desire for union with strangers—simultaneously minimum and maximum exogamy.

7 Birth, and Copulation, and Death

1. The Facts of Life

To produce a child is a lengthy job, requiring frequent copulation and a great expense of semen (*ta'i re*)[1] in order to heat up and develop the fetus. All the potential components of the person are contained in the paternal semen. The genitor is conceived to be the one who makes (*mõñĩ*) or gives (*mẽ*) the child. The mother is a *ta'i re riro*, receptacle of the semen, where its transformation (*heriwã*) is processed.

My attempts to clarify the nature of this transformation were thwarted. Menstrual blood is not thought to play any role. When I remarked on the physical resemblances between mothers and children, everyone agreed, giving a grammatically abstract explanation: the resemblances were due to the fact that the semen becomes a child *ohi ropĩ*, "through (along) the mother."[2] This was the same reason adduced to explain why the circle of abstinence for disease includes matrilateral relatives. In sum, the patrilateral "theory" of conception coexists with a general bilaterality in the recognition of filiation, the interdiction against incest, and abstinence.

I sometimes wondered whether Araweté ideas about conception were similar to the Aristotelian theory of animal generation, where the father contains the "motor and generator principle" (efficient cause), the mother the "material principle." However, for the Araweté the mother does not contribute any "material" to the seminal "form"; to the contrary, it is in her body that the semen, the exclusive material, is *transformed*. As the site of transformation or as the transformer herself, the mother exercises a metonymical causality over the material she receives in her depths. The idea of an exclusively masculine genesis must be viewed with caution, either because our conceptions of substance and causality are inappropriate for capturing Araweté ideas, or because something is both denied and admitted at the same time: the female role in generation. In addition, although the sperm lies at the origin of the child's body and soul, certain proverbial expressions characterize maternal milk as an affective ("spiritual") substance. I think, furthermore, that it is not by chance that women have female semen (beer); as we will see, they also have a female penis made for them.

In fact, when asserting effective and affective siblingship, it is more common to stress provenience from the same matrix than a community of seed (capable of mixture and division). Uterine siblings are thought of as parts of a whole and as successive occupants of the same place: they refer to each other as *he kɨre,* "a piece of me"; *he rene'e pe here,* "the one who took my place"; or *he pɨrɨ here,* "the one who substituted me." Those who share only what was given by the same genitor specify their status by the *difference* between their matrices: *hiro amɨ̃te pa re,* "coming from another body." This is an expression of the strong matrifocality of their social life.[3]

As I mentioned earlier, more than one inseminator can cooperate (*oyo pitiwã,* also said of men who open the same garden—a comparison made by the Araweté) or take turns in producing a child, in a process called *dɨ̃ mõ,* to enlarge. The ideal number of genitors seems to be two or three; more than this leads to a painful childbirth or splotchy skin.[4]

When a shaman is conceiving a child, his nightly songs cease. Repeatedly "eating" his wife makes him soft; he sleeps a lot and does not dream. One of the jocular nicknames for the vagina (or for an *apĩhi*) is specifically *aray mo-pẽ hã,* "that which breaks the shaman's rattle"—a rather clear allusion to the phallic quality of the rattle, an instrument of male creativity. Female sexuality not only breaks rattles metaphorically, but also other male objects, literally: when a man is carving a piece of *Tabebuia* wood to make a bow, he must abstain from sex or else the piece will split.

The couple involved in the work of conception observes few precautions during pregnancy. Some will continue after childbirth, when many others will be imposed. They should not eat tapir, since its spirit would trample on the mother's belly; nor should they eat the thighs of deer or curassow, which would weaken the child's legs; nor should the man eat pregnant female animals. They should avoid using maize carried in a basket that has split. Men should be cautious in the forest, since snakes will try to bite them.

Childbirth (*mo-ã,* to cause to fall) usually takes place in the nearby brush. The husband of the woman in childbirth can assist her, picking up (*hopĩ*) the child and cutting the umbilical cord. The placenta is buried where the birth occurred. In most cases, however, the one who picks up the child and cuts the cord is a woman, a relative of the mother or her husband. Ideally, I was told, boys had their cord cut by a woman; girls, by a man. The cutter of the umbilical cord (*ipiri'ĩ kã he re*) has a matrimonial right over the child. If it is a girl, she will be an *ipa̲'ï pi*, "one taken care of": she should be fed by her future husband until puberty, when she will be handed over to him. In the case of boys, they will later on provide their future wives with meat.

Currently, there are no *ipa̲'ï pi* children in the village, but there are various "cutters of the navel cord" who maintain their right to reserve the boy or girl, a right the parents recognize. In all the cases I recorded, they were classificatory mother's brother, father's sister, or grandparents of the children. The woman who lifted up the child does not appear to have any special relationship to him or her; but everyone knows who cut their own navel cord and who lifted them up when born.[5]

As soon as it is born, the infant is bathed in lukewarm water; its father then pierces its ears and shaves any hair that grows beyond the temples. Some experienced person then *mo-katɨ*, "repairs," the child: he or she flattens its nose, bends its ears outwards, massages its chest, plucks its eyebrows, straightens its lower jaw, pushes its arms and fingers towards the shoulders, squeezes its thighs together, and separates its damp hair with a stick.

The parents then enter into seclusion, spending most of their time at home and depending on relatives for certain essential domestic tasks, such as cooking and fetching water. A few hours after the birth, they must drink a bitter infusion of the bark of *iwirara'i* (*Aspidosperma* sp.)—the same that is drunk upon the first menses and the killing of an enemy. This measure would thus appear to be associated with the blood that accumulates in the body during these states, which should be purged. But the Araweté do not explain the practice in this form: they say, rather, that *iwirara'i* should be drunk "in order to eat tortoise," otherwise one may suffocate from a swelling of the glottis. This refers to the red-footed tortoise, a meat prohibited to parents during the couvade, women during their first menses, and killers.[6] All the men who participated in conception should drink the infusion, but only the principal genitor rigorously follows the rest of the restrictions.

On the night after the birth, the mother should undergo an *imone* operation, a shamanic return of the soul to the body. All physical or psychological traumas produce this dangerous liberation of the soul; *imone* is performed "to make the person stay," "to make him/her heavy." But the combination of *imone* with the drinking of *iwirara'i* marks only three particular states: maternity (childbirth), first menses, and homicide.

The postpartum restrictions are varied and taken seriously above all by the parents of a firstborn child. The rules are more rigorous while the navel cord has not yet dried up and fallen off; they begin to relax as the child comes to have a "firm neck," and then relax further when it begins to laugh and to walk. The termination of the restrictions is imprecisely marked; the definitive consolidation of the child takes much longer than the couvade period.

Some of the restrictions aim at protecting the parents themselves, now defined as *ta'i ñã* (the F) and *memi ñã* (the M), "child owners" or "masters of children." They should not expose themselves too much to the sun or moon, or else the excrement of the astral bodies will blacken them; they may not carry water or walk on rocks or rough soil, or else the *Iwirã ñã* spirits and their kind will shoot arrows at their feet. The most important precaution is observed by the father: he may not go to the forest before the navel cord has dried and dropped off, or he will attract multitudes of bushmasters and boa constrictors that will bite him or swallow him alive. This means that the man finds himself unable to exercise the activity that defines his gender identity and his main economic responsibility: hunting.

Other restrictions protect the baby: the parents do not touch mirrors or combs, since this would provoke fever and aches, nor do they touch jaguar skins, since the child's skin would become splotchy. They avoid exertions that may have repercussions on the child: carrying heavy loads, grinding maize, or felling trees.

The restrictions on ingesting substances are more numerous. The parents may not cook or eat hot foods. The mother may not smoke, while the father may do so only through a wad of cotton. In general, a distinction is made between, on the one hand, actions and foods prohibited during the period immediately after the birth until the navel cord drops off, and, on the other, long-term interdictions. The majority of immediate prohibitions (*hopï we*—see note 2) are for the health of the parents (as in the case of red-footed tortoises); all long-term ones are for the protection of the child. Thus, the meat of paca, capuchin monkey, collared peccary, and certain fish (peacock bass, matrinxã, and dogfish) may be consumed only after the child has begun to "laugh"; toucans, macaws, parrots, a type of tinamou, razor-billed curassows, electric eels, and the liver of both species of tortoises may be eaten only after it begins to walk. Pregnant female animals are not eaten until the child is three years old (pregnant women, however, may eat them). Some types of honey are prohibited, since their consumption would produce pustules; papaya would make the child's skin peel off; bacaba palmfruits and two types of yam would cause swelling.

Consuming these meats and performing activities such as boiling or smoking lead to *hapi*, the "burning" of the child. This involves a sort of internal combustion that is manifested as fever, desiccation, and weight loss. The underlying idea seems to be that the newborn is a volatile being who must remain far from contact with hot things. Nor should the child be painted with annatto, lest its skin peel off as if scorched in a fire.[7]

I was unable to discover any principle underlying the foods prohibited to the parents. To the contrary, I was surprised that animals such as piranha, trairão, and foods that are shamanized in *peyo* rites, such as xupé honey and howler monkey, are considered neutral. Notably, with the exception of tortoise (liver), the main animals hunted by the Araweté (especially armadillos and white-lipped peccaries) are not on the list (which I do not believe is an exhaustive one).[8]

While they are still small, children are often made to undergo a shamanic operation that "closes the body" (*hiro rī̵*; cf. rī̵, "to heal over, form scar tissue") or "seals it off" (*hakapetĩ*). Its aim is to permit the parents to gradually resume their activities once again and to prevent the child from suffering "flesh-ache" (*ha'a rahi*). The symbolism is obvious: the child is open and the parents' actions and substances penetrate its body. The treatment is repeated over several months upon any sign that the infant is indisposed, and it is especially necessary when the parents intend to engage in sexual activity and drink strong beer again.

Beer festivals and sex are the object of the strictest prohibitions. Both activities may be pursued only after the child begins to crawl (according to fathers) or to walk (according to mothers). Before this—and even afterwards, if a shaman does not close its body—the infant would die in a fit of convulsions and vomiting. Sexual abstinence seems to be more drawn out for the mother than for the father. The latter, after a few months, may seek out another woman "to cool down." The mother's actions are more directly harmful to the child, who is always clinging to her. Mothers are the ones who take on the task of asking a shaman to close their children's bodies; the reason is that they nurse them. Everything the woman ingests, including semen, passes (*mo-wã*) through her milk. Affect also passes through it: daughters do not marry virilocally and men always return to their village of origin, because "one does not forget the milk one drank." Another proverbial expression is: "She who nursed us makes us nostalgic."[9]

Two weeks after birth, infants begin to eat yams, potatoes, and bananas premasticated by the mother. Manioc, maize, and other fruits and meat are introduced into their diet only when the child is "finished" (*aye*), that is, when it begins to manifest "consciousness." This is when it receives a name and can be painted with annatto, the color of health (sick people must not paint themselves) and humanity. No shamanic operation is linked to the introduction of meat into the diet. Rather, the operations for closing the body were always explained to me as a means of blocking contagions from the parents to the child.

The notion of "having consciousness," the most general translation of the verb *kaakĩ*, defines the degree of the humanity of the infants. It is not the same thing as the ability to speak (*ñe'e*), since it is chronologically prior. It apparently designates the capacity of the child to respond to communicative stimuli; the principal sign of this is the smile. If a baby dies before manifesting consciousness, even its parents will not weep. Speech is nevertheless an important and anxiously awaited sign of maturation. An operation intended to facilitate linguistic learning consists in breaking leaves of the *kã'ã ñe'e ato* bush next to the infant's mouth while words of the language are repeated.

But for a few more years, the personhood of the child is still not entirely stabilized. Its soul/vital principle (*ĩ*) is easily detached from the body, especially by the covetous Master of Water. For this reason, children between one and four years old are frequently made to undergo the *imone* operation, when the shaman brings back the wandering soul and consolidates it (*mo-atĩ*, to harden), making the person heavy (*mo-pohi*) again.

The parents avoid a new conception until their child has reached the age of three or four years, during which time it continues nursing. Until then, they resort to coitus interruptus, the sole birth control method they claim to know (*ta'i re hakawa*, "to spill semen"—a technique which, as far as I know, has only been recorded among the Txicão for Brazilian Indians—Menget 1977: 108).[10] Abortions are provoked by abdominal pressure. But undesired children are usually killed after birth (sometimes having been suffocated by the mother) and buried with the placenta.

There are various reasons for abortion or infanticide: the divorce of the couple during gestation (a rare occurrence); the death of the husband during this period; gestation in young women, who are "too lazy to nurse" and afraid to undergo the restrictions; children conceived or born during epidemics, especially if the parent took medicines from whitemen; deformations of the child (attributed to Western medicines, to the semen of the Master of Water, or left unexplained); a pregnancy that is too premature relative to the prior one; and even quarrels between the spouses, when the wife takes revenge by killing the child. Unmarried women attempt abortion upon the first signs of pregnancy.

Although the Araweté are anxious to space births, they consider having children an essential value. Children are adored and spoiled by the entire village; women and men compete over the privilege of walking about with the newborn on their hips. If a woman dies and leaves behind a small child, others will assume the responsibility of nursing it (in general, a sister of the deceased). Everyone says they prefer male children over female, because men hunt and will provide for the parents when they become old.

From the time they are three years old and begin to exercise autonomy in their movements, children are referred to as *ta'i roho,* "big offspring," or as "little men" and "little women." Between seven and eleven years old, boys are classified as *pɨrɨ ači,* literally, "green (new) people." During this phase, they go out to hunt and fish in the surroundings and accompany their fathers on expeditions preceding beer festivals. They also begin to build their small house next to their parents'. Around twelve years old, it is time for the boy's prepuce to be tied; the penis is already "full" and the glans might be exposed, a cause for shame. A boy's penis cord (a fine strand of cotton) is put on discreetly. Any man who is not his genitor or mother's husband may perform this operation. If the latter do it, they will die of *ha'iwã* illness.

Before wearing the cord, boys must not have sexual relations. Nevertheless, from a young age boys and girls play together, and older girls usually initiate boys into sex. Until puberty, girls are in general considerably more extroverted and bold than boys of the same age.

There is no food prohibition marking male adolescence, except that they have to avoid eating the *yɨrarã* turtle, or they will easily tire when adults. But two musical interdictions are imposed: they may not repeat the songs of the god *Tepere,* or their pubic hairs will not grow; and they may not participate in songs and dances commemorating the death of a jaguar, or the felines will attack them in the forest.

This is extended to the commemorative dances for the death of a human enemy. Unmarried youths may drink beer, but only in small quantities.

Starting at twelve years old, youths initiate a long series of tentative marriages with girls of their age or a little older. Until around fifteen years old, they greatly resist marrying, doing so only when no adult is available who can remove a girl about to have her first menses from the house of her parents. At this time, the girls move into the small houses of the youths. These trials generally do not last more than a few weeks.

Between fifteen and twenty years old, the youths engage in more serious marriages than when they were boys, but these are no less unstable. Few youths have not had at least five wives during this phase—having gone to reside uxorilocally almost every single time. They marry young women their own age and ones who are much older. The matrimonial circulation is very accelerated as the exchanges of spouses among young people undergo cycles almost every year.

From fifteen years old on up to their early thirties, young men are classified as *pɨra'i oho* ("a grown-up child"), a term that continues to describe all men who do not yet have married children. The youngest segment of this category is turbulent and venturesome; it provides numerous *tenotã mõ* for hunting parties and those most disposed to embark on war expeditions. Various shamans belong to the oldest segment of the *pɨra'i oho.*

Men between thirty-five and fifty years old are defined as "ripe" (*dayɨ*). This is the phase when they constitute their extended families, attracting sons-in-law and leaving their own uxorilocal situation. Mature men form an influential segment, especially when they are leaders of important residential sections and when they are shamans. Above this age, they are "elders" (*tapïnã*).

Araweté elders have no special power, but neither are they in a liminal position. The two oldest men of the village still hunted, had large gardens, and had families who helped them. Aya-ro, one of these elders, was still an active shaman, but he did not sing often; his services were solicited mostly for closing the bodies of children and for snakebite cases, operations that do not necessarily involve the presence of gods. The other man, Meñã-no, had already been "left behind by the *Ma̲ï*"—that is, he no longer sang.

Girls between seven and eleven years old are called *kãñĩ na'i roho,* "child woman." Many of them are handed over to an elder or someone who is physically handicapped and unable to obtain an adult wife.

These men "raise" (*ipa'ï*) the girls, initiating them into sexual play.[11] As mentioned earlier, a girl cannot have her menses in her parents' house, lest they suffer the same death by *ha'iwã* that befalls incestuous couples, a father who ties the penis cord on his son, and so on. Thus, her parents must arrange a husband for her quickly.

The Araweté believe that girls only menstruate if they have been previously deflowered (they show no interest in submitting such a dogma to a countertest). The beginnings of the sexual life of *icĩ papa re* girls ("with budding breasts") is conceived of as a time when their bodies are being manufactured by the men. They pierce (*momo*), excavate (*maya*), and fabricate (*mõñĩ*) the vagina and the labia of the vulva. Along with the seminal nurture they receive, the progressive elongation of the labia minora of adolescents is considered essential for their growth and maturation, besides being a favorite technique in the erotic arts. The length of this part of the female anatomy (which is hidden by the girdle) is an obsession peculiar to the Araweté: all men were able to remember the particularities of women who had died a long time ago, and such memories led rapidly into erotic fantasies. I had the distinct impression that having big "little lips" was a measure of a woman's prestige and influence. I recall that one of the nicknames for female souls and female *Maï* was *hamã kɨcã mi re*, "decorated vagina"; this refers to the idea that the large, hanging labia of female gods and deceased women are decorated with fine geometric lines in genipap. The penis, on the other hand, is not the object of special attention in the sky; it is simply reinvigorated as part of the process of rejuvenation.

The labia minora are, in effect, the female analogue of the penis (*nakãy*): the name of the labia minora is *kãñĩ nakãy*, female penis. The penis and labia, moreover, are usually called the "weapons" (*irapã*, bow or shotgun) of each sex.

It seems to me that a series of paradoxes are involved in this symbolic valorization of the labia minora. In contrast to practices of the African type that aim at a maximal differentiation between male and female genitalia—through circumcision and clitoridectomy—the Araweté fabricate a female penis at the same time that they open and enlarge the vaginal canal. It is, moreover, a double penis and incapable of erection (the clitoris—*ičire*, "bud"—is not important in their sexology, as far as I can tell). On the other hand, as in the majority of Lowland South American cultures, the opposite of circumcision is practiced on men: the stretching and binding of the prepuce. But instead of the elaborate penis sheaths of some tribes, the Araweté have a sort of "sheath" of the female penis, the tight girdle, an article of great symbolic importance. Also, in contrast to the conspicuous plugs in men's lower lips among the Gê groups, the female "lowest lips" are kept strictly hidden. The contrast between the sober male nudity and the complicated female clothing among the Araweté is striking to any observer.[12]

The girdle/labia complex marks the female gender by its sexuality. The construction of women's sexuality is the responsibility of men: they cause women to menstruate, which leads to the imposition of the girdle that hides the labia they have stretched. Perhaps in all this there is an obscure relation with another Araweté paradox of gender, seen earlier in the analysis of maize beer. If women have an artificial female semen with which they orally inseminate men (and which is always fabricated by married women and excludes sex and menstruation), it would therefore be logical that men fabricate a female penis on unmarried women, at the same time as they inseminate them naturally, facilitating their menstruation and habilitating them to adult life.

It is also possible that this complex of the female penis is related to the dogma of exclusive masculine conception. Another name for the labia minora is *hapïnã,* which also applies to the two internal sacs in the male body where semen is stored. Does this indicate that the labia have a procreative function?

In any case, if the skirt/girdle and labia complex characterize women, men have its equivalent: the *aray* shamanic rattle. Every married man, shaman or not, has an *aray. Aray ñã,* "masters of the rattle," is a synecdoche for the male portion of society, parallel to that of "masters of the diadem" (see chap. 2, sect. 3). There is no analogue for women, who are instead metonymized by the maternal state, their collective name being "mistresses of children." But the inner girdle, sign of the adult female state capable of procreation, is no less a means of characterizing them. Thus, instead of the Aché bow and basket (P. Clastres 1987: chap. 5), the Araweté gender symbols are the rattle and the girdle: the first, a metaphor of the phallus in both appearance and creative function, owned by every married adult man; the second, a sheath covering the vagina and the female penis, things that "break the rattle" (and the bow) of men.

The manipulation of the labia minora, if done too enthusiastically, can sometimes lead to their being lacerated. The erotic techniques include the plucking of female pubic hairs and caresses that are somewhat violent. The hairs may be saved as a souvenir of a sexual adventure and are occasionally tied to the shaft of arrows, a form of boasting that arouses general curiosity about the identity of the one so honored. And, to bring this fetishistic excursion to a close, it is worth noting that I was once told that nostalgic widowers cut the labia minora of their dead wives, cure them over smoke, and wrap them in cotton. This memorial is kept in the *patọã*, a straw storage box for men's treasures (feathers, earrings, children's hair). I never saw such a memento. *Se non è vero . . .*

Duly deflowered, girls menstruate, *heyi*, a verb meaning simply "descent" (of the blood); the expression *yahi herowarɨ* is also used, "the moon initiated her." Upon the first menstruation, the girl drinks an infusion of *iwɨrara'i* and undergoes the *imone* treatment; besides this, she drinks a mixture of ashes with cold water to prevent excessive bleeding. The flowing blood cools the menstruating girl, who is *hakɨ*, hot. A girl in this condition (in fact, any menstruating woman) cannot take baths in the river—it would cause strong rains—nor have sexual contact, since this would cause *ha'iwã* (illness), but she may cook. The most important sign of the catamenial rite of passage is the imposition of the girdle, woven by her mother, a prospective mother-in-law, or another female relative. The names for this article of clothing are: *tupãy hete*, "true clothing" (in contrast to the external skirt, sling, and head covering); *wɨ hakawa hã*, "blood absorber"; or *ii re*, "inside thing." It cannot be taken off in front of a man without this being interpreted as a sexual invitation.

Prepubescent girls should not eat too many eggs or else they will have multiple births; nor the hearts of turtles, deer, or other game—pieces that usually bleed a lot—or else their menarche will be abundant and painful. They enjoy considerable sexual liberty, usually taking the initiative in such matters. While they are still prepubescent, their parents do not interfere. But when they begin to approach puberty, control over their behavior intensifies. Girls who are especially "prone to wander" (*ɨatã me'e*)—those who circulate in gleeful bands at night—are feared by prospective spouses. Young husbands are extremely jealous of any extramartial affair outside the friendship system, as in the case of sexual adventures by young wives with single youths. Brothers, especially those who still depend on their sisters to obtain a wife, also control their movements.

From puberty until thirty to thirty-five years old, women belong to the class of *kãñĩ moko*, "big women." They marry very young but only begin to bear children relatively late, at about eighteen to twenty years old. The change in lifestyle after the birth of the first child is much more radical for a woman than for her husband. She ceases to be an appendage of her mother and turns towards her own household; she also ceases to belong to the turbulent band of girls, adopting instead a calm and serious attitude, always attentive to the needs of her child. From being the object of her husband's jealousy, she becomes the one who tries to control his adventures. The *memi ñã* (owners of children) are accorded respect, even when young, and the balance of domestic authority tips noticeably to the feminine side after the first child.

Mothers are very zealous of their children, blindly taking their side even when they cause damage to other people's possessions or when they conduct themselves in a manner intolerable to village peace. On the other hand, their parental authority is not much greater than that of the fathers, and both are constantly trying to contain their children, frightening them with tales of *ta̲'o we* (specters of the dead), the *Ãñĩ*, and enemies.

Around thirty-five years and up, women are classified as "adults" (*o̲dï mo-hi re*) and, after menopause, as "elders" (*tapïnã*). Middle-aged women possess enormous influence in daily life. A residential section revolves around the eldest woman and is normally identified by her name. The tendency for the principal couples of the village to be composed of ex-widows who are older than their current husbands only augments the power of these women. Such women, besides having an active voice in village negotiations, are the main source of squabbles and intrigues. It is they, more than their husbands, who argue over the postmarital destinies of young couples. It is very rare to hear men publically expounding their differences or conflicts; on the other hand, ignoring their husbands' cautious aloofness, the five or six grandes dames of the village set the tone of day-to-day life, mobilizing relatives to antagonize some against the others, in an ever-changing system of alliances.

Seen from the village, life is feminine; one could even say that society is feminine—but it is such precisely because it is only part of an encompassing whole from which meaning emanates, and this whole is masculine. If humans were immortal, perhaps society could be confounded with the cosmos. Since death exists, it is necessary for society to be linked with something that is outside itself—and that it be linked *socially* to this exterior. Here is where men enter, charged with two functions that are their exclusive province: shamanism and warfare. In the interior of the *socius*, male authority can only be based on an association with women: the leader of an extended family controls daughters and gardens, feminine things he obtained through his married status. On the other hand, the power of magic and the force of the warrior exist "independently" of women; they express a movement outwards from the *socius,* required because it is necessary to administer (in both senses of the term) death. Finally, negated or disguised in its own domain—the internal elaboration of the social fabric—affinity will be used to domesticate this founding bond, the bond with death and exteriority.

2. Passions

The notion of abstinence, *koako hã,* plays an important role in marking kinship bonds in the context of sickness. The restrictions of the couvade are only part of this more general attitude, involving abstinence from actions that introduce harmful substances or manifest malignant principles in one's own or others' bodies. *Koako hã* is the active and physical counterpart of a psychology of passions, that seeks to thwart sentiments that cause a person to become "estranged from him- or herself." The physiology of abstinence, as well as the psychology of joy, seeks to avoid Illness, *ha'iwã,* that which destroys the health of the body or disrupts the link between body and soul.

A person may undergo abstinence for his own sake (*oyi koako*) or to benefit some relative, such as a newborn child, a sick sibling, or an ailing parent. The object of all abstinence is anything said to be *me'e a'ï:* actions that may cause harm to newborns, certain foods (especially meats), and sex. Although the verb *koako* is used for all types of abstinence, its focus appears to be the complex of "eating": nourishment and sex. The *a'ï*-thing par excellence is the vagina, and sexual activity is designated in general by a negative circumlocution: *koako ï,* "to unabstain."

Violating the couvade abstinence, as we saw, precipitates the baby's death through a fiery desiccation or suffocation by beer and semen. When the abstinence concerns an adult relative, the effects are more varied. Meats such as trumpeter bird, deer, tapir, tinamou, or razor-billed curassow, if ingested by the relative of an ill person (a fortiori by the latter) can provoke weakness in the legs (in the case of the first two kinds of meat), strong pains in the belly (the third), and deafness (the last ones). When the disease is grave, the result of incontinence is death by *ha'iwã.* The same effect results from sex, if it is practiced during illness or while a close relative is sick: *tamã bïde rero-kãñĩ*— the vagina kills us (literally, "it makes us get lost"). Some of the above foods liberate a malignant agent, the *ha'o we* (spirit) of the animal. Thus, the Araweté say that when we suddenly become sick, *me'e ra'o we bïde reti,* "the spirit of something is pummeling us"; this can always be attributed to the incontinence of some relative, if not to our own. Another dangerous thing to ingest is any animal found dead in the forest; this provokes dizziness and fainting among the kindred.

This community of similars is thus defined by a negative norm: *oyi koako me'e,* "the interabstainers." To this circle belong the *bïde dĩ,* one's equals: parents, children, siblings. Spouses are not obliged to interabstain; being by definition an *amĩte,* what a spouse does or eats will not affect the health of the other (except, of course, sexual relations). All *close* classificatory consanguines are interabstainers. It becomes clear that here the circle of abstinence coincides with that of incest; the boundaries of the first are as fluid as those of the second, depending on the gravity of the relative's disease, the actual or affective distance of their relations, and so on.[13] An infraction of abstinence can affect nonsubstantial relatives, understood in the strict sense: thus, the death of a man in 1980 was associated with the fact that his wife's daughter had had sexual relations when he was sick (even though he was not her father or father's brother). Similarly, if a girl menstruates in her natal house, it may kill her mother's husband, no matter who he is.

The paradigms for similarity and abstinence are small children and the couvade. The Araweté always resorted to this context to explain the reasons for abstinence in cases of illness: an invalid is like a baby, since he is weak and his soul is not firm (he is in a "lightweight" state). Note that husband and wife abstain at the same time only on behalf of their children. In turn, a child's responsibility to abstain on behalf of a sick father or mother is strongly emphasized and is conceived as the counterpart (*pepi kã*) of the couvade.

Referring above all to sex, abstinence includes the period of menstruation, the occasion when sex becomes, so to speak, potentialized. Although the *ha'iwã* illness that befalls infractors (the man *and* the woman) is in this case attributed to the blood, it punishes other sexual infractions in which blood does not appear: contact with a son's penis while binding the prepuce, incest, or sex during illness. Sex is the principal *causa mortis* when *koako* rules are not observed. During the epidemic of 1982, all sexual activity ceased for two months.

The generic term for illness is *me'e rahi,* "pain." The causes of illness are many: whitemen, the present locale of the Araweté on the edge of the earth, mist over a river at dawn, spirits of ingested animals, arrows of tortoise and honey, contagion by a pain substance (*hahi we*) present in beer and rotten things (especially graves). But no one dies *of* a disease. There are many material causes of death, but the efficient cause of all deaths, other than those derived from enemy arrows or assaults by the *Ãñĩ*, is *ha'iwã*, a term that designates Illness, that which removes the person from the state of *hekawe*, life.[14] *Ha'iwã* entails sudden weight loss and internal combustion. All "nonartifical" deaths can be attributed to a *ha'iwã*-effect produced by some agent or action. Those with which I am familiar include: the spirit of the trumpeter bird, if this animal is eaten in any form other than roasted; incest (which also provokes enemy attacks); the menarche in the natal house; sex with menstruating women or during illness; copulation with the Master of Water; the incorrect burial of the dead, with excessive handling of the corpse; certain dangerous musical emissions; the sky and the *Ma̱ï*.

The mention of the sky as *ha'iwã hã*, lethal, is somewhat obscure to me. It appears to refer to a type of cause of death in which the sky rumbles and opens, fulminating the victim, but such a type gets confounded with deaths caused by *tatã na'iwã hã*, the invisible celestial fire of the gods hurled against the living. This divine fire (which has nothing to do with lightning) is blamed for every death without an obvious immediate cause—even for those for which the efficient causes were diseases brought by whites. In truth, every death is the result of this kind of divine *ha'iwã*: the passage from the state of the living to that of the dead—death as an ontological alteration—is caused by the celestial fire of the *Ma̱ï*. For that matter, reasoning in the Azande mode, the Araweté muse that everyone gets sick, but the only ones who die are those who are struck by the *Ma̱ï đatã*, divine fire. The sky and the gods are thus the ultimate *ha'iwã* behind every efficient cause, be it arrows, capture by *Ãñĩ*, or *ha'iwã* caused by other sources.

To the extent that it is possible to compare the Araweté's causal system (which I only understand imperfectly) with our own (which is admittedly quite foreign to theirs), I would suggest that the *Ma̱ï* (and their fire) are the final (and efficient) cause of every death. Even further, the gods are the formal cause of death: immortal themselves, it is they who define humans as mortals, hence, it is they who kill us, revealing our essence. Finally, the idea that the sky is lethal in itself (as distinct from the divine celestial fire) is associated with the feared apocalypse when the firmament will break open and annihilate humanity (see chap. 3, sect. 1). Some say that every death is caused by both the divine fire and a sudden opening and closing of the sky. This is another way of indicating that the human predicament, that is, mortality, is the inevitable correlate of the "forsaken" condition of all terrestrial beings, those left behind in the original separation.

I discussed with the Araweté the singular paradox of deriding the

Maï as "eaters of raw flesh" or "beings bereft of fire" (see chap. 3, sect. 2) and at the same time attributing to them the power of this lethal fire. They explained to me that the fire the gods were ignorant of was cooking fire, while this celestial fire was their own kind (*e'e apa te*), inherent in their *aray* rattles and the shininess of their bodies.[15]

□

The attitude expressed in *koako* points to another concept, that of *kaakĩ hã*, "consciousness." *Kaakĩ* is a verb that signifies thinking, remembering, knowing, manifesting intentionality; prefixed with the causative *mo-*, it connotes ideas such as evoking and convincing. The attribute *kaakĩ hã* appears to play the same role in Araweté psychology as the notion "word-soul" does for the Guarani (*ayvu, ne'e*). Its corporal seat lies in the chest and ears: it is thus associated with the soul/vital principle, which, when present in the chest, marks the normal state of the person (health and alertness); its link with the ears is underscored in the expression *apihã-ĩ*, "deaf," used to describe someone who is acting erroneously or who is beside himself with rage. *Kaakĩ-ĩ*, "unconscious," refers as much to people in shock as to children before they begin to react to deliberate stimuli. Anyone who is not yet conscious or who has fallen unconscious is in danger: either he is not yet a complete human being or he is on his way towards ceasing to be one, since his vital principle is poorly attached to the body.

Certain emotional states cause the *kaakĩ hã* to leave the body. Anger is one of them. When someone is *ñarã*, irate, he hears the noise of babassu palmfruits falling, the sun appears red, and his throat closes. Four types of beings are especially prone to anger: enemies, killers of enemies, the *Maï*, and the recently deceased. Shamans are constantly singing about the anger of the *Maï* and the necessity of placating them, embracing them, and thus "cutting" (*mo'ĩ*) their anger.

Another dangerous state is nostalgia for a loved one. In such a case, our *kaakĩ hã* exits, we are "somewhere else" (*ĩẽ te ete*), our thoughts "make us reach" the place where their object is found, and the sun looks red to us. This is why the recent dead are dangerous: already beside themselves with anger over their death and angrily coveting their relatives left behind, they *mo-a'o* ("make absent" or "spiritualize") the living, causing them to become estranged from themselves. The dead, celestial gods, and absent beings in general have this power of making others self-estranged through the affective suction they exert. Sadness or mourning (*ho'irã*), a sentiment close to nostalgia, makes us lose the indispensable fear of the dead and renders us liable to follow them. A person who is sad is "empty," his soul having left his body.

Sexual desire, *ha'irã*, is another passion that leaves us unconscious. It is related to wrath: an erect penis is an "angry penis." It is said jokingly that female desire is the equivalent of homicidal rage—it is no accident, then, that women have their weapons.[16]

Of all these passions, nostalgia and sadness are unambiguously negative. These two feelings place someone in a particular psychophysical state. Sadness and nostalgia make us lightweight, *mo-wewe*, and make us transparent, *mo-kɨyaha*. The first notion can be found in other Tupi-Guarani psychologies (Kracke 1978: 25, 280); the second is apparently exclusive to the Araweté. The term *kɨyaha* has an ample spectrum of meaning: it can be glossed as diaphanous, open, exterior, and insomniac. The state of *kɨyaha* suggests a transluscence produced by the exiting of the soul. Being lightweight indicates the same thing: the soul, like a balloon attached by a fine cord to its corporal ballast, risks getting loose and floating away.

Such states of being can be provoked by other factors: strong, sudden frights, too much sun, certain Western medicines, birth, the first menstruation, or homicide. All of these unfasten the *ĩ* from the *hiro*, the soul from the body. The *imone* operation (a term referring to the act of carrying something protectively, shielded from harm, used here for bringing the soul in the *aray* rattle) seeks to make a person "heavy" and "hard" again. It is always undertaken when a shaman sees a soul wandering in the sky or when a patient is wasting away and listless. The most frequent object of this intervention are children up to three years old and women; I never saw it performed for a man. Children are always on the verge of losing their unstable souls; women are coveted by the *Maï* who try to capture them. This is why women may not be shamans: the gods would not let their souls return from the sky.

While heaviness and opacity characterize the healthy state by imparting density and substance to the person (preventing him from becoming a body without a soul, a *ta'o we*), lightness and transparency are states sought by shamans, who are the only ones who can attain them without risk. For this they use tobacco, which "refines" them and makes them "lightweight." The shaman is a man capable of controlling the connection between soul and body, becoming disembodied actively, not passively.[17]

The sentiment that makes us heavy and dense is joyfulness, *tori*. It makes us forget (*mo-raarãy*) absent people and returns us to society. This is why *apĩhi-pihã* always intervene after a partner has been mourning for a few weeks, in order to cheer him up; the *apĩhi* is also the main pacifier of a killer overcome with fury (induced by the dead enemy). Also, it is the friends of the dead in the sky, the gods and goddesses, who make them forget the living, "breaking their sadness."

Joyfulness is thus associated with the capacity to forget—an essential theme in the relationship between the living and the dead—and with sexuality. Although sex involves a state of "unconsciousness," it is positive in that it brings joy; although it is *me'e a'ï*, dangerous, it is also what makes us weighty. Its ambivalence does not lack parallels with anger, a disembodying passion, but also an affirmative impulse. Sexual desire and anger, moreover, characterize the *Ma̲ï*.

3. Death

Manĩ, to die, refers to all loss of *kaakĩ hã* consciousness: drunkenness from beer, tobacco narcosis, shamanic accidents (when the gods knock out the shaman), traumas such as illness and grave wounds, and the temporary situation of a slayer. Rushing things, the Araweté decree that people in such states are "dead" (*imanĩ če*), even though they may be far from it. One time, a simple conjugal brawl was amplified to such a point that news reached the other side of the village in minutes that so-and-so had been torn to pieces by his wife. Another case I witnessed was that of a woman, very ill with pneumonia, whose wardrobe was divided up by her weeping sisters. When she recovered, she had quite the chore recouping her belongings.

One of the principal characteristics of humans, however, is that they do not "truly die," even when they truly die. An actual death is simply a more violent instance, from a certain point of view, among the many deaths and resurrections that a person suffers. From a certain point of view—that of the dead person, since for the living, it is a serious matter.

Accordingly, various euphemisms are used to mention the fact of death: "He got tired," "she got lost," "he went to join the gods," or "she went to the place of the good life" (*teka katɨ we*). The precise moment of corporal death is associated with the loss of cardiac pulsations (*ɨpa-ɨpa me'e*) and respiration (*pitowo*), both signs of the *ĩ*, the soul/vital principle. Death overcomes the person either when the shaman is no longer able to keep the *Ma̲ï* at a distance, who come down to earth in their vehicle, the *ĩã* (something similar to a canoe, but made of cotton) to fetch the dying person, or when the shaman is no longer able to keep the corporal envelope sealed, letting the soul escape.

No one likes to approach a dying person, fearing some harmful *hai'iwã.* The corpse is an *a'ï*-thing and is guarded from the view of "owners of children," especially mothers. Only very close relatives and the spouse will embrace the invalid out of grief. After death has been pronounced, the displays of sorrow are quite discreet, limited to a short, low weeping by the deceased's spouse, siblings, and *apĩhi-pihã.* The entire village gathers in silence in the patio of the stricken house and, at a prudent distance ("just like when the gods come to eat"), behold the preparation of the cadaver by the siblings and spouse. Despite their evident consternation, everyone makes an effort to minimize the importance of the event. Phrases addressed to no one in particular are exchanged in that same neutral tone with which women repeat the words of shamanic songs (see chap. 5, sect. 1): "Who said anyone really dies?"; "He was simply carried away by the *Maï*; soon he'll marry in the sky and then come back to take a walk on the ground he used to tread, when he'll eat with us."

The body is carried out of the house to the patio, where it is handed over to a relative (a sister of the deceased or of his/her spouse, or the mother, if it was a child that died) who daubs it was annatto, coats its hair with eagle down, and puts earrings on it. Then, wrapped up in an old hammock, the corpse is quickly transported to the burial site in the *ɨwehe* style: the burden is supported on the carrier's back, with the ends of the hammock coming over his shoulders and grasped together in front—the same way that maize, game, and older children are carried. Ideally, the ones who transport and bury a man are his brothers; in the case of a woman, her husband (or father, if she was single). A man who performs such a service for his brother can claim a right to succeed to the dead man's widow.

Deceased children who did not yet have a name are buried inside or nearby the house; those who were a little older are buried in the nearby brush. Adults are interred at least five hundred meters from the village along a hunting path that henceforth will be abandoned. Although the death of a small baby arouses little emotion, its burial may draw many people; by contrast, the retinue for the funeral of an adult is small. When Awara-hi was buried, the adult members of her section attended: her husband, who carried her corpse, a brother and sister of his, one of her sisters, and the sister's husband. One of her "brothers" who was married to a "sister" of her husband, as well as an *apĩhi-pihã* couple, came from other sections. In general, a minimum of people get involved in the event. It was common, as I came to see, to ask the employees of the FUNAI Post to perform some of the main steps—opening the grave, carrying the body—for deaths that had occurred since contact.

Circular graves are opened (unless the hole left by a rotted tree is utilized), and lined with old *tipe* mats. The cadaver, wrapped in the hammock, is laid on its side with the legs flexed, one arm under the head and the other crossed over the chest—the position used by the Araweté when they lie down on the ground. The face should be turned towards the setting sun, but it does not matter on which side the deceased rests. Another old mat or cloth is placed over the body and it is covered with earth. Graves are rather shallow.

A few objects are placed in the grave—a mirror, comb, machete, some clothes—which will be useful in the afterlife. A small fire is lit by the side of the tomb to keep away coatimundis (necrophagous animals and the favorite game of the *Ãñĩ*) and to illuminate the dark path to the sky.

If the deceased was an "owner of children," especially a mother, the grave is not covered with earth; it is closed with a framework of lashed poles similar to the racks used for smoking meat. Without it, they say, the earth would weigh down on the chest of the deceased's child. Such a framework is called the "grill of the *Ãñĩ*," since these spirits gather around it at night to devour the corpse. The grill is a typical feature of the *Ãñĩ*, who are *me'e hehi a re*, "eaters of the roasted."

A curious system of permutations can be seen here. The "grill of the *Ãñĩ*" is an antigrill, where the meat is underneath the rack and the fire above; and it is rotting, not roasting—a caricature of the human method. For its part, the epithet "eaters of the roasted" corresponds in a no less paradoxical way to "eaters of the raw," which refers to the *Maï*—who eat celestial souls that are boiled, not raw, and who afterwards resuscitate them so they will become incorruptible. There is a play between the oppositions of rotten and boiled, on the one hand, and the roasted and the raw, on the other, and between literal and metaphorical modes of cannibalism.[18]

The death of Awara-hi, as an "owner of children," required a shamanic intervention. Bringing up the end of the funeral procession was one of her sons, who carried her small daughter Awara as far as the edge of the forest; there, the shaman Yiriñato-ro performed an *Awara mo'ï*, the "separation of Awara," in order to prevent the girl from following her mother into death. The movements of the *aray* rattle, sweeping from above to below in order to cut the space between the girl and her mother, were evocative of the rupture of invisible bonds—done, I was told, "because of the milk" (see above, sect. 1).

A few months after the burial, the graves are reopened "to look at the cranium," that is, to make sure that the soft parts of the corpse have disappeared. The graves of "owners of children" are exposed sooner; even the wooden framework weighs down upon the children. In the case of Awara-hi, I was told that, since it had rained a great deal in the weeks following her death, the body decomposed rapidly. I was invited to attend a periodic inspection of the grave, which had been exposed while I was in the city. The couple who undertook the task (the man being a classificatory brother of the deceased) spent a long time stirring the bones around with a stick, looking for signs of predators, verifying that the bones were free of flesh, and reflecting on the remains: "Here is the *hiro pe* ('ex-womb') of Tato-awĩ, Morekati, Awara . . . ," recalling that these children had emerged from those pelvic bones. Such inspections are the fruit of curiosity mixed with nostalgia, as well as a means of guaranteeing that the flesh has disappeared; they are dangerous in cases of recent deaths.[19]

With the passage of time, the graves that have been exposed and left open are regarded with indifference, as are the remains of the skeleton. In the middle of a garden cleared in November 1982 was the open grave of a man who had died five years earlier; the children of the garden owner played there, once they had lost their fear of the bones.

The period following the death of an adult is extremely dangerous. A death triggers the immediate flight and dispersal of the villagers into the forest, from which they will not return until at least a month has gone by; they stay in the forest "until the body is finished." As I stated earlier, the Araweté said that a village was definitively abandoned when it was struck by a death, which does not seem very likely. What can be verified is that the temporary dispersal into the forest is respected to this day. The path leading to the tomb is avoided for a long time and comes to be called by the name of the deceased.[20]

Such abandonment of the village and the fear that descends upon everyone after the burial, especially at night, contrasts sharply with the show of indifference during the moments of death and the exposure of the body. If on these occasions what is sought is some means of marking the nonessential character of death, such an attitude gives way to a barely contained panic as soon as the body exits from the scene. When I returned from the burial of Awara-hi, not a living soul could be seen outside the houses. For several days afterwards, flu symptoms were matched by profound melancholy: many said they were dying "like Awara-hi" and "because of Awara-hi." Since everybody was too sick to go out to the forest and the head of the FUNAI Post insisted they stay, no dispersal took place this time, but for an entire month no one went out to the patios at night.

Fleeing from the village is compared to the dispersal prompted by an enemy assault and by the arrival of the cannibal *Iaracĩ*. In the case of death, everyone flees the *ta'o we*, the cadaver's double, the malignant specter that wanders in the vicinity of the grave and in the village at night, throwing stones at the living, grabbing them with its cold hands, and paralyzing them with terror. During the dispersal, shamanic songs and sexual activity come to a halt. The *Maï* are said to be furious; they close off the eastern path to the sky, as if this route and the western one where the dead ascend could not operate at the same time. Sex is banished as if a superdisease coupled the deceased with all the survivors, except that here it acts to the contrary: sex would kill the healthy. Finally, while the gods close themselves off, the *Ãñĩ* exhibit intense rage in the forest camps; the shamans do battle every night to kill them. Death is a cosmic catastrophe that disorganizes everything: humans go to the forest, the path to the sky closes, the *Ãñĩ* multiply, and an ex–fellow human, the deceased, becomes a dangerous enemy.

Decorating and interring the cadaver convey the right to inherit a few possessions of the deceased; these objects are *naĩ me'e* (a term I do not know how to translate), relics kept "in order to weep." Only consanguines may keep them, but I observed that the belongings of dead persons could be found dispersed to some degree throughout the village. Ideally, the bow of a man passes to a brother or son; the clothes of a woman, to her sisters or daughters. Notably, in contrast to the majority of Amazonian peoples (see Albert 1985 for an analysis of the Yanomami case), the Araweté show no desire to extinguish the material traces of the deceased; just as his name is evoked, so too his belongings are not destroyed, and he will return in the shaman's songs.

Two objects, however, can never be inherited because they cannot be owned by more than one person: a woman's girdle and a man's *aray* rattle. Dead women are buried with their girdle (and old clothes); the *aray* is left hanging inside the deceased's house, "so people will know." If it was a shaman who died, his house is demolished with his rattle inside. The girdle and the *aray* are *itoyo me'e rĩ*, "things that will rot"—things that should rot. We can see here how these two articles, sexual emblems of the two genders, are also nontransferable emblems of individual singularity. They indicate the nature of that which *should* disappear—all that concerns the terrestrial portion of the person and what is incarnated in the *ta̲'o we,* the specter.

The period of mourning is marked not by any formal termination but, rather, by a gradual extinguishing of sadness. A mourner ("a sad one") does not paint himself, sing, or have sexual relations. Little by little he resumes all such activities, thanks especially to the diligence of his *apĩhi-pihã.* When shamans begin to *mo-ñĩña,* "make him sing," referring to the celestial spirit of the deceased, it is a sign that he is already installed in his new status, his anger has passed, and the terrestrial specter is gone. The "secondary funeral rites" are over, having been performed in both the sky and the forest. As an imprecisely defined process—the Araweté decidedly abhor drastic cuts in the flow of things—the consolidation of the soul and the dissolution of the specter are concomitant and progressive phenomena. It is not enough for the shaman to merely make the deceased sing for the first time, or for the families to return to the village when they think the *ta̲'o we* has gone away, in order for equilibrium to be restored. Time, more than ritual, heals the wound.

The deceased is remembered for a long time and for any reason. Years later, a relative may suddenly recollect him. Then a low, grievous weeping can be heard from within the house, along with the lamenting repetition of the loved one's name. It is difficult to forget the dead—since only the dead forget.

4. Only the Bones Forget

Death disperses: both society, which abandons the village, and the person, who fragments. *Ɨmanĩ đïđĩ bïde ɨwawa kã:* "As soon as they die, humans divide." The components of the person take diverse directions and are submitted to new deaths and new syntheses. The motif governing such transformations is a generalized cannibalism. While it cannot be said that the Araweté consider every death to be a cannibal act, as the Yanomami do, every death nevertheless unleashes a series of cannibal acts.

In its general lines, the conception of death closely follows the Hertzian canon (1960 [1907]), especially in the connection between states of the body, soul, and society, and in the ambiguous situation of the person up to the point when natural and social processes resynthesize what death disaggregated. Although Araweté ideas about these matters are distinct, their particular concepts are obscure and, being few, are endowed with a polysemy that makes them difficult to translate. With this necessary proviso—that terms such as "body," "soul," "shadow," and "vital principle" are rather inappropriate—let us explore how death leads to a logical and literal analysis of the person.

The person decomposes into three elements: the corpse, the terrestrial specter, and the celestial spirit. The first—*te'õ me'e*, "dead thing"; *hete pe*, "ex-body"; or *hiro pe*, "ex-container"—is what rots. The body, or rather, the part of the person that is transformed into a cadaver, is referred to as *itoyo me'e rĩ*, "that which will rot."[21] But this does not mean it is not devoured. Rotting is the visible sign of a shamanic cannibalism conducted by the *Ãñĩ* and by *Iwi yari*, Grandmother Earth. The former roast the corpse, the latter boils it. If the matter is pursued in greater depth, the Araweté say that these beings eat the image (*ĩ*) of the body; what consumes its material is the earth or the "flesh of the earth" (*iwi ra'a*). "Flesh of the earth" means the physical materiality of the earth, as opposed to its eponymic spirit. Such distinctions are analogous to that present in the *peyo:* the gods shamanically eat the *ĩ* of the food, while humans eat the flesh (*ha'a pe*).[22]

The corpse and its rotting are thus the site of a cannibal transubstantiation. Although the *Ãñĩ* and *Iwi yari* are not derided as "eaters of the rotten" (like vultures), since they roast or boil the flesh, they are nonetheless *me'e ɨmanĩ če a re*, "eaters of things (found) dead"; in other words, they are necrophagous, a contemptible form of predation, opposed to the nobility of the hunter, who, like the *Ma̲ï*, kills what he eats.

Another circumlocution to designate the physical (living) body is *iwi pipe hã nĩ*, "what will go inside the earth." *Pipe* is a locative connoting interiority; *he pipe* designates as much "my house" as it does "my grave." *Iwi pipe hã* are terrestrial beings, as opposed to birds and inhabitants of the sky. Humans are in general *iwi pipe hã*, but only fully so when they are dead. Death "divides the person in the middle" (*bïde ɨweyere*): one part is of the earth (*iwi apa*) and will go inside it; the other is celestial (*iwã hã*). The living are thus found between the bowels of the earth and the other side of the sky (*iwã haipi ti*, the world of the gods), residing upon this fine membrane, the ground: "We are in the middle."

The period of the rotting of the body corresponds to the time that the village disperses to the forest and to the reign of the *ta̲'o we*, the specter. Some people assert that the specter rises up (*ɨpoĩ*, a verb with an aggressive connotation; see chap. 4, sect. 3) at the time and place of death; others say it does so at the gravesite.

"Specter" is a poor translation. Although it is called (like the corpse) a *hete pe*, ex-body, and *bïde pe*, ex-person, the *ta̲'o we* is not an immaterial entity: it *is* a body in the physical sense of the term, a *hiro*, endowed with materiality and form. *Hiro* is here opposed to the notion of the *ĩ* as a shadow or incorporal image. If the specter is a representation of the dead person, it is a free representation, endowed with a modicum of being of its own: the *ta̲'o we* is a double.[23] A figuration of the invisible, what the *ta̲'o we* incarnates is death itself. The specter is not a double of the person, but of the cadaver—of the deceased as the nonliving or nonpresent.

A semantic digression: one time, returning from the city, I found out that something had disappeared from my house. Resignedly, I commented that my *ta̲'o we* was surely the thief (since the living who are absent can also liberate the specter, as we will see), but others countered, "*Te, hiro*," "No, it really was a person." *Hiro*, body, is here being used in opposition to *ta̲'o we*; nevertheless, what defines a *ta̲'o we* is that it is a *hiro*, a real thing, not an image (*ĩ*). *Hiro*, like *ĩ*, has a positional meaning. A living person is a *hiro* in opposition to a specter; a specter is a *hiro* in opposition to an *ĩ*-image; and an image is a *hiro* in opposition to that which has neither form nor cause, that which is subjective. Thus, when I asked if the shamanic songs were taught to novices by elders, I was told, "Not at all; the gods are not inside our flesh, they are *hiro*." This meant that the songs, in manifesting the objective presence of the gods, were not the product of the shaman's mind (of the flesh, as they say), but of the very existence of the *Ma̲ï*. What is "inside the flesh" (*ha'a iwe*) is sensation, memory, and spontaneous sentiments lacking an external cause (a person who is in a bad mood without any reason is said to be angry inside his flesh). In turn, although what ascends to the skies is our *ĩ*, there it becomes a *hiro*, a body that is fully real. The concept of *hiro* (a generic term for any container) thus connotes the objective mode of existence, reality. But reality may be more or less real, as the contrastive use of the term *hiro* suggests.

The *ta̲'o we* is a body, rather than something that has a body; it is a pure in-itself, a body reduced to the state of an object without a subject. It is generated from the *ĩ* of the living, the visible shadow of the body, also called *ta̲'o we rĩ*, "what will become a specter." A paradoxical object, the *ta̲'o we* is a body generated by a shadow; it is the inverse of the living, whose body projects a shadow that is servile to it. The *ta̲'o we* is a free-moving shadow, projected by an immobile dead body.

After the specter emerges—a movement signalled by the wind or the flight of blue-headed parrots—it begins to wander in the forest. It tries to follow the footsteps of the villagers in flight. The specters of deceased shamans have the peculiarity of singing and shaking the *aray,* but such songs are mere repetitions of what the shaman sang when alive, never a new manifestation of the *Ma̲ï.* All other specters simply emit a syncopated, hoarse sound. They have cold hands, bulging eyes, and bare foreheads (in contrast to the living, who always make sure their bangs cover their foreheads).[24] They may suddenly appear before people and throw rocks and sticks at them. Although their appearance can kill through fright or contamination (a type of illness that makes us *mo-a̲'o we,* turn into a specter), they are not intentional assassins. They manifest a kind of viscosity, adhering to the living in an automatic way; they are grotesque and repetitive caricatures, bearing none of the deceased's attributes other than occasionally a deformed version of his appearance. Nevertheless, it is said that a specter is ferocious and that it adheres to the living out of rage at having died and out of *haihï,* "jealousy" of, or displeasure in being separated from, its relatives, especially its spouse and children. None of this means that the specter has consciousness: it is a living dead that reacts mechanically.

After a death, rarely does a day pass without someone running into a specter wandering in the forest or the village, or even emanating from the domestic fire as a small image. The *ta̲'o we* are proteiform, and the fact of being the "ex-body" of the deceased does not impede them from appearing in the form of some animal, sound, or movement; they grow and shrink, penetrating the smallest slits in the walls. A specter may in fact be anything whatsoever, less the person proper.

The specter is furthermore defined as "the companion of the *Ãñĩ,*" "the fire-bearer of the *Ãñĩ,*" bearing the torch of these spirits in their nightly forays. Specters eat coatimundis, like their masters. Although they are not properly *Ãñĩ*—they do not "become *Ãñĩ*" like the celestial souls "become *Ma̲ï*"—they do belong to the universe of these beings. (The necrophagy of the *Ãñĩ* is purely destructive and their connection to the liberation of the specter is not clear; if it is so connected, it is redundant, since the specters are active during the rotting of the body. Celestial cannibalism, on the other hand, is the condition of immortalization.)

Specters have a limited life span. Their death coincides with the disappearance of the soft parts of the cadaver. After a period of wandering, the *ta̱'o we* undertakes a solitary journey towards the deceased's birthplace. Arriving there, it extinguishes itself, "transforming itself into something similar to a dead opossum." Such a destiny is a redundant image of rottenness: the corpse of a stinking and rotten animal, a double corruption. The *ta̱'o we* takes over the rottenness and incarnates it: it ends up as the simulacrum of a dead opossum, the imprecise remains of nothing.

The journey to the deceased's village of origin thus retraces the route taken by the living person in the opposite direction. It separates the living and the dead: the first leave the villages where the dead have been interred; the second return to the villages where they were born. In the vacuum left by this double dispersal remains the abandoned village, henceforth named for the deceased who is buried there. To live is to leave behind the dead: "*Ta̱'o we ɨre račipe*," "The specters are behind our backs," chronologically and geographically speaking.

Despite the association of the specter with the deceased of whom it is the double, it has something impersonal about it. Although its appearance is reminiscent of the deceased (and then, not always), its actions are typical of any specter whatsoever. Although it is highly mobile, it manifests a diminished being if compared to the living: a *ta̱'o we* does not act, it merely repeats.

The extinction of the specter liberates another double, even more distant from its origin: the *apoyiči*, the night monkey (gregarious and noisy monkeys of the Cebidae family, with bulging eyes and speckled faces). These small animals are considered to be manifestations of the dead. It is said that as soon as the *ta̱'o we* leaves for the deceased's village of origin, the *apoyiči* appear in the vicinity of the grave. The shadow cast by our hands is the "future night monkey." The shadow that generates the specter is the silhouette of the entire body; the shadow of the hand, part of an extinct part, generates this final avatar. Night monkeys are nicknamed "moonlight killers" or "crest of the *Ãñĩ*," since they perch on the heads of these spirits. They suffocate sleeping people.[25]

The impersonal nature of the *ta̱'o we* and *apoyiči* is associated with a notion of multiplicity. To each dead person there does not actually correspond *one* specter and *one* night monkey; this last animal is always thought of as part of a band. The specter, for its part, is a principle of plurality. Proteiform, it is also ubiquitous. "There are many *ta̱'o we* of a person," I was told, when I tried to correlate an individual and his double. The specter is thus the opposite of an individual image: a double, it is multiple.

□

The *ta'o we* is the mark of an absence, hence the living can also generate one. When someone goes out on a long expedition in the forest, his house becomes full of specters that make noise and break and rob things. These phenomena are all ascribed to the absent person. One time when the entire village went to fish in a nearby lake, someone made a comment about the commotion and animation in the clearing where we rested: "Tonight this place is going to be full of *ta'o we* [after we leave]." When a child is thwarted by his parents, his *ta'o we* commits small acts of revenge, such as digging up potatoes in the garden and throwing palmfruits against the walls of houses. The *ta'o we*, in this case, marks the insistence of an unsatisfied desire—a psychological absence, so to speak. People who are gravely ill also liberate specters, through which they reveal their proximity to death.

All of these spectral manifestations of absent beings occur outside their consciousness or will: one knows nothing about one's own *ta'o we*. It is intrinsically unconscious; I would even say it corresponds closely to the Freudian unconscious in its exteriority to the subject, its relationship to desire, its inherence in the body, and its compulsion to repeat. The specter is *bïde pe* in the strong sense: an ex-person, separated from itself, absent.

The *ta'o we*, in sum, is something that, rather than existing, inheres or subsists on the surface of reality, in the manner of the "incorporeal" entities of ancient Stoicism (Deleuze 1990:4–11). It is a sterile shadow of an absent body, projected by memory, the effect of a cause that derives its effectiveness from acting *in absentia*. It is something from the past, which pertains to negative repetition. It is at one and at the same time a death instinct manifesting itself in the compulsion to repeat and a marginal persistence of life, a kind of incarnated death throe.

A shadow of memory—not, as the Araweté theory would have it, the memory of the dead person, but rather, the memory of the survivors. Small children do not spawn specters when they die (nor are they devoured in the sky). Their deaths cause little commotion and subsequently little fear: someone who has lived little does not leave marks in memory, prompt weeping, or persist in the world. On the other hand, the death of a person who is aged and important produces specters that are especially conspicuous and dangerous, a function of the size of the gap they fill.[26] Araweté psychological fetishism attributes to the deceased an effect that in truth is generated by and for social consciousness: it is absence, not the absent, that brings forth the specter. Yet again we can see the analogy of the *ta̲'o we* to the unconscious: individual but impersonal, it expresses the libido of others. The specter is where the person is not: it is an antisubject, impersonal and unconscious. The ones who generate someone's *ta̲'o we* are others, but the blame falls on him.

An Araweté proverb says: *Bïde čĩ ñẽ'ẽ mo-kãñi,* "Only the bones forget" (literally, "[Dead] people's bones lose speech"). It is used whenever someone alleges to have forgotten an important fact in his own life, especially past love affairs and long-dead *apïhi-pïhã* relationships. The living do not forget, since *kaakɨ hã* memory remains deeply embedded in their flesh, *ha'a iwe* (delightfully appropriate to carnal affairs). Only the bones forget because what remembers is the flesh; memory is an attribute and a burden of the living. The rotting of the flesh is the disaggregation of the deceased's memory, the "dual and painful" work of oblivion (Hertz 1960: 86), the reciprocal forgetting of the living and the dead. Thus, it is only after the flesh has decomposed that the specter is detached from the living and undertakes its trip to the natal village, in a mechanical and obscure "anamnesis," where it is extinguished. Recall that the items that cannot be transferred through inheritance, the female girdle and the male *aray,* bear a sexual connotation, manifesting an adherence to their owners that is almost an inherence; they should be consumed, as should the flesh.

This is linked to the idea that nostalgia for the dead is something that makes us "absent" or "estranged from ourselves" (*mo-a̲'o*), separating our soul from our body and making us become lightweight. The wish of the living is that the dead forget them so that they in turn can forget the dead. Nostalgia, as we saw, is thought to be caused by the absent person; thus, when the memory lying in the flesh of the deceased dissolves, we no longer run the risk of following him, responding to the call of the flesh (ours and his) and becoming nonflesh, i.e., spirit and bones. Memory, in the context of death, is corruptible and corrupting.[27]

The notion of *ta̲'o we* can sometimes be employed to designate the celestial part of the person, but with a significant difference. The possessive inflection of the type *he ra̲'o we* ("my *-a̲'o we*") is not admissible except to denote this celestial part. The personal inflection of the terrestrial specter requires the affixing of *-reme,* "deceased," to the subject noun or pronoun. On the other hand, the absolute form marked by an initial *t-* is not used to speak about celestial souls in general; the relative or personal inflection *ha'o we* is employed, which is not used to speak about terrestrial specters. Another way of indicating this differential distance of the celestial and terrestrial *-a'o we* relative to the subject is by another contrast in the possessive inflection: *bïde apa ta'o we* (person-thing-specter) means "our terrestrial specters," while "our celestial souls" is expressed as *bïde ra'o we*. The first form suggests an extrinsic relation between subject and object, and maintains the absolute inflection of the root. The second is the form of the inalienable possessive, utilized for parts of the body, kinship positions, and all relations of intrinsic or inherent possession. The inflection in *r-* used to speak about a specter is found only with the apposition of *-reme* to the subject, a suffix that expresses its absence (see chap. 6, sect. 2). In sum, the subject and the specter cannot be co-present, even linguistically.

Some animals also give rise to *-a'o we*. In this case, the term is always marked by the determinative *h-*, entering into genitive constructions. An animal's *ha'o we* is referred to as *ihi*, the "adult," in relation to the real animal, which is thus thought of as its offspring. Poisonous creatures must have their *ha'o we* killed by a shaman as part of the treatment for the person who has been attacked. The *ha'o we* is responsible for the persistence of pain after the animal has been killed; it is what lingers after the suppression of the agent. In principle, every animal supposedly has a *ha'o we*, but this is not an especially developed theory among the Araweté.[28] Another animal has a powerful *ha'o we*—the jaguar. But the spirit of a dead jaguar is not the object of any protective shamanism. It belongs to the system of warfare and the *ha'o we* of dead enemies.

Finally, let us look at the general meaning of the concept of *ta'o we*. The Tupi-Guarani languages make use of two forms for ideas referring to the incorporal aspect of animate beings or to the representational mode of things; let us write them as **anga* and **-a'uva*. The first is more stable and appears in a series of nouns that connote representation; the second is more elusive, entering mainly into verbs and aspect morphemes that connote immateriality. Both can receive suffixes that indicate the past or separation (like the Araweté *-we*), and in many cases they cannot stand without such an inflection.[29] In Araweté, the root **-a'uva* is found in the verb *mo-a'o*, "to suffer nostalgia"; it also forms a verbal aspect that indicates the quasi actualization of something, an intention that was not accomplished (cf. the Guarani *ra'u* [Cadogan 1950:245]). In all cases, what is connoted is a potential separation between a spiritual or mental principle and its physical support. Thus, the concepts of -*a'o we*—the separated *a'o*—refers precisely to the last residue of this separation.

□

An Araweté concept derived from the other Tupi-Guarani protoform (**anga*) is the preeminent term for designating the celestial portion (*iwã hã nĩ*) of the person: *ĩ*, the "soul."

Ĩ, shadow, image, reproduction (visual or sonoral), also refers to the throbbing of the blood, the vital pulsations of the body. I would here translate it as "vital principle," since the pulsation is both the presence and the index of the presence of the *ĩ*. In the eschatological context, this *ĩ* receives various epithets: *ɨha me'e rĩ*, "that which will go (to the sky)"; *Maï pihã nĩ*, "future companion of the gods"; *Maï dĩ*, "future divinity"; and *bïde rĩ*, "future person." This last one contrasts with *bïde pe*, "ex-person," applied to the specter.

The notion of *ĩ* refers as much to the vital principle as to the image-shadow. But such a principle is not an abstraction; it corresponds to a corporal image (*hiro*) when it is encountered apart from the body—in dreams, death, or soul-loss. It is necessary to distinguish *two* meanings of *ĩ*: the active *ĩ*, the "vital image," and the passive *ĩ*, the "shadow image." The first belongs to the order of causes; it is interior (the body, *hiro*, is its envelope) and it leads an autonomous existence. The second, generator of the specter, belongs to the order of effects; it is exterior and its "autonomy" is more accurately an automatism.

The vital image is generated concomitantly with conception. One of the names for semen is *bïde rĩ*, "future human being."[30] Souls simply begin, they do not have a past, and they are strictly individual. The principal seat of the active *ĩ* is the trachea; other notable points are the chest, wrists, and the fontanel. A child whose fontanel is still open (having a "soft head") is easily captured by the Master of Water, who removes its soul through that spot. Each of these points is spoken of as if it were a distinct *ĩ* (*ĩ dɨ̃*), but they are synthesized in a single corporal image, once the *ĩ* is thought of as separate from the body. The multiplicity of *ĩ* in the body simply indicates that their presence infuses it; this is different than the qualitative, exterior, and essential multiplicity of the *ta'o we*. The *ĩ* outside the body is singular; the shadow of a dead body is multiple.[31]

The essential attribute of the active *ĩ* is *kaakɨ̃ hã*, consciousness. It is thus clearly distinguished from the notion of the *ĩ* as a reproduction, a tangible image. It is, rather, the *bïde* proper. If we try to find out what aspect of the shaman travels to the skies and deals with the gods, we will be told that it is the *peye e'e te,* the "shaman proper." In fact it is his *ĩ*, but not an "image" of the shaman, rather, his personal principle. Similarly, what we are seeing when people appear in our dreams are such people themselves, not their images. The active *ĩ* is full presence: wherever it is, there the person is. (The *ta̲'o we,* product of the passive *ĩ*, is where the person was—*Wo es war, soll ich werden . . .*) The active *ĩ*, "what will be above," is a trait of the living, that is, of those who are present. In Araweté, *ĩ* does not receive a temporal inflection; it coincides with life. Separated from the body, it is transformed and transforms the corpse into the *-a̲'o we,* dividing itself into two parts: on the one hand, a past and passive shadow, a dead and extrinsic repetition of the body; on the other, a future and active vital principle, a living and internal repetition (the life force) of the person.

The ambiguity of the concepts of *ĩ* and *-a̲'o we*—designating opposite but intimately interconnected principles—reveals that the person is something split or prone to fissioning along various dimensions: body and spirit, exterior and interior, past and future. But such a division is not simple: although the terrestrial specter, the emanation of a body without a soul, is pure negativity, the celestial principle is not pure positivity. Araweté dualisms cannot be easily reduced to Cartesian figures.

Upon death, the *ĩ* escapes through the trachea or the upper part of the cranium (cf. the fontanel), embarking in the cotton canoe of the *Ma̲ï.* As it ascends, it pauses for a bit at the height of the tops of the tallest trees, the sky of *Đa̲'ï ñã,* the Master of the Birds.[32] There the *ĩ* stops and listens to the lamentations of its relatives on earth. Then it heads west. In the domain of the western Master of Peccaries (*Mo'iročo*), it drinks some maize beer and then continues its ascent. At the portal of the sky, the soul is received by the Master of Vultures, who blows on its face ("Come on, grandchild, let's revive!"), removing its mortal stupor.

Reanimated, it is led by the Master of Vultures to the village of the *Ma̲ï hete,* who trample each other in their rush to meet the visitor. The *ha̲'o we* is then painted with genipap in thick lines (in the pattern called "new soul") by the "sons" and "daughters" of the Divinity. The male *Ma̲ï,* approaching the deceased, make him give them presents of feathers of cotinga, toucan, and macaw. If the soul is feminine, they propose that she copulate with them. Since the dead *always* refuse—out of fear, avarice, stupidity, or anger for having died—the gods kill them: they shoot the men with arrows and break the necks of the women. The dead conduct themselves without civility in this foreign land, refusing to enter into a relationship with the owners of the sky according to the only possible mode for a stranger—giving what he has as a sign of goodwill.

The Araweté would compare this aggressive reception of the gods to what they themselves used to do when they came across white hunters in the forest before contact. And they would elaborate for my sake (note my hosts' ironic subliminal propaganda): the *Maï* do to us what we do to you every time you arrive here—ask for things, shout excitedly, snatch things for ourselves. But since the *ha'o we* are stingy (the female souls are "overprotective of their vaginas"), they are killed. The dead soul in the sky is therefore a stranger, an enemy. On the other side of the mirror of death, the gods are the "we" and humans are the "other"—a variation of the theme "the dead are the enemy" found in societies that consider death to be a desertion to the other side, the enemy camp (Carneiro da Cunha 1978:143ff.; H. Clastres 1968; Lévi-Strauss 1974:234ff.).

It is not only because of this avarice, inadmissible when one is among others, that the dead are treated as enemies. The gods manifest a double aggressivity: they are angry *with* the souls for being dead—a dead being is ugly, smells bad, and is himself a choleric being that is recalcitrant in accepting his state—and they are angry *because* of the souls, that is, they avidly covet them. The gods *ha'o we pɨtã hetĩ*, "desire the souls greatly."

The solution to this ambivalent desire is death and devouring. Once executed, the victim is quartered and cooked in a huge stone pot by the *Maï đari*, Grandmother Divinity—the equivalent of the cannibal Grandmother Earth. All the *Maï hete* eat the flesh. The skin has already been removed and put out to dry in the sun; it is kept as a kind of trophy by the gods. Shamanic songs often mention the buzzing of the eternal bumblebees that alight on the old skin of the souls. The bones are separated out and carefully arranged (revealing a solicitousness that contrasts with the conduct of the *Ãñĩ*, who gnaw and scatter the bones of the corpse). From them, the god *Tiwawï* recomposes the body of the soul, now free from all human flesh. The body is then carried over to the *ođïpïđa kã*, a bath of effervescent water (in other words, boiling without fire) that "changes the skin" of the soul and revives it, making it strong, young, and beautiful. A male soul is painted with genipap in a pattern of fine lines; a female soul has her vulva painted. Henceforth the souls are immortal, or rather, eternally young: as soon as they start to age, they are submerged in the *ođïpïđa kã* to change their skin, foster the growth of new teeth, and allow the penis to recuperate its elasticity.[33] The locale of this bath is compared to the circular depressions that are found in the large flat rocks in the Ipixuna River, where fish are killed with fish poison. The motif of effervescent water appears to be a compromise between stagnant and running water: it flows in circles and it makes noises like rapids, but it is not a river, rather, a natural "pot." Among the Krahó, there is a correlation between stagnant water/running water and the dead/the living (Carneiro da Cunha (1981:168–70). We can extend the Gê association between immersion in running water and maturation and say that the immersion of dead Araweté in a body of circulating water signifies a process of initiation. This revitalizing water that "boils" without a fire underneath is a symmetrical inversion of the *Ãñĩ*'s grill, the grave, the apparatus of a process of rotting that "roasts" with the fire above (see sect. 3)—a funerary *cuisine croisée.*

According to some shamans, small children (who do not liberate the terrestrial specter) are not eaten; they are rubbed with the juice of the *aracï* fruit, which changes their skin, and are placed in the resuscitating bath. What the gods kill and eat thus appears to be an equivalent of the terrestrial *ta̲'o we,* the mortal aspect of the person.

Following a death and for quite a while afterwards, lightning bolts, thunder, and rainbows are interpreted as indices of the transformative processes the deceased undergoes in the sky. Every loud peal of thunder is followed by the comment, "Someone has just been eaten by the gods."[34]

The devouring of the dead soul's flesh and its resuscitative "cooking" is thus a double cooking that replicates the double rotting of the corpse, which has been devoured by the earth and whose double (the specter) has then been transformed into "something similar to a dead opossum." Both steps are essential for it to be transformed into a divinity and consequently forget the world of the living. Such a process is prolonged and coincides with the time it takes for the cadaver to putrefy. But it is conceived as independent of the latter process; there is no notion of an articulation of the corruption of the corpse with a "purification" of the soul (Bloch & Parry 1982:26). The necessity of divine cannibalism derives precisely from the fact that the rotting has not been sufficient for the transfiguration of the person.

For a long time, the soul of the deceased exerts a kind of suction on the *ĩ* of the living. The first shamanic descents of a soul are also operations that bring back the *ĩ* of the deceased's children and spouse, which had escaped to follow his or her *ĩ* during dreams. The shamans must convince it to let go of its relatives and remain in its new and splendid situation. A recently divinized soul functions like a *Ma̲ï,* that is, it exercises an irresistible fascination over the *ĩ* of the living. The ones who do not forget the dead are the living, as the Araweté know only too well. The most frequent reason given for a "natural" death is this: *Maï demiyika pitã mõ*, "Because he [the deceased] wanted to be with the gods." This kind of nostalgia for the future is the secret perdition of every human being. The fondness the deceased has for the earth does not contradict this impulse towards the realm above that inexorably moves the soul, insofar as this sentiment is what attracts the living to the sky. In truth, they want both things, heaven and earth.

After consumption and the bath of youthfulness, the deceased's anger comes to an end. He takes a celestial spouse, and the "heavenly bliss"—the friendship relations he establishes with the gods—as well as the perfumes with which his new abodes are impregnated, make him forget the earth. The *odïpïda kã* is a bath of forgetfulness. The notion of consumption, by fixing the deceased to the sky, is a substitute for the idea common in other eschatologies that it is the acceptance of food from spirits that marks the definitive entrance of the soul into the beyond—in this case, he is the food. In turn, the celestial perfumes are opposed in their amnesiac function to the stench of death, the smell of rotten flesh, the substratum of memory. The odor of sanctity (if we may put it that way) is the sign of a reincarnation in a new ontological mode, incorruptible divinity.

We can finally understand the ultimate sense of the proverb about the forgetfulness of the bones, which inverts the Guarani attempt to "make the bones continue to listen" (H. Clastres 1978 [1975]:104) but manifests the same desire: resurrection. It is not enough that the corpse be cleaned of all flesh in order for the dead to leave the living alone; it is also necessary that there be a consumption of the "spiritual flesh" the souls have when they arrive in the sky, in order that, from a pure skeleton, a god without memory is reborn. To be transformed into a divinity is to forget. Inverting the Pythagorean theme of anamnesis as regressive identification with the divine, the Araweté propose an inherently divine amnesia facing the future. The undesirable adherence of the dead to society is prevented by their transformation into the very beings that devoured their memory: a cannibal god.

None of this is as simple as it seems. Neither do the dead forget the living all that quickly; nor do the latter want to drastically break the bond that links them to the former. For several years, shamans bring the deceased to earth so he can come eat with the living, narrate what is happening in the sky, and speak with his relatives.[35] One day, after becoming less and less frequent, his visits cease. It is only then, when the living have finally forgotten the deceased, that one may say the latter has truly forgotten the living. He has been transformed into a generic *Maï* as well as a generic "ancestor" (*pirowĩ'hã*). His name remains, which can be put back into use. He has died, at last: the work of mourning has come to an end.

But by that point, other dead will have appeared, since they are necessary to the living. Celestial cannibalism and divinization are not merely a pious fraud used to try to convince the dead that they are doing fine and should thus leave us in peace. Nor can shamanism be reduced to a struggle with the dead for the souls of the survivors. If the dead are dangerous because they extract the living from the present, they also permit the appearance of those who are supremely absent: the *Maï*, who abandoned the earth in the beginning of time, giving rise through exclusion to the human condition.

8 Alien Words

1. The Marriage of Heaven and Earth

Devoured and resurrected, the dead marry the *Maï*. This does not mean they are lost to the living; they are the pawns in an exchange relationship that transforms the *Maï* into allies of humanity. In contrast to the Tupinamba, who turned enemies into affines, the better to eat them, the *Maï* devour enemies, the better to affinize them.

The "transformation into divinity" that benefits the dead is the result of this consumption by and marriage with the gods. But it is progressive or incomplete—this is a fundamental point. The dead must retain some human quality or else they cannot serve as a bridge. For this very reason, they do not eat the flesh of souls who have recently arrived in the sky: one does not eat one's own relatives. Only the *Maï hete* do so, although it is quite possible that the ancient dead, who have already forgotten the living (and been forgotten), have been completely assimilated into divinity and have thus turned into cannibals.[1]

Spouses of the gods, the dead are not exactly their affines; they constitute a *relation*, not a term. The dead are there so that the living and divinities may become allies through marriage; these are the two relevant parties, linked by the ontological ambiguity of the dead. Ingeniously, the Araweté put cannibalism—that "negation of alliance" (H. Clastres 1978 [1975]:47)—to the service of an alliance between heaven and earth.

At first sight, Araweté cosmology seems to contradict the idea that the other world is a world without others—an idea that equates the world of the beyond with the end of affinity and which, be it a secret dream or a didactic *reductio ad absurdum*, stamps the eschatology of so many human cultures. Similar in this respect to anthropologists (to ironically beg the question, as Lévi-Strauss once did [1973:234]), such societies would assert, directly or obliquely, that difference and alliance are the necessary conditions of social life. Accordingly, the

Other world, releasing men from the excessive humanness of exchange, returns them at last to the safe haven of the Same. In this world, the dead, finally absorbed in their singularity or dissolved in generality, oscillate between incest and auto-cannibalism on the one hand, and the blessed absence of desire and necessity on the other. Worlds of extremes, in which all difference is abolished, either because the differences interwoven in life become fixed and incommunicable, or because they blend and dissolve in an entropic chaos. In one way or the other, by excess or absence of distance, what the world of the dead represents is the converse of the social: a terrible or blissful indifferent identity. Such a notion is widespread: among the Shavante (Maybury-Lewis 1974), the Krahó (Carneiro da Cunha 1981), the Tukano (C. Hugh-Jones 1979), the Piaroa (Kaplan 1984); but also among the Merina, the Melpa, the Gimi, on Dobu, in India . . . It may even be universal, to judge by the frequency with which the last paragraph of *The Elementary Structures of Kinship* is cited, that sociological Critique of Pure Reason which, after having brought men to the symbolic tribunal of reciprocity, concedes to them the imaginary *sursis* of posthumous incest. There seem to be, indeed, "no others in eternity" (Block & Parry 1982:8).

In fact, others do exist in Araweté eternity; furthermore, it is precisely there that they are found. Affinity has been transported to the heavens, or rather, to the relations between heaven and earth. Death permits the great cosmological chasm to be bridged. Divine cannibalism, in transforming humans into divinities, does something even more important—it humanizes the gods, that is, socializes them.

In contrast to what is supposedly the eschatological norm (Humphreys 1981:275), marriage and procreation exist in the Araweté Beyond. But the salient mode of relation between gods and the dead has the tenor of friendship (*apĩhi-pihã*), and in this sense there are, in effect, no "others" in the sky. Actually, no one has much interest in things like celestial children of the souls or other such matters; what is pertinent are the kinship relations between the living and the dead, and the affinal relations between the living and divinities. Properly speaking, there are no dead in and of themselves, but only for us and for the *Ma̱ï*.

For this reason, the problem is not so much one of discovering the fate of affinity in the Beyond or of investigating analogic correspondences between the world of the dead and the world of the living—reflection, inversion, sanction, or whatever. Rather, the problem is to understand the cosmological function fulfilled by cannibalizing and divinizing the dead. The relationship between the living and the dead is not a speculative problem for Araweté reason, but a practical one. It is in this relationship that affinity emerges: not on earth, where it is diverted and disguised by the dominance of the friendship system; nor in the sky, where *apĩhi-pihã* friendship is also what counts (it is actually an attribute of the gods); but rather, *between* these two worlds. The Araweté gods are affines; they are not food, like the Tupinamba affinal enemies, but eaters, the cannibals in person. *Ɨre Maï demï-do rĩ*, "we are the future food of the gods"; but we also will be gods. Araweté cosmology is immediately a sociology, not some ghostly emanation of it.

Who are the *Maï*? In general, they are called "our big grandfathers," since they are ancient, great, and powerful—and still half savage. Many of the divine races are also *ñañe rati pɨkɨ*, "our tall fathers-in-law." This does not involve the notion of giving wives to humans, although this epithet is also applied to the gods who raised the firmament and who were in fact allies of humans before the separation; what it indicates is the superiority of such beings, the danger they represent—and our obligation to feed them. The Jaguar-Thing that comes to eat tortoise is the prototype of these heavenly fathers-in-law, petulant and voracious.

The *Maï hete*, the most important and exemplary divinities, are defined as *ɨre tiwã oho*, "our gigantic potential affines." *Tiwã*, as we saw, is a "middle term" of kinship that designates nonrelatives, potential allies, and cross-cousins: something between a brother and an enemy, it indicates an internal exteriority, so to speak. The *Maï hete* are the archetype of *tiwã:* they are from "the other side," but are linked to the living. They are "like enemies," but we will be transformed into them and by them, by marrying them. Death is like marriage (indeed it is a marriage): it transforms *tiwã* into actual affines.

Shamans and the *Maï hete* never address each other as *tiwã* (a vocative that only appears in the warfare complex). These gods are either referred to simply as *Maï* and address the shaman by his personal name, or they stand in a specific affinal relationship with the shaman or with other living persons to whom they speak through the former. The *Maï* take pleasure in mentioning the relatives of the dead: male gods speak to or about their brothers-in-law, fathers-in-law, and sons of their human wives; female gods converse with their sisters-in-law, mothers-in-law, etc. Notably, terms of consanguinity are never used, even if pertinent; a shaman, for example, will mention a *Maï* as *mãy nerekɨ̃*, "husband of my mother," not as "father." The divine spouse also enjoys underlining the rupture of the relationship between the deceased and his or her terrestrial spouse: "Your ex-wife is delicious," he tells the widower, speaking through the shaman's mouth.

When a shaman makes one of his deceased female friends (*apĩhi*) sing, he is occasionally considered an *apĩhi-pihã* by the god that accompanies her. During the *peyo,* the joyful *Maï* like to call the shaman by this term. But in contrast to what happens in the interior of human society, friendship relations between gods and the living are clearly subordinated to those of affinity: the necessary mutuality of the *apĩhi-pihã* system is absent here, *et pour cause.* Death is the unilateral and definitive transference of the deceased from sexual commerce with the living to that with the gods; through it, the possibility of exchange is instituted. On the superior level of the relations between gods and men, affinity encompasses anti-affinity: thus, the negation of affinity, essential to the internal fabric of the human *socius,* is in turn negated on the cosmic plane. This is equivalent to saying that society is not complete on earth: the living are one part of the global social structure, founded on the alliance between heaven and earth. The cosmology of the Araweté is its sociology.

It is easy to see that there is one affinal position that the *Maï hete* cannot occupy vis-à-vis the living: precisely that of father-in-law. They are spouse-*takers:* typically they are conceived of as males who takes sisters and daughters from humans, thereby becoming brothers-in-law (ZH) or sons-in-law of the living. When female gods appear, they question living women about dead men. The structure is a "alliance of marriage" in Dumont's (1983) sense: it links partners of the same sex.

This inversion impresses me as essential: while they are cosmological "fathers-in-law," that is, dangerous and cannibalistic beings to whom one owes food prestations, the *Maï hete* are sociological "sons-in-law." This gives humans a strategic advantage. The problem is thus one of knowing *what* humans receive in exchange for the spouses and foods they give to the *Maï.* This is a question for which I have no ready answer, but let me return to it later for reconsideration.

2. Shamanism and the Music of the Gods

The gods and the dead are *marakã me'e,* "musical things," or musicians. Their mode of manifesting themselves is through song, and their vehicle is the shaman, a man who is a *Maï de ripã,* "support of the gods."

Although women see gods in dreams (as do all humans), they cannot interact with them. If they dared to sing, the gods would break their necks, confining them in the sky forever. Only men are able to control their own disembodiment. But more is involved in this: only men are shamans because the relations between gods and humans are seen through a masculine lens: women are the pawns of alliance, not parties to it. They are the gods' favorite food, in both literal and metaphorical senses. For this reason, the "ideal deceased" is a woman and death is a feminine movement, since it entails being devoured. Men can travel to and from the sky without having to die (as shamans) or they can die without being eaten (as warriors). Women must stay put on earth while living, and be eaten in the sky once dead. Although living women do not sing (merely repeating male songs), dead women sing profusely through the mouths of shamans.

Shamanism does not involve any formal initiation. Certain recurrent dreams, especially those featuring the Jaguar-Thing, may be signs of a shamanic calling.[2] But what distinguishes a shaman is not his capacity for dreaming (which is also important for a killer), but rather, his association with tobacco. The usual way of saying that someone is not a shaman is *petĩ ã-ĩ*, a "noneater of tobacco." Shamanic training involves a series of sessions of becoming intoxicated by this plant until the person is "made translucent" and the gods come to him.

Everybody smokes socially, men, women, and children. The thirty-centimeter cigar, made of leaves dried over a fire and rolled in bark of the tauari tree, is a supremely social object. The first gesture of hospitality is to offer the guest a puff on the house cigar lit expressly for him. A request for tobacco is never refused, and one never smokes alone except in shamanic rites—but then the cigar is being shared with the gods.

One of the favorite nighttime activities is the collective session of tobacco inebriation, which also gives shaman initiates an opportunity to become more "translucent." Night after night, a good part of the village convenes in some patio for these sessions. The patio owner furnishes the tobacco and a few men are considered the *tenotã mõ* of the session, those who receive the most massive doses.

The session of tobacco eating ("to smoke" is literally "to eat tobacco") take place in complete darkness, since tobacco abhors light, and may flash and strike like lightning (*hapi*, as do so many things in Araweté culture). The cigar may not be held by the person who smokes it; each must be served by someone else, as occurs with strong beer. The person who consistently serves a man until he becomes translucent enough to experience shamanic visions is called *mo-petemo-hã*. As a rule, this is a woman: the wife or a female friend. Many people become inebriated during these sessions. "New smokers" (shaman initiates) stop filling themselves with smoke only at the point of fainting, "killed" by the tobacco. The ambience is reminiscent of beer festivals, the difference being that no one sings or speaks loudly; only the labored breathing of intoxication can be heard.

A "killer of people," tobacco is also the main instrument for reviving those who have fainted.[3] Tobacco smoke is used to resuscitate the dead in the sky. This substance is a two-way converter between life and death, and a commutator between domains (see above, chap. 5, sect. 2).

Novice shamans usually try out *payikã*, the hallucinogenic seeds of *Anadenanthera peregrina*, which are toasted and mixed with the tobacco in cigars. This drug is capable of making the most "ignorant" man become transparent and able to perceive the gods. It is never consumed by women. Tobacco and *payikã* are given names that indicate their deadly character: "wedges" or "mallets" (to strike the head), or "dissolvers of the earth." *Payikã* is not widely used. The oldest shamans declare that they do not need it, since the gods have already passed "into their flesh"; they are, so to speak, impregnated with divinity.[4]

Shamanic initiates must abstain from sex and certain foods: the giant armadillo (because of its "stench"), foreign foods and condiments, and raw fruits. All these "break the transparency" and "extinguish" the shaman, making him "stay put." The idea of being extinguished refers to the fact that the skin of shamanic initiates shines and gives shocks like the electric eel; such luminescence is attributed to the tobacco, a thing that illuminates (*me'e e'e pe hã*) and a thing of knowledge (*me'e ko̲ã hã*). Things of knowledge are everything that puts us in contact with the gods: dreams, death, traumas. Thus, for example, someone who is bitten by a poisonous snake is visited by a "thing of knowledge," the creature's *ha̲'o we;* men who survive this accident become shamanic candidates (the type who bring rain; cf. chap. 7, note 8).[5]

This might lead us to consider the shaman as a "wounded healer," someone who has experienced disembodiment and successfully controlled it. But such an idea receives little elaboration among the Araweté, in contrast to other Amazonian societies. Nor do they have the notion of the shaman being trained by some spirit. Tutelary spirits do not exist: a generic relationship links every shaman to the entire supernatural universe. It is true that certain shamans are more likely to perform *peyo* for certain foods and that some "do not know how" to serve strong beer. No reason was adduced for this; some shamans are polyvalent, but are not thereby the most prestigious.

Besides tobacco, the other emblem of shamanism is the *aray* rattle. Every married man has an *aray* in his house. It may be used by non-shamans as an instrument for minor cures and as accompaniment for the nocturnal songs of men who see the gods from time to time. Shamanic ability is an attribute inherent in the status of male adulthood, not something monopolized by a special role; this is what possession of the *aray* indicates. Some men have not sung for years, others very rarely have visions, and some youths have only begun to sing—all of them are "a little bit shamans." But only those who sing often and perform *peyo* are ordinarily designated as *peye.* In other words, some men (in 1982–83, twelve of the forty-four married men) realize this potential more fully than others—just as only a few men possess the ideal status of killer.

The *aray* has the shape of a narrow inverted cone with a convex base; the inner structure is woven by women of thin basketry strips of itiriti cane. Pieces of shells of a forest snail (*yaračitã*) are put inside. Cotton thread is wound around the container, completely covering it except for the broad base of the cone at the end opposite from where the rattle is grasped. Between the base and the body of the rattle, wads of cotton are attached like a collar, hiding the points where four or more red macaw tail feathers are inserted. All such finishing work is done by men. When it is complete, the *aray* looks like a theatrical prop representing a flaming torch. The sounds it makes are not adequate for marking strong rhythms, being sibilant and somewhat garbled; it is not a musical instrument of accompaniment, but a magical tool. It contrasts with the dance *marakaʾi,* a simple object made from a small gourd and filled with soapberry seeds or glass beads, which has the subordinate function of accompaniment. It is possible to dance a *pirahẽ* without a rattle, but not possible to summon the *Maï* without an *aray,* which can be used without singing.

Āray iwe or *aray we,* "inside the rattle" or "through the rattle," is the laconic explanation given for any question about how various operations are effected, such as mythical operations of metamorphosis and resurrection, mystical ones of food consumption by the gods, or therapeutic ones of returning souls or closing bodies. The *aray* is a receptacle of spiritual forces: lost souls are carried inside it and returned to their seat, while souls captured by the spirit *Ayaraetã* live inside his rattle. In this sense, the *aray* is a kind of mystical body (*hiro,* container) of invisible things: it is the support of the *ĩ,* the *Maï,* and the *ipeye hã* force that resides in and is activated by the *aray*. It is also a "thing of knowledge" and an eminently fiery object; it flashes like lightning and ignites the earth when handled by shamans and gods. It is a "container of lightning bolts" (*tatã ipe riro*), an epithet that renders it, besides a body, a phallus; the scrotal sac is given the same designation. Also, the rattle, as we have already seen, is something that a vagina "breaks" (see chap. 7, sect. 1).

Although it is a phallic body, the *aray* nevertheless appears to be endowed with a mystical creativity of a *feminine* type, different from and complementary to the biological creativity of the masculine, seminal type. I can find no other reason for why this emblem of masculinity is woven by women (after all, men work with itiriti and weave mats), if it is not to equate their fabrication with conception, a process that differentially involves both sexes.[6] The manner in which souls and other spiritual entities are captured and transported by the rattle is as mysterious as the transformation that semen undergoes inside the female body: "through the rattle" and "along the mother." This metaphor of the phallus, which has its body fabricated by women and "clothed" in cotton by men, perhaps corresponds to the masculine fabrication of the female penis, the labia of the vulva. As a phallus, the *aray* would also be a *son* made *by* women *for* men. So, not only are there female penises and female semen, but now we encounter a female son. A complex process of symbolic exchange appears to operate between the two sexes, which I can only glimpse but which goes far beyond a simple "patrilateral theory of conception."

The Tupinamba also had rattles: "They put their faith in a thing shaped like a pumpkin, the size of a pint pot. It is hollow within, and they put a stick through it and cut a hole in it like a mouth, filling it with small stones so that it rattles. They . . . call it Tammaraka, and each man has one of his own" (Staden 1928 [1557]:148). The chroniclers described these maracas, periodically animated by the powers of wandering prophets, as a receptable of spirits who spoke to their owners (Léry 1990 [1573]:145). Notably, the owner of a rattle called it "*son*," caring for it like a human (Thevet 1953 [1575]:117). Each man had one of his own, as among the Araweté. The rattles are to men as children are to women: two figurations of the Phallus, as psychoanalysts would say. Could it be that because the Araweté "really know" that children come from women, that women must be the ones who makes these "children" for men?

I cannot resist pushing the matter further and suggesting a correspondence between the *aray* and the uterus (*memi apo hã*, "wrapping of the child"), a correlate of the explicit equation penis = labia minora. In this case, we would have an opposition between, on the one hand, interiority and creative concavity (rattle, uterus), and, on the other, exteriority and aggressive convexity (penis, labia). Note the curious inversion between the cotton covering that encloses the shamanic tool, leaving only the broad upper end exposed (from which emerge red feathers protected by a collar), and the manner of treating the male penis, leaving it exposed and uncovered except for the glans, which is protected by the stretched prepuce that is tied with a single cord. A metaphorical penis, clothed with a tight "girdle" of cotton, the *aray* can be seen, finally, as the masculine double of the girdle—something that we already established following another line of reasoning.

I did not discuss these ideas with the Araweté; I doubt they would receive their stamp of approval, even if I were able to formulate them in an intelligible manner. But they seem to me to ring true and serve to set the stage for an important distinction, internal to the male gender, that I will take up again: the notion that the shaman and his rattle occupy a feminine position relative to the killer and his bow. Recall that "bow" is the general term for the penis and the labia minora.[7] Maybe it is no accident that the three distinctive objects displaying the greatest refinement in Araweté material culture, objects that moreover are quite different from their Tupi-Guarani analogues, should be precisely these three: the *aray,* the bow, and the female girdle.[8]

□

With such equipment, his tobacco and rattle, the shaman executes various operations of prevention and curing: fumigating with tobacco, cooling through breath, sucking out pathogenic substances (for curing poisonous bites and extracting arrows discharged by certain foods), dispersing malignant principles from foods, killing animal spirits, closing bodies, and returning souls.

The closing of the body is undertaken to prevent substances from entering or the soul from leaving. The first case usually involves children (protecting them from semen or beer); the second, people who are very ill. The *imone* operation, which returns the soul, is the opposite of the operation of closing, or rather, is prior to it; the shaman resituates the *ĩ* and then closes the patient's body so it will not escape again.

The killing of animal spirits—tapir, deer, but also venomous creatures—is identical to the killing of terrestrial spirits. The shaman locates and "ties up" the spirits (usually with the help of the *Maï*), making them stumble and fall. They are then killed by beating, machete blows, or arrow shots, aimed at a spot on the ground indicated by the *aray* movements. Usually the shaman's wife or the patient's spouse does the job of killing.[9]

But the most frequent and important activity of a shaman is chanting. Shamanic songs are probably the most complex item of Araweté culture, being also the sole source of information about the state of the cosmos and the situation of the dead.

There is no adult man who has not sung at least a few times during his lifetime and none, therefore, who has not used the *aray*. But the *peye* are those who sing almost every night. Normally a song is generated according to the following sequence: a man sleeps, dreams, wakes up, smokes, and sings, narrating what he saw and heard in his dream. Sometimes the song includes the descent of the inhabitants of the sky. This sequence reveals a progression of intensity (which is not, however, always completed): singing in his hammock, singing inside his house using tobacco and *aray;* and going outside to the patio, using dance and song that manifest the arrival of the night's visitors. The sessions when food is shamanized or souls returned involve the maximum intensity, as the shaman leaves his patio and acts on objects and people of the village at large.

Maï marakã, "music of the divinities," is an expression that is both genitive and possessive. The songs belong to the gods: they are not learned from another shaman nor are they thought of as "composed" by the singer. When I asked for the first time if I could record a song, I was told that "the music is not ours, it belongs to the *Maï*"; men had no role in deciding such a question. When I committed the blunder of making a comment to a shaman about something he had sung, the evasive reaction was, "I didn't sing anything, the *Maï* were the ones who sang." Such exteriority of divine music is manifested in other forms: the songs of deceased shamans are frequently remembered, but rarely is the singer's name given. This contrasts with the "music of enemies," always linked to the name of the killer. This extrinsic character of shamanic songs does not mean, however, that shamans do not know what they are singing or that they are not judged by the quality of their songs.

"The shaman is like a radio," I was told. By this comparison, they meant that he was a vehicle and that the subject of his voice comes from elsewhere, not from within himself. The gods are not "inside his flesh" nor do they occupy his body. During his dream, the shaman's "ex-body" (*hiro pe*) remains in his hammock while his *ĩ* travels. But it is only when the *ĩ* returns that the shaman sings. When the gods descend to earth with him—he being the one who "makes them come down" (*mo-eyi*)—they descend in person, not into his person.[10]

The shaman depicts or represents the gods and the dead, narrating their actions and words. He is conscious of what he is singing and he knows what is happening around him during the song; for instance, he responds to the spectators' requests to close the bodies of their children. Such requests are made to the shaman, not to the spirits. He can also clarify ambiguous points of the song, although he only does so to his wife at home; this makes the shaman's wife a privileged interpreter of the songs' messages. One time when I asked a girl the name of the person who had appeared in a shaman's song, she said she couldn't know this, "since I'm not his wife"—even though she knew the song by heart.

Shamanic songs lend themselves to joking variations and adventitious adaptations, being a great source of metaphors employed in daily discourse. But a song, insofar as it is a divine manifestation, cannot be "reutilized" by anyone. The words of the song can be repeated, but the original enunciative situation cannot. The songs of enemies, by contrast, exist in order to be repeated in the same situation, the *pɨrahẽ*; they create a musical repertoire, while the music of the gods is a sedimentation of a cosmological repertoire. A *Maï̲ marakã* is the materialization of a historical singularity.

A shaman is evaluated according to his timbre and vocal style and the originality of his songs. Full, deep voices are the most appreciated. People pay attention to his control over the vibrato of his singing; characteristic of shamanic songs, the vibrato should not be exaggerated, or the singer is disdained as a "trembler."

The *Maï̲ marakã* is a vocal solo, assisted by the *aray*, that follows a fixed pattern for all shamans. The style does not sound very melodious to Western ears; it plays with microtonal intervals and its rhythm is weakly marked, based on the shaman's breathing as he forcibly exhales, such that every phase ends up out of breath, falling in volume and strength. The overall melodic contour is always a descending one.

The songs exhibit a structure of verses or sentences. Each sentence is opened with a short refrain, usually having no lexical meaning but serving to identify the divinity involved; there follows a complete linguistic-musical phrase that ends with the same refrain. The verses form blocs that are linked thematically; it is common to change the refrain in the middle of a song, introducing another thematic and melodic bloc. The verses that name a character in the song are distinguished as *papã* or *henɨẽ,* "to name" or "to utter" (cf. Seeger 1981:99).

Although considered extrinsic to the person who emits them, songs are evaluated by their originality. This is due to the obvious fact that certain songs repeat phrases, tropes, and themes that have already been sung, so everyone is aware that shamanic plagiarism exists. While this does not discredit the ontological authenticity of the song, so to speak (a problem that would take us far off the topic), it diminishes its aesthetic merits and the singer's prestige. Thematic innovations, when skillfully done, are greatly appreciated. A good song is one that rearranges themes and tropes with grace, and especially one that contains cosmologically salient utterances, portraying the dead in the midst of specific situations.

The rhetorical repertoire of songs is extensive. Using parallelism as a basic stylistic resource, it makes use of characteristic metaphors, mythical allusions, and exemplary images. A fixed set of epithets are used that recall Homeric poetry or Scandinavian *kenningar* (or, less exotically, the sacred chants of the Mbyá-Guarani [Cadogan 1959]): "eaters of tiny tortoises" are humans; "divine flowers" are celestial women with their earrings; the "fragrant canoe" is the vehicle of the *Maï̱*; and so forth.

But the essential complexity of the shamanic song lies in its enunciative schema. Although the music of the gods is a vocal solo, it is linguistically a polyphony where various characters speak in diverse citational registers. In general, the shaman does not change his timbre or rhythm to indicate the entrance of a new "voice"; this information depends in part on the internal context, in part on the external, and in part on a procedure referred to earlier (chap. 1, sect. 2), the embedding of citations through the appostion of formulas of the sort "thus spoke X." The music of the gods is a narration of the words of others.

Typically, there are three enunciative positions: the deceased, the *Maï̱*, and the shaman. The deceased is the principal enunciator, transmitting to the shaman what the *Maï̱* have said. But what the *Maï̱* have said is almost always something addressed to the deceased or the shaman and referring to the deceased, the shaman, or themselves. The normal form of each sentence is thus a complex dialogical construction. The shaman, for example, may sing something said by the gods, cited by the deceased, referring to the shaman. In simpler constructions, the shaman may sing what the gods are saying about humans in general; in more intricate forms, the deceased may tell another deceased what a divinity is saying about some living person (other than the shaman).

□

The following is a free translation and simplified presentation of a *Maï marakã* sung by Kãñĩ-paye-ro (literally, "father of Kãñĩ-paye," a deceased daughter who, as we will see, is the main enunciator of the song) during the night of 26 December, 1982, the fruit of an inspiration unassociated with any ceremony but which developed into a therapeutic *peyo* for his wife, who had pains in her chest. Elsewhere (Viveiros de Castro 1986: 550–52) I have presented the original version with additional commentary. The sentences between double quotation marks are uttered by the dead; those between single quotation marks, by the *Maĩ;* and those without any, by the shaman.

I

(1) "Why are you feathering the big Brazil-nut tree?"
(2) "Why are the gods feathering the big Brazil-nut tree, Modïda-ro?"
(3) "Why are the unmarried gods feathering the face of the Brazil-nut tree?"
(4) "Here come the gods, to feather the face of the Brazil-nut tree, Arariñã-no."
(5) "Here are the gods feathering the big Brazil-nut tree."

II

(6) "Here are the gods feathering the face of the Brazil-nut tree, here they are!"
(7) "Why are the gods doing that, feathering the big Brazil-nut tree?"
(8) *[Loud and deep]:* "Here are the gods! Here they are, feathering the face of the Brazil-nut tree, here they are, here are the gods!" *[Stamping his foot repeatedly.]*
(9) "It's because he desires your daughter, the god said, that's why he said, 'Let's go feather the big Brazil-nut tree!'"
(10) "This is what the god said: 'No one has eaten the thing,' said the god . . ."
(11) "Why are the gods doing that? Why did they say, 'Let's go feather the big Brazil-nut tree!'?"
(12) "Here they are, look at the gods feathering the face of the Brazil-nut tree, Modïda-ro!"
(13) "'Light my cigar that was thrown away,' said the god."

(14) "There are the gods, feathering the face of the Brazil-nut tree, look, Araríñã-no."

(15) *[Loudly, shaking the rattle over his wife's chest]:* "Here are the gods feathering the big Brazil-nut tree, here they are!"

(16) "Here is what the gods said: 'Let's go feather the big Brazil-nut tree,' they said to each other."

(17) "It's because they want our little daughter, that's why the gods said, 'Let's go feather the big Brazil-nut tree.'"

(18) "Why are the gods doing that, feathering the face of the Brazil-nut tree?"

III

(19) "Why are you feathering the face of the Brazil-nut tree in the morning?"

(20) "Why are you feathering the face of the Brazil-nut tree?"; "'Light my neglected cigar,' said the god."

(21) "Why are you feathering the face of the Brazil-nut tree?"; "Because he desires our little daughter, the god said to himself, Araríñã-no."

(22) "Why are the gods doing that, making their arrows miss the big toucans?"

(23) "Why are you, god, feathering the face of the Brazil-nut tree?"; "'Come on, hand your little daughter over to me,' said the god."

(24) 'It's because of you, really, that the Brazil-nut trees are being feathered.'; "'I haven't been served anything whatsoever,' said the god."

(25) "Why are the unmarried gods feathering the face of the Brazil-nut tree like that, Moďïda-ro?"

(26) *[Loudly]:* "Why are the gods feathering the face of the Brazil-nut tree like that?"; "'I'm going to eat the deceased Kãñĩ-paye-ro!' said the god."

(27) *[Loudly]:* So the god will carry me off, to cook me in his big stone pot . . .

(28) *[Loudly]:* "'We shall eat your deceased father,' the gods said repeatedly." They are going to cook me in their stone pot, the gods said . . .

(29) *[Loudly]:* So, yet again the gods are going to devour me on the other side of the sky—that's what they said . . .

(30) 'Ask your little daughter to come,' said the god. 'So the two of us can go shoot big toucans,' said the god.

(31) "Why are you painting annatto on the face of the Brazil-nut tree?"
(32) *[Loudly, stamping his foot]:* "Here are the gods, painting the face of the Brazil-nut tree completely!"
(33) "Why are the gods lighting up the face of the Brazil-nut tree like that, Yowe'ï-do?" 'Come on, hand your daughter over to me!'
(34) "'Eeeh! An eater of tiny tortoises frightened the big cotingas!' said the gods. 'Our future food made the big doves fly off,' said the gods."
(35) "'The feathers of the big eternal-canindé-macaws and the cotingas,' said the gods. 'Come on, let's go shoot the big toucans!'"
(36) Eeeh! As for that 'hand your daughter over to me' that the gods said, I think the gods were just talking [unnecessarily].
(37) 'Nothing has been offered to me, go on, [get] some tiny tortoises for me!' said the god.
(38) "Why are you feathering the face of the Brazil-nut tree?"
(39) 'Eeh! Our future food made the big doves fly off!'
(40) "Why are you feathering the big *iĉiri'i* tree?"
(41) He wants to take his wife hunting, that's why the god is feathering the face of the Brazil-nut tree . . .
(42) "Why are you painting the big *iĉiri'i* [with annatto]?"
(43) Why are the gods using up my tobacco?
(44) "'Our ground is perfumed,' said the god. 'As soon as he has painted the big *iĉiri'i,* we shall perfume each other [with the tree's resin],' said the god."
(45) "Why are the gods feathering the face of the Brazil-nut tree?"

This song, with its economy of vocabulary, is a good sample of the enunciative schema of the *Maï marakã.* The main enunciator is not named at any time: it would be Kãñĩ-paye, one of the shaman's daughters, who died at two years of age in 1978. Following a question-and-answer format that organizes the whole song, she addresses the gods, her father, a dead "grandfather" (Modïda-ro), and a brother of her father, Arañĩnã-no—or rather, the *ĩ* of this man, who would be in the sky along with the shaman.[11] Besides the girl, her deceased "father" Yowe'ï-do speaks, who will not be named until verse 33 but who already spoke in verse 17. This character, like the other deceased mentioned in the song (Modïda-ro), has close relatives in the shaman's residential section. The song thus portrays members of a restricted kindred.

All the sentences are introduced and concluded with refrains (not transcribed) that also appear in the middle of verses that have two sentences. The refrain of blocs I and III has no meaning; it belongs to the *Maï hete*'s songs. The refrain of bloc II is the name of a goddess, Canindé-Macaw-Woman. She is not a character in the song, but she is somehow manifested in it in a way I do not understand.

All the sentences of bloc I are uttered by the dead girl. The first verse is a question asked of a *Maï*. The listeners will only know that it is a female soul, specifically that of the shaman's daughter, beginning in verse 9; until then, there is nothing to indicate that it is not the shaman who is the enunciator. The focal image is that of a big celestial Brazil-nut tree that is being decorated with white harpy eagle down by the gods, which thus makes its "face" (leaves) shine at a great distance. The gods are doing this because they are "irate" (*e'e*) over the dead girl, that is, burning with desire for her. I was unable to find out the relationship between the act of feathering the tree and this sentiment. The image associates two canonical themes of discourse about the sky: Brazil-nut trees (the tallest trees in Araweté country) and harpy eagles.

Bloc II is introduced after a pause, which then leads to an increase in the vocal volume and affective intensity of the song, marking the arrival of the gods on earth. The enunciative situation becomes more complex. Verses 6 and 8 are accompanied by foot stamping, indicating the presence of the enunciators on earth. The speaker of these verses is apparently still the dead girl, or some sort of synthesis of the shaman and his daughter. Verse 9 is stated by the girl and refers to herself: the gods say (to you, the shaman) that they desire your daughter (me, who is speaking), having said that it is out of such desire that they are feathering the Brazil-nut trees. Verse 10 offers another motive for the anger of the *Maï*: the girl says that the gods said "no one has eaten the thing"—that is, that they haven't been invited yet to eat tortoise. At the time, preparations were underway for the collective tortoise hunts, but no *peyo* had been held yet. The song thus sends a message to the village. Verses 11 and 12 are uttered by the girl. The first is a generic question; the second, a *deixis* directed to Modïda-ro. In verse 13, the girl transmits the god's request to her father that he light his (the god's) cigar. This is a gesture of cordiality, suggesting that the shaman should offer his cigar to the *Maï* ("my cigar" is actually the shaman's cigar). At this moment during the song, Kãñĩ-payero's cigar had gone out and his wife had to light it. The verse presents a labyrinthine construction: the god's request is a request by the shaman to his wife through the medium of his daughter. Verse 14 is similar to 12. Verse 15 was uttered while the shaman shook his *aray* over his wife's chest, closing her body after having resituated her soul. The phrase was stated by the girl; she would thus be the one who brought the soul back: "*Ohi mone,*" "She was carrying (the soul of) her own mother," was the interpretation I was given.

Verse 16 involves the girl reciting to her father what the gods said. Verse 17 brings another enunciator to the stage. The one who says that the gods said that they desire "our" (inclusive plural) little daughter cannot be the girl or the gods. This is an instance of an indirect linear style of construction, similar to that of verse 9 (through which a complex self-reference emerged), that indicates that the enunciator is Yowe'ï-do, the shaman's deceased "brother." This interpretation is retrospective, relying on verse 33 where this person is named; until then, everything is ambiguous. The commentators were unanimous in declaring that the expression "our little daughter" was not a phrase directed by the shaman to his wife, as I had thought. With the possible exception of verses 6 and 8, the shaman does not occupy the position of enunciator in bloc II. He cites citations: he says what his daughter or brother say the gods said. Verse 18 returns to the girl's speech.

In bloc III, the number of "voices" and the emotional intensity of the song reach their climax. A direct confrontation takes place between the gods and the shaman, and the latter will go on to speak for himself a few times. Verse 19 is the usual question by the girl to the gods, and underscores that it is daytime in the heavens, alluding to the brilliance of the Brazil-nut tree in the morning light. The first part of verse 20 repeats 19; the second repeats the situation of 13, as the shaman's cigar has gone out again. Verse 21 brings in two voices directed to two parties: first, the girl asks questions of the god; then Yowe'ï-do repeats what he said in verse 17, but now addressing another brother. Verse 22 is interpreted (by the listeners) as a question the girl puts to the gods concerning other gods. Verse 23 starts with the theme question, then conveys an order from the gods (using an imperative form of the verb) to the shaman, referring to the enunciator, the girl. The first part of verse 24 is direct speech from the gods directed to the girl; the second part has the girl citing to her father the gods' complaint that they haven't been served anything, that is, tortoises. Note that the insertion of this theme of tortoises assimilates this food to the shaman's daughter: both things are demanded of the men by the gods. Verse 25 takes up the theme of the unmarried (therefore young) *Maï* again, who covet the shaman's young daughter (after the resuscitating bath, dead children become adolescents).

Verse 26 reveals the threat that lies behind the entire game of requests, questions, and answers: one of the *Maï*, naming the shaman and already referring to him as "deceased" (attaching *-reme* to his name), announces that he is going to eat him. The shaman's daughter is the one who says "the god said" and thus cites her father's name. Through this double mediation, the shaman names himself and anticipates his own death.[12] He sang this verse and the following ones in a loud voice using the lowest register with a macabre intonation. At this moment, the listeners (of the tape of the song) became enthusiastic; Kãñĩ-paye-ro's "self"-naming was undeniably the high point of the song. Verse 27 contains the shaman's voice as subject for the first time: he says that he will be devoured. In the first part of verse 28, the shaman's daughter cites the gods, who say they will eat her "deceased father"; the second part brings back the shaman's voice in a fine example of the indirect style. Verse 29 uses the same style: the shaman cites the gods and alludes to the numerous occasions when he ran into this danger. The "other side of the sky" is the reverse side of the visible sky, the plane of the *Maï*.

Verse 30 bears the request that, if met, will guarantee the invulnerability of the shaman in the sky. The *Maï*, cited here by the shaman, orders him to convince his daughter to go with the *Maï* "to shoot toucans," a metonymy for taking her "out to the forest," which in turn is a metaphor for sexual relations and, as we saw, is evocative of the theme of sexual friendship.

Verses 31 and 32 bring back the girl speaking. The theme of painting the Brazil-nut tree with annatto introduces an olfactory motif, that of celestial fragrances. While singing verse 32, the shaman stamped his foot loudly and renewed the *peyo* motions over his wife. As in verse 15, the deictic construction manifests the presence *hic et nunc* of the gods and creates an impression of cosmic interference, since the gods are here but at the same time in the sky painting the Brazil-nut tree: two images coexist in the canvas of the singer's voice. The first part of verse 33 is a question by the girl to Yowe'ï-do; the flashing of the Brazil-nut tree is magically produced by the gods in their anger-lust.[13] The second sentence is a literal citation of what the gods are saying to Yowe'ï-do. Verse 34 is uttered by the dead girl, who cites the comments of the gods who become agitated and alert: a human being ("eater of tiny tortoises") is approaching and his presence scares off the birds from the bush encircling the village of the *Maï*. The expression "our future food" is a classic motif: this was what the Tupinamba called their war captives. The shaman is thus entering the celestial village at this moment. Verse 35 is stated by the girl, who cites the gods inviting her to go hunt toucans, macaws, and cotingas, birds with feathers that are used on earrings and serve as gifts from hunters to their *apĩhi*.

Verse 36 is decisive in the plot. Citing what the gods told him, the shaman remarks that such a request is unnecessary. The gloss of the listeners was: "Kãñĩ-paye-ro said to the *Maï̱*, 'You can take Kãñĩ-paye, she no longer belongs to me, but to you; I did not come to take her back.'" The verse is a sort of elliptical summary of what happened in the sky. Two central ideas are revealed here: the dead girl belongs to the gods, not to her father, but the gods recognize the shaman's power over his daughter, so he has to reiterate that he is ceding her to the *Maï̱*—an act that guarantees him invulnerability in the sky. The shaman accepts the "virilocality" of his daughter; the gods accept him as their affine.

Another bargain underlies this song, which was suggested by the commentators but which is more explicit in other songs. The performance involved an *imone* for the soul of the shaman's wife. In effect, the permanent residence of the dead girl in the sky is the counterpart (*pepi kã*) of the return of the mother's soul, liberated by the gods. The great majority of *imone* bring forth deceased persons, not simply because their souls attract the *ĩ* of the living, but because the shaman engages in a game of "give-and-take" with the gods: keep one of the truly dead and give us back one of the living.

During an intense electrical storm in February 1988, I heard this same shaman violently scold the *Maï̱*: he'd been minding his own business, eating agouti in his patio, but if the *Maï̱* insisted on thundering and hurling dangerous lightning bolts, he would ascend and take back Počihe (another small daughter who had died a year ago). "Kãñĩ-paye-ro is furious with his son-in-law," people commented. Here we can begin to perceive what it is that humans gain in ceding their dead to the gods: life.

We are near the end of the song. Verse 37 is an arrogant solicitation by the gods to the shaman, who add to their demand for his daughter a request for tortoises; here the singer cites them directly. From verse 38 to the end, utterances by the girl alternate with statements by the gods and the shaman. The *ičiri'i* tree yields a highly fragrant resin used by women or quartets of friends. Verse 41 is a generic and concluding statement by the shaman: he answers the theme question of the song. It no longer concerns merely his daughter, but humans in general. "He wants to take his wife hunting" refers to sex. Verse 43 prepares the way for the end of the song: the gods have consumed all of the shaman's cigar; his inspiration is coming to a close. Verse 44 allows a final glimpse of the celestial scene: the girl tells her father what the gods say to her about the perfume that impregnates the very ground they tread.

□

The *Ma̱ï hete,* like the dead, are present in almost all songs, even those uttered by other divinities. Thus, for example, an *imone* song performed in March 1982 for a boy had the following arrangement: the refrain identified the song as one expressed by the "Owl-turned-divinity," who told the (living) father of the boy what the *Ma̱ï hete* said about statements by *Iraparađï,* who is a kind of celestial transfiguration of killers. Another *imone* song was uttered by the dead woman Awara-hi, with a refrain that mentioned the Master of Parakeets and the same theme as the song analyzed above: the dead woman told the shaman (her brother) that a *Ma̱ï* wanted to go out to the forest with her and that he had asked her to ask his brother-in-law (the shaman) for permission.[14]

Both women's and men's souls sing. The only difference is that male souls tend to speak about hunting, war, and celestial battles against cannibal spirits. The songs of *Iaracï̃* always bring the soul of some killer, as do the songs during the *đokã* of strong beer. I observed a much higher frequency, both in songs produced and those remembered during my stay, of manifestations of female souls (I exclude here the fact that the death of Awara-hi generated many of the songs in which she appeared). This may be due to the greater sociological yield of a female soul from the shaman's male point of view: she brings to the forefront the question of the affinity of gods and humans.

One of the functions of the souls' visits is to comment on current events in the village. One time Awara-hi spoke of her fear when approaching the shaman (her "ex-father-in-law") because she saw that he and everyone else in the village were armed with shotguns, resembling whitemen. In fact, the first distribution of arms had occurred the day after her death. Another time she jokingly commented on her widower husband's marriage to a certain girl by speaking of the hairless vulvas of the goddesses.

All the shamans active in 1982 brought the soul of this woman. Some were her "brothers"; others, "fathers-in-law," "parents," "lover," etc. This brings us to two questions: who is being manifested through whose mouth? My impression that is every dead soul comes forward at least once through some shaman's mouth during the period after mourning and the villagers' dispersal. Some of the dead, however, persist in songs, and some even reappear after years of absence. Certain dead, especially children, are sung only by their fathers or close relatives, whereas others are sung by everyone. Some dead, I was told, never appear in songs. All of this is ascribed to the will of the deceased. When two or more souls appear together, they may bear any of the most varied relationships: father and child (as in the case of the song analyzed above), siblings, uncle and nephew, sisters-in-law, and so on. Besides this, it is common for a shaman to sing a soul whose kinship relation to him is not important: he can thereby serve as a bridge through which the visitor addresses a relative.

In short, I do not believe that any significant regularities underlie such relationships. If the tendency is for a shaman to sing the dead of his kindred, the very fluidity of this category makes it possible for him to sing any dead person. Accordingly, shamanic songs do not constitute an "ancestor cult." Rather, a generic relationship exists between the dead and the shamans. The "specialization" of certain shamans in certain dead appears to be a phenomenon similar to their predilection for certain divinities, types of *peyo,* themes, and figures of speech. The immediate cause of the manifestation of the (individual) dead appears more psychological than ceremonial, since it springs from a dream experience. This experience is, of course, subject to interpretations by both the shaman and the listeners of his often ambiguous words, and the songs are the sedimentation of socially given experiences—but this is beyond my reach. Maybe we should leave things where the Araweté let them stand: who sings are the gods and the dead, not the shamans.[15]

The phenomenon of the persistence of certain dead and the absence of others is furthermore analogous to the issue of criteria for choosing eponymous dead for each abandoned village: it appears to be a function of the objective and subjective importance of the deceased. Note also that there are divinities who are rarely sung or who never descend to earth.

Two traits nevertheless characterize every shamanic song. First, no song refers to the process of the gods devouring the dead—the souls who come forth have already "become *Maï.*" Second, a shaman only brings those dead whom he knew while they were alive. The first characteristic is associated with the closing of the gods' path during the village dispersal, causing songs to cease; it also indicates that only divinized souls sing. The act of consumption creates a disjunction between the dead and the living: the soul's song is the voice of someone who is already on the other side of the mirror, even if he still has fundamental social ties with earth. The second trait shows that the participation of the dead in the discourse of the group lasts only as long as the experiential memory of the living. A deceased soul only remembers those who remember him and only reveals himself to those who saw him alive. As their contemporaries gradually join them, the dead are dissolved into the generality of the divine state; hence they are not ancestors.

The shamanic song puts individual temporality—the movement that leads each person to his or her death—to the service of a synchronic connection between the two halves of the cosmos, separated in diachrony: sky and earth, gods and men, those "who left" and those who were "forsaken." The absence of the dead is the guarantee of the presence of the gods in the here and now, and the means of making them part of society. The transformation into divinity that benefits the dead is not intended to ancestralize them, but rather, to affinalize the gods.

If the shaman is a *Ma̲ï dečã̲ka*, a "reflector of divinity," it is because the entire system is put together as a play of images, as Hubert and Mauss said of sacrifice; shamanic discourse is a vertiginous play of reflections of reflections, echoes of echoes, an interminable polyphony where the one who speaks is always an other speaking about what yet others say. The words of others can only be apprehended *per speculum in aenigmate*. And the words of the shaman establish constant and shifting differences among the voices that reflect each other through his own voice, which forms yet another link in the enunciative chain. Just as a person can never pronounce his own name without citing someone else, so the shaman can never speak without it being what others are saying to him; when he speaks *for himself*, it is as the topic of the discourse of others—as a potential cannibal victim. He exists in someone else's sphere of discourse; his words in turn will be recited later on. Even if the singer is rarely identified with the songs, he is accountable for the information contained in them. "So-and-so (a soul) said thus-and-such (something a *Ma̲ï* said), that shaman said," people say. It is always someone in particular who speaks (see chap. 1, sect. 2), but it is never the particular one who is speaking. Just as it is paralyzing to initiate something and assert oneself as the agent of an action that concerns others in concert (see chap. 4, sect. 4), so it is equally difficult to say something that has not been said by someone else. For this reason, if the *tenotã mõ* are indispensable, lest no one do anything, shamans are also indispensable, lest no one say anything. This is the reason, in short, for my suggesting that the role of headman in Araweté society is more compatible with the shaman's position than with the warrior's: the village leader and the shaman are the ones who are entrusted with the actions and words of others.

So, if village leadership is founded on the leadership of an extended family, and if this position implies a reference to the feminine world, the position of the shaman also maintains a fundamental relation to the domestic group. Every married man has an *aray*, the emblematic object that is the fruit of a couple's labor; the domestic interior is the shamanic "temple" par excellence; the shaman's wife is his main assistant and interpreter. Every residential section has at least one important shaman; we could say that the *aray* of each of the conjugal houses is to the *aray* of this shaman as each house is to the section's main house. The correspondence is certainly not perfect: for instance, some leaders of extended families are not shamans, some sections have more than one shaman. Nevertheless, I would suggest that the shamanic unit is the couple, not the individual, and that the proliferation of shamans among the Araweté indicates that this unit is a function that unifies the collectivity (notably in the representative position of the shaman in the alimentary rites, where he is the generalized "owner" of the food relative to the gods), just as much as it works towards its dispersal. A shaman, his wife, and their children are the potential embryo of a local group.[16]

Even if Araweté shamanism is an exclusively masculine attribute—the woman being a mere assistant or a patient—such a position, when compared to that of the warrior-killer, is relatively feminine. This is due not simply to its connection with the domestic structure, but to the very nature of the relationship of the shaman to the gods.

Shaman status does not assure a privileged posthumous destiny, contrary to the majority of other Tupi-Guarani groups. Shamans will be devoured like everyone else, or almost everyone. The sole peculiarity of dead shamans is that their specters exhibit the trait of singing, but this appears to be a marginal phenomenon (and even so, it evinces the terrestrial side of the person).

The shaman naturally has something of the warrior in him. He risks his life among the heavenly cannibals; only his male status saves him from being permanently disembodied. But his very capacity of constant disembodiment, his lingering among the gods, his function as support of the words of the dead—all this characterizes him as a sort of *prospective deceased human*. His position relative to the gods is not much different from that of the souls who have recently arrived in the sky, and his role as host of the community in the food *peyo* situates him as a "nourisher," a position analogous to the owner of beer relative to the rest of the men and people invited from outside villages. Being a man, the shaman is able to carry out the mediation between the feminine world of the village and the hyper-masculine world of the sky. It is a male function, but also a human function: shamans stand, in a certain respect, between women and the gods, just as deceased women, in another, stand between men and the gods.

This ambivalence of the shaman, his role as a "support" or "reflector" of Divinity, can be compared with another sort, that of the killer. If the shaman is a kind of other, a dead being, then the killer is another other, a *Maï*. As a living being, the shaman is a man who links himself to the gods through a structure of affinity (perhaps this is why he sings more female than male deceased), even enjoying the privileged position of "father-in-law." But as a dead being (prospective or definitive), he stands in a generic feminine position relative to the gods: he is someone to be eaten. If the position of the shaman is a complex reflection on mortality, the status of the killer is a prospective vision of immortality. If the shaman is the support of the singing function of the gods, the killer symbolizes their cannibal side. Finally, if the shaman is the instrument through which the gods speak (of sex and food), the killer speaks as the enemy and is inedible.

3. Killers and the Music of Enemies

Although the dead are, in their own way, enemies (either as the terrestrial specter, enemy of the living, or as the soul, received as an enemy by the gods), and the gods too, in their way, are enemies (since they treat us as strangers in paradise), there is no place in the Beyond for the Araweté's real enemies. The souls of enemies, upon arriving in the *Maï*'s village, are hurled back down to earth, where they perish for good. In this sense, enemies only have, or are, *ta'o we:* being deadly, they die. And in this sense, the Beyond is a world without others; enemies, not properly human, have no celestial soul, the principle of the person.

But although dead enemies, as *killers* of the Araweté, do not go to the sky, the *shamans* of enemies are there. They form the class of *Awĩ peye,* "enemy shamans" or "shamans of the enemies," gods who went up to the skies with the *Maï* during the original separation and who frequently come to earth to eat and sing. Just as gods with animal names are animal-modulations of Divinity, so the *Awĩ peye* are a shaman-modulation of enemies. As such, they participate in Divinity at the same time that they implicitly exclude the enemy-aspect that Divinity contains: they are not dangerous. They are foreign gods—included as if to underscore the essential polytheism of the Araweté pantheon.

Such a situation radically inverts the posthumous destiny of *Araweté* shamans and killers. Their shamans, as we saw, receive no special treatment in the sky: they are food for the gods and will be transformed into the *Maï hete,* generalized divinities who are in a certain sense the "shamans of the Araweté," by analogy with the *Awĩ peye.* By contrast, killers and the spirits of *enemies whom they killed* not only ascend to the skies, but also enjoy a special situation: they are transformed into a type of being who is spared consumption and who merges the positions of *bïde* and *awĩ* into a single figure.

To prepare for war, the tradition has been to choose a leader who has the status of a killer, *moropĩ'nã.*[17] The assailants paint themselves black and wear wristbands, headbands, and kneebands of babassu leaflets. The traditional weapons were bows and large arrows with bamboo points and harpy eagle tail feathers (more recently, shotguns have been used). They leave behind their babassu ornaments on the enemies' corpses; when possible, they recoup their arrows (the point of an arrow that had killed large game or enemies would be painted red). Usually they also bring back the enemy's humerus and scapula as trophies, which form part of a dance ornament made with grebe feathers. I was unaware of the practice of decapitation until I heard about the events of 1983 when they brought back the head of a slain Parakanã; the explanation they gave, however, was that it was "to show to the whites."

Neither dead enemies nor Araweté who succumb in war are buried. The reason for the latter case, I was told, is fear; those killed by enemy arrows "belong to the vultures." People killed by enemies are treated in the sky like every other deceased person. The only difference is that when an attack causes many people to be sent there at the same time, their bodies are submerged in the resuscitating bath all together. The specters of war victims apparently have no peculiarity that would distinguish them. Some people, however, ventured the hypothesis that the *ta'o we* of victims killed by enemies stayed with them, a notion consistent with the destiny of enemies killed by the Araweté.

The Araweté say they go to battle to take revenge (*pepi kã,* counterpart) for attacks they have suffered, or out of the simple desire to kill enemies. Someone who is already a killer has this desire "inside his flesh."

After killing or simply wounding an enemy, the killer "dies." As soon as he gets back to the village, he withdraws into his house and lies as if unconscious for several days without eating anything. His belly is full of enemy blood and he vomits continually. This death is not a mere disembodiment, although he must undergo the shamanic *imone* operation; it is a state in which he actually becomes a corpse. The killer hears bumblebees and beetles buzzing and vultures flapping their wings as they approach "his" dead body—that is, the enemy's cadaver—in the forest. He feels "as if he is rotting" (*itoyo herĩ*) and his bones become soft. The *Iwirã ñã* spirits and their kind blow over his face to revive him (see chap. 3, sect. 3).

When the enemy has actually been killed, the period of the killer's "death" lasts three to five days, especially when it is his first homicide. He must drink *iwirara'i* tea, used for menstruation and childbirth, as well as an infusion made from monkey ladder vines (*ihipa-pepe*) "in order to be able to eat tortoise." He may not go out into sunlight, eat green maize, matrinxã fish, a certain type of yam, or red-footed tortoise. Nor may he touch any part of the enemy: he is not the one who cuts off the arm from the cadaver or assembles or dances with the trophy ornament; if he did, his belly would swell up and he would explode. The killer's abstinence and seclusion last only a short time. One restriction, however, is more prolonged: for several weeks afterwards, he may not have sexual relations with his wife. The enemy's spirit is "with him" and would be the first one to have sex with his wife; the killer, coming "behind" him, would be contaminated with the enemy's semen and he would die of *ha'iwã*.

The period of sexual abstinence comes to a close when the *ha̱'o we* of the enemy leaves, heading out to the ends of the earth "looking for songs." Returning quickly, he transmits these songs to the killer through his dreams, as well as the personal names that the killer will confer. One night, he wakes the killer up and violently exhorts him, "*Eya ča-poĩ, tiwã! Eya tere-pɨrahẽ!*": "Come on, get up, *tiwã!* Come on and dance!" The enemy is furious, but he is indissolubly linked to his killer. With time, his hatred ceases, and he and the warrior "mutually cheer each other up," an expression that is evocative of friendship relations. We can thus see a progression: someone who was an enemy becomes a *tiwã*, then an *apĩhi-pihã*, and later in the sky, part of the killer's person.

Thus, the dead enemy is the one who "makes the killer get up" to dance. It is also he who is behind the singer who "makes men rise up" during the *pɨrahẽ* (see chap. 4, sect. 3). He is literally behind them (while during the seclusion phase it was the killer who was behind him—recall the sexual interdiction): indeed, the dead enemy is called *marakã memo'o hã*, the "song teacher," a term that refers to the dance position directly behind the singer, occupied by an experienced man who "breathes" the songs on him. It is thus the dead enemy who makes the killer rise up who in turn makes everyone else rise up. Yet again, it is an other who begins: the history of a song begins with an enemy, its first enunciator.

Prompted to rise up by the enemy, the killer gathers around himself all the men for a commemorative dance when he utters the songs that were revealed to him. Traditionally this first dance was not accompanied by beer-drinking, since it was performed a few weeks after the homicide, but as soon as possible a great beer festival had to be prepared, during which the songs would be repeated. This is why enemies are called "the seasoning for beer" (see chap. 5, sect. 2).

But the typical metaphor for an enemy in general is *marakã nĩ*, "what will be music." Seen from his good side—his dead side—the enemy is the one who brings music. Dance songs are *awĩ marakã*, songs *of* the enemy, sung *by* the killer.

□

Dance songs (*pɨrahẽ marakã*, or *marakã hete*, "true music") have few lyrics (four to eight verses, repeated dozens of times), a well-marked binary rhythm, simple melodic line, and a two-part structure marked by a difference in pace. They are sung in a low register by all the men in unison.[18] This musical genre systematically contrasts with the shamanic solo. Each shaman sings only one song at a time (during his nocturnal solo or a *peyo*), although several shamans may sing simultaneously and independently, filling the night with a kaleidoscopic polyphony. On the other hand, one dead enemy teaches several songs to his killer, and even to other people: everyone who had any sort of close contact with the enemy (exchanging shots, inflicting or suffering wounds) receives songs, such that the *pɨrahẽ* dance festivals involve the collective and unanimous enunciation of diverse melodies woven together sequentially.

The tripartite division that presided over the Araweté naming system is once again encountered in the three types of music: the music of the gods, that is, the shamanic song; the music of enemies, the killer's songs; and the "music of ancestors," *pɨro̱wĩ'hã marakã*. The last two categories are sung during the *pɨrahẽ* and have identical structures and contents. Just as names conferred by the criteria of *pɨro̱wĩ'hã ne* ("after a deceased") largely belong to the divine and enemy semantic classes, so the music "of the ancestors" has a heterogeneous origin. The *pirowĩ'hã marakã* comprise: (1) music of enemies (*awĩ marakã*), originally sung by mythical ancestors or long-dead predecessors; (2) songs of mythical enemies, that is, foreign music (the majority belonging to "ex-Araweté" who departed and "became enemies"); and (3) a small number of songs attributed to mythical animals, all these songs being dangerous and subject to restrictions on their performance.[19]

None of the songs in the *pirahẽ* festivals mention the *Maï* or celestial souls, but refer instead to animals, enemies, Araweté who died in war, arrows, vultures, etc. Although songs of the "music of the ancestors" category are frequently sung during the annual beer festivals, the *awĩ marakã* proper, i.e., songs inspired by recently killed enemies, are the preferred ones. Interestingly, a woman once told me that the "good" songs in a *pirahẽ* are "ancestral" ones (their origin as enemy songs is recognized but not emphasized), since the *awĩ marakã* are sad and frightening. Once again we witness the feminine preference for the *pirowĩ'hã* criterion, directed towards the interior of the *socius,* which we saw operating in the naming system. But here things are inverted: the *pirahẽ* songs are a masculine affair, and men prefer enemies. When I returned to the Ipixuna in February 1988, the first thing I was asked was to record the *awĩ marakã* obtained from the dead Parakanã, for which they improvised a *pirahẽ.*

The acquisition of songs from dead enemies seems more fundamental than the acquisition of names: enemies are called "future music," not "future names." Although he is an important name-giver, the killer is above all a singer. Finally, even though names are inspired by shamanic visions and dreams about enemy spirits, they are conferred by Araweté, but songs bring in the words of others directly: the ones who speak are the gods, the dead, and enemies.

Some shamanic songs do not involve manifestations of souls, but rely heavily on fragments of myths instead. But even this variant (judged very poor) of the music of the gods is not a myth in song form; it is always considered to be a divinity manifesting himself. The *Maï marakã* are never commemorations, but epiphanies. In contrast, dance songs, except for the moment of their first enunciation, are always literal repetitions of a certain repertoire. They are by definition "repeated," sung by a choir of men. Although they are identified by their author-singer (in contrast to shamanic songs), they build up a collective musical memory. The only way of composing new dance songs is through the death of an enemy (the death of a jaguar is commemorated by a traditional song), while the music of the gods undergoes continual invention. In a certain sense, all enemy music becomes "ancestral music" as their composers die off.

Compared to the music of the gods, enemy songs have restricted informational contents. In them the visual propensity of Araweté poetry is exploited to a maximum, producing synthetic and vigorous images. The important difference between the two major poetic-musical types lies, as should be expected, in the enunciative format. While in the music of the gods the enunciative positions were differentiated in such a way that the "voice" of the shaman could be distinguished from the rest, thereby creating a polyphony, the *awĩ marakã* are always sung from the point of view of the enemy. He is the subject of the utterances pronounced by the singer. Since the *awĩ marakã* also feature embedded citations, the result is thus a phenomenon of identification of the deceased with his killer by means of another complex play of mirrors. Let us turn to some examples. The first is a song performed by Yakati-ro-reme, taught by a Parakanã killed in 1976:

(1) "'I'm dying,'
(2) said the deceased Moiwito;
(3) thus spoke my prey;
(4) thus spoke the deceased Koiarawï;

(5) "In your great patio,
(6) 'Eeh!' said the *Towaho,*
(7) 'Here is my prisoner
(8) in the great bird's patio.'"

The deceased who said he was dying is Maria-ro, an Araweté man killed by the Parakanã shortly before the counterattack that resulted in the death of the enemy who speaks in this song. He is called by his childhood name (Moiwito) and a nickname (Koiarawï), with the suffix for "deceased." In this way, the enemy-singer defines himself as being the killer of Maria-ro (verse 3), and cites what his victim says: "I am dying." In the second part, the enunciator changes. "Your" great patio refers to the vultures, mentioned by the epithet "great bird" in verse 8. The vultures' "great patio" is a macabre metaphor for the clearing opened by these birds around a cadaver in the forest—here, referring to the site of the body of the enemy who is singing, not that of Maria-ro. The words of this second part are attributed to the *Towaho* mentioned by the dead enemy in verse 6. *Towaho* is the name of an ancient tribe of archetypal enemies. It so happens that this "*To-*

waho" is none other than Yakati-ro himself, that is, the Araweté who is singing, the killer of the enemy. From the point of view of the enemy, his killer is a *Towaho*. The killer thus cites himself, having the enemy say what he *himself* would be saying. We could call this process "reverberation": the enemy cites a dead Araweté (verse 1) and then cites his own killer (verses 5–8), all through the mouth of the latter, who globally "cites" what the enemy is saying to him. The ones who end up being cited, twice, are Araweté: the dead one, in the first part, the killer in the second, always from the point of view of a third party, the dead enemy. Who is actually speaking? Who is the deceased, who the enemy?

This is the song of Kããĩwïdĩ-no-reme, taught by an Asuriní wounded in the 1970s:

(1) "'The *tata* hawk is joyous,'
(2) said the cotinga [perched] on the small bow;
(3) he is joyous on the branch of the *yočĩ*,
(4) that's what my wife heard";

(5) "'The small bamboo is deflected,
(6) it is deflected away from us;
(7) it is deflected away from our path,'
(8) that's what my wife talked about."

Here the spirit of the enemy, who escaped with his life from Kaniwïdi-no's arrows, is rejoicing over his good luck. He cites what his wife said or heard. The first part of the song portrays the small *tata* hawk hopping about joyfully on the branch of a tree; a cotinga, perched on the singer's bow, is the one who tells this to the enemy's wife. The second part commemorates the bad shot of the singer, whose arrow ("small bamboo," an ironic expression) is deflected from the enemy and his wife. Here too the enemy cites his wife.

But eventually the Asuriní was shot when he was alone in the forest. Who, then, is this "my wife" who sings? None other than Kããĩwïdĩ-hi, that is, the wife of the Araweté singer. Everybody explained to me that "my wife" referred to the singer's wife, but *the one who said* "my wife" was the enemy's spirit. The song is enunciated from his point of view: the arrows are deflected from him. But the enunciative format is such that the singer, referring to his wife as "my wife," is actually citing the enemy's words. We have already seen how the killer must take precautions about having sex shortly after the homicide: his wife in fact becomes the enemy's wife.

This is the song of Moneme-do, taught by a Parakanã he killed in 1976:

(1) "These *aramanã* beetles,
(2) the dangling *aramanã*,
(3) these mamangaba bumblebees,
(4) [dangling] from our long hair."

The spirit of the enemy alludes to his condition as a corpse: beetles and bumblebees alight on his putrefying body. The pronoun "our" (inclusive plural) indicates that it refers to the hair of both the dead man and his killer, beings who are interwoven, so to speak, like the locks of hair in this song.[20]

The identification of the slayer with the victim, which was set up with the simultaneous "death" and "putrefaction" of both, is pursued further in the songs. Through the mouth of the killer, the one who speaks is the deceased, but in a manner different from the play of citations in shamanic music. The shaman portrays and transmits; the killer incarnates and becomes his enemy, reflecting him in such a way that the other who speaks is the other speaking as if himself, and vice versa.

□

This identification of the slayer with the dead enemy, generating the paradoxical situation of the war dance in which the male community unites around the killer so everybody can repeat the words stated by the enemy, is an identification that has a price. It entails an alteration, an Other-becoming. The killer becomes an enemy, for the spirit of the victim will never leave him. Shortly after the homicide, the killer's weapons must be taken away from him, since the *awĩ na̲'o we* (enemy's specter), lusting for revenge, inspires in him a blind desire to continue killing, but now directed against his fellow tribesmen. The warrior will remain exposed to this danger for a long time; he is seized by fits of fury, and his *apĩhi* lovers have to come to his aid, embracing him and calming him down with gentle words. At times he must flee to the forest: the enemy "feathers the killer's head" (compare what the *Ma̲ï* did to the Brazil-nut tree) and makes him deranged. "When he comes over the killer, the enemy's spirit transforms him into an enemy of ours." The spirit cannot take revenge directly on the killer, since he is an appendage of him. Only many years later, it seems, does he become quiescent and leave the slayer in peace.

Even so, killers are considered temperamental people, prone to come to blows when irritated. This distinguishes them from "harmless" people (everyone else, in essence, except for sexually voracious women). In 1982–83, there were five living killers; only one was an active shaman, but this was a coincidence, since numerous killers who had recently passed away had been prestigious shamans, and the killer of the Parakanã in 1983 was one of the most important shamans of the village.

The position of *moropï'nã*, killer, does not confer ceremonial privileges. Its only visible mark is patchy bangs, since the enemy's spirit makes the slayer's hair over his forehead fall out in clumps—the same effect produced by large game (tapir and deer) in accidents occurring in shamanic rites. But the position does convey an honorable status, and *moropï'nã* are admired and slightly feared; the five killers were among the few people who never became the object of the usual mockery that otherwise spared no one, not even great shamans. The demographic collapse upon contact made the Araweté lose eight killers in a short space of time, something that was frequently recalled. A long time ago, "all the men, without exception, were killers." Although certainly an exaggerated statement, it does express an ideal.

The essence of the person of the killer is revealed posthumously. The enemy's spirit, which always stays "with" (*-rehe*) or "in" (*-re*) the killer, ascends to the sky with him. The killer and his enemy become an *Iraparadï*, a kind of being feared by the *Maï*. An *Iraparadï*, the soul of an Araweté with an enemy component added to it, is not eaten by the gods. He goes directly to the bath of immortality; he is transformed into a *Maï* without passing through the trial of consumption. Sometimes this used to happen without passing through the trial of death tout court; just as "a long time ago every man was a killer," so it is said that various warriors of long ago did not die, but ascended to the skies in flesh and soul. The dogma is sometimes expressed literally: "A killer does not die."

We saw how, upon killing an enemy, the killer dies and then resuscitates; henceforth he is "immortal"—that is why he is not eaten. He is himself already a cannibal (his belly is filled with the enemy's blood)[21] and he is already an enemy, or an ambiguous fusion of *bïde* and *awï:* in other words, he is already a *Maï*. If the shaman is a prospective deceased, the killer is a prospective god: he incarnates the figure of the Enemy at the same time that he is an ideal Araweté.

The cannibalistic consumption of the dead is the precondition for their transformation into incorruptible Divinity: immortal beings endowed with "glorious bodies," as theologians would say. But because the killer is an other—being an enemy—he has already suffered this apotheotic transubstantiation. A killer does not putrefy in death. In the idealized past, he went up to the skies incarnate; nowadays, his buried body rots (as everyone can see) but it does not liberate a specter. Some say that it does, but that his specter is "inoffensive" (*marĩ-ĩ me'e*), precisely what he was not when he was alive.

We can thus see that the Guarani concept of *kandire,* the state of the "nondecay of the bones," is attained in the Araweté case by the *hubris* of the killer, not by the asceticism of the shaman (Cadogan 1959: 59, 143–48; H. Clastres 1978). After all, the killer has already rotted (his *bones* get soft) along with the cadaver of his victim; resurrected, raised up by the spirit of the other, he henceforth has an imputrescible and inedible body. The entire Guarani symbology of resurrection as a means of "keeping the skeleton erect by means of the flow of speech" is here shifted to the killer complex: it is the enemy's voice that keeps him erect. He is not eaten for the same reason that he does not rot on earth or in the sky: homicide is the Araweté route to what the Guarani term *aguyje,* that is, maturation. *Aguyje,* a state of completeness and perfection that allows one to attain immortality without dying (H. Clastres 1978: 97), refers in the first place to the ripeness of a fruit (Cadogan 1959: 191; Dooley 1982: 26). Common mortals are thus "green"—children, as the Araweté would say (see chap. 3, sect. 1); death and divine cooking are necessary to make them mature. But the Guarani shaman and the Araweté warrior have already been transformed—they are no longer raw—and hence they will not rot or be cooked.[22]

Children do not produce a *ta̲'o we* because they are on this side of the human condition—they are too "green"; killers do not produce one because they are on the other side—they are already gods. This helps to clarify at least one of the motivations behind Tupinamba cannibalism and the haughtiness of the war captives:

> and some are as contented though they are to be eaten, that in no wise they will consent to be ransomed for to serve; for they say that it is a wretched thing to die, and lie stinking, and eaten with Wormes (Cardim 1906 [1584]:432).

Whereas the Tupinamba were eaten in order to avoid rotting, the Araweté killer is not eaten because he does not rot. Among the Tupinamba, only a killer is immortal, and only a cannibal victim does not rot; among the Araweté, only a killer is immortal and is not eaten. Cannibalism is a metaphysical cuisine.

□

The spirit of a jaguar, *ñã na'o we,* is treated in the same way and has the same fate as the spirit of an enemy. Yet again we encounter a theme of the Tupinamba, who executed jaguars with all the honors of a prisoner of war, taking names on their heads.[23] Like the enemy's spirit, the *ha'o we* of a jaguar cannot be killed shamanically. It remains with its killer and turns into a sort of hunting dog for him: it sleeps below his hammock and, through his dreams, directs him towards sites of abundant game, especially tortoises (compare this with the "Jaguar-Thing" god, the main eater of tortoises). The song performed upon the death of a jaguar obeys the same process of reverberation found in the *awĩ marakã:* the singer is called the "jaguar's future prey" and he brings forth the jaguar speaking of the humans it will eat (representing a temporal inversion as well).

A dead jaguar is thus the inverse of a living jaguar, a wild animal and competitor of man. This is exactly like the transformation in the enemy's spirit: from a threat to life, the enemy becomes a guarantee of life; from a cause for fear, he turns into a means of inspiring fear in celestial enemies, the *Maï.*[24] If the killer is transformed into an enemy upon killing one, the latter becomes something else when his murderer dies—a part of him. From metaphor to metonymy, one would be tempted to say (Lévi-Strauss 1966 : 106).

4. The Enemy's Point of View

The word *Iraparadï* appears to be a poetic form of *irapã,* bow, and is thus a synecdoche of the warrior status. It is the term for *awĩ,* enemy, in the language of the gods. The *Maï* use the term to refer to the *Awĩ peye,* whitemen and other enemies, and Araweté killers.[25] The generic figure of *Iraparadï* or its specification as the soul of a certain killer always intervenes when songs bring forth dangerous divinities or when the gods and the dead have something to say to a living killer.

As a designation for the status of the Araweté warrior, the concept of *Iraparadï* is revealed to be essentially a perspective. If the *Maï* are one and the same time the celestial parallel of the Araweté and a figuration of the Enemy, that is, if they contemplate us with the eyes of an enemy and we eye them as enemies, the *Iraparadï* are the Araweté actively thinking of themselves as enemies. They are something that the *Maï* fear, just as the common dead fear the *Maï*. This capacity to see oneself as the enemy, which is at the same time the ideal angle of viewing oneself, strikes me as the secret to Tupi-Guarani anthropophagy. The cannibal enemy is always the other; but what else is an *Iraparadï* if not the other of others, an enemy of the *Maï* who are the masters of the celestial perspective?

The ideal that long ago all men were killers is an implicit translation of a situation in which only women would be eaten by the gods (since small children are not)—or rather, of the idea that the position of "food of the gods" is feminine, and hence the status of living humans is feminine. The typical deceased is thus a woman, just as the ideal immortal is a warrior. Ideal, but paradoxical: this immortal is a dead warrior, a being who only realizes his full potential through a dual relationship with death. A killer dies when he kills his enemy, he identifies with him, and he is able to truly benefit from these deaths only when he truly dies: confronting the gods, he is not treated *like* an enemy because he *is* an enemy, an *Iraparadï*, and thus immediately a *Maï*.

During the time that I lived with the Araweté, the position of the killer was less important and conspicuous than that of the shaman (although the effects of the slain Parakanã on the naming system observed in 1988 suggested that things could be different). The place of the singer in *pɨrahẽ* dances was vicariously occupied by any adult capable of remembering the songs. On the other hand, the daily exercise of shamanism could not simply rely on memory: it needed individuals capable of actually communicating with the gods.

This differential importance of the two modes of masculine being may be due to the peace that characterized Araweté life at the time, but I believe it has a structural foundation. Although the Araweté shaman is a prospective deceased—since, as C. Hugh-Jones (1979) said of his Tukano counterpart, he is capable of *being divided in life*, metaphorizing death—he nevertheless plays a vital social function: he is a "being-for-the-group." Although the Araweté killer is a prospective god—since, like the Guarani shaman, he is capable of *not being divided in death*—he manifests a mortal and individual function: he is a "being-for-himself." The shaman is a living entity par excellence, the representative of the living in the sky, and the channel of transmission (what the Araweté once called a "radio") of the celestial dead. He is a mediator, ubiquitous but always distinct from what he communicates, communicating what is separate. His efficacy depends on his being alive and bringing the dead. On the other hand, the killer represents no one, but incarnates the enemy with whom he is confounded; he is the place of a complex metamorphosis that only benefits himself. The potency of his status is only actualized after he is dead. Although shamanism bears a latent potential encouraging dispersal, it is nonetheless through the shaman that the Great Alliance between heaven and earth is brought about, manifested in banquets and songs. Although the complex of homicide, for its part, unites the community around the death of an enemy (inverting the dispersal triggered by the death of a member of the group), it inevitably alienates the killer, separating him and estranging him. Clearly the ideal of a society composed of warriors is present in Araweté culture and must have been doubly "vital" in their long history of wars. But from the point of view of individual eschatology, a killer is someone who has already passed to the other side, becoming an enemy and becoming a divinity. For this reason, if the shaman is to the deceased as the killer is to the divinity, the shaman is to the living as the killer is to the dead. Society would be impossible without shamanism; but masculinity would be unthinkable without the figure of the killer.

The *Maï̱* are at one and the same time shamans and killers, life and death. They are the archetype of the shaman, since they hold the science of resurrection; they are also the archetype of the killer, in that they represent an ambivalent fusion of *bïde* and *awĩ*, transforming the dead into themselves through consumption, exactly as the slayer transforms the enemy, transforming himself into the latter. But the status of shaman does not make a dead person distinguished, while that of a killer does. Although there is no place in the sky for enemies (who are killers of Araweté), there is one for the "enemy shamans" and for Araweté killers—and both are seen by the *Maï̱* as *Iraparadï*, "enemies of the gods." The shaman-aspect of enemies and the enemy-aspect of the Araweté are partial realizations of the divine synthesis in the figure of the *Maï̱*—shamans, killers, enemies, and Araweté.

Araweté gods are essentially warriors, and I believe that their position as affines of humans is linked to this quality. The Araweté "man-god" is a slayer, not a priest. It is in this sense that women, doubly noncelestial, doubly unconnected to death (a male province), incarnate life and the human condition. It is also for this reason that they will become the ideal food of the gods. The shaman, located between life and death, but on the side of the living, thus occupies an intermediate position between the deadly, individual, and posthumous world of the warrior, and the vital, present, and collective world of femininity. Women are the mistresses of this world. (See Fig. 2.)

The intermediate situation of the shaman confers on him his political value and his capacity for representation, exercised between cos-

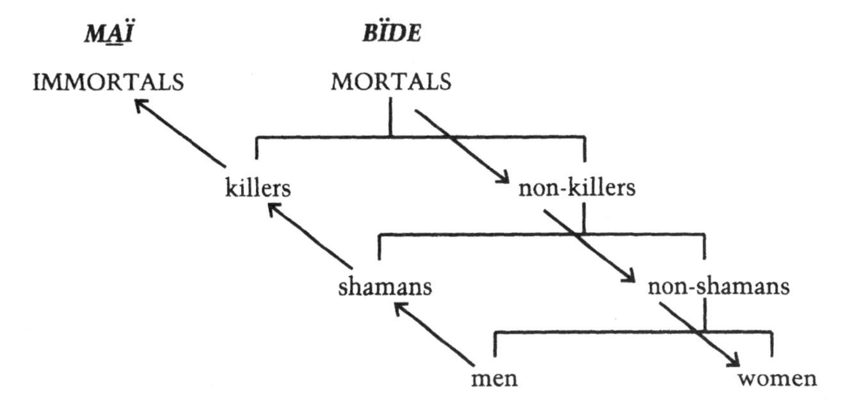

FIGURE 2. Men and women, gods and humans

mic planes and within society. He is materialized in the enunciative structure of his song, an echo chamber where nevertheless one always knows that another is speaking. On the other hand, the liminal and excessive place of the killer is marked by his exteriority to the social, in the quasi-incestuous reverberation that he maintains with himself and that is consummated only in death. This is the paradox of the Araweté warrior: pure spirit, a man without a shadow and without flesh, he is his own enemy and the center of a society without a center.

9 Beings of Becoming

1. The Cannibal *Cogito*

Death produces a division of the person and renders it something doubly separated. The *ĩ*, the principle that gives the living entity its sense (that is, the principle underlying the unfolding of life), generates *qua* material shadow, the terrestrial spectral double, and *qua* vitality and consciousness, the celestial soul. The first accompanies the *Ãñĩ*, the regressive image of wild nature, and prevails during the rotting of the flesh; the second is transformed into a *Maï* from the bones by undergoing consumption and a resuscitating bath. Both are *-a'o we*, divided or separated persons: the first, a soulless body or a kind of anti-soul, the animated emanation of a corpse; the second, a bodiless soul or a kind of incorruptible and supernatural anti-body. The first is absence and faces the past: *bïde pe*, ex-person. The second is presence and looks towards the future: *bïde rĩ*, what will be a person.

The terrestrial *-a'o we* suffers a double rotting—first of the body and then through the degeneration of its double into a dead opossum. The celestial one suffers a double cooking: once prior to being devoured and again through immersion in an effervescent rejuvenating bath. These transformations of the substance of the living form a ternary system, as shown in figure 3. This is clearly a dynamic figure, incapable of being stabilized by reducing the third term (the celestial principle) to a function of mediation. The celestial soul is not a mediator between the living and the dead; it incarnates the meaning of the person more intensely and perfectly than the living. Here is yet another example of the structure of hierarchical opposition, dynamic and asymmetrical (Dumont 1980), which has repeatedly emerged throughout this analysis of Araweté cosmology. It is the living who constitute a middle term between the pure negativity of the terrestrial double, and the presence and plenitude of the celestial principle. The opposition between the living and the dead is not static and horizontal, but

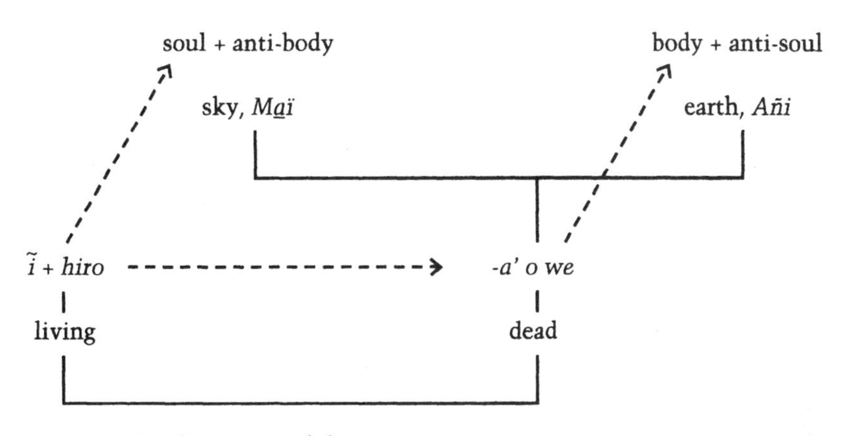

FIGURE 3. Triadic system of the person

unfolds in pairs on distinct levels: life/death and, within death, Life/Death. Within death, the opposition Life/Death is *maximal:* the difference between the celestial and terrestrial principles of the person is *greater* than the difference between the living and the dead. In sum, death is the encompassing term; life, the encompassed.

The life of souls in heaven is not an inversion or a negative of the living state, but rather, of the dead—of the solitary, poor, nasty, brutish, and short life of the specter. The celestial *modus vivendi* is an amplification of the earthly good life. In this sense perhaps it is possible to understand the equivalence between the concepts of *bïde rĩ,* future person, and *Maï̲ dĩ,* future divinity, that designate the active soul. The true *bïde* are the *Maï̲,* the gigantic *tiwã* of humans, and the person is only completed in his becoming, necessarily, an Other: a deceased, an enemy, a god. Between what was once a person and what will be a person, there is poised, fleeting and neutral, the person. Having been, going to be, it is not, properly speaking, anything: it becomes.

Manuela Carneiro da Cunha aptly summarized the dialectic of the Gê *cogito* in the conclusion to her analysis of Krahó death: "Seen as fundamentally diverse, the dead serve to affirm the living. Krahó thought seems to proceed . . . by complementarities, by negations: I am that which I am not is not" (1978:143). This strikes me as a perfect example of analytic judgment. The Araweté and the other Tupi-Guarani seem to prefer the supplementary of a priori synthetic judgments, where one must go beyond the given concepts in order to produce something new, a movement foreign to identity and to contradiction.[1] Cannibalism offers an ideal schematism for such synthetic judgments that construct the person by making *time* intervene: the I is something that is not yet, and that which I shall be is all that I am not—an "ambiguous and tempting" god, as Nietzsche said of another eater of raw meat, Dionysius. I shall attain fullness of being only after having been devoured by my enemy—because, as a deceased, I am an enemy of the celestial Subject (*bïde*)—or after I have devoured (slain) an enemy on earth, which turns me into an enemy, then a god. The system is like a twisted circular band with no reverse side: the deceased is the enemy, the enemy is the god, the god is the deceased, and the deceased is the self. The cannibal *cogito* does not express the narcissistic geometry of representation, but the topological torsion of other-becoming. The peculiar inversion of Araweté perspectivism, which posits the human subject as the object of divine anthropophagy, suggests something that was already evident in the Tupinamba case: that Tupi-Guarani cannibalism is the opposite of a narcissistic incorporation; it is an alteration, a becoming.

Death—another name for time—constitutes the person as an intercalary relation. The opposition between the celestial and terrestrial principles of the subject is not synchronic, but diachronic, suggesting a play of differential repetition, where the repeated "term" does not exist outside repetition. *Bïde,* the person, does not have a conceptual place of its own; it is *in between,* divided between the naked, dead repetition of the terrestrial double (a larval shadow that repeats an absence) and the living repetition of the celestial soul (a future position that displaces presence to a beyond and identity to an other-becoming). Alterity is intrinsic to the Araweté person; as we have seen, here the Other is not a mirror, but a destiny, and is thus not an entity in a field of identities, but a pole of attraction, a source of inchoateness, the becoming of being.

To be sure, the *ta̲'o we* as well as the *Ma̲ï dĩ* are in the future, since what *is,* that which is present, are the living, and death is the future. But there is a difference between a future perfect (that which will have been) and a simple future (that which will be): the shadow that retreats, the divinity that advances. This future is also an absolute past, or rather, a nontemporal state: before the Separation that created death and difference, humans were (since they were with) the gods. This is what humans are: "those who will go," *ɨha me'e rĩ.* But this is death.

Panta rhei? The return of the dead, in the shamanic song, is a most precarious form of perpetuity. The celestial souls are not ancestors; their personal principle does not wait more than two generations to plunge into oblivion and to silence its voice. The bones are dispersed on earth, the living go forward, names return only erratically and sporadically, signifying almost nothing. The living are under the aegis of impermanence.

But death assures another continuity: between heaven and earth, gods and humans. Araweté society persists because it is composed not only of men, but of gods as well. It is, in the final analysis, a dualistic society: a terrestrial moiety, as it were, and a celestial moiety, linked by matrimonial alliance. Humans give mates and foods to their cannibal brothers-in-law. In exchange they receive songs, a supplementary presence of their dead, an ideal of immortality, but above all, I believe, life: this present life. I suspect that the dead die so that we may continue living. Here I touch on a question about which the Araweté do not like to speak: the collapse of the sky on their heads. The living ally themselves with the gods by means of matrimonial and alimentary prestations so that the latter will not decide to demolish the firmament and thus annihilate humanity. And yet, they know that the weight of the dead must inevitably cause the sky to split open one day.

This "dual organization" of humans/divinities, asymmetrical and diachronic, is in essence the Araweté *social structure.* The founding principle of their metaphysics is that Being is constituted only by projecting itself through exteriority, entailing the lack of elaboration of differences internal to the social body, which in this sense has no interior. Its morphological acentrism is a function of the vertical and diachronic structure of the cosmos, and society is part of the cosmology, in the strict sense of the term. Here, a functionalist or sociocentric perspective would be doomed to contemplating nothingness, or else to take refuge in "fluidity," in "individualism," or, who knows, in historical degeneration.

□

But after all, why cannibalism? It appears that Araweté cannibalism has not always been "merely" metaphysical. Their sagas are peopled with accounts of cannibalism. My data here are scarce and ambiguous. Even those people who denied categorically that their group was cannibalistic—underscoring instead their status as victims of the *Towa̱ho, Todï,* and other former enemies—admitted that not a few of their recent forefathers were *awĩ a re,* "eaters of enemies." In their wars in the Ipixuna region against the Asuriní, Kayapó, and Parakanã, they never ate enemies; but long ago, say some, they did so. My impression is that anthropophagy was, at least in this century, a restricted and infrequent practice. But the expression *awĩ a re* is current, and *awĩ kã'e*, "smoked enemy," is a personal name. A certain traditional belief is revealing: an eater of enemies lives a long time, is immune to diseases, and is physically strong. "Real" cannibalism thus produces a kind of relative immortality, which evokes the actual immortality of the celestial cannibals and the transcendental condition of the killer. The flesh of an enemy, in this case, would be the opposite of *ha'iwã hã* (lethal) meats. We could therefore surmise that the vigor of the *Maï* is due as much to their warrior diet of human flesh as to their shamanic science of eternal youth, a theme present in Tupinamba cannibalism (discussed below).

The longevity of the elders who survived in 1981–83 was jokingly attributed to this *awĩ a re* condition. Queried, the elders laughed loudly and denied it; only the venerable Pãñorã-hi (who died in 1987) willingly accepted the opprobrious label, saying that indeed she was. But I never managed to get much out of her about this, nor out of others. Perhaps my intimacy with the Araweté had not yet reached such a point. They would say, "That ended a long time ago, now we are 'harmless' . . ." One thing is definite: even if the *bïde* are not devoted cannibals, their gods certainly are, and their chosen victims are the *bïde*. Let us now explore divine cannibalism.

□

The Araweté triad of the person fits into the Tupi-Guarani cosmological tripartition proposed in chapter 3, as can be seen in figure 4. In this schema, culture appears as a state that is at one and the same time ambivalent and neutral. Let us consider which values fall under its rubric. The double cooking of immortality and the double rotting of death (both involving cannibal transubstantiations) determine as if by elimination the distinctive character of the provisional life of humans in the present, made of flesh and bone, existant between sky and earth: they are the *raw*. If the dead are twice rotten and the immortals twice cooked (instead of "twice born," as in Hinduism), it is because the living are "twice" raw: something incomplete, ambiguous, and immature, which only death will elaborate.

This illuminates further meanings of that epithet of the *Maï* as *me'e wi a re*, "eaters of raw flesh." The gods in fact eat cooked food—they cook us, since *we* are the "raw flesh." Their epithet expresses this: the gods are anthropophagi. They are, to be precise, *jaguars with fire*. The system operates through an inversion of perspectives. From

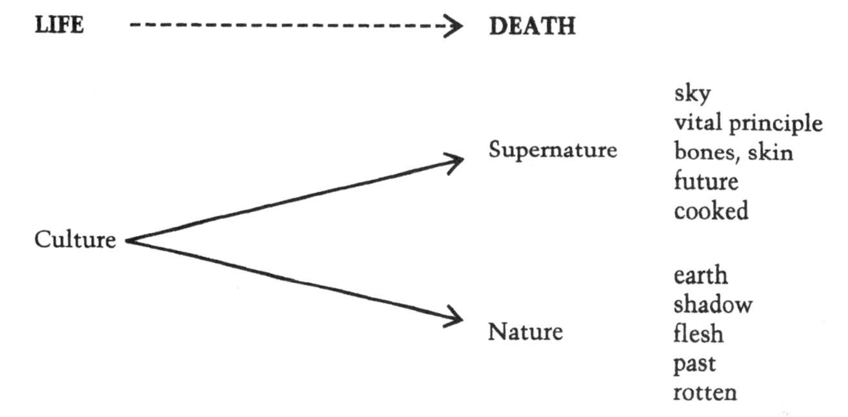

FIGURE 4. Triad of the person within the cosmological tripartition

the humans' point of view, the gods are eaters of the raw because they formerly did not have cooking fire. In Tupi-Guarani mythology, fire was stolen from Vulture, Master of the Rotten, not from Jaguar, Master of the Raw, as among the Gê (Huxley 1956: 14–15; Lévi-Strauss 1969b: 139–42). That is, Araweté gods "are jaguars." From the gods' point of view, humans are raw, food that needs to be cooked twice to be free of corruption. Drawing on Lévi-Strauss's model (1969b: 143; discussed here in chap. 7, note 18), I propose:

(Nature:Rotten) :: (Culture: Raw) :: (Supernature:Cooked)

This system is not stable, however, and, in the Araweté case, appears overdetermined. The ambiguity of humans—as subjects, they are the masters of the cooked; as objects, they are something raw—is repeated on the plane of the gods. A jaguar with fire is nothing else but a cannibal human. Cannibalism, the "fourth alimentary diet" (Lévi-Strauss 1987: 40), merges the raw and the cooked in a complex figure.

This allows me to suggest a hypothesis. In the Tupi-Guarani myth of the theft of the civilizing fire, the losing side, symbol of Nature, is the vulture (the central opposition being rotten/cooked). Could this be because another function is reserved for the jaguar and the raw, that of positively incarnating cannibalism? Another classic motif of Tupi mythology is the mythic twins, associated directly or indirectly with the pair jaguar/opossum (Araweté, Kaapor, Tupinamba, Guarani, Shipaya, etc.). We saw how the opossum, sign of the rotten, is linked to the spectral double of humans; hence the jaguar, symbol of the raw, marks the function played by the *Maï* in eschatology: celestial cannibalism.[2]

Accordingly, in the Araweté tripartition, Culture is an ambivalent and neutral state, Supernature is ambivalent but positively connoted, and Nature is nonambivalent and negatively connoted as unequivocal and malignant rottenness. In other Tupi-Guarani cosmologies, these values are distributed in different ways. The ambiguity of the *Maï* appears to be a distinctive trait of Araweté thought.

Women, necessarily nonkillers, are inevitably the victims of celestial cannibalism. In this sense, only they are necessarily raw. This is consistent with the idea that the world of the human *socius* is fundamentally feminine:

(Human:Divine) :: (Women:Men) :: (Raw:Cooked)

The opposition between soul and specter expressed in terms of skin and bones versus flesh suggests the theme of the "secondary burial" and its dialectic of death and regeneration. Bloch and Parry (1982: 20–21) advance the hypothesis that such an opposition—to which they add yet another, men (bones) versus women (flesh)—would be operative only in social systems where the distinction consanguines/affines is fundamental, which is not the case in endogamic or strongly cognatic systems. The opposition appears to be valid for the Araweté: the distinction consanguines/affines is unmarked inside human society, which is endogamic and cognatic, but it nevertheless structures the relations—equally sociological—between the sky (masculine) and the earth (feminine). This provides an additional argument for the idea that society is complete only at the level of cosmology.[3]

□

The cannibalism of the *Maï* connotes various determinations of alterity. The dead are eaten because they refuse to enter into alliance relations with the gods: they are thus like enemies for the latter, who occupy the position of celestial *Bïde*. But the gods, in relation to us, the dead—who are, after all, humans—are cannibals because they are enemies. This cannibalism appears as a synthetic solution and as a condition for the possibility of alliance between the living and the gods: it transforms some humans (the dead) into *Maï*. The gods, transcendental affines of humans, are above all *those who eat:* on earth, the food of humans; in the sky, humans themselves.

Araweté divine cannibalism transcends the distinction between "exo-" and "endo-cannibalism." What is inside, what is outside, who is the other, in the relation between humans and divinities? What is eaten is always the other: a deceased of one's group, an other, must be devoured by the gods; the enemy, an other, must be killed (eaten) by an already-god, the warrior. Neither "endo-" nor "exo-," this cannibalism, like that of the Tupinamba, Yanomami, or Pakaa-Nova (Albert 1985; Vilaça 1989) links affines or transforms into affines those whom it links. Between gods and men, via the dead, a process of reverberation is established where the position of alterity circulates incessantly. The dead, others, are eaten by the others, gods, in order to be transformed into Us—enemy gods. The living, in the final analysis, are something between two others: the deceased that was, the god that will be. The being of the living is the product of this double alterity brought about by cannibalism. That is why the gods devour the dead: so that the Araweté can be—can be real.

2. Spiritual Dualism and Cosmological Triads

The posthumous disaggregation of the person into two polar aspects is a theme that runs through all Tupi-Guarani cosmologies, marking a double difference in relation to the state of the living: a principle of regression towards Nature, a principle of progression towards Supernature. This movement is associated with various other polarities already mentioned. Depending on the cosmology, such a division of the person may either be inherent in every human being, or it may differentiate sociometaphysical positions and statuses. The Araweté put these two possibilities together: every living being has a potential spectral-aspect and a potential soul-principle, but killer status "sublimates" the terrestrial portion of the subject and transforms him into a prospective god. In the majority of the other Tupi-Guarani societies, it is shaman status that distinguishes the person posthumously. Perhaps this is why Schaden (1959: 119) asserts that the "mythic hero of the tribal tradition" for all the Tupi-Guarani is modeled on the figure of the shaman, not that of the warrior. Here we must recall that the peculiar situation of the *Maï* as affines of humans contrasts with the paternal position of the rest of the Tupi-Guarani "cultural heroes": the former are essentially warriors, the latter, shamans.

A preliminary hypothesis, therefore, would articulate Tupi-Guarani spiritual duality with the basic functional pair of these societies: shaman/warrior. But this pair orients the masculine position, determining the feminine position by exclusion. The pair is linked to another masculine position that, first in the order of the real, is overdetermined in the symbolic order by the values of shamanism or warfare: the position as head of the extended family or village chief—the "father-in-law function," linked to femininity. Accordingly, I advance a general model:

Men		Women		Men
(Nature:Warrior)	::	(Culture:Father-in-law/Chief)	::	(Supernature:Shaman)
Rotten, death		Raw, life		Cooked, immortality

This model does *not* summarize any concrete Tupi-Guarani cosmology, nor is it a syncretic inductive generalization, but a deductive construction from which transformations can be derived. These transformations will depend on the specific modalities of hierarchical encompassment among the three domains and on the consequent assimilation among certain positions. Among the Araweté, for instance, warrior status connotes immortality (by means of a previous passage through rottenness), shaman status is associated with village leadership, and celestial cannibalism involves an interference between the raw and the cooked. What is invariant for the Tupi-Guarani is the subordination of the central complex—society—to the other two, which divide the world of exteriority (see chap. 3, sect. 4). This matrix can be compared (if need be, to allay suspicions of smuggling in a Dumézilian tripartition) to the model of the five functions of Tukano social structure (C. Hugh-Jones 1979 : 54–75) or to the Gê dualist matrix that distributes the above values differently (Turner 1984).

Two additional points. First, it is necessary to examine carefully the modes of subordinating one dimension of the extrasocial to the other, in order to reveal what secondary encompassments are operating. Thus, for example, among the Araweté, it is Supernature that encompasses Nature: the best example of Others for humans are the *Ma̲ï*. Similarly, the positive correlation between the jaguar (master of the raw) and cannibalism, which seems to me to be valid for the Araweté and the Tupinamba, is redistributed in other cosmologies. The contemporary Guarani place the "jaguar-function" on the side of Nature and the rotten; among the Kaapor and the Parakanã, warfare is positively associated with the vulture and rottenness. Finally, the women: there are cases, rare or theoretical, of female shamans, chiefs, and even killers. But such functions are eminently masculine, except that of the village leader; its exercise by a woman (as among the Kaapor studied by Balée [1984 : 172]) strikes me as a logical step in uxorilocal societies, where the sociopolitical world falls in general under the aegis of the feminine.

□

The Kaapor and the Akuáwa-Asuriní illustrate the case of the generic dual destiny of the person: the terrestrial specter associated with the rotten, the *Ãñĩ*-beings, and the corpse; and the immortal celestial soul associated with the *Maï*-beings and the vital principle (Huxley 1956: 126–27; Andrade 1984). The chief's position is associated with shamanism for the Akuáwa, and with warfare for the Kaapor. Huxley (1956: 71) mentions an ethos of sexual continence for Kaapor chiefs that calls to mind the shamans of other Tupi-Guarani. Note that the Kaapor have lost shamanism (becoming dependent on Tembé specialists) and that the war chief is the one who initiates adolescents (1956: 153, 191–93).

The Wayãpi, in principle, would also illustrate the canonical case of the division of the person (Campbell 1982: 270–72; 1989; Gallois 1985). But recently, Gallois (1988: 183–95) reported a peculiarity of the shaman after death: the terrestrial portion of his person does not disintegrate after the specter travels to his birthplace, as occurs with lay persons, but goes to join *Moju*, the anaconda Mistress of Nature, remaining active and dangerous. There is some doubt about whether shamans have celestial souls like other mortals. It is important to note that the Wayãpi shaman does not intervene in the relationship between humans and the celestial world (the abode of souls and *Ñandejara*, the Master-Creator of Humans). Rather, this relationship is established by the *aporai* ritual dance and flute music, enacted when humans wish to pay homage to the Creator or when epidemics increase the weight of the sky with the numerous dead and threaten to make it burst. The shaman handles relations with the world of Nature: human enemies, specters, animal spirits, and Masters of Animals, who are encountered much more frequently than the distant inhabitants of the skies.

In Wayãpi society, the roles in shamanism and warfare appear to be related more through superimposition than through opposition. Defined as "the two specialists of Wayãpi society" (Grenand 1982: 238), both shamans and warriors are guided by dreams. A shaman is a kind of warrior—either because he confronts the spirits of nature or because "shamanism is a continuation of warfare" by magical means. The data leave the impression that the permanent character of the shaman-function (versus the temporary reign of the war chief) places it at the foundation of village leadership.

Among the Kayabi, a people with a tradition of bellicosity, the headman's position is modeled on the warrior:

> The Kayabi see their ideal society as directed by an old and embattled chief, who can fully exercise his purely political and coordinating function only when many good shamans guarantee transcendental assistance to all the members of the group. Thus, chief and shaman correspond to the ideal image of a personality, but the power of the shaman acts independently of the chief while, to the contrary, the chief cannot fulfill his function without shamanism (Grünberg n.d. [1970]: 126).

Grünberg observes that warrior-killer status was a prerequisite for the foundation (chieftainship) of a village. However, the shaman's position enjoys a spiritual distinctiveness (the passage above evokes the relations between kings and brahmans in ancient India). There seems to be only one spiritual principle (*ai'an*, name-soul) of the person, which goes to the celestial world. But the souls of shamans are transformed into the *Ma'it* (cf. *Ma̲ï*), that is, celestial shamans who are the main assistants of living shamans.

The association between a single spiritual principle and the posthumous distinctiveness of shamans is particularly clear among the Tapirapé. The souls of laymen (*anchynga invuera*—cf. *Ãñĩ*) lead an errant existence in the forest, while deceased shamans inhabit their own village in the West (Wagley 1977: 169). He expands on this point:

> The greatest prestige which Tapirapé culture offered accrued to its shamans. That prestige was reflected in the concepts of a separate afterlife for shamans and in the identification of ancestral culture heroes as shamans . . . While a Tapirapé layman was thought to become a disembodied soul at death, the afterlife of a shaman was only a continuation of his present life, but under ideal circumstances (1977: 195–96).[4]

The souls of dead shamans (*panče invuera*) are the familiars of Thunder, against whom living shamans must battle during a ceremony linked to the maturation of maize and the initiation of shamans. The ambivalence of the Tapirapé shaman is a strong version of the enemy-becoming of the Araweté killer. The shaman is the warrior of Tapirapé society, protecting it against cannibal spirits, souls of the dead, Thunder, and deceased shamans. But insofar as he is the friend of the enemies of the living, he is both a protector and a threat: his visits to demonic beings confer dangerous powers on him and, in a certain respect, transform him into one of them (Wagley 1977: 182).

The enormous power of the Tapirapé shaman—he is responsible for the conception of children, the abundance of game,[5] the security of the group—reveals a malignant side when confronted with the living. He is the typical assassin, sorcerer, and kidnapper of souls. Wagley observes that the three most powerful shamans in 1939 were themselves *killers* of earlier shamans—since a powerful shaman is destined to be executed by sorcery. His power is his perdition, and his destiny in the afterlife under "ideal circumstances" is the consequence of his transformation into an enemy. An ideal shaman is a dead shaman; shamanic initiation occurs through the death of the novice by the arrows of Thunder and his accomplices, defunct shamans. (Wagley's description [1977: 201–9] of the possession of novices by spirits who drive them crazy resembles the furor of the Araweté slayer.) But only deceased shamans are immortal, while laymen transmigrate into animals and are extinguished: Supernature (Thunder—cf. *Mai̱*) versus Nature.

Finally, shaman status is one of the determinant factors for leadership of the domestic group (there is no village chieftainship, in Wagley's view). A powerful shaman, being the potential target of sorcery accusations, strives to have a strong domestic group to protect him.

Among the Tenetehara, Wagley and Galvão (1949) reported an association between shaman status and leadership of the extended family; the warrior values disappeared a long time ago. Two forms of differentiation of the person in the afterlife appear to coexist, both starting from a single spiritual principle, the *ekwe*. The first distinguishes between those who died a natural death and those an ugly death (committers of incest, executed sorcerers, or sorcery victims). The souls of the first go to the "Village of the Supernaturals," joining the creators and cultural heroes (*Tupan, Maíra*) in a place of abundance. Those of the second turn into malignant specters, linked to abandoned villages and graves—they are the *Azang* (cf. *Ãñĩ*), who control the growth of maize. Shamans combat the *Azang* as well as the spirits of dead animals, the Owner of Water, and the Owner of the Forest. The god-heroes and the "good dead" are distant and neutral; Tenetehara cosmology, like the Wayãpi, directs shamans toward a confrontation with Nature. In both these cases, it is the pole of Nature that encompasses that of Supernature (following the definition of these terms in chap. 3, sect. 4).

Upon this distinction good dead/bad dead[6] is superimposed another one, briefly indicated by Wagley and Galvão (1949: 104): only shamans could enter the village of *Maíra* and other culture heroes. Finally, the authors present evidence that a dual destiny, sky/earth, existed for all humans, but they hasten to take into account some Christian influence.

Shamanism involves possession by spirits of animals, the dead, and other entities. Only the shamans who controlled certain spirits were capable of curing the diseases caused by them. The most powerful animal spirit is that of the jaguar; he penetrates the body of other animals, "jaguarizing" them and making them monstrous. This idea (which inverts the role of the dead jaguar's spirit among the Araweté) calls to mind the Mbyá monsters, animals with names followed by the modifier *-jagua,* jaguar; to each animal species corresponds one of these solitary exemplars (Cadogan 1959: 104). A Tenetehara "jaguar shaman" (which no longer existed during the time of Wagley and Galvão's research) would thus be a kind of super-shaman, capable of incorporating the essence of animality. The shaman, finally, is also exposed to accusations of sorcery, but rarely is he killed, since he would turn into a vengeful *Azang.* In any case, he shares the ambiguity intrinsic to the focal masculine role in Tupi-Guarani societies, shaman or warrior: protective but threatening, associated with the dead and wild beasts, having a special destiny after death.

The Parintintin materials (Kracke 1978) do not permit a correlation between posthumous destiny and personal status. All humans are transformed into *añang,* earthly specters. However, shamans (no longer present at the time of Kracke's research) had more than one spiritual principle *during life,* in contrast to laymen: besides a *ra'uv,* soul, they were endowed with a *rupigwara,* a spiritual double that was responsible for their power. The destiny of the *rupigwara* after the death of its carrier is unknown.[7]

As for factors that lie at the base of headmanship (in our terminology here, village "chief"), Kracke has demonstrated the operation of a double ideology: the chief as *warrior* or as *provider* (as singer-slayer or as owner of the beer, as the Araweté would put it). I would suggest that the provider aspect is associated with the figure of the shaman, given that he was a kind of "spiritual father" whose dreams introduced spirits desiring to be born into the uterus of women. The ambiguity of the village headman's position—at the same time a father-in-law and a father (Kracke 1978: 34)—may be correlated with the pair warrior/shaman.

□

The ethnographic data on the contemporary Guarani (Ñandeva, Mbyá, Pãi-Kayová) reveal the greatest elaboration among the Tupi-Guarani of a theory of the person, developing the distinction between the celestial and terrestrial principles of human beings to the maximum. Schaden (1969: 136) said that the Guarani conception of the soul was the "key to the religious system" of this people, a religious system which in turn dominated social life. Moreover, the Guarani case is where the most complete operation of the triadic matrix Nature/Culture/Supernature is found. Finally, it is where the shaman's position sees greater prominence and less ambiguity—but where ambivalence unequivocally characterizes the cultural state.

The Guarani distinguish between a soul of divine origin and destiny, linked to the personal name, individual "prayers," speech, and breath, and a soul with an animal connotation and a posthumous terrestrial destiny, linked to individual temperament, eating, the shadow, and the corpse. The first is given complete at birth; the second grows with the person and manifests his/her history. These distinctions are similar in all respects to the two *-a̱'o we* of the Araweté, although more elaborated.

Accordingly, Schaden says that the *ayvú*, the Ñandeva language-soul, "is of divine origin, that is, it shares the nature of the supernatural spirits" (1969: 145); its seat is the chest; it is "given" by the great god *Ñanderú* ("Our Father"—cf. the Araweté idea of a father "giving" a child) and at death returns to him. On the other hand, the *atsyguá*, the other personal principle, "represents the animal character of the person." Its seat is the mouth: "The *atsyguá* nourishes itself from what the person eats." It manifests itself in the resemblances between a person's physical attributes and conduct and those of the animal he "incarnates" (it is not "given" by this animal, but, rather, concerns a resemblance that is literally natural); it develops from an almost-nothing, growing according to the excesses committed by its carrier. The *atsyguá* emanates from the corpse when it decomposes, then it wanders about at night, returning by day to the grave. It "only walks in the places where the body walked when alive." The separated-*ayvú* (*ayvú-kue*), the celestial soul, thus incarnates the *person* properly speaking, while the *atsyguá*, becoming an *anguêry* ("ex-shadow") upon death, incarnates the *individual*, his history, and his necessary disappearance (Schaden 1969: 143–51).

Nimuendaju (1978) says that for the Ñandeva-Apapokuva, the *ayvykué*, the celestial soul that is incarnated in a child, must have its divine source identified by the shaman, which thus determines the personal name. Associated with good and gentle sentiments and with vegetable foods, it is opposed to the *asyiguá*, "animal soul," the source of bad or impetuous sentiments and the appetite for meat. When the person has an *asyiguá* of a predatory animal, this will predominate entirely over the *ayvykué*. Such was the case with the Kaingang, the Apapokuva's enemies, who not merely had, but were, pure *asyiguá* of jaguars. Transformed after death into *anguêry*, the animal portion is very dangerous and must be killed by lesser shamans (while the principal shaman has the task of identifying the divine soul at birth and leading it back to the sky at death).

The potential for reincarnation by the *ayvykué* manifests the presence of the celestial souls among the Ñandeva in its strongest form and is due to the tenacious grip of the person to his life and his relatives. Note that this "adherence" is the opposite of the mechanical and mortal repetition of the specter: it is a rebirth within the kindred. Other Guarani tribes do not appear to have such a belief. For the Kayová, the *ayvú*-portion is the incarnation of a *tavyterã*, one of the celestial beings who are the supernatural correlates of the living (Schaden 1969: 155); after death, this soul returns to its origin. The *anguêry*-portion is released only by adults; since a child "did not travel through places," it does not have a history or a specter. The Kayová personology described by B. Meliá, F. Grünberg and G. Grünberg (1976) has the same dualism: the *ñẽ'ẽ*, "spiritual soul," or speech-name, goes to paradise, and the *ã*, "body soul," becomes the *angue* specter and can incorporate itself into an animal.

Cadogan (1959:chap. 19) describes the same dualism for the Mbyá: on the one hand is the *ñẽ'ẽ*, soul-breath-speech of a divine origin; on the other, the "telluric or imperfect soul," the result of the life of passions and appetites, the "imperfect way of living"—the human condition in general. This portion of the person becomes the *angue*, the assassin specter responsible for the dispersal of the living after a death.[8]

The animal portion of the person is associated with another concept, the *tupichúa*, which for the Pãi-Kayová is an animal spirit that accompanies a man seated on his shoulder and governs his appetites (its other name is *juru-tau-gue*, "ghostly month"). For the Mbyá, the *tupichúa* is a malignant spirit that, incarnated in an individual guilty of transgressing social norms, converts him into a "jaguar-man, an eater of raw meat." Cadogan (1962: 81–82; 1968: 7) also translates *tupichúa* as the "soul of raw meat," that which is incarnated in a person who consumes meat in this form and which, by inducing him to copulate with a jaguar-woman, transforms him into a jaguar.

Here we can see how the jaguar-function, which for the Araweté is incarnated by the *Maï̱*, "eaters of raw meat," and for the Tupinamba by humans themselves *qua* cannibals, is for the Guarani transferred to the pole of Nature, as an active counterpart of rottenness (the terrestrial specter) and the polar opposite of the personal principle (soul, name, vegetable, song, skeleton). This derives from the radically anticannibal ethos of the contemporary Guarani, and from the displacement of transcendence to the ascetic side. The figure and value of the warrior have disappeared altogether; shamanism has hypertrophied. The shaman is the foundation of the tribe, the leader of ceremonies that reunite dispersed local groups, to such a degree that it has been said that a Guarani society is a religious association unified by the shaman (Nimuendaju 1978 [1914]: 92ff.; Schaden 1969: 22, 119). The political arena has become thoroughly overtaken by religion.

Assuming what we know about the Tupinamba to be valid as well for the early Guarani, it could be said that the father-in-law/warrior, paradigm of the village chief or, in any case, the leader of the men of his house in war, disappeared in modern times to be replaced by the shaman-father ("our father" is also the title of current Guarani leaders). Without necessarily accepting the thesis of H. Clastres (1978) on the "contradiction between the political and the religious" that was supposedly the motor of Tupi-Guarani prophetism, it is impossible to overlook this notable inversion of the functional structure between the sixteenth-century Tupi-Guarani and the modern Guarani. If for the former, political power rested on the control over women and on the symbolism of the warrior (Fernandes 1963: 325ff.), the role of the shaman in its maximal expression, that is, as prophet (*carai*), was marked precisely by his physical and social exteriority to the group—and, as H. Clastres observes (1978: 41–45), the status of chief was incompatible with that of prophet. But the contemporary Guarani merged these two functions in the figure of the religious chief, and nothing more remains of the warriors of antiquity.

Hélène Clastres has shown how contemporary Guarani cosmology not only reveals the same desire that propelled early Tupi-Guarani societies—a rejection of Society as the space of impermanence, a rejection of the mortal human condition—but also conceives of Culture as an ambivalent position, an ambivalence expressed in spiritual duality:

> Culture is the mark of the supernatural on the imperfect earth, the sign of an election that separates men from animality . . . But at the same time, culture is also what separates men from the immortals since, for the Guarani of today as for the Tupi of the past, the path to the Land without Evil lies in the renunciation of social life . . . Between these two poles, men

> occupy a middle position that makes them ambivalent . . . They have, therefore, a dual nature . . .
>
> Seemingly paradoxical, the place occupied by social life in Guarani thought is at one and the same time the sign of their disgrace and the sign of their election: it is defined as the necessary mediation between a beneath (nature, which is immediacy) and a beyond (the supernatural, which is a surpassing). Their dual being thus situates men between two possible negations of society: the first, pointing downwards, so to speak, consists in ignoring the exigencies of social life, in trying to avoid exchange . . . it resolves in the negative sense the ambiguity inherent in man by situating him on the side of nature and animality . . . The other consists, not in disregarding the social order that defines the human condition, but in surpassing this condition, that is, in being liberated from the network of human relations . . . it is the renunciation of the well-being of this world, the necessarily solitary search for immortality (H. Clastres 1978: 92–95).

Thus, a regression towards Nature, involving submission to the terrestrial-animal portion of the person, produced by the infraction of the norms of culture (use of fire, alimentary reciprocity, sexual temperance), is counterposed against an ideal ethic of asceticism (abstinence from meat, sexual continence, abundant use of tobacco, absolute generosity, song and dance)—the inverse form of exiting the human condition, achieved by making the body lightweight, sublimating the flesh, achieving maturation and imputrescibility. As the author observes, we have here a double ethic: one simply human, consisting of respect for norms, which seeks to *avoid* animal regression; the other, the ethic of the renouncer who seeks to *overcome* the mortal condition, progressing towards divinity. In contrast to the former collective renouncer, the nomadic society created by the prophetic movements, the modern Guarani renouncer is always an individual and individualistic:

> Relations with the sacred are always personal . . . The individualistic character of Guarani religion . . . assumes here the form of an imperious necessity . . . It is the essence of a religion that seeks to make man into a god and to be a reflection on immortality. And immortality is conceivable only as a counter-order . . . To be mortal or to be social: two expressions of the same reality. This means that it is possible to think of

> man's relation to death as unnecessary only insofar as it is possible to think of his relation to others as unnecessary (H. Clastres 1978 : 99–100).

If the world of Nature is solitary death, ferocity, and rottenness, the world of Supernature is a no less solitary, perfect immortality: they are symmetrical forms of resolving the ambivalence of the human. Man is something between two Others, which the Guarani would posit as the Jaguar and Divinity, the cannibal beast and the masters of abundant words. The human condition is pure potency and dissimilarity with itself: among the Guarani, as among the Araweté, its destiny is achieved only elsewhere.

But significant differences lie between the Araweté and Guarani philosophies: the former does not proceed to a negative moral evaluation of the condition of the living, and its conception of Divinity is itself ambivalent. For the Araweté, reciprocity is not only something that can be circumvented on earth, but is above all a mechanism that establishes alliance with the gods. Consequently, the Araweté gods, notwithstanding the "extraordinary predominance of the religion in all spheres of the culture" that Schaden (1969 : 49) saw among the Guarani, are much closer to man than is the Divinity of the latter.

Finally, while the Guarani developed an anticannibalistic ethic, the Araweté invented a cannibal eschatology—alternative transformations of the cannibal anthropology of the early Tupinamba.

3. My Brother-in-law the Jaguar

Anthropophagy, emblem of the Tupi in the Western imagination since Montaigne, has always posed a certain enigma for anthropology—due less, I believe, to phagic reasons than to a sort of logical repugnance. After all, cannibalism is like incest, impossible: impossible in the sense of making bodies and signs, persons and names, coincide (Deleuze & Guattari 1983 : 161). The very act of eating transforms what is eaten into something else: the symbol escapes from under the gesture. If ritual is "essentially the art of the possible" (C. Hugh-Jones 1979 : 280), then cannibalism is not a ritual. As the real, it is the art of the impossible.

Although Tupi-Guarani cannibalism operates within the same field as the dialectic of Gê identity, so well described by my colleagues of Central Brazil as the constitution of the "I" through the "Other," I do not believe it can be placed in a continuum with the play of double negations that reign among the Gê. Cannibalism is not an extreme or literal instance of the dialectic of the subject, but something that extrapolates from it. It is perfectly consistent with the complex of forces that led many of these societies towards destruction and echoes the observation of H. Clastres on the impulse that moves Guarani religious philosophy:

> A logic that refuses the principle of noncontradiction appears to operate in this thought, which at one and the same time opposes the extremes and yearns to make them compatible or co-possible (1978 : 89).

Neither identity nor contradiction, but indeed refusal: a refusal to choose, fostering an ontological restlessness indeed. In order to achieve what they intended, the Tupinamba weighed their acts very carefully, as the Araweté do with their ideas; cannibalism is not a maniacal exaggeration of some symbolic necessity that could be satisfied in other ways.

To eat the other is certainly to exaggerate, to commit a sacrificial excess. It establishes a maximal continuity with the victim, creating an animal immanence between the devourer and the devoured, and at the same time presupposes a discontinuity, no less absolute and transcendent, between both, since what one eats is by definition the non-self, a "thing" (Bataille 1989 : 17, 39). To eat a similar (of course he is a similar, or else it would not be a *ritual* cannibalism laden with precautions and mystic dangers) is precisely to prevent him from reflecting an image and thereby serving as a support for the eater's identity. It is a way of breaking the mirror of the imaginary function, destroying representation. Ritual cannibalism is in no way a "*fantasme agi*" (Green 1972), like those to be found on psychoanalytic couches, but a symbolic mechanism of other-becoming. And if the explicit motivation of Tupinamba cannibalism was vengeance, it is because vengeance, like cannibalism, is impossible and interminable, another figure of becoming. It is more than a mediation through alterity, seeking to constitute an identity; it is an inescapable passage towards alterity. I am the Enemy. This is what the Araweté are saying through their gods.

Did Cunhambebe say anything different? The Tupinamba chief did not say that what he ate was not human, that it was a thing, an animal. He said the opposite:

> This same Konyan Bebe [Cunhambebe] had then a great vessel full of human flesh in front of him and was eating a leg which he held to my mouth, asking me to taste it. I replied that even beasts which were

> without understanding did not eat their own species, and should a man devour his fellow creatures? But he took a bite saying, *Jau wara sehe:* "I am a tiger [jaguar]; it tastes well," and with that I left him (Staden 1928 [1557]:110).

□

Cunhambebe's repartee cited by Hans Staden was certainly a burst of humor: black or Zen, it was unquestionably Tupinamba. Even if it did not illuminate the German, it involves a declaration of a revealing *non-sense.* Asked about what he was eating, the Tupinamba warrior defined his perspective: he was a jaguar, because his food was a man. If the leg he ate was from an enemy, the mouth that ate it (and spoke) was of the Enemy. "Isn't the cannibal always the other?" asked Clastres and Lizot (1978:126). Indeed, but not simply in the banal ethnocentric sense: when one is a cannibal like Cunhambebe, one is the Other—a jaguar, that inedible cannibal. Naturally, a civilized jaguar: he ate cooked flesh—a jaguar with fire. The anthropophagy of Cunhambebe, thus, was neither an allelophagy (devouring a similar) as Staden thought, nor an omophagy (eating the raw), to use the vocabulary of Greek cannibalism (Detienne 1972:235). It was a feline-becoming, but refined by a human cuisine.

Cunhambebe's *boutade* does not seem to me to be a good candidate for the anthology of memorable phases of the savage mind, of the sort "Bororo men are parrots" or "Nuer twins are birds," with which Von den Steinen and Evans-Pritchard heated up the intellectualist debate between totemism and mystic participation, metaphor and prelogical thought. The cannibal-as-jaguar was perhaps a metaphor, since it certainly was not a belief: the postlogical humor of Cunhambebe would not be a good example for Lévy-Bruhl. But more than a mere metaphor: Bororo men and Nuer twins do not fly, whereas the Tupinamba "jaguars" really did eat human flesh, not being contented with figures of speech.[9] Nor did it here concern either an imaginary "turning into a jaguar" or a mere "acting like" a jaguar—jaguars do not cook. But perhaps a jaguar-becoming, where "jaguar" is a quality of the *act,* not of the *subject* (Deleuze & Guattari 1983). Even if the object of the becoming is imaginary, the becoming is real, and the ferocious alterity is a quality of the verb, not its predicate. Cannibalism replaces the problem of identification with that of alteration; it is not so much concerned with predication as with predation.

A metaphor, however, for me. For the "Cunhambebe equation" suggests to me the idea that Tupinamba cannibalism implied a feral transformation of society. An eminently cultural phenomenon, it is not for all that any less a questioning of culture (Pouillon 1972: 16), a mode of transcending it. The elaborate symbolic machinery of the rites of capture, captivity, and execution of enemies ended in something which, the more it made hypotheses proliferate, the more it escaped them: cannibalism. One wonders why the Tupinamba ate their enemies instead of simply killing them, adopting them, or anything else. Perhaps the Araweté cosmology has begun to clarify the matter.

10 The Anti-Narcissus

1. Vengeance and Sacrifice

Tupinamba eschatology combines the motifs discussed earlier for contemporary Tupi-Guarani societies: although there may have been a single spiritual principle, the *An* (Evreux 1929 [1615]: 294), its posthumous destiny was differentiated according to a "good" or a "bad" death (at the hands of enemies or at home) or according to the personal status of the deceased (whether he was a manslayer or not). The souls of "cowards" (nonkillers) went to the *Anhanga*, the "demon"; only the brave could enter the world of the ancestors, heroes, and gods (Thevet 1978 [1557]:121; 1953 [1575]:84–86; Léry 1990 [1578]:136). Métraux (1979 [1928]:11) associates this with the numerous trials the dead faced during their trip to paradise, adding that women were rarely able to enter unless they were wives of great warriors—a transformation of the Araweté theme that only women are necessarily devoured by the *Maï*.

But it was not only personal eschatology that depended on warfare. "Since the Tupinamba are very bellicous, all their motives are how they will make war on their adversaries ['contraries']," Soares de Souza (1971 [1587]) tersely summarized the situation. Without death in foreign hands, the *perpetuum mobile* of revenge would be paralyzed:

> And do not suppose that the prisoner is shocked by this news [that he will be eaten shortly], since in his opinion, his death is honorable, and he would much rather die in this way than at home by some contagious death; because (they say) one cannot take revenge on death, which offends and kills men, but one can certainly avenge those who have been slain and massacred in an act of war (Thevet 1953:196).

A perfect complicity between victims and executioners. If for the former this was a death that overcame death by permitting vengeance, from the point of view of the latter, the ritual execution of the enemy consummated vengeance for past deaths and at the same time guaranteed the access of young men to the status of slayer, that is, a full person, capable of immortality in the afterlife. Once again, past and future came together in the act of ritual vengeance. Only a killer could marry and have children, since the Tupinamba, like so many other peoples, equated the warrior function of a man with the reproductive function of a woman. The rites of the first menstruation were identical with those of the first homicide; the girls "undergo the same ritual as executioners" (Thevet 1978:133): scarification, tatooing, seclusion, abstinence. Both women and killers spilled a blood vital for the reproduction of society.[1]

Tupinamba cannibalism is but an element of "an infinitely complex system" (H. Clastres 1972:81) that cannot be reduced to a simple function. As in any central complex of a culture, it has no privileged level of explication, since, extrapolating what Lévi-Strauss (1977a:65) said about myth, it consists "in an *interrelation* of several explanatory levels." As a restorative cannibalism, it cancels out the "heteronomy" produced by death within society and rescues the group's relation with its past. As a funerary cannibalism, it is where enemies serve as transubstanciators, producing the "good dead," beings who can be vindicated. Finally, as a productive cannibalism, it impels the social machine towards the future by creating the spiral of vengeance and producing complete adults.

□

Much has been written on Tupinamba anthropophagy, most of which is of mediocre quality. The work truly worth discussing is the sumptuous and impenetrable thesis of Florestan Fernandes (1970 [1952]). Assuming what the chroniclers identified as the motor of Tupinamba warfare—blood revenge—Florestan (as he is most commonly known in Brazil), armed with a resolutely functionalist disposition, submitted it to the Maussian theory of sacrifice. He argued that the system was centered on the deceased members of the group, who occupied the position of beneficiaries of the "human sacrifice," which was at the heart of the Tupinamba bellico-religious complex.[2]

Florestan argues that anthropophagy, the culmination of Tupinamba warfare, was the logical consequence of this religious drive. The captives, overdetermined and ambivalent figures, as befits sacrificial victims, were the means of communication between the living and the dead (the recent dead, to be avenged, or the mythic ancestors, to be commemorated):

> Everything revolved around the collective communion, promoted by the ingestion of the flesh of the victim, with the supernatural entity as the beneficiary of the sacrifice . . . Tupinamba cannibalism had a religious function: to promote a collective modality of direct and immediate communion with the sacred (Fernandes 1970:326–27).

Florestan is suggesting that those who ate the captives were the deceased members of the group: the "supernatural entity" refers to the spirits contained in men's rattles, which supposedly incited them to war. In them our author sees ancestors, represented by the sacrifier (society) and incarnated in the sacrificer (the executor). Moreover, what they ate was their own "substance" (Fernandes 1970:325). Cannibalism furnished a kind of mystical body to the souls or spirits to be avenged or commemorated. Essentially funerary, therefore (but not in the sense alluded to above), Tupinamba cannibalism was a recuperation of the dead, through enemies, by society—a "restoration of the collective We" (Fernandes 1970:332, 336, 339).

The determinant relation, the distance to be spanned by the sacrifice, was thus between the living and the dead of the group, putting into action an "internal dialectic of human sacrifice" (1970:319). Death and the dead carried with them what we could call, following Bataille, "the truth of society," producing an unbearable heteronomy. In this way,

> the sacrifice of the victim was part of the funerary ceremonies owed [to the deceased] relative, and instead of being a consequence of the imperative of *revenge,* it was its cause . . . Sacrifice was not caused by the action of enemies, but by the necessity of the "spirit" of the relative killed by them . . . What could be interpreted as being the "master idea" of the Tupinamba notion of *revenge* translates essentially as: *the intention of aiding the spirits of a relative killed under conditions that placed the integrity of his "person" at risk, or to satisfy the necessity for a sacrificial relation on the part of the "spirit" of a forebear or mythic ancestor* (Fernandes 1970:318–20; italics in original).

With this, Florestan gives his interpretation of revenge. It is a scapegoat theory, where the victim both incarnates and placates the deceased or the ancestor. The latter is the true enemy; it is he who, imposing on the living the categorical imperative of revenge, keeps them in a kind of fundamental state of unrest. "It cannot be denied that in fact the texts reveal the Tupinamba as mentally tormented beings" (Fernandes 1963 [1949]:303). Extending a generalization of Lévy-Brühl, Florestan attributes to "blood sacrifice" an expiatory value: "The fear inspired by the spirits of the dead taking revenge, being much greater than the corresponding fear instilled by the expectation of subsequent revenge by the enemies, is what gives to revenge the character of an 'essential obligation'" (1970:345). However, no source confirms such a threat or authorizes such a conclusion. To find it, Florestan must resort to theory, since it is essential for the closure of his model of sacrifice to the ancestors.[3]

Fruit of the exigencies of the dead, human sacrifice is "the alpha and omega of war" (Fernandes 1970:351), a system of second burial, similar to Malayan practices of hunting heads to conclude the period of mourning and placate the soul of the dead (Hertz 1960 [1907]:31, 40). Being a collective communion, it was not a refinement of cruelty, as Hertz said of exo-cannibalism, contrasting it to the devotional ethos of the endo-cannibal "sacred feast." To the contrary, it was an act of filial piety: the death of an enemy was the "immolation" of a victim—a transference of energies, a recuperation of a vital essence—a sacrifice *to* the dead relative (Fernandes 1970:210, 324, 332). The model that orients Florestan is that of an ancestor cult, the central rite of which is anthropophagy. War, *instrumentum religionis,* seeks to restore to the *socius* the autonomy and coincidence with itself that were lost upon death. Thus, it is a matter of yet another one of those machines to suppress time: what was devoured was Becoming; revealing itself as death, it was the Enemy.

□

To what extent does Tupinamba warfare actually conform to the sacrificial Procrustean bed of Hubert and Mauss? Florestan never asks this question; to the contrary, he treats the ethnographic materials like raw gems, cutting and filing to make them fit into the jewelry box of theory and shine there as exemplars. Through the shamans, the "spirits" asked for "victims," inciting warfare. The killer, on the other end of the chain, caused captives to pass over to the Sacred (the ancestors); he thus officiated over a funerary rite. The shaman summoned the dead; the killer sent them sacrificed enemies. *Voilá.*

Tupinamba cannibalism presents, no doubt, a type of sacrificial logic. It involves a whole play of identifications and substitutions, beginning with the widespread practice of exhuming enemies to smash their skulls, the last resort in the absence of live enemies (Anchieta 1933 [1565]:236–37). This exhibits the casuistry typical of the sacrificial game,[4] in which the wild card of death is alternately played by the captive, the slayer, and the deceased member of the group, in a process of reverberation analogous to that described earlier for the Araweté. But Florestan, in his zeal to make anthropophagy out to be a "communion with the ancestors," tries to tailor the customer's body to fit the ready-to-wear suit.

□

The crucial ethnographic source of Florestan's sacrificial theory is the Franciscan friar André Thevet, *cosmographe du Roy.* Thevet (1953: 193–95) says that a captive, before being brought to the village, should "renew the grave" of the dead man in whose memory he was to be executed.[5] After that, the personal possessions of the deceased were handed over to him for his use. The deceased's weapons, which would be passed on to his relatives, were first washed by the prisoner to free them of "corruption." The nimble friar likened these operations to a sacrifice: the captive acted "as if he were a victim who should be immolated to the memory [of the deceased]" (Thevet 1953: 193). Thevet also describes a process of substitution that was occasionally brought about by the capture of a prisoner: he could be granted to a war widow as compensation until the day of his death (and would be killed by one of the deceased's brothers, thereby entitling the latter to leviratic succession [1953: 105–106, 194]).

Based on this text, Florestan begins to weave his theory. He argues that the execution of a victim situated the deceased in the position of an ancestor, placating his thirst for revenge, and restored his lost "substance" to him. The deceased's spirit instilled certain "qualities" in the victim, who was thereby both his incarnation and his means of appeasement. Eating the victim returned to the group the "energies" lost in the person of the dead relative.

But Florestan overestimates, if not simply assumes, the importance of the dead as the beneficiaries of the sacrifice. Data regarding the intervention of *spirits* of *individual* dead in the system are nonexistent; the same holds for any relationship between the killer and the deceased to be avenged. Although shamanism certainly involved communication with the souls of the dead, in no place in the extensive documentation of the sixteenth century did I find "imperatives of revenge" imposed by the dead. All we have is Staden (1928 [1557]:149) attributing the desire to eat human flesh to the spirits placed in each man's rattle by a shamanic transfusion that served as a prelude to war. Nothing guarantees that this concerns the spirits of the dead.[6] As a matter of fact, Thevet (1953:76–78, 81–84, 117–18) clearly distinguishes the spirit "*Houioulsira,*" the source of shamanic powers used when conducting war expeditions, from the souls of the dead, "*Cherepicouare,*" about whose state in the Beyond the shamans informed the living. Note that the rattles were called "beloved child" by their owners, not "ancestor," "grandfather" or something along such lines (see chap. 8, sect. 2).

In the second place, vengeance does not appear to have been exercised on the basis of a zero-sum reciprocity. The vicarious and global nature of the retaliation and the generalized evocation of the "dead" who should be avenged were all parts of the usual manner of conducting war and exercising vengeance. The substitution of *one* dead for *one* captive, as well as the motif of individualized vengeance, seems to have been the exception rather than the rule. Cannibalism, as the maximal socialization of revenge, involved the same kind of dispersion, since it included in the potential field of "compulsory revenge" (Fernandes 1963:123) the hundreds of people who ate the flesh of a single captive. Who avenges, who was avenged, and on whom vengeance was exercised, all suggest an element of generality (Carneiro da Cunha & Viveiros de Castro 1985). Rather than a juridical system based on a restorative vendetta, it was a war of ontological predation, formulated in the idiom of vengeance—the idiom of the social relationship of reciprocity.

Of course, there was always someone to be avenged (perhaps even those who died peacefully in their hammocks): distant kinsmen, the kinsmen of one's affines, political allies, and so on. But above all, there was always someone who *had to avenge,* someone who had to obtain a name on the head of an adversary. As an imperative that was, in effect, categorical, inculcated since birth, vengeance did not depend on any specific dead person who required it; to the contrary, everything else depended on vengeance, the embodiment of the three characteristics of an authentic Kantian a priori: it was universal, it was necessary, and it was independent of experience. To characterize the ritual execution as a funerary sacrifice, Florestan had to minimize its productive and initiatory value, suggesting that this was a "derivative function of human sacrifice" (Fernandes 1970:201, 215). He had to subordinate the prospective to the retrospective function, production to recuperation, the future to the past. To postulate a functionalist cult of ancestors, it was thus necessary to reduce vengeance to a mechanism of mystical compensation, a homeostasis of the Imaginary.

We have already seen how homicide was the necessary action to attain the status of an adult man able to procreate, and how courage in warfare produced the ideal personal status. For the Tupinamba, the accumulation of names by the death of enemies was "their greatest honor" (Staden 1928 : 148). One killed for vengeance, but also to obtain names; these two motives were inseparable. Everyone killed and ate as many enemies as possible—a prospective vengeance, or a "transcendental induction," where it was the *propter hoc* that created an *ergo post hoc.* After all, it is up to the enemies, not to us, to find the reasons for the deaths we inflict on them. Positive predation, accumulation: "Of all the honours and pleasures of this life, none is so great for this people as to kill and get a name on the heads of their Adversaries, neither are there among them any Feasts, comparable to those which they make at the death of those which they kill with great Ceremonies, which they doe in this manner" (Cardim 1906 [1584]:431).

The status of the victim was irrelevant: "to kill a child of five yeere old, they goe so prepared as for to kill some Giant" (Cardim 1906: 438). Women and children were killed and eaten; if a prisoner became ill, anxiety spread and a hurried decision was made, "Let us kill him before he is dead" (Staden 1928 : 99); people disinterred enemies to crack their skulls and take names.[7] Without enemies, there would be no proud recitation of names, no bodies laboriously marked with commemorative incisions, no mouths ornamented with precious stones for authoritative public speech, no honorable destinies in the afterlife. Without dead enemies, there would be, literally, no one living: there would be no legitimate children. The restorative function of the cannibal system simply cannot be privileged in the face of its creative and dynamic function.

Significantly, only one characteristic of enemies (beings whose main value lay in supplying names) guaranteed that they would be unharmed: good singers or musicians were pardoned (Soares de Souza 1971 : 316; Cardim 1906 : 428). This brings us back to the "oral" complex and to the pair song/cannibalism. H. Clastres (1978 : 41ff.) interprets these references as applying only to the *karai,* the prophets, according to her theory of the extraterritoriality of these personages. This seems forced to me. It was verbal-musical excellence in itself—the Tupinamba esteemed highly the "masters of speech," men skilled in discourse and song—that conferred immunity from consumption. As Monteiro (1949 [1610]:415) observed incisively, "While their second beatitude is to be singers, the first is to be slayers." Such "beatitudes" are evidently linked: if the latter was the great obstacle to conversion, the former provided a powerful tactical weapon for the Jesuits, as history attests. One way or the other, the Tupinamba ended up dying (and came to an end) because of the mouths of either their enemies or the fathers of the Society of Jesus.

2. A Rare Bird

The value of the enemy as a source of names illuminates an association that has received little attention, due perhaps to the more spectacular character of his qualification as a "brother-in-law." The captive was an *avis rara*.

Upon entering the village, the captives were received by the women in a ceremony that inverted the welcome of tears with which they greeted visiting friends, when they wept over past sorrows. The captives were reminded of their destiny as "future food" (Staden 1928: 70) in a fierce and graphic manner; they were showered with threats and blows by their female hosts, who thereby took new names (Monteiro 1949: 411). As soon as they were led over to their hammocks, however, "the insults ceased" (Magalhães de Gandavo 1922 [1575]: 103). The captives were well treated: they were given women, they enjoyed a semiguarded liberty, and they were fed by their owners (their captor or the one to whom they were given) until their time came, something which could be delayed for years. Revenge, as the Brazilian proverb goes, is a meal that is best savored after it has cooled.

Meanwhile, they were treated like pets, *schere inbau ende* (or, more properly, *xe-reimbab*, "my pet"), as they were jocularly called (Staden 1928: 68). This symbolism is strategic for understanding the captivity. Since their entry into the village, the enemies were subordinated to the feminine portion of society. The captive was brought there under such a pretext; Staden, for instance, was spared and taken to the village "so that their women might see me and make merry with me" (1928: 64). Received by the women, linked to the group by a woman, prepared for his death ceremony by the women, the captive, after being killed by a man, was eaten by everyone—but preferentially by the women, according to the descriptions of the notorious voracity of the old women (Léry 1990: 126), in a ritual for which they had contributed an essential product, beer.

The favorite pets of the Tupinamba were beautifully colored birds that furnished feathers for the ornamentation used in the rites of execution. The songs that preceded the captive's death compared him to one of them: "If thou hadst beene a parrot annoying us, thou wouldest have fled," the women sang. "Wee are those that make the necke of the bird to stretch" (Cardim 1906:435).[8] If we search for contemporary parallels, we see that pets, parrots and macaws in particular, are feminine property. Even if their feathers go to ornament the men, they are raised and fed by the women. The captives of Tupinamba wars could have said, with as much cause as Bororo husbands, that they were parrots—and for some of the same reasons (Crocker 1977).

We may ask, then, what the homologue was of the bird feathers furnished by the enemy. The answer seems simple: names.[9] These were given in the first place to the executor and secondarily to various other people: those who had captured him, those who had recaptured him in a ritual pursuit that preceded the execution, the women who greeted him, the wife of the killer. Furthermore, if war and killing *in situ* can be metaphorically likened to the hunt (as among the Mundurucu; see Murphy 1958:60), then the imprisonment of enemies would correspond to the capture of ornamental birds. The enemy would onomastically adorn his slayer like the feathers of the birds to which he was compared.[10]

Note, however, that pet birds were not eaten, while the prisoners were. More than a parrot, the captive was a kind of tortoise with feathers, raised for his adornments (names) and for his flesh. His person underwent a differential appropriation according to gender. The women could also take names from him, and even kill him when furious (but they had to call on a man to break his skull [Anchieta 1933:203]); for their part, the men also ate the flesh of their adversary. But the renown and renaming of the women was clearly secondary in comparison to that obtained by the killer. On the other hand, the cannibal repast was dominated by the women: it was the form par excellence of their participation in the system of vengeance. The nominal value of the captive was the part that fell to the killer; his substantial value fell above all to the women. Thus, the bones (the skull) and names went to the men, who had captured the enemies; their flesh went to the women, who had raised them like pets.

As among the Araweté, there seems to have been an exchange between men and women expressed as meat versus beer. The rites of Tupinamba childbirth—as in all aspects of their society—mobilized symbols of war. Boys received bows and arrows and were associated with jaguars and birds of prey; girls received a necklace of capybara teeth (the large South American rodent) to make them good chewers of mash for beer, the ceremonial cannibal drink. Again as among the

Araweté, certain details suggest a strong sexualization of the beer/cannibalism complex: women ate the genitalia of the executed enemy (Thevet 1953: 50, 203; Soares de Souza 1971: 321; Ramirez 1852 [1528]: 17).

There are no truly domesticated animals native to Lowland South America, as is well known. But the Tupinamba apparently developed a technique of domesticating their enemies: the captive produced children by the women he was granted, and they would later be killed and provide new names. The practice of handing over women to captives, considered an honor for the women and their relatives, had this objective, among others: "On the night that [the prisoners] arrive, they give him as a wife a daughter of the man who captured him, or one of his closest female relatives; it is a cause for honor should a birth result from that marriage, because in having children by a *tapuia* [enemy], the same names will be taken and with the same solemnity as with the father" (Monteiro 1949: 411).[11] A partial explication, insufficient to cover all the significations behind this granting of women, but it unveils themes that are unequivocally indigenous.

The prisoner's "marriage" should be inserted in a system of multiple finalities. It appears to be associated above all with the linking of the captive to the feminine domain (Lévi-Strauss 1987: 113–17). After all, the case was just as much a matter of granting a woman to the captive to serve him, as it was of delivering the captive to a woman to guard him. What is at play is a relationship between men of two enemy groups (where the captive is a term and the woman granted him is a sign, which transforms him into a "brother-in-law"), as well as a relationship between the men and women of the captor group by means of the captive. Here the captive is what ends up being the "relationship"—value. An affine, perhaps, a term, but above all a relationship—the captive is an anti-affine.

3. On Dialogical Anthropophagy

Honors, names, vengeance—none of this is sufficient to account for the way the Tupinamba treated their enemies: eating them. Why did they eat their "pets"? Florestan, criticizing the classic idea of an "incorporation of the virtues" of the enemy, develops a spectrum of explanations: a defensive destruction of the corporal support of the victim; a recuperation of the "substance" of the deceased person being avenged; finally, a "communion with the supernatural entity" leading to a "magical superiority" over the enemy group achieved through the act of consumption. This is supposed to explain why the community was associated with the sacrificial triad captive-killer-deceased, eating from the flesh of the first:

> The collectivity was associated with the process of mystical recuperation, because what it signified for the supernatural entity, it also signified for the group. If the former recuperated its integrity, the collectivity would recuperate its own. This is why the sacrificial relation, as a form of *revenge,* would be incomplete without anthropophagy. The collectivity needed to participate in the process of mystical recuperation because only such participation could assure it magical autonomy in the face of a particular hostile group and provide it with effective magical control over it. The deceased relative, whose integrity was reestablished as a consequence of the mystical recuperation, returned to form part of "our group" as a potential member of the society of mythical ancestors and forebears; the mystical unity of "our group" was recomposed at the same time as that of the hostile group was broken. Anthropophagy, returning those who ate to a state of magical autonomy, conferred upon them control or magical power over the enemy collectivity (Fernandes 1970:327).

This paragraph represents the synthesis of Florestan's theory. Despite what he meant to demonstrate, he ends up revealing the opposite: that the Tupinamba system was in a perpetual disequilibrium. The "autonomy" of some could only be obtained at the expense of the "heteronomy" of others—we must not forget that the wars of vengeance and cannibalism were directed mainly towards groups of the same linguistic and cultural background who recognized a common origin and who in many cases had recently broken off alliance and coresidence relations.

Just as Araweté society includes the gods, Tupinamba society should be understood as including its enemies. It constituted itself through its relationship with others, in a regime of generalized heteronomy. The "dialectic" of human sacrifice was external, not internal, insofar as it manifested a social form that included its exterior or was only realized through it. Dead foreigners and death at the hands of foreigners were inseparable from each other, and both were indispensable to social "reproduction." Fernandes' notion of restoring group identity via revenge, the ideal of autonomy, relies on a perspective that *confounds the local and the global.* This treats the viewpoint of each avenging unit (kindred, village, or bloc of allied villages) as if it coincided with the global structure. However, although necessarily "ego-centered" at the local level, the Tupinamba *global* social structure had neither subject nor center, being constituted as a relation-to-the-enemy: vengeance was its foundation.

Indeed, Tupinamba society seems to have been strikingly amorphous. There were no internal segmentations based on lineages, age grades, or ceremonies (not that they have not been sought or postulated by generations of anthropologists). No "dialectical" arrangement contraposed parts of a totality that had been posited a priori as Principle in order to be reconstituted as a system of differences. Their thorough internal undifferentiation, which so surprised observers (as did their urbanity and exemplary cordiality among relatives), was accompanied by a projection of differences "outwards" and the transformation of all alterity into hatred. Yet the Others returned, indispensable unifiers of the *socius* ("neither are there among them any Feasts, comparable to those which they make at the death of those which they kill with great Ceremonies"), and differences became ordered in a ritual exchange of dead bodies. The ceremonial execution of the enemy founded the ever-labile village unity and kept the global machine of differences operating—an inverse alliance ("anti-affinity"). If society included and implied the Enemy, then this position was necessarily the ground of all that was social, being therefore a reversible and generalized point of view, the dominant perspective of Tupinamba social life. One is always, and before all else, the enemy of someone, and this is what defines the self. The transformation of the captive into a brother-in-law expresses this paradoxical "internal exteriority" of enemies, the true *place of honor* that they occupied in society: honor in granting a sister to the enemy, honor in killing him, honor in dying in this fashion. The relationship to the enemy was the supreme social value.

□

Among the innumerable hypotheses about the reasons for Tupinamba cannibalism, the one rejected by Florestan, that of an "incorporation of the qualities" of enemies (Métraux 1979:82; 1967:69) seems too facile, but it is not absurd. H. Clastres notes that it would be consistent with the Tupinamba alimentary analogies, which forbade the flesh of slow animals to youngsters and prescribed for future shamans a diet of songbirds and water from cascades (1972:82). In effect, *"They believe that the nature and condition of what they eat gets passed on to them"* (Monteiro 1949:419 [emphasis mine]).

This poses a general question. Consumption, cannibal or otherwise, is just as much an encompassing of the devoured by the devourer (which would bring us back to Florestan's idea of "magical superiority") as it is a determination of the devourer by the devoured. What is eaten indeed becomes part of he who eats; but then again, as the Chinese say, vegetarians repeat, and Amerindians widely maintain, one is what one eats. This dilemma calls to mind the problem of how logicians interpret the classic attributive proposition: is the subject included in the predicate, or is the latter an attribute of the subject? Turning from predication to predation, let us adopt an intensional interpretation consistent with Tupinamba ideas and ask what, or *which qualities,* are incorporated through the consumption of the enemy.

An old idea—the same that Florestan developed at the abstract or "religious" level—holds that the Tupinamba, in the final analysis, practiced endo-cannibalism by means of an interposed enemy stomach: we eat those who ate our relatives, therefore . . . This goes back to Montaigne's famous essay, "Of Cannibals," where he cites the song of a captive about to be executed:

> "These muscles," he says, "this flesh and these veins are your own, poor fools that you are. You do not recognize that the substance of your ancestors' limbs is still contained in them? Savor them well; you will find in them the taste of your own flesh" (Montaigne 1943 [1580]:89).

We cannot judge the fidelity of this gloss, but it fits very well into the dialogic complex of the ritual execution and does *not* serve as evidence for endo-cannibalism. Obviously it portrays a challenge flung by the prisoner at his captors: the "endo-cannibalism" it implies is an ironic and insulting final result of the system of exchanging the dead, not its "emic" motivation. After all, if the question were one of recycling the dead, it would be simpler to eat them directly and better to die at home.

Thus, the hypothesis of indirect endo-cannibalism hardly seems tenable; no chronicler ever reported anything that could be interpreted in this sense. Let us consider, therefore, the idea that the aim of cannibalism was the appropriation of the qualities and virtues of the enemies as such. Métraux suggests, for example, that the cannibal voracity of the elder women was due to the necessity of "recharging their energies." Put in such a blunt way, this hypothesis makes one think of Wittgenstein's observation (1979 [1931]) that Frazer was more "savage" than the majority of his savages . . . One wonders why enemies would have such geriatric virtues and why human flesh would contain such metaphysical proteins.

Although the preferred victim was an adult man of valor, the Tupinamba killed and ate anyone who fell into their hands. In other words, all that the victims had in common—their "nature and condition," as Monteiro says—was the fact of being enemies. So let us venture the hypothesis that what was eaten was this condition. The quality incorporated would thus be the enemy position, not the "substance" of the enemy; he was not extended matter, but intellectual relation. The nature of what was eaten was an abstraction, a "spiritual" cannibalism. What one eats of man is always a relationship: manducation can only be "according to the spirit" when what is in one's mouth is man.[12] It is an incorporation of something incorporal, of Enmity, and not consumption of the imaginary substance (or a substance that is "imaginary," an image) of *an* enemy: it is generality and abstraction. What does the analogic principle of the alimentary theory have to say? That the nature and condition of what is eaten passes to the one who eats. That is, if someone who eats a slow animal becomes sluggish, then someone who eats an enemy changes into . . . an enemy? The virtue of enemies that was necessary to incorporate was precisely that of being enemies: this is what was eaten. Instead of a "magical superiority" obtained by the dissolution of the enemy's identity in the belly of the society of eaters, such a superiority would be derived from a determination *by* the enemy, a cannibal transformation *into* the enemy. The contrary of an identification—literally, an identification *to the contrary.*[13]

As Sahlins (1983: 88) said, "The problem, of course, is that cannibalism is always 'symbolic' even when it is 'real.'" I would rather say that it is symbolic especially when it is real. Cannibalism is inevitably a semiophagy.

This hypothesis is consistent with what we have seen among the Araweté: there, too, the killer becomes an enemy, and this makes him become immortal. I also suggested that the inexhaustible vigor of the *Maï* is perhaps due to this anthropophagous ambrosia. Likewise, Tupinamba cannibalism was an incorporation of enmity that sought immortality—for the eaters and for the eaten.

□

Against death, the Tupinamba adopted the best defense: attack. Making a virtue of necessity and a necessity of virtue, they transformed the natural given of death into a social necessity and a personal virtue: warfare vengeance was a method of instituting society. Indeed, vengeance was not made necessary *because* men die and need to be rescued from the flux of time; rather, it was necessary to die *in order that* there could be vengeance—and to die, preferably, in enemy hands. This was what Anchieta called the "handsome death," unwittingly echoing the *kalos thanatos* of the Greeks (Vernant 1984); the stomach of one's adversary was the "bed of honor," says Evreux (1929). This was in fact a "life-giving death" (Coppet 1981): it permitted vengeance and thus permitted the production of persons, names, honors. Heteronomy was the condition of autonomy; what is vengeance, if not a mode of recognizing that the "truth of society" lies in the hands of others? Vengeance was not a consequence of religion, but the condition of the possibility and the final cause of society.

In this case, the dead were the instrument, not the subject of Tupinamba religion, a religion of the living in search of immortality. The dead were the connection to enemies, not the contrary. The sacrificial triangle of Florestan must be reorganized: the enemy was not the means, but the end—the Other was destiny. Deadness was a vicarious and fluctuating position, occupied by all the participants of the warfare-funerary system, and not its center.

An enemy was a dead person in many ways. The process of substitution described by Thevet illustrates how the captive at the same time cancelled out and underscored the absence of the deceased member of the group. But what he represented was the deceased *as such,* a dead being: for this reason, he had to be killed and not simply adopted as a substitute—he was a kind of *ta'o we.* In fact, from the moment of his capture, he was considered to be dead by his group of origin (Métraux 1967:52). He could not escape: he would not be taken back by his own people, who would feel insulted, thinking that this would make their enemies think they were not capable of avenging themselves (Magalhães de Gandavo 1922:171; Abbeville 1975 [1614]:231). A prospective deceased, existing in the interval between his own people and his enemies.

Here it may be possible to do something with Florestan's ideas about the necessity of "placating" the spirit of the deceased in cases of individualized vengeance. The central duo of the sacrifice, captive and killer, could be thought of as incarnating complementary facets of the deceased, unfolding and actualizing the absence and division of the person produced by and in the deceased. The deceased *as a living being* would be represented by the killer-avenger; as a dead being—as an enemy, then—he would be represented by the captive. The pair killer/captive would thus incarnate the two faces and the two phases of the Tupinamba person, which is whole, but divided, only in the deceased—in absence. The person thus appears as pure limit, an imaginary congealing of a becoming that is established between the captive and his slayer. The deceased is a *pretext*, something that must be done away with in the end.

A dead person was an enemy in many ways. Concerning the funerary customs, Cardim (1906:428–29) observed: "After he is dead they wash him and paint him verie bravely, as they paint their enemies." That is, the dead of one's own group were painted with the ornamental pattern used on captives for the execution festival. They were thus transformed into posthumous images of enemies ready to die. Since death at home was improper, this funerary decoration might suggest that every person who died (at home) was an enemy. Or rather, it might imply that every man must *die as an enemy*, as if he died in a foreign village, decorated for a public, proper, and handsome death. Thevet reports that the captive who was delivered to a war widow spent some time "married" and was then executed by a brother of the dead warrior; only in this way was the brother qualified to assume levirate succession. *Who*, in the final analysis, was being killed in order to be succeeded—the enemy or the dead man?[14]

The treatment of the body of those who died an undignified death at home, "in the hammock like weak women" (Magalhães de Gandavo 1922:105), presented another notable aspect. The corpse was firmly tied and covered with cotton threads (Cardim 1906:429; Monteiro 1949:416). Thevet explains that this was aimed at impeding the return of the specter, something the Tupinamba feared enormously (1953:97). Thus, whereas dead enemies were dismembered in order to be eaten after a beer festival, the group's own dead were kept whole, sometimes being buried inside beer cauldrons. Whereas the dead enemy was eaten, the burial of a group member enjoined the daily placing of foodstuffs on the grave (until the flesh disappeared) so that the *Anhang* would not disinter and devour the cadaver (Léry 1990:176). Someone who died at home was therefore an enemy: painted as one, feared as one, evoking the *Anhang*, demons that prefigured a bad death. But those who died in foreign hands, as enemies of one's enemies, were esteemed as heroes, since they died a non-natural death. In other words, they died with meaning—justifying the vengeance that would justify them—leaving behind the *memory of their names* among the living (Fernandes 1970:255) instead of the bad memory of rotten flesh, something which, in the Araweté case, generates the specter.

If ritual death is a *kalos thanatos*, consumption must be seen as a direct funerary practice (and not as part of a hypothetical rite of secondary burial). Enemies were the gravediggers of this society, their stomachs the most secure tombs; the names they took and the marks they inscribed on their bodies were the most effective memory that a man could leave of himself. If good enemies are dead enemies, the good dead are ones who died by the clubs of their enemies.

Tupinamba funerary "exo-"cannibalism depends on a system of beliefs to which this book has alluded several times. Léry, noting that foodstuffs were placed on the graves out of fear of the necrophagy of the *Anhang* (something that was done on a daily basis "until they think the body is entirely decayed"), draws a parallel to beliefs of "Judaic theologians or rabbis," who maintain that "since our body is created from the mud and dust of the earth . . . it is subject to it until it is transmuted into a spirit" (Léry 1990: 176). So, from the point of view of the cannibal victim, his consumption was something that would save him from putrefaction and the *Anhang*, transforming him directly into a "spirit," as Léry would have it. As cited earlier, Father Cardim remarked that, for the Tupinamba, "it is a wretched thing to die, and lie stinking, and eaten with Wormes" (1906: 432). Jácome Monteiro was even more explicit. Speaking of the "auguries of the heathens" in their wars, he relates that one of the things that would cause a war party to desist from the enterprise was the rotting of the provisions they brought:

> If the meat, after being cooked, had maggots, which occurs very easily because of the great heat of the land, they say that just as the meat has maggots, thus their enemies ['contraries'] will not eat them, but will leave them to become filled with maggots after they kill them, which is the worst dishonor there is among these barbarians (Monteiro 1949: 413).

So it was necessary to be eaten; the Tupinamba manifested a horror of burial. Anchieta wrote:

> The prisoners nevertheless believe that in this way they are treated excellently and with distinction, and ask for such a . . . glorious death, inasmuch as they say that only the weak and cowardly in spirit die and go, buried, to support the weight of the earth, which they believe to be extremely grave (1933: 45).

"Extremely grave," in this letter translated from the Latin, means very heavy (*gravissimum*), but to be interred is equally grave in the current sense in Portuguese and English. If the earth is heavy, we could say (using an Araweté conceit) that the cannibal death makes the person light, detaching the soul from its ballast more quickly: it liberates the spirit from the body's gravity.

As a funerary rite, therefore, Tupinamba cannibalism is inserted into the Tupi-Guarani problematic of immortalization through sublimation of the corruptible portion of the person. It is the supreme form of spiritualization: the ideal warrior has no body, since it was eaten. Such is the Tupinamba mode of accomplishing what the later Guarani shaman-ascetics strove to gain by rejecting all carnivorous food, by fasting, and by dancing—divinization as transcendence of decay.

But the objective of the sublimation of the person could have been obtained by less violent means, for example, by endo-cannibalism, as Thevet said that "Tapuia" (non-Tupinamba) did, who ate their dead because the earth was not fit to rot them, and as so many other peoples did. But the Tupinamba coupled their horror of the earth with their passion for war, the will to immortality with the impulse for vengeance, by positing individual death as the fuel for social life. Hence the separation between the portion of the individual and the portion of the group, the strange dialectic of honor and offense: to die in foreign hands was an *honor* for the individual, but an *insult to the honor* of his group, which enjoined an equivalent response. It was an honor to be the cause of an offense to one's own group[15]—because in contrast to natural death, this was an offense that could be redressed. To be eaten was better than rotting in the ground; but one was eaten out of vengeance, not pity or piety. Honor, in the end, rested on being able to be the motive of vengeance, contributing to the perseverance of society in its own becoming. The mortal hatred linking enemies was the sign of their indispensability. This simulacrum of exo-cannibalism consumed individuals in order to maintain what was essential to their groups: the vital *conatus* of vengeance. Between the death of enemies and one's own immortality lay the trajectory of each and the destiny of all. Each man's deadly pursuit of vengeance might well have been guided by an ideal of personal immortality, but in the end what was actually produced was immortal, endless social vengeance.

□

The sacrifice of the prisoner operated in two fundamentally distinct dimensions, one "logical" and the other "phagical." The cannibal anthropology was preceded and prepared by a dialogical anthropophagy, a solemn battle of words between the protagonists of the ritual drama of execution. The captive and his killer undertook a verbal duel that crowned the numerous discourses exchanged between the enemy and his captors ever since his arrival in the village.

This dialogue was the culminating moment of the rite. It was moreover what made the Tupinamba famous, thanks to the "chivalrous" reading of Montaigne, who concentrated on this aspect of the cannibal complex and treated it as a kind of Hegelian combat for mutual recognition, a death struggle waged through the medium of discourse.

On the face of it, the dialogue does lend itself perfectly to a reading in terms of honor in warfare, but to little more than this. In the examples recorded by the chroniclers, there are no religious evocations, no mention of "supernatural entities," and nothing about the destiny of the victim's soul after death. On the other hand, all the examples deal with an issue that nobody seems to have noticed: the production of time.

The dialogue opened with a harangue by the killer, who asked the captive if he was indeed one of those who had killed members of his tribe and if he was prepared to die; he exhorted him to fall as a brave man, "leaving a memory" (Monteiro 1949:411). The captive retorted proudly: he affirmed his status as a killer and a cannibal, recalling the enemies he had slain in the same circumstances as he now found himself. A ferocious version of the "acquiescent victim," he demanded the vengeance that would strike him down, warning: kill me, so my people may avenge me; you shall fall in the same way.[16]

The dialogue seems to switch the positions of the protagonists. Anchieta (1933:224) was astonished: the captive "acts as though he were going to kill the others rather than to be killed." In fact, "as these captives see that the hour has arrived when they must suffer, they begin to proclaim and speak great praises of their person, saying that *they had already taken revenge* on the ones who were about to kill him" (Soares de Souza 1971:326 [emphasis mine]). The verbal combat stated in a few deadly words the temporal cycle of vengeance, encapsulating it, as it were, inside an absolute present: the past of the victim was that of a killer, the future of the killer would be that of a victim; the execution would weld past deaths to future deaths, giving meaning to time. Compare this discourse, which contains only past and future, with what H. Clastres said about the sacred Guarani songs:

> [In this sacred language], the one who speaks is at the same time the one who listens. And if he asks a question, he knows that there is no other answer besides

> his own question . . . A question that asks for no answer. Better yet, what the beautiful words appear to indicate is that both question and answer are equally impossible. It is enough to pay attention to the tenses and verb forms: affirmation is only in the past and the future; the present is always the time of negation (H. Clastres 1978:114–15).

For the Tupinamba, to the contrary, the present is the time of *justification*, that is, of vengeance—of the affirmation of time. The captive/killer duel indissolubly associates the two phases and two facets of the warrior figure, which reflect and echo each other (the questions and answers can be interchanged in time), thereby making possible a relation between past and future. Only he who is about to kill and he who is about to die are effectively *present*, that is alive. This dialogue is the transcendental synthesis of time in Tupinamba society. The a priori category of vengeance requires this double schematism, verbal and cannibal, that makes the temporal dimension intervene. Before eating, it is fitting to engage in conversation—and these two acts *explicate* temporality, which emerges from the relationship with enemies. Far from being a device for recuperating an original wholeness, thus the negation of becoming, the cannibal complex, through this agonistic exchange of words, brings forth time: the rite is the great Present.

A semiophagy. The greatest care was taken so that the entity about to be eaten was *a human being*, a being of words, promises, and memories. Innumerable details of the rite, culminating in the dialogue, testify to this effort of constituting the victim as a thoroughly human and social subject (his transformation into a brother-in-law of his captors should also be interpreted in this sense). In a fine analysis of Montaigne's essay, Lestringant points out how it reduces cannibalism to a mere "economy of the word," which conceals the savage dimension so clearly present in the chroniclers' accounts. He argues that Montaigne proposed a nonalimentary version of Tupinamba cannibalism, thoroughly "idealizing" it.[17] Be that as it may, I find that Lestringant's characterization of the Montaignian shift expresses beautifully what was really at stake in this moment in the Tupinamba rite, so let me put his words to my service:

> The flesh of the prisoner that is going to be eaten is in no way a food, but a sign . . . The cannibal act *represents* an extreme vengeance . . . this [is an] effort to find in the practices of the cannibal the permanence of a discourse . . . Without lingering over the sequels

> to the massacre, Montaigne stays with the challenge to honor, the exchange of insults . . . He ends up forgetting that the mouth of the cannibal is provided with teeth. Instead of devouring, it only utters [*profère*] (Lestringant 1982:38–40).

There is no doubt that the mouths of the cannibals had teeth, besides tongues; but Lestringant is unaware of the fact that it was the Tupinamba who themselves separated the mouth that eats from the one that utters: the killer was the only one who *should not eat* the flesh of the enemy. The discourse, as a representation of vengeance, transformed the flesh that was going to be eaten into a sign: the dialogical cook did not taste it.

Between the captive and the killer, a process of reverberation was established analogous to that linking the captive and the deceased. An entire series of cabalistic gestures performed with the club, the weapon of death (decorated like the captive and treated like a person by the women who prepared it) that was passed between the legs of the captive and the slayer, united these two men. Before the fatal blow, the victim was given room enough to dodge and retaliate; this simulacrum of a physical confrontation appears to have been intended to affirm the equality of the antagonists. And finally, there was the rigorous seclusion of the killer: withdrawing to his house after the final blow, he not only did not eat the captive, he wore around his wrist the lips cut from the victim, as if inverting the cannibal relation (S. Carvalho 1983:45). Fasting for days in his hammock, with a cotton thread tied around his chest (like a corpse?), his goods were freely appropriated by everyone—whereas his enemy, during captivity, could appropriate freely the foods of everyone else if something was denied him, and appropriated the goods of the deceased whom he "substituted." Finally, the killer was scarified (so that his blood would not rot in his belly [Thevet 1953:206]) and submitted to various mystical precautions against the soul of the victim. This seclusion was a mourning: the feasts that closed it were identical to those held by the relatives of someone who died. And he reemerged with a new name—transfigured, like his victim, for whom, as the chroniclers said, he had mourned.

4. The Anti-Social Contract

Let us take up a classic problem—the definition of the war captive as a brother-in-law—and see how this elucidates the fundamental thrust of Tupi-Guarani cosmology.

Hélène Clastres (1972), hesitating over the explanation for cannibalism ("les Tupi étaient des gens très compliqués"), underlines the semantic and objective relationship between enemies and brothers-in-law, both called *tovaja.* The objective of Tupinamba warfare, she notes, was the exact opposite of that usually considered characteristic of "primitive" societies, the capture of women. Instead of trying to obtain women without the burden of affinity, the Tupinamba went after brothers-in-law—enemies to whom they gave women before killing them. She wonders if this was not a devious way of expressing the same thing. If so, warfare for the capture of "brothers-in-law" to be devoured would be a translation of the yearning for an ideal world where affinity—dependency on others—would not exist. Hence, the Tupinamba would be carrying out vengeance not against their enemies, but against their affines, or rather, a vengeance against affinity. This takes us back to the theme alluded to so many times in this book, the world without affines. Creating a ritual simulacrum of affinity in order to deflect towards it the perverse desire to annihilate real affines, the Tupinamba practiced a "ritual negation of alliance" (H. Clastres 1978:47)—a ritual of rebellion, inspired by the demon of incest.

This is an intriguing hypothesis, consistent with the ideological complex of prophetism and the myth of the "Land without Evil" of the early Tupi-Guarani. The author shows that in their general suspension of social rules (carried out during the Tupinamba's and Guarani's delirious transcontinental migrations), the prophets spared only two customs: while work, political authority, and the rules of matrimonial exchange were banished, warfare and cannibalism were maintained. It was as if prophetism put into practice that which cannibal warfare only dared to manifest ritually and indirectly: the end of society, law, and alliance. A vengeance against death, as Thevet observed, and a vengeance against affinity, as H. Clastres suggests, Tupinamba "vengeance" would thus be a two-pronged combat against the bases of the human condition: submission to others and to death.

We must ask if it is really possible to read Tupi-Guarani prophetism through such a bias of negativity. If what its discourse retained was vengeance and cannibalism, then prophetism was not a negation of the foundations of society (a negation that H. Clastres believes was an antidote to the negation lurking in the "State" emerging among the Tupi-Guarani in the sixteenth century), but an affirmation of what remained essential for this society (Carneiro da Cunha & Viveiros de Castro 1985). Fundamentalists more than revolutionaries, what the prophets announced was a contamination of the entire social body by the principle guiding the personal trajectory of each man: access to the Land without Evil, the horizon of warrior prowess and death. Prophetism is a denial only insofar as vengeance, that Anti-Social Contract that makes enemies more necessary than brothers-in-law, already is.

It is curious that through prophetism and cannibalism, the Tupi-Guarani made a reality of what other human societies have merely imagined, either as an impossible dream or as a somber nightmare: to do away with death and reciprocity, finitude and mediation. Even if this realization of the impossible found its greatest expression—and thus its necessary failure—in the maelstrom of prophecy, it never stopped guiding the plot of life: "All their motives are how they will make war on their adversaries."

As a "negation" of alliance, the system of cannibal vengeance was the ritual that united all the Tupinamba, enemies of themselves. Ritual, unquestionably, but not a mere representation: although they did not kill their real affines, they really ate their symbolic ones.

□

The woman given to the captive (or the other way around, as we have seen) is variously characterized by the chroniclers: sister or daughter of the captor, of the future executor, of the chief of the village, or the widow of a dead man to be avenged. The prisoner maintained a specific relation with the men who would kill him. The paradigmatic case seems to have been delivering him to the safekeeping of the killer's sister; parents usually reserved prisoners for the initiation of their sons, at the same time that they gave the prisoners their daughters. Thus, the captive was a sister's husband; the killer, the wife's brother.

But the prisoner was an affine *sui generis*. Instead of performing brideservice, as befell youths who requested wives, he received a woman for whom he had not asked, and was maintained and fed by his affines ("who would rather go hungry than fail to ensure that their prisoners were well treated" [Thevet 1953:273]). Instead of being the obligatory participant on war expeditions commanded by the father-in-law, he was the very war booty itself. Instead of being a provider of food, he himself was the "future food." And finally, instead of being a term in a relation of matrimonial exchange, the captive was the object of prestations within his captors' group.

One of the obligations of a newlywed man was to present his young brothers-in-law with gifts of enemies so they could be initiated or avenge their father. The captive was a matrimonial prestation, the equivalent of the wife his captor had received. But the captive also served as a present between people who esteemed each other or as something given to someone to whom one owed a debt. Enemies consolidated many relations: between men and women,[18] relatives, affines, friends. They were, in sum, a precious gift, use value and exchange value, a thing of honor and a thing of vengeance.

The equation "enemy = brother-in-law" perhaps says more about the position of the actual brother-in-law (sister's husband) than about that of captive enemies. Captivity under a woman's surveillance was the extreme instance of "temporary" uxorilocality to which every youth was in principle condemned. The man who took a woman to whom he was not related was at the mercy of his affines, living in a foreign house, incorporated into the domestic and war economy of the father-in-law. He enacted an attenuated version of the drama of the captive, an enemy uxorilocalized without his consent and destined to die at the hands of the wife-givers. A typical phantasm of an uxorilocal society, it was less a matter of a captive being a "brother-in-law" than of an in-marrying brother-in-law (ZH) being a "captive." But each leads into the other: in order to obtain a wife, it was necessary to have killed an enemy; in order to escape uxorilocal captivity, it was necessary to offer enemies to one's brothers-in-law (WB). This is, at least, what Tupinamba ideology asserted.

Monteiro (1949: 408) mentions a curious myth of the origin of cannibalism. A brother once injured his sister, "whose husband, unable to suffer it, killed him and ate him," and so the primal society split up and people began to eat each other. An ideological *tour de force,* this brief story begins with something unthinkable for Tupinamba kinship customs, an exchange of insults between brother and sister (a relationship ideally marked by a "very particular love," as Anchieta put it); it then sets the sister's husband to eating the wife's brother. In other words, an inverted incest ends in an inverted cannibalism. Thus it is understandable why everything falls under the rubric of vengeance: the initial act of cannibalism was of a sister's husband against a wife's brother; henceforth, it will always be the wife's brother who will eat the sister's husband.

If the enemy as a generalized nexus was the symbolic foundation of Tupinamba sociability, uxorilocality was its political foundation. Here it is necessary to discuss the relation between the two most famous practices of this people: the cannibal captivity of "brothers-in-law" and avuncular marriage. If captivity is the maximal case of uxorilocality—at the same time temporary and final, one might say—then marriage with sister's daughter is the minimal limit of this residential form, or the mode of escaping from it.

Someone who took his sister's daughter as a wife did not have to leave his residential group. On the other hand, someone who granted a daughter to his wife's brother was relieved of part of the debt owed to his affines. Thevet (1953 : 130) is explicit: the granting of a daughter liberated the father from his "servitude." It may be too much to suppose that this prestation of a daughter was the only condition for escaping the uxorilocal situation (much less that it cancelled the duties of reciprocity among affines). But the granting of a daughter *or* the prestation of a captive were the counterparts of a wife; if such prestations were not honored, the woman could be confiscated by her brothers (Rodrigues [1552], in Leite 1956–58, 1 : 307).[19]

All in all, it is as if the structures of Tupinamba matrimonial exchange drifted towards two polar opposites. To one side is a ritual hyperexogamy, where women are temporarily granted to enemies, paradoxical brothers-in-law; to the other is an endogamous avarice that is hardly distinguishable from incest (Lévi-Strauss 1969a : 448, 454), marriage with sister's daughter. Anti-affinity and counter-affinity: it is as if there were no stable place for affinity in the system. Between the "privileged union" of avuncular marriage and the "underprivileged" situation of the captive-husband, it is as if affinity disappeared, torn to shreds between opposites. This may also help to explain the notorious instability of the terms for cross-cousins—middle-distance affines—in Tupinamba terminologies.

Between these extremes of exogamy and endogamy were common and initial marriages, of a moderate exogamic coefficient: the higher it was, the more it imposed uxorilocal residence. These marriages, however, were merely that, common or initial. The entire apparatus of warrior renown had as a consequence or objective the overcoming of uxorilocality. The polygamy of chiefs and eminent killers was an essential value, implying virilocality as well as the inversion of the hierarchy between givers and receivers: to grant daughters to chiefs and heroes was an honor (Abbeville 1975 : 223).[20]

Both the avuncular union and the polygamy of great men thus appear to be forms of escaping the gravitational field of uxorilocality. Far from being an automatic rule that would allow a calculus of its effects on the social structure to be derived, uxorilocality was an effect of the political system (and this, a function of the "cosmology" of vengeance). Each time it was practiced, it represented a negative limit that depended on the historical state of the system. In other words, those who resided uxorilocally were those who had no other way out. That is why the textbook notions usually applied to the Tupinamba—"temporary uxorilocality," "uxorivirilocality"—are inadequate. They assume a nonexistent mechanical normativity. The uxorilocal axiom was an initial situation that posed the problem of how to escape it, something that was not always possible to achieve, such as cases where the father-in-law was powerful or the kindred of the son-in-law weak.[21]

Fernandes (1963:215–32) undertook a survey of Tupinamba matrimonial and residential forms reported in the literature. Strict uxorilocality prevailed in the case of youths unrelated to the woman's family; this suggests that the avunculate was the limit of a broader endogamous tendency, and that the possible existence of symmetrical exchange was also intended to repeat ties between kindred groups. The avuncular union, although being the preferential form (but not "prescriptive," as we knew from Anchieta), was practiced especially by primogenitors and residential leaders' sons as a strategy of virilocal succession. The avunculate was articulated with polygamy, a function in turn of warrior renown. Warfare was inscribed directly in the marriage system; its effects went beyond the qualifying rite of homicide. Uxorilocality was not "temporary," but *temporal*—it was the point of departure that opened up onto the event, generator of a dynamic of differentiation dependent on prowess in warfare (of ego or his ascendants or both). Here again, I am drawing conclusions from what Tupinamba ideology seems to have maintained.

Thus the Tupinamba, instead of obtaining the women *of* enemies, obtained and accumulated them *through* enemies (or brothers-in-law, who yielded sisters' daughters). Instead of killing the male relatives of the women whom they might take in war, they gave female relatives to the captured men and, killing them, obtained women of their own group. Endogamy depended on exonymy and the death of outsiders. Escaping the uxorilocal "servitude" by renown in warfare, a man would be capable of imposing this subjugation on his young sons-in-law, husbands of the daughters generated by his many wives: "And so whoever has more daughters is honored by the sons-in-law they acquired, who are always subject to their fathers-in-law and brothers-in-law" (Anchieta 1933:329). The "uxorilocalization" of the captives was a dramatic caricature of an internal situation, the means for everyone to escape it, and the instrument with which to impose it on others.[22]

□

Marriage and residence patterns impress me as much more important for understanding Tupinamba society than the sometimes imagined groups of patrilinear descent, which no information substantiates. The social units were the *malocas* (longhouses): the men of each one formed a core band of warriors; the houses were the production units for beer and the hosts for cannibal feasts; their leaders formed the "council of chiefs" (Fernandes 1963: chap. 5), the maximal political body of the village. The data suggest that these residential units were centered on a polygamous family headed by a war leader who was able to "acquire" numerous sons-in-law and who at the same time attempted to keep some married sons living virilocally. Some information indicates that marriage within the same house was possible, which thus sheltered a bilateral kindred. The political bond that founded this unit was the dependency of the son-in-law (or an aspirant—bride service began before marriage) on the father-in-law and brothers-in-law who were unmarried or living virilocally. The village was no more than the aggregation of these houses, founded on affinity and dedicated to war: "In general, having a great number of sons-in-law supported the attempts . . . by certain family heads to found a new collective house . . . This was very important . . . since the men he attracted would constitute a group of warriors subordinated to him" (Fernandes 1963:72–73). The village was a unit subordinated to the collective houses; it was an unstable aggregate, merging and exchanging its members with neighboring villages. Fission from internal dissension was common, and many times the fiercest enemies were adjoining groups that had once formed a single unit and that recognized kinship ties—the opposite of a segmentary organization. The war between the Tupinamba of Itaparica and those of Salvador, for instance, stemmed from a fission over a woman (Soares de Souza 1971:301). The peace ceremony between enemy chiefs witnessed by Father Leonardo do Vale was possible because "even though they went to war for a better life and as a pasttime, they do not fail to recognize the tranquility that is born when their wars cease, especially because of the kinship and marriage alliances that exist among them and the friendship they had in earlier times" (Vale [1562], in Leite 1956–58, 3:478). Anchieta was amazed that the war of Piratininga opposed uncles and nephews, fathers and sons, and cousins (Anchieta [1563], in Leite 1956–58, 3:551).

But at the same time, the solidarity of the longhouse seems to have been uneven. The great matrimonial instability of the Indians, so lamented by the Jesuits, suggests that even the *maloca* was a fluid grouping. Its composition, the result of the prevailing bonds of affinity, depended on, or was manifested in, warfare activity. Tupinamba society, considered from an institutional point of view, relied entirely on the "external dialectic" of capturing enemies for vengeance and renown. War produced the society, at the level of persons, houses, villages, and blocs of allied villages—the maximal level, created by the cannibal ceremony that qualified all the participants as possible objects of vengeance by the victim's group.

So what about the famous patrilinearity of the Tupinamba? It is indisputable that they professed the dogma of exclusive patrilateral conception. The consumption of the sons of enemies attested to this; the licitness of avuncular marriage was justified along the same idea (Anchieta 1933:448–56). But from patrilaterality of conception to patrilinearity *lato sensu* and from there to the existence of corporate patrilinear groups spans a distance that no source allows us to bridge. It is useless to try to derive "jural" rules of descent from theories of conception (Goodenough 1970:39); in various cases, the line of "blood" and that of "rights" are opposed or independent. In the sixteenth-century Tupinamba sources, there is a clear disproportion between the abundance of texts on patrifilial conception and its effect on avuncular unions (which it more likely *rationalizes* than *explains*) and the absence of any indication whatsoever of corporate action on an agnatic basis.

The atom of the unit of warfare was the pair wife's father/daughter's husband (or sister's husband/wife's brother), just as the minimal pair of vengeance was the killer/captive duo conceptualized in the same idiom of affinity. Tupinamba vengeance does not point to a "descent theory," but rather to an "alliance theory." The association between vengeance and the manifestation of lineage-based collective identities must be discarded—but not in favor of the idea of groups constituted by marriage alliance, where the exchange of women would be duplicated by the exchange of captives. Even if these prestations were superimposed, they did not define groups internal to the society. The institutional centrality of warfare may have derived from the fact that no other mechanism competed with it to assure the viability of large villages: no unilinear skeleton, no system of perpetual alliance between groups. Without the relationship to the exterior and the omnipresent ontological predation, society would not be possible. The absence of an "internal dialectic" projected difference to the exterior at the same time that it required a passage through this exterior in order to constitute the "interiority" of the *socius.*

In short, *the enemy was the center of the society.* Isn't this what was expressed in the solemn execution in the central plaza of the village, where the victim stood resplendent, superbly feathered as if he were the guest of honor? If, as Lévi-Strauss showed, the relation of alliance is logically superior to that of filiation, since it rescues the latter from its continuity with nature and institutes society, here we have the same thing. The relationship to the enemy is anterior and superior to society's relationship to itself, rescuing it from an indifferent and natural self-identity—one where others would be mirrors and reflect back the image of a Subject posited in advance as *telos.* Every origin was an answer; every gesture, vengeance. Free and fierce, inconstant and indifferent, the Tupinamba were servants of warfare: this pushed them into the future. Inhabitants of a society without corporations—incorporal, so to speak—and cannibal (thus incorporating), its being was time.

5. Eaters of Raw Flesh

If alliance and mortality define the space of Culture—the first differentiating men from animality, the second exiling them from divinity—Tupinamba cosmology explored the frontiers of this double boundary. We have seen how this is still echoed in Araweté thought. If their gods, immortal mortals, are affines par excellence, Tupinamba enemies were too: good affines are dead affines, and the good dead are gods.

Let us consider cannibalism from the perspective of the desire to go beyond the human condition. The Tupinamba's anthropological cannibalism, the Araweté's divine cannibalism, and the anticannibal religion of the Guarani are all transformations of the same theme: the instability of Culture between Nature and Supernature. Thus, we can recuperate the meaning of cannibalism as a sacrificial structure without resorting to the notion of communion with the ancestors.

The presence of the collectivity in the ceremony of execution can be explained in another way than Florestan did. It must be remarked that he does not address the problem of the difference between the conduct of the killer and that of the other participants: why does the former not eat his victim while the others do? Why is the mouth that utters not the mouth that eats? And why, after all, *does* the latter eat?

One aspect of Tupinamba cannibalism should be pointed out that, although perhaps exaggerated by the chroniclers and difficult to deal with, is nevertheless essential. I am referring to ferocity: the orgy of blood relished by the small children, the infamous gluttony of the old women, the use of the enemies' flesh as a consolation for the sick and afflicted (quite like the Trobriand *vaygu'a*), the rampages of fury, the vivid hatred for the enemy, the unbridled and brutal climate—qualities that emerge in all the descriptions of the anthropophagic feasts. The sacrifice of the enemy involved what Florestan mentioned in passing as the "animal plane" of Tupinamba warfare, which he then cast aside as useless for explaining the causes of the phenomenon (1970:44–47). Useless, undoubtedly, if the idea is taken literally, since warfare was not hunting and anthropophagy was not alimentary, but ritual. It was nonetheless an alimentary ritual—which implied a "symbolic" animalization.

"The essential rule of [Tupinamba] anthropophagy," says H. Clastres (1972:80), "may be the requirement that everyone participate in it." Only the killer, withdrawn at home, fasting and maintaining absolute silence, is an outsider to the feast. While everyone crowns the days of drunkenness by staging the maximal display of collective ferocity, the killer is the image of measure and caution. Clearly, there is a division of ritual labor in all this. While the executor enters into a "liminal state"—dead, temporarily without a name, dispossessed of everything he owns, filled with the victim's mystical blood, which he must purge to lighten his body—the society is in the midst of full and exuberant activity. But things can also be seen in the opposite way: it is the slayer who incarnates the part of structure; it is he who exercises the work of the symbol, supporting the process of the "reproduction" of society. Operator of the sacrifice, he is the pivot in the play of images, staging vengeance, mirroring the enemy and perhaps the deceased relative being avenged, manifesting the central values of the group: the warrior and the person, the name and the numen. Meanwhile, liberated from the burden of representation, the collectivity outside is the opposite of a society, engaging in a destructive and savage cannibalism. While the killer is spiritualizing himself at home, entertaining an obscure commerce with the soul of his victim, out in the patio the others are "animalizing" themselves—they are all, as Cunhambebe would say, jaguars. While only a short time before, vengeance required an elaborate exchange of words between slayer and victim, whose mouths articulated a dialogue that produced social time, now vengeance is located in the mouths that eat. The killer represents; the others pursue the real. But in order for them to leave, someone has to stay. Cannibalism is possible only because *someone* does not eat. The collective acting out requires that someone take care of the symbol. Quiet and reclusive, the killer is the one who afterwards will sing and utter his name. Ritually dead, he is the only one who is truly human during the cannibal feast—the warden of the Symbolic. While the community "incorporates" itself by incorporating the enemy during this anthropophagic carnival, he is pure spirit. Those who eat are still the others.

This does not mean that Tupinamba ritual anthropophagy is a recuperation of a mystical or moral substance lost by the group, nor an imaginary (that is, "false") assimilation of the enemies' powers. It consists of an enemy-becoming, which translates alimentarily into an animal-becoming. What is incorporated is the ontological position of "Enemy." If war can be seen as vengeance against affinity, the act of consumption is an incorporation of enmity: a transformation into Enemy.

The opposition between the killer and the cannibal community is the axis of the system. The killer enters into a mirror chamber with his victim and together with him stages the mortal ballet of the person, producing the attributes of the self. The community incarnates—incorporates—the Other, the enemy as position. The liminality of the slayer and the death of the victim extract them from society and direct them towards the side of Supernature; the ferocity of the community pushes it towards the side of Nature. The ceremony creates a double distancing of Culture. For this reason, it is not an operation of a Durkheimian religiosity—the restoration of collective moral harmony—but a philosophical enactment: an anthropology. Cannibalism is an animal critique of society and the desire for divinization.

These extremes meet up. Combès (1987) recently elucidated something that I only suspected regarding the Araweté *Maï*: that the cannibal diet is itself immortalizing and that therefore the eaters and the eaten meet up with each other in the end. The chronicles about the Chiriguano (Tupi-Guarani of Bolivia) attest that cannibalism made the body become lightweight: "They say it is to make them light." Human flesh was thus the opposite of those foods that make the body gravitate towards corruption; its consumption entered into the diet prescribed by the prophets, capable of rejuvenating elderly women, making them able to procreate—the specifically feminine form of immortality. The victory over death was achieved through cannibalism from everyone's point of view: the one who killed, the one who died, the one who ate. Human flesh was the ambrosia of the Land without Evil. Through Supernature or through Nature, as spirit or as flesh, the enemy is a promise of immortality—because through him, one obtains the power to be the other. Something the *Maï*, as gods and cannibals, know very well.

□

Let us conclude with an evocation of the ancient Greeks, who also founded their anthropology on a dual contrast of the human condition with the beasts and the gods. Marcel Detienne (1972, 1977, 1979, 1989) showed that in Greek thought, the human condition depended on a politico-religious system anchored in the sacrifice of foods to the gods. To humans went the flesh, putrescible like themselves, and to the inhabitants of Olympus, the smoke of calcinated bones and their perfume, sign of their immortality. On the other end, humans distinguished themselves from animals by having fire and laws. Without fire, animals are omophagi, eaters of the raw; without *dike*, justice, they are allelophagi, devouring each other.

The position of humanity as a function of the sacrificial fire, where fire distinguished it from animality and where sacrifice evoked their lost commensality with divinity (Vernant 1989:27), and the construction of the *polis* around this fire were factors that came to be questioned between the sixth and fourth centuries B.C. by four "anti-systems," movements to reform or renounce civic and religious life. Such movements resorted to the language of cannibalism. Thus, Pythagorism and Orphism intended to break down the line that separated men from gods by denouncing the carnivorous diet as anthropophagy and preaching a vegetarian asceticism. Detienne observes that there were two variants of Pythagorism and their followers: the "Pure," rejecting all blood sacrifices and all meat, who embarked on a radical project to form a sect of renunciators (Detienne 1989:6; 1972:239), and the other camp, the reformists, who professed an alimentary casuistry that refused only certain types of victims (especially the paradigmatic one, the draught ox). The asceticism of the Pythagoreans and followers of Orpheus manifested the same impulse as the Guarani: the overcoming of the human condition "by the high road," through Supernature. The differentiation internal to Pythagorism resembled the dual Guarani ethic: one followed by commoners, who were content to maintain their distance from "the soul of raw meat"; the other practiced by shamans, who sought the lightness of immortality through mortification of the body (H. Clastres 1978). The discourse of Guarani prophets, in its antipolitical radicalism, approximates that of the disciples of Orpheus in their total critique of society and their marginality, wandering, and esoteric theology (Detienne 1989:7; 1977:45).

From the other end were the movements that sought to overcome the human condition "via the low road," through bestiality: Dionysianism and Cynicism. The Dionysian sacrifice, the savage devouring of the raw flesh of an animal pursued outside the walls of the city, inverted the sacrificial norm of the *polis;* legend attested that this omophagy terminated in allelophagy—in cannibalism (Detienne 1972:241; 1979:89; 1989:8). Dionysius, the god who manifested an "inveterate oscillation between the twin poles of savagery and paradise regained," received exactly the same epithet as the Araweté gods: *ōmēstēs* or *ōmádios*—"eater of raw flesh" (Detienne 1979:62, 92).

If it is possible to think of the Pythagoreans and the followers of Orpheus as Hellenic equivalents of the Guarani, then perhaps it is possible to see in Tupinamba cannibalism and its eschatological shift among the Araweté the same impulse towards transcendence, merging the divine and the animal, that Dionysianism manifested. The coincidence of epithets between Dionysius and the *Mai̱'* is eloquent. But starting from the same triadic matrix that situates men between beasts and gods, Tupi-Guarani cosmology approaches the *anti*-systems of Greece, not its official religion. It conceives of the human condition not only as intercalary, but also as precarious. The space of Culture is not a bastion to be fortified, but, rather, a passageway, an equivocal and ambivalent place. We know little, after all, about Tupinamba religion; but prophetism and cannibalism appear to be the two sides of a synthesis that sought to overcome the human condition from above and from below. The words of the prophets preached the abolition of work and incest laws, exhorted people to nomadism and dance, but maintained and exalted cannibalism, that obsession that stamped the entire Tupi-Guarani cosmology. We know little about this religion; but its impulse can still be encountered in the religion of the Araweté, where only a killer approximates the cannibal and immortal gods. Just as Dionysius, eater of raw flesh, was the central character in the mythology of the Orphic vegetarian renunciators, so, too, Araweté Divinity joins extremes: it is both the mouth that devours and the mouth that speaks, cannibal and singer; both raw flesh and perfume, mortal and immortal, the Golden Age and Savagery—the animal and the divine in a single figure, the extra-human. The Araweté with their *Mai̱'*, their perfumed jaguars, preserve the distant echo of what once belonged to Tupinamba wisdom: the truth always lies with the Other and always in the future—which is one and the same thing.

APPENDIXES

Appendix 1-A

Araweté Villages in 1981–83

In map 5 note the concentration of houses 7–10 around a single patio, like that of houses 14, 16–20. The space between houses 1, 2, 4, 11, and 5 serves not only as this group's patio, but also as the spot for holding the shamanic rites for mild beer and tortoise. At the end of 1981, the families of this village moved to the other village at FUNAI Indian Post (see map 6). The correspondence between house numbers in this village and house numbers in the one by the Indian Post is as follows:

House Numbers

This Village	Village by Post	This Village	Village by Post
1	20	10	10
2	37	11–12	28
3	1	13	29
4	43	14	30
5	42	15	44
6	19	16	24
6	34	17	33
7	36/23 (remarriage)	18	34
9	26	19–20	9

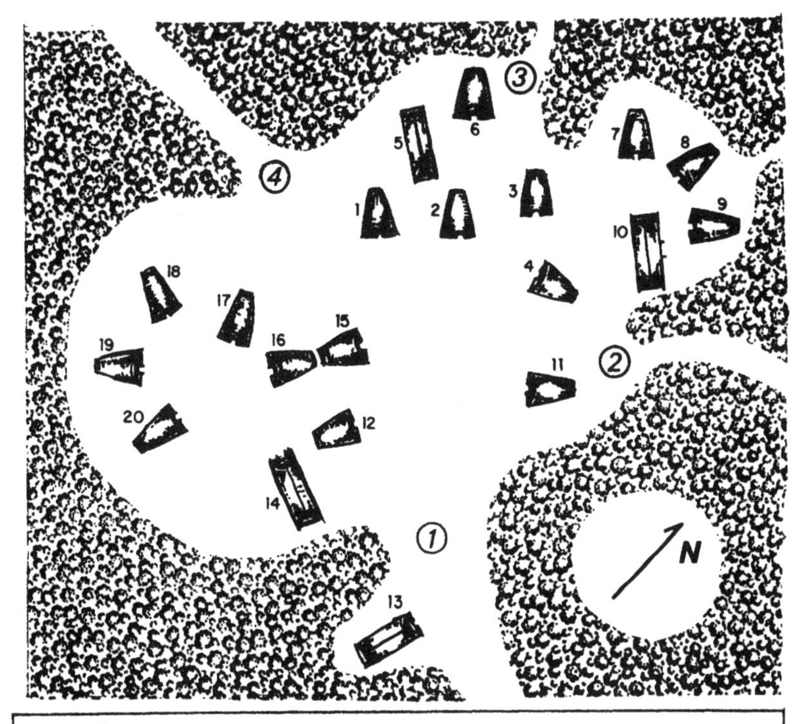

MAP 5

Araweté village on east bank of Ipixuna River (1981)

① Hunting trail

② Path to gardens

③ Path to gardens and water hole

④ Trail to river, water holes, village at FUNAI Post

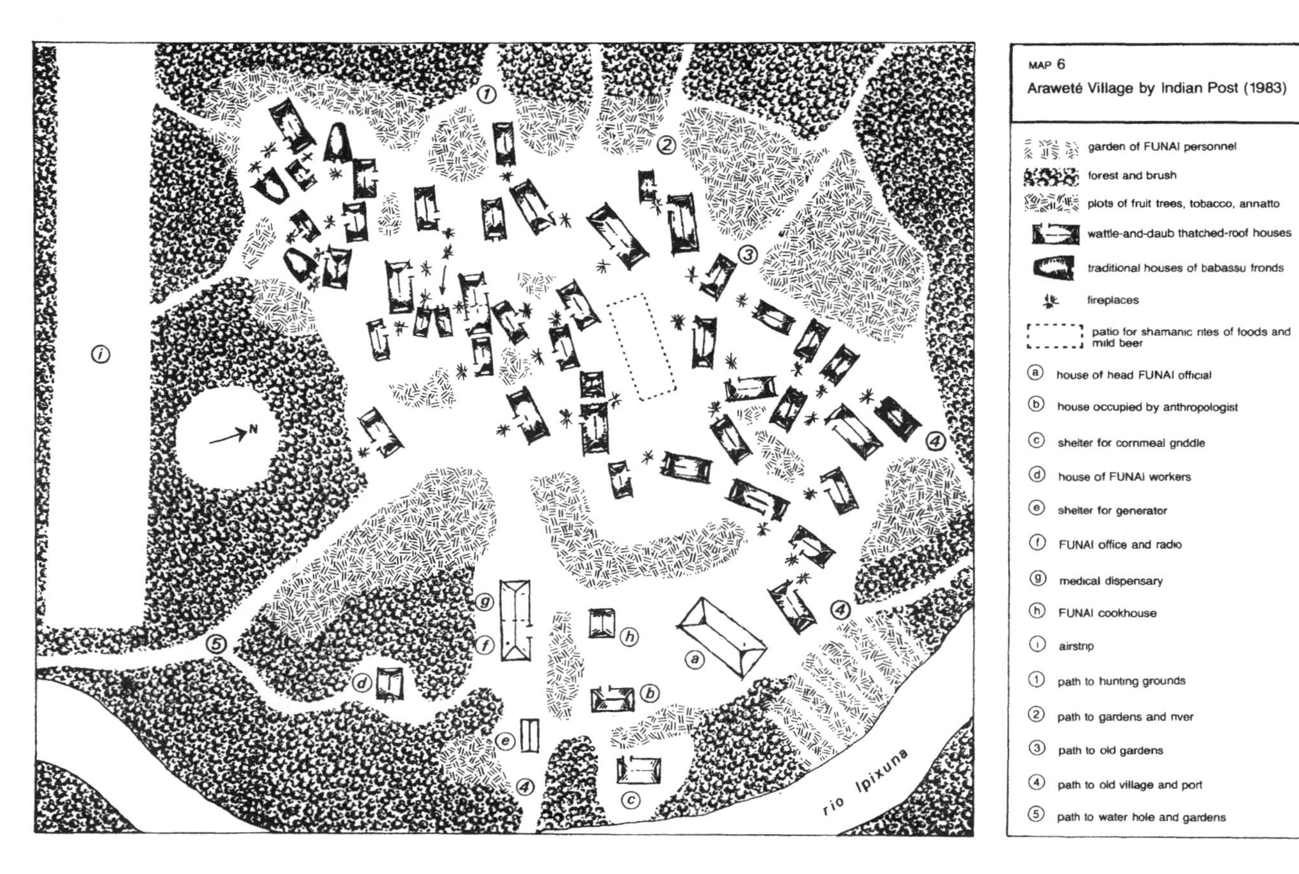
rio Ipixuna
N
a
b
c
d
e
f
g
h
i
1
2
3
4
5
MAP 6
Araweté Village by Indian Post (1983)
garden of FUNAI personnel
forest and brush
plots of fruit trees, tobacco, annatto
wattle-and-daub thatched-roof houses
traditional houses of babassu fronds
fireplaces
patio for shamanic rites of foods and mild beer
a house of head FUNAI official
b house occupied by anthropologist
c shelter for cornmeal griddle
d house of FUNAI workers
e shelter for generator
f FUNAI office and radio
g medical dispensary
h FUNAI cookhouse
i airstrip
1 path to hunting grounds
2 path to gardens and river
3 path to old gardens
4 path to old village and port
5 path to water hole and gardens

Appendix 1-B

List of Historical Araweté Villages

This list of villages begins about 1940–1945, when the main informants for this aspect of group history were born. To the extent possible, the list is ordered temporally, although it also includes coeval villages of different territorial blocs. Each entry indicates the village name, river basin where it is located, and, if available, information on year founded, enemy attacks, or group fissionings. All untranslated names take the form "(Personal name) + *hɨpã*," which means "So-and-so's place, support" and indicates that this person was buried there.

1. Iatadĩ *nɨpã:* Bacajá; founded 1940
2. Mada'i-hi *rɨpã:* Bacajá
3. *Yɨta'i oho rɨpã* ("Place of big courbaril trees"): Bacajá
4. Irayiwã-hi *rɨpã:* Bacajá
5. Ararĩñã-no *rɨpã:* Bacajá
6. Tiapï *dɨpã:* Bacajá
7. Moy-reme *rɨpã:* Bacajá
8. Takara-hi *rɨpã:* Bacajá
9. Tapïnã-no *rɨpã:* Bacajá
10. Pekã-hi *rɨpã:* Bacajá
11. Kãñĩnadĩ-no *koï* ("Kãñĩnadĩ-no's gourd"): Bacajá
12. Ñãmire *rɨpã:* Bacajá
13. *Itã pɨkɨ'ï* ("Long rock"): Bacajá
14. *Itã pïdĩ* ("Red rock"): Bacajá
15. Torowa *rɨpã:* Bacajá
16. Iareakã-no *rɨpã:* Bacajá
17. Matadï-hi *rɨpã:* Bacajá; Kayapó attacks c. 1955
18. Apite *rɨpã:* Bacajá
19. Ñã-toti *rɨpã:* Bacajá; fissioning of group
20. Matadï *dɨpã:* Bacajá-Ipixuna
21. Paratacĩ *nɨpã:* Ipixuna
22. *Iwã pite pehã* ("Of the middle of the sky"): Piranhaquara
23. Takara'i-toti *rɨpã:* Bom Jardim
24. Nãñã-no *rɨpã:* Bom Jardim
25. Taramĩ-hi *rɨpã:* Bom Jardim
26. Yakoati-ro *rɨpã:* Bom Jardim; fissioning of bloc

27. Ođïđï-kãñĩ *nɨpã:* Jatobá
28. *Yaatïnã ti we* ("Mosquito place"): Jatobá
29. Todïnã-hi *rɨpã:* Bom Jardim
30. Tayopi-hi *rɨpã:* Bom Jardim; founded c. 1962
31. Tawičire-hi *kã̱'ɨ̃ naka̱wa he* ("Where Tawičire-hi spilled beer"): Bom Jardim
32. Tiwa̱wĩ-no *iwã-iwã he* ("Where Tiwa̱wĩ-no was shot"): Piranhaquara; existed 1965–67
33. *Awĩ ka pe* ("Enemies' clearing"): Piranhaquara; Kayapó attack 1967; fissioning of group
34. *Tã i̱i̱aho* ("New village"): Piranhaquara; Kayapó attacks; major fissioning of northern and southern blocs
35. Irawa̱dï-do *rɨpã:* Ipixuna
36. *Ka pite i̱i̱aho* ("New garden"): Ipixuna; Kayapó attacks
37. *Awacï đo he* ("Where maize was eaten"): Ipixuna
38. Arananĩ *nɨpã:* Ipixuna
39. Takawi *rɨpã:* Ipixuna
40. *A kãy hã we* ("Where the house burnt down"): Ipixuna; contacts with fur hunters, conflicts with Asuriní
41. *Ia'i rɨpã* ("Place of Brazil-nut trees"): Ipixuna
42. *Ara̱ho'i rɨpã* ("Place of frutão saplings"): Ipixuna
43. *Paranĩ nehã* ("River bank"): Ipixuna
44. Madïma *rɨpã:* Ipixuna
45. Ođïđã-kãñĩ *rɨpã:* Ipixuna
46. Nãñã-hi *rɨpã:* Ipixuna
47. Kãñĩ-ma̱ï-hi *rɨpã:* Ipixuna; first Parakanã attack c. 1974
48. *Tayipa rɨpã* ("Place of bow wood trees"): Ipixuna
49. *Arakaiyi'i ti* ("Place of *arakaiyi'i* trees"): Bom Jardim; southern group, separated since 1960
50. Yorodĩ *nɨpã:* Bom Jardim
51. Iwarawi-hi *rɨpã:* Bom Jardim
52. Amiyiti-hi *rɨpã:* Bom Jardim; Parakanã attack 1975–76
53. Kãñĩna̱dĩ-no *rɨpã:* Bom Jardim
54. *Pïdã ihi pi* ("Place of the fishing line"): Bom Jardim
55. *A đarã nenã* ("Place of the round house"): Bom Jardim
56. Ma̱dĩ-hi *rɨpã:* Ipixuna; founded 1976
57. Mere-hi *rɨpã:* Ipixuna
58. *Yɨta'i cïmõ he* ("Where the scaffold in the courbaril tree was"): Ipixuna; former Asuriní village
59. Kãñĩ-moko-ro *rɨpã:* Ipixuna
60. Toropa'i *rɨpã:* Jatobá
61. *Oyo we me'e rĩ:* Jatobá
62. Mađïpa-do *mo-pe he* ("Where Mađïpa-do broke his leg"): Jatobá

Appendix 2-A

Araweté Population

In the following list, the individuals numbered from 001 to 136 constituted the Araweté population in January of 1983. The enumeration starts from House 1 (in Sectors F/H) and continues to House 45 (in Sector G). The data indicated for each individual are the following: most commonly used personal name; sex; house number; village sector (A–H) where the individual is represented and approximate location on the page (I–IV); and estimated age.

From number 137 onwards, deceased persons are listed, and so house number and age are no longer indicated. Of the deceased, I have listed only those who had living descendants in 1983; on the other hand, I have not listed unmarried deceased children among those Araweté who were alive in 1983. In the genealogies a few individuals are shown on more than one page in order to display their connections to other people. The numbers at the end of each horizontal line in the genealogical diagrams (sibling group) indicate the closest sibling connections and/or folio (f 1–8) where the group is shown again. Dotted lines for filiation, siblingship, or marriage indicate classificatory or putative relations. Closed lines drawn around groups of living people indicate the house in which they live.

001. Moidïma-ro	m / 1 / F III–IV / 30
002. Moidïma-hi	f / 1 / F III–IV / 25
003. Mi̱rã	m / 1 / F IV / 5
004. Kadĩ̱ne-kãñi	f / 1 / F IV / 3
005. Irã̱no-ro	m / 2 / G-H III–IV / 35
006. Yowe̱'ï-hi	f / 2 / G-H III–IV / 30
007. Iadïma-ro	m / 3 / F III–IV / 25
008. Iadïma-hi	f / 3 / F III–IV / 18
009. Iadïma	f / 3 / F IV / 3
010. Towãñiwãy	m / 3 / F IV / 1
011. Toroti-ro	m / 4 / G-H III / 35
012. Tapïdorĩ-hi	f / 4 / G-H II / 40
013. Ma̱ï-kãñĩ	f / 4 / G-H III–IV / 7
014. Kãñĩ-pokã̱'e	f / 4 / G-H III–IV / 4
015. Iriwɨpa̱i-ro	m / 5 / F III / 40
016. Iriwɨpa̱i-hi	f / 5 / F III–IV / 35

017. Kɨrereti	m / 5a / F IV / 12
018. Tareara	f / 5 / F IV / 4
019. Kãñĩ-paye-ro	m / 6 / G-H II–III / 35
020. Tawičire-hi	f / 6 / G-H II–III / 40
021. Ayo	f / 6 / G-H IV / 5
022. Počihe	f / 6 / G-H / 2
023. Kamarãčĩ̈	m / 7 / G-H IV / 14
024. Yowe̲'ï	f / 7 / G-H IV / 12
025. Aritã'ɨ̃-no	m / 8 / G-H IV / 18
026. Aritã'ɨ̃-hi	f / 8 / G-H IV / 18
027. Arariñã-no	m / 9 / G-H II–III / 40
028. Arariñã-hi	f / 9 / G-H II–III / 30 (see A–B #102, 108)
029. Mɨrɨakã	m / 9 / G-H IV / 8
030. Iči-kãñĩ	f / 9 / G-H IV / 5
031. Pičinga	m / 9 / G-H IV / 2
032. Ia̲pï-do	m / 10 / D IV / 25
033. Iapï̲'ï-hi	f / 10 / D IV / 25
034. Maiyičičĩ̈-kãñĩ	f / 10 / D IV / 4
035. Kãñi-newo-ro	m / 11 / D IV / 25 (see A-B, #136)
036. Kãñĩ-newo-hi	f / 11 / D IV / 18
037. Kãñĩ-newo	f / 11 / D IV / 1
038. Toiyi	m / 12 / D III / 35
039. Marɨpã-no	m / 13 / D III / 45
040. Tapaya-hi	f / 12 / D III / 50
041. Kɨnay	m / 13 / D IV / 4
042. Araiyi-kãñĩ-no	m / 14 / D III / 50
043. Iwã-Mayo	f / 14 / D III–IV / 30
044. Moneme̲'ï-do	m / 15 / III–IV / 30
045. Moneme̲'ï-hi	f / 15 / D III–IV / 28
046. Moneme̲'ï-ti-pihã-kãñĩ	f / 15 / D IV / 5
047. Kãñĩ-marã-no	m / 16 / E III–IV / 30
048. Moy-pɨkɨ	f / 16 / E III–IV / 10 (see A-B, #108)
049. Moyna̲i'o-ro	m / 17 / D III–IV / 40
050. Madïpa̲'ï-hi	f / 17 / D III–IV / 35
051. Temekɨ	f / 17 / D IV / 6
052. Taramĩ	m / 17 / D IV / 2
053. Irawa̲dï-do	m / 18 / D IV / 20
054. Irawa̲dï-hi	f / 18 / D IV / 20
055. Tičineã	m / 18 / D IV / 2
056. Ta̲'ia-ro	m / 19 / E II–III / 40
057. Ta̲'ia-hi	f / 19 / E III / 35
058. Kano̲e	m / 19 / E IV / 6
059. Moiparã-no	m / 20 / C III–IV / 50
060. Apïdï̲ma-hi	f / 20 / C IV / 18
061. Arawete	m / 21 / C III–IV / 25
062. Teredetã-kãñĩ	f / 21 / C III–IV / 35

063. Moiparã	m / 22 / C IV / 20
064. Yɨrĩñato	f / 22 / C IV / 15
065. Na̲ʻï	m / 23 / C IV / 14
066. Iwã-kãñĩ	f / 23 / C IV / 13
067. Arariñã	m / 24 / C IV / 13 (see G-H #27, 28)
068. Arariñã-kãñĩ	f / 24 / C IV / 11
069. Yɨrĩñato-ro	m / 25 / C II–III / 35
070. Arado-hi	f / 25 / C III–IV / 45
071. Moiwerã (Maria-hi pihã)	m / 26 / A-B III–IV / 30
072. Maria-hi	f / 26 / A-B III–IV / 40
073. Ñeñahi	f / 26 / A-B IV / 7
074. Kanopia-ro	m / 27 / A-B III–IV / 40
075. Kawiayi-hi	f / 27 / A-B III–IV / 40
076. Eyo	m / 27 / A-B IV / 9
077. Kanopia	m / 27 / A-B IV / 6
078. To̲đïnã	m / 27 / A-B IV / 3
079. Moira̲wï-do	m / 28 / A-B III–IV / 45
080. Mopitã-hi	f / 28 / A-B III–IV / 45
081. Kɨpe̲irã	m / 28 / A-B IV / 11
082. Kãñĩ-ma̲ï	f / 28 / A-B IV / 8
083. Kacï-oho	m / 28 / A-B IV / 3
084. Tamo-ro	m / 29 / A-B III–IV / 50
085. Tamo-hi	f / 29 / A-B III–IV / 45
086. Apo	m / 29 / A-B IV / 6
087. Moiyiwã	m / 29 / A-B IV / 4
088. Yaraiyi-kãñĩ	f / 29 / A-B IV / 3
089. Merereti	m / 30 / A-B IV / 18
090. Kɨrere	f / 30 / A-B IV / 14
091. Mitã-hi-pihã	m / 31 / A-B III–IV / 55
092. Mitã-hi	f / 31 / A-B III–IV / 40 (see D #49)
093. Patekã	m / 31 / A-B IV / 8
094. Kãñĩ-ayo	f / 31 / A-B IV / 8
095. Tapïda̲iwï-kãñĩ	f / 31 / A-B IV / 4
096. Takayama-ro	m / 32 / A-B IV / 28
097. Kãñi-wïdĩ-hi	f / 32 / A-B III–IV / 30
098. Madehã	m / 33 / A-B III–IV / 20
099. Apite	f / 33 / A-B III–IV / 15
100. Meñã-no	m / 34 / A-B II / 75
101. Pãñorã-hi	f / 34 / A-B II / 80
102. Heweye-ro	m / 35 / A-B III–IV / 28
103. Heweye-hi	f / 35 / A-B III–IV / 25
104. Heweye	f / 35 / A-B IV / 2
105. Pïnãhã	m / 36 / C III–IV / 30
106. Iarã̲ʻɨma	f / 36 / C III–IV / 20
107. Mođï-do	m / 37 / A-B III–IV / 35
108. Moiyi-hi	f / 37 / A-B III–IV / 28

109. Movđï f / 37 / A-B IV / 5
110. Kãñĩ-kɨcã-yo f / 37 / A-B IV / 3
111. Tato-awĩ-no m / 38 / F III–IV / 35
112. Madïpa'ï f / 38 / F IV / 15
113. Tato-awĩ m / 38 / F IV / 11
114. Matehã'ï f / 38 / F IV / 8
115. Morekati m / 38 / F IV / 6
116. Awara f / 38 / F IV / 2
117. Tiwawĩ-no m / 39 / F III–IV / 45
118. Ñã-maï-hi f / 39 / F III–IV / 50
119. Irãyi-oho m / 39 / F IV / 9
120. Čere'ï-mïdï m / 40 / F IV / 13
121. Yapïdaïwï-kãñi f / 40 / F IV / 12
122. Iatadĩ-no m / 41 / E III / 30
123. Homi-hi f / 41 / E III / 40
124. Kãñĩ-bïđï f / 41 / E IV / 9
125. Yato f / 41 / E IV / 6
126. Hɨerã m / 41 / E IV / 4
127. Ođođo-ti-pehã-kãñĩ m / 41 / E IV / 1
128. Ñapɨrɨ m / 42 / E IV / 18
129. Kãñĩ-ti f / 42 / E IV / 13
130. Awe m / 43 / E II–III / 45
131. Pačĩčĩ-hi f / 43 / E II / 55
132. Kãñĩ-atã-no m / 44 / E III–IV / 25
133. Kãñĩ-atã-hi f / 44 / E III–IV / 22
134. Kãñĩ-atã f / 44 / E IV / 1,5
135. Aya-ro m / 45 / G-H II / 80 (see A-B)
136. Hɨãto f / 45 / G-H IV / 9

Deceased Persons

137. Maria-ro m / A-B III–IV
138. Homi-ro m / E III
139. Kanopia-hi f / A-B IV
140. Kawiadï-do m / A-B IV
141. Araiyi-kãñĩ-hi f / D III–IV
142. Moirawï-hi f / A-B IV
143. Mopito-ro m / A-B IV
144. Moirã-hi f / A-B IV
145. Mitã-no m / A-B IV
146. Iwã-no m / A-B II
147. Iwãñi-hi f / A-B II
148. Temekɨ-hi (#202) f / D II
149. Pãñorã-no m / A-B II
150. Madewe-ro m / A-B II
151. Madewe-hi f / A-B II

152. Karama-ro	m / A-B I
153. Torowa-hi	f / A-B I
154. Mɨrɨakã-no	m / F II–III
155. A̱đï-do	m / A-B I (see F I–II)
156. Aiyi-hi	f / A-B I (see F I–II)
157. Kã̱'ɨ̃mea-hi	f / A-B II
158. Meñã-hi	f / A-B II
159. Moy-pɨkɨ-ro	m / A-B IV
160. Tapaya-ro	m / A-B I (see F I–II)
161. Moiparã-hi	f / C II
162. Iara̱wï-do	m / C II
163. Arado-ro	m / C III–IV
164. Amiyiti-ro	m / C III–IV
165. Amiyiti-hi	f / C III–IV
166. Iraia̱tĩ-no	m / C II–III
167. Ira̱iyi-hi	f / C II–III
168. Yetewerĩ-no	m / C II
169. Tayopi-hi	f / C II (see E I–II)
170. Đïtã̱i-hi	f / C II
171. Iwarawi-ro	m / C I
172. Iwarawi-hi	f / C I
173. Moy-kato-ro	m / C I
174. Moy-kato-hi	f / C I
175. Nãñã-hi	f / C I (see G-H I)
176. Moy-pɨkɨ-ro	m / C I–II (see G-H I)
177. Yɨrɨa̱i-ro	m / C I (see G-H I)
178. Mere-ro	m / C I–II (see G-H I–II)
179. Mere-hi	f / C I (see G-H I)
180. Yarɨwã-no	m / C I (see E I, G-H I)
181. Yarɨwã-hi	f / C I (see E I, G-H I)
182. Moyna̱i'o-hi	f / C II
183. Ta̱pïnã-no	m / C II
184. Tođïnã̱nĩ-no	m / C I–II
185. Tođïnã̱nĩ-hi	f / C I–II
186. Mađïpa̱'ï-do	m / D III–IV
187. Temekɨ̃-no	m / D III–IV
188. Iareakã-no	m / D I
189. Iareakã-hi	f / D I
190. Tapaya-ro	m / D III
191. Tiapï	m / D I
192. Yičirepa-hi	f / D I
193. Takara-ro	m / D I
194. Takara-hi	f / D I
195. Kãñĩ-a̱wï-hi	f / D I–II
196. Kãñĩ-a̱wï-do	m / D I–II
197. Karamirã-no	m / C II–III

198. Dece-hi	f / D I
199. Dece-ro	m / D I
200. Ipe-pɨkɨ-ro	m / D I–II
201. Temekɨ̃-no	m / D I–II
202. Temekɨ̃-hi (= #148)	f / D I–II
203. Ka̲yi-hi	f / D II–III
204. Itã̲'i-hi (= #277)	f / G-H I–II
205. Mãmãñã-yo-kãñĩ-no	m / D II–III
206. Kãñĩ-kɨcã-hi	f / D II
207. Ã̲ymi-hi	f / E I
208. Ã̲ymi-ro	m / E I
209. Toiyi-ro	m / D II
210. Kãñĩ-ma̲ï-hi	f / D II
211. Moko-ro	m / D II
212. Ireyere-hi	f / D I
213. Ireyere-ro	m / D I
214. Ipekɨ̃-hi	f / D supra I
215. Koira-ro	m / D supra I
216. Mođï-do	m / C I
217. Mođï-hi	f / C I
218. Dači-ro	m / C supra I (see F I)
219. Dači-hi	f / C supra I (see F I)
220. Ara̲dïma-hi	f / E II
221. Mãñato-ro	m / E II
222. Mãñato-hi	f / E II
223. Tĩara̲yi-hi	f / E I–II
224. Tĩara̲đï-do	m / E I–II
225. Moneme-ñã-kãñĩ-no	m / E I
226. Moneme-ñã-kãñĩ-hi	f / E I
227. Pačĩ̈čĩ̈-no	m / E II
228. Aradïma-ro	m / E II–III
229. Tare̲pï-no	m / E I–II
230. Iwã-mayo-ro	m / E I–II
231. Tare̲pĩ̈-hi	f / E II
232. Iwã-mayo-hi	f / E I–II
233. Mo-iwito-ro	m / F II–III
234. Mo-iwito-hi	f / F II–III
235. Mikɨrã-no	m / F II
236. Mikɨrã-hi	f / F II
237. Tayopi-ro	m / F II
238. Taranĩ-hi	f / F II
239. Ira-kɨčã-no	m / E II–III
240. Ira-kɨčã-hi	f / E II–III
241. Koho-hi	f / E I
242. Kãñĩ-na̲dï-no	m / D II (see E I–II)
243. Kãñĩ-na̲dï-hi	f / D II (see E I–II)

244. Marɨka̲i-ro — m / F II–III (see D II)
245. Arãcĩ̈me-ro — m / E supra I
246. Arãcĩ̈me-hi — f / E supra I
247. Parapičĩ̈-hi — f / E I
248. Irayiwã-no — m / F III
249. Iwã-topĩ-hi — f / F III
250. Irayiwã-hi — f / F III
251. Yɨrĩñato-hi — f / F II–III
252. Yɨrĩñato-ro — m / F II
253. Mɨrɨakã-hi — f / F II
254. Ta̲pĩ̈nã-hi — f / F II–IV
255. Ta̲pĩ̈nã-no — m / F II–IV
256. Ñã-ma̲ï-do — m / F III–IV
257. Mana̲yi-hi — f / F I–II
258. Tana̲yi-hi — f / F II–III
259. Tana̲yi-ro — m / F II–III
260. A̲wïnã-no — m / F I–II
261. Mano-hi — f / F I–II
262. Mano-ro — m / F I–II
263. Koira-hi — f / F I
264. Yowe̲'ï-do — m / F II–IV (see G-H III–IV)
265. Moirã̲'ɨ̃-no — m / G-H II
266. Moirã̲'ĩni-hi — f / G-H II
267. Mođïda-ro — m / G-H I–II
268. Ta̲wï-no — m / G-H supra I
269. Ta̲wï-hi — f / G-H supra I
270. Mođïda-hi — f / G-H I–II
271. Kãñĩ-wi̲dĩ-no — m / A-B III–IV (see G-H II–III)
272. Iakoati-ro — m / G-H I–II
273. Iakoati-hi — f / G-H I–II
274. Tapïdorĩ-no — m / G-H I–II
275. Tawičire-ro — m / G-H II–III
276. Itã-no — m / G-H I–II
277. Itã'i-hi (= #204) — f / G-H I–II
278. Tapaya-hi — f / A-B I
279. Itã-nopï-do — m / F II
280. Itã-nopï-hi — f / F II
281. Tamo̲i-ro — m / A-B I
282. Mađapï-hi — f / A-B I
283. Tiwa̲wĩ̈-hi — f / F III–IV

Appendix 2-B, Genealogies, follows on next page.

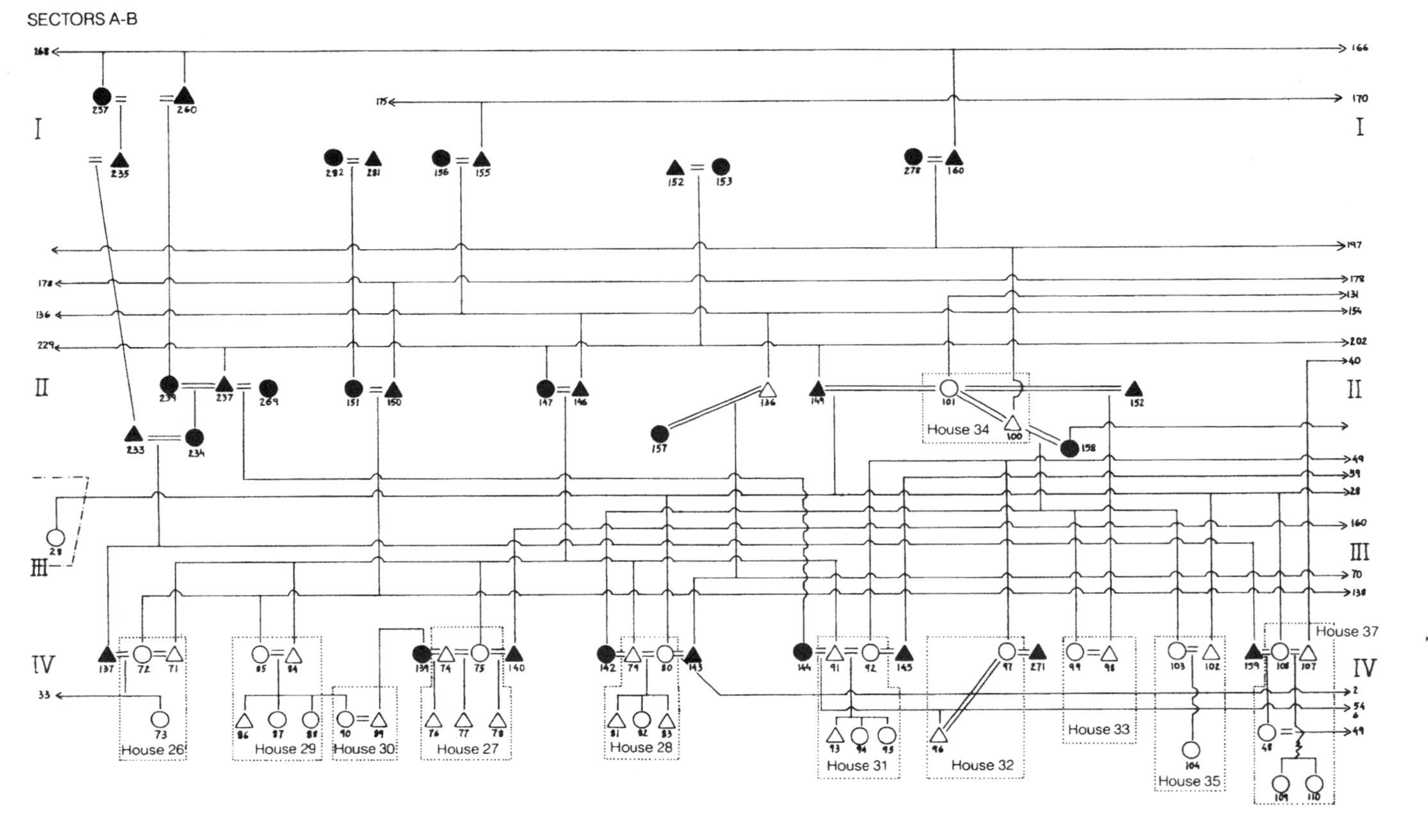
SECTORS A-B
I
II
III
IV
House 26
House 29
House 30
House 27
House 28
House 31
House 32
House 33
House 34
House 35
House 37

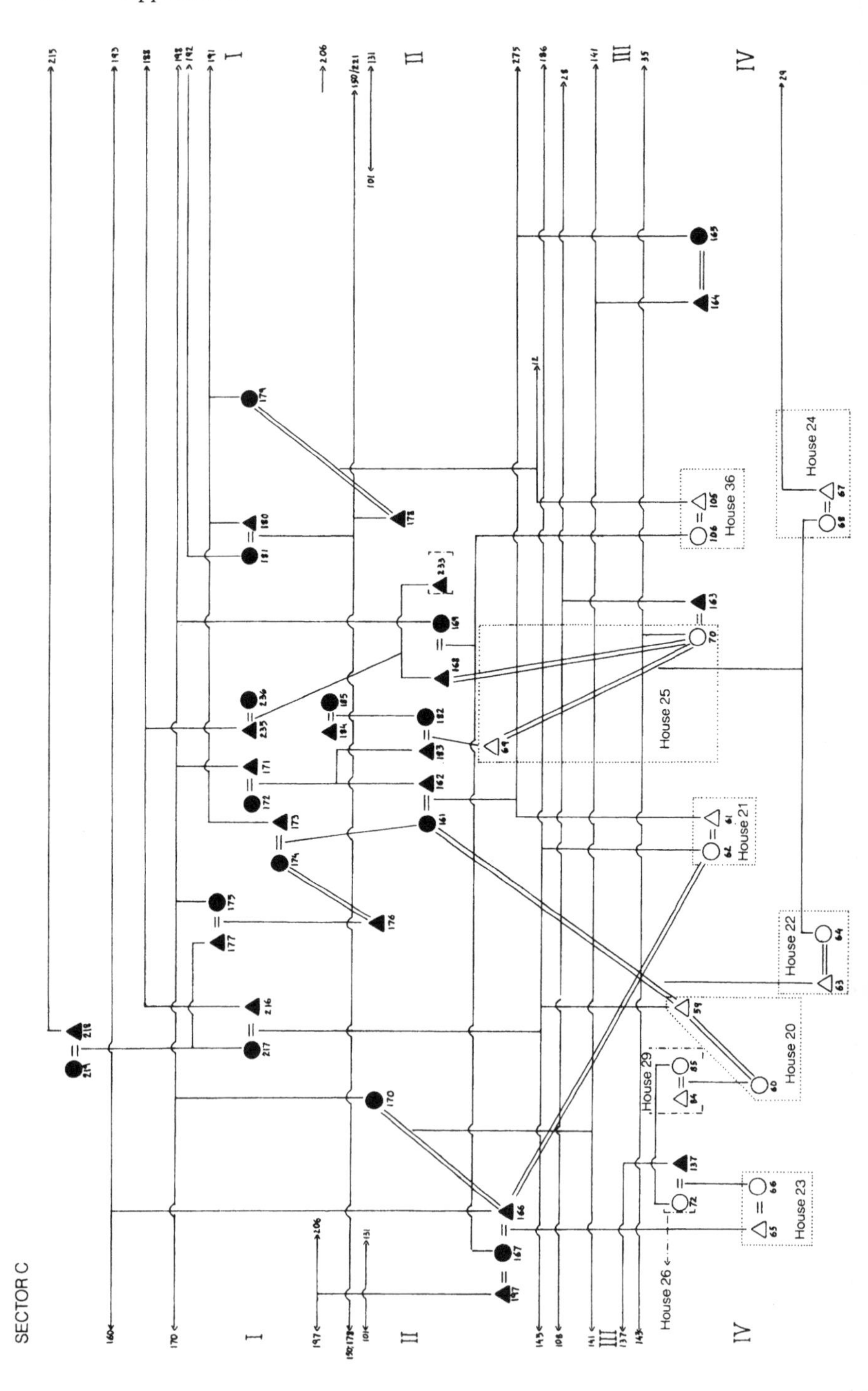
SECTOR C
I
II
III
IV
House 20
House 21
House 22
House 23
House 24
House 25
House 26
House 29
House 36

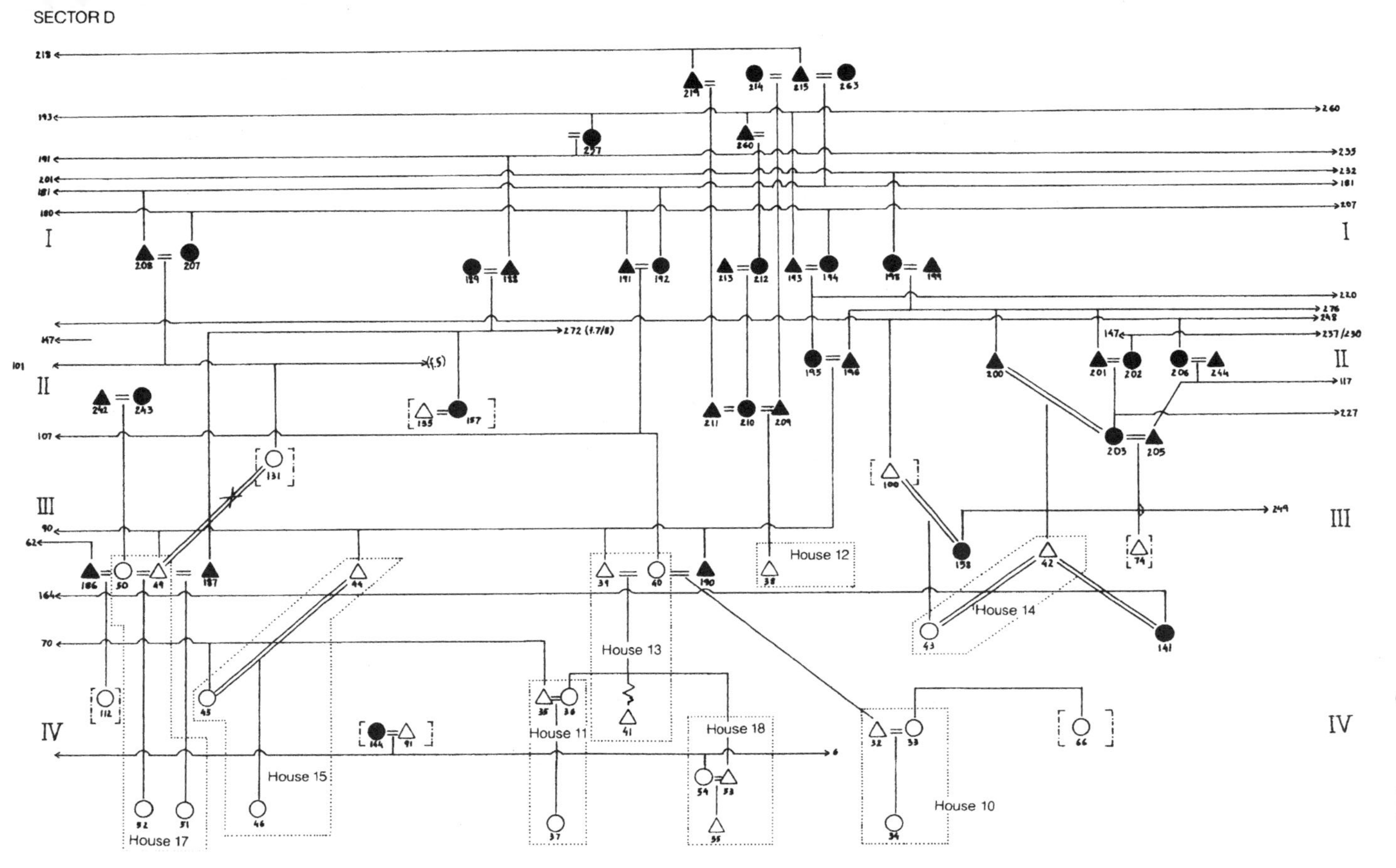
SECTOR D
I
II
III
IV
House 10
House 11
House 12
House 13
House 14
House 15
House 17
House 18

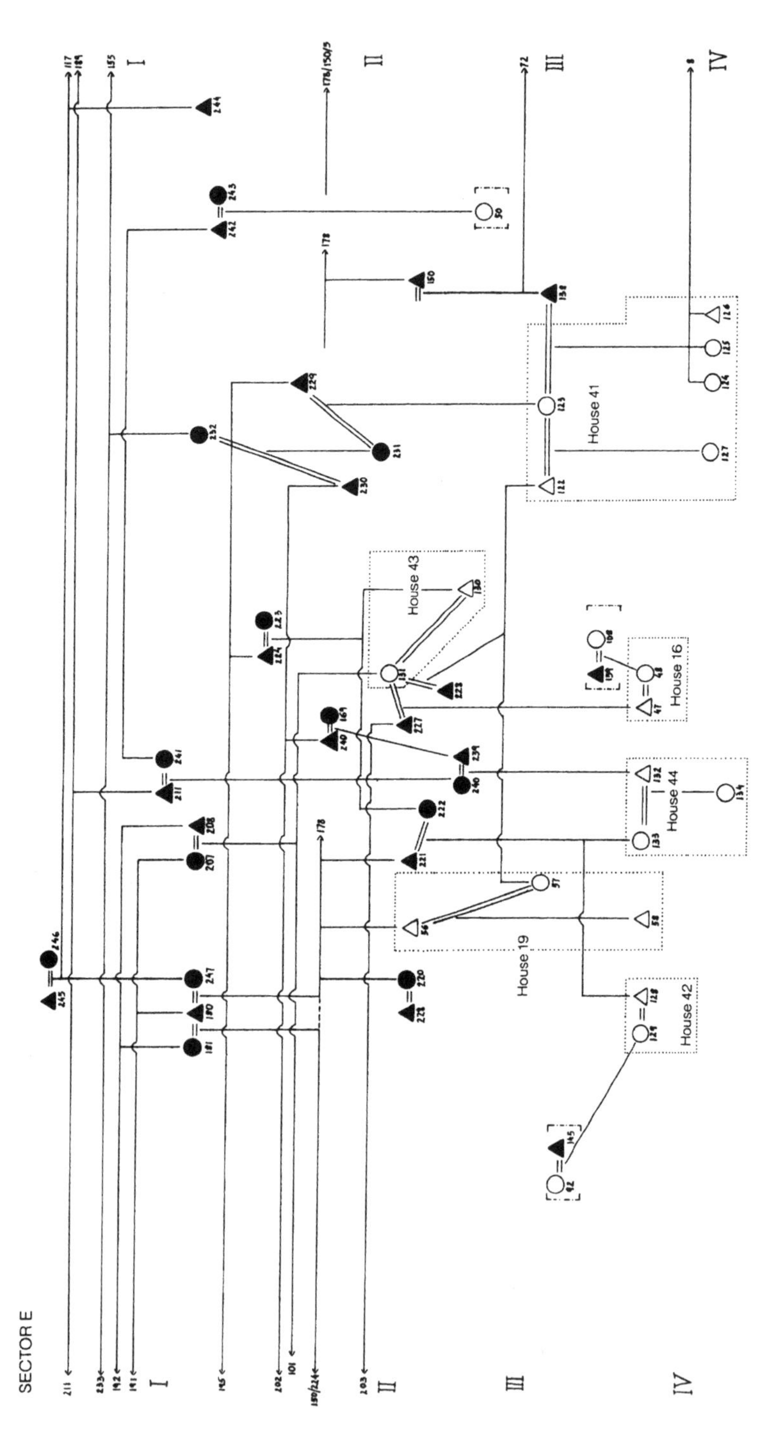
SECTOR E
I
II
III
IV
House 41
House 43
House 16
House 44
House 19
House 42

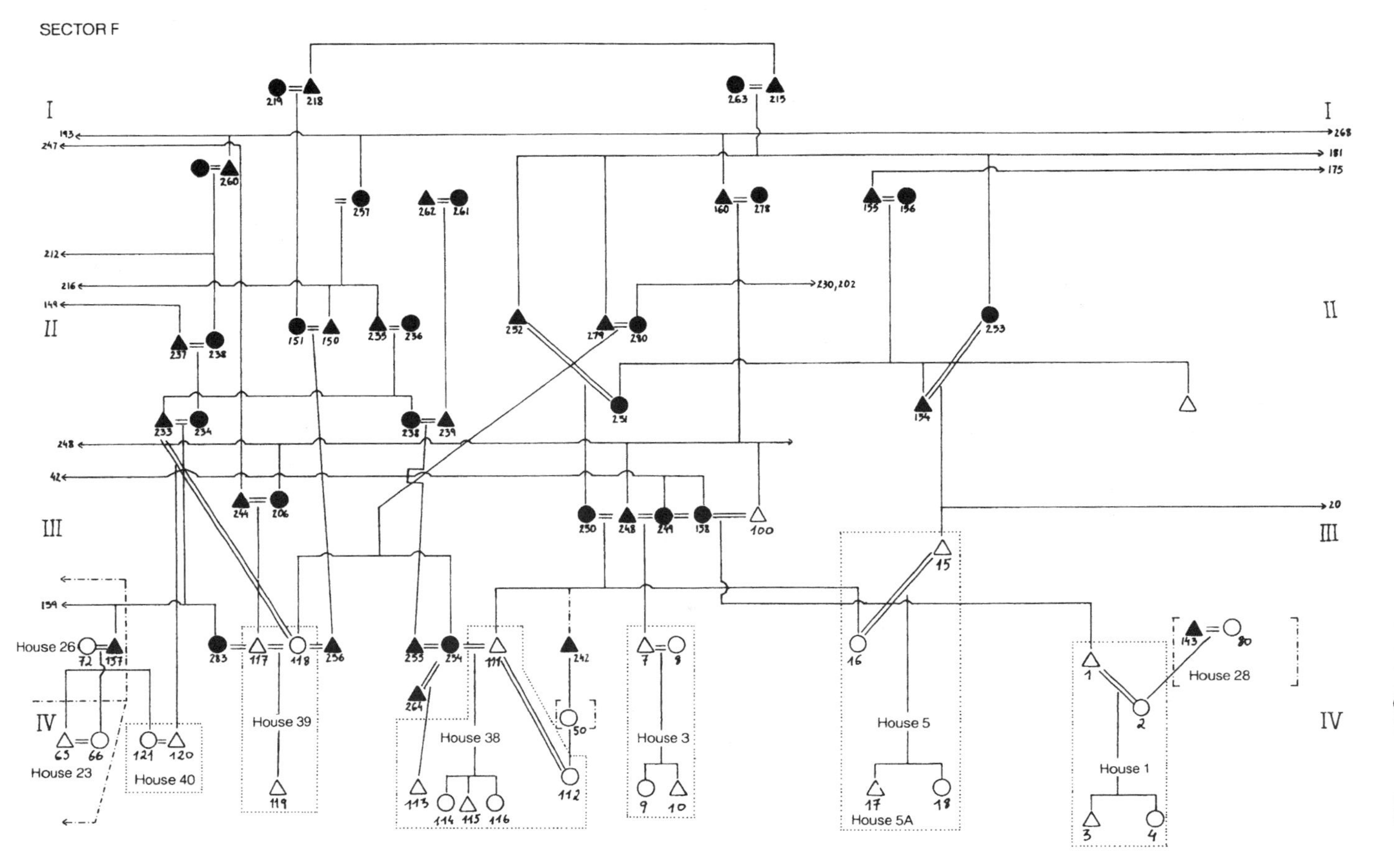
SECTOR F
I
II
III
IV
House 26
House 23
House 40
House 39
House 38
House 3
House 5
House 5A
House 1
House 28

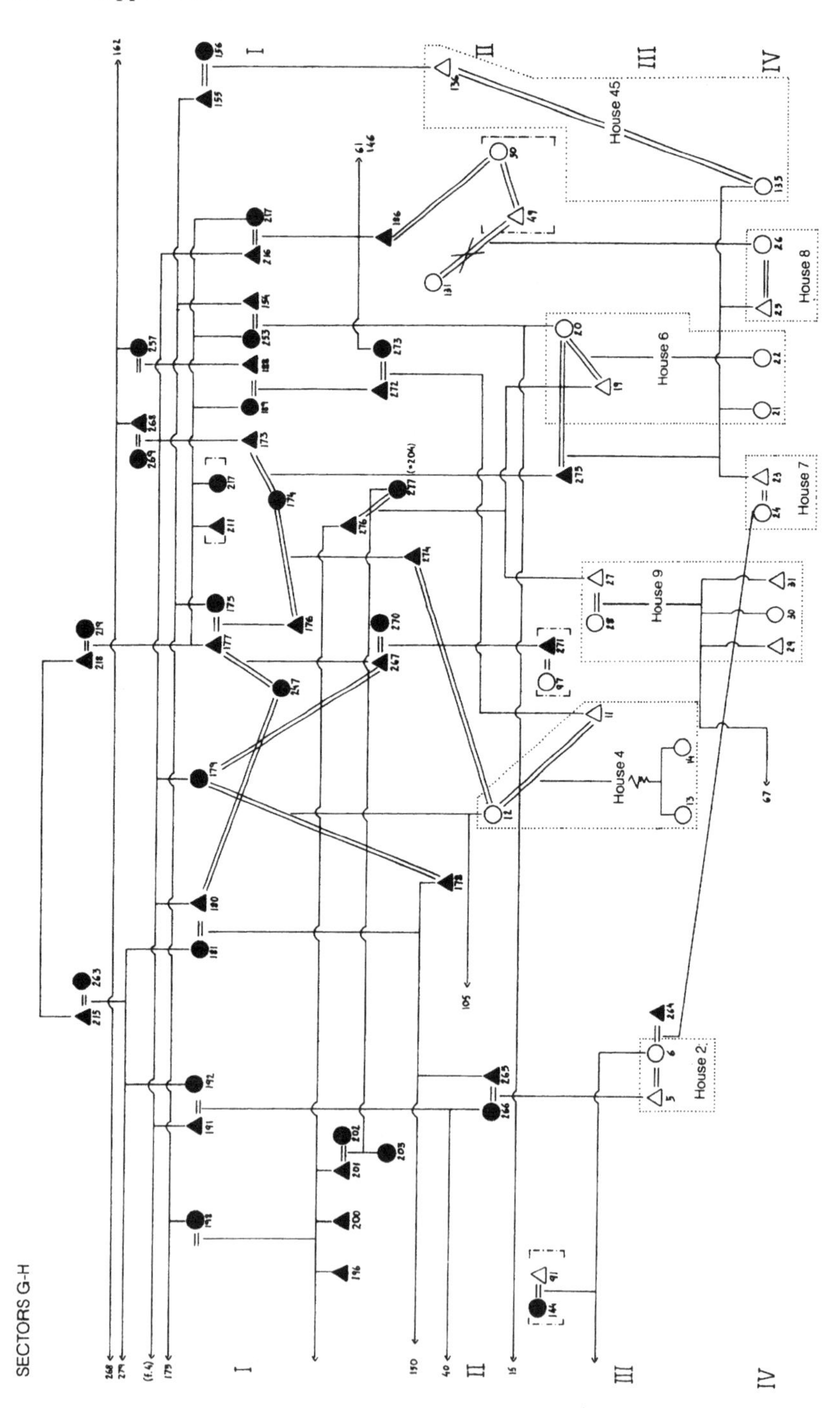
SECTORS G-H
I
II
III
IV
House 45
House 8
House 6
House 7
House 9
House 4
House 2

APPENDIX 3

Botanical and Zoological Terms in English, Portuguese, Araweté, Latin

This list includes only those animal and plants cited in the text for which I could establish some type of identification that would be more precise than vague translations like "lizard," "palm tree," and so on. The degree of precision of each entry varies between certainty and educated guesses. My knowledge of Araweté ethnobotany and ethnozoology is quite limited. I would like to thank William Balée for his inestimable assistance in drawing up this list, especially for the botanical vocabulary. A number of plants mentioned here were collected and identified by Balée and his colleagues; the reader should consult his articles (some of which are listed in Works Cited) for further information. The botanical terms in Araweté that have the suffix *-i* designate the plant ("*X*-stem"). I have not listed the numerous Araweté terms for varieties of cultivated species. For animals, in some cases I list only the generic names.

English	Portuguese	Araweté	Latin
	Plants		
nnatto	urucu	*iriko*	*Bixa orellana*
ssai palm	açaí	*ačai'i*	*Euterpe oleracea*
abassu palm	babaçu	*nata'i*	*Orbygnia phalerata*
acaba palm	bacaba	*pĩdowa'i*	*Oenocarpus distichus*
amboo	taboca	*kɨre'ĩ*	*Merostachys* sp.
amboo	taquaruçu	*ta'akĩ*	*Guadua* sp.
anana	banana	*padɨdɨ̈*	*Musa paradisiaca*
anana (wild)	pacova-sororoca	*pakoã*	*Phenakospermun guianensis*
ow wood	pau d'arco	*tayipa*	*Tabebuia serratifolia*
razil-nut tree	castanheira (castanha-do-Pará)	*ya'i* (tree) *ñi* (nut)	*Bertholletia excelsa*
acao (wild)	cacauí	*aka'awi'i*	*Theobroma speciosum*
alabash tree	cuieira	*koy'i*	*Crescentia cujete*
okerite palm	inajá	*naya'i*	*Maximiliana maripa*
otton	algodão	*miniyo*	*Gossypium barbadense*
ourbaril	jatobá	*yɨta'i*	*Hymenaea courbaril*

English	Portuguese	Araweté	Latin
		Plants (*continued*)	
cupuaçu (relative of cacao)	cupuaçu	*kopi’i*	*Theobroma grandiflorum*
dog bane family	araracanga	*iwirara’i*	*Aspidosperma* sp.
fish poison (vines)	timbó	*cïma*	at least two species of *Sapindaceae*
genip (genipap)	genipapo	*yanipa’i*	*Genipa americana*
hog plum	cajá-mirim (taperebá)	*akaya’i*	*Spondias mombin*
ingá	ingá	*ña pɨkɨ’i*	*Inga* sp.
itiriti (arrowroot family)	arumã	*ɨrɨ’i wï* and *ɨrɨ’i*	*Ischnosiphon obliquus* and *I. puberulus*
maize	milho	*awacï*	*Zea mays*
manioc (bitter)	mandioca brava	*mađïđa*	*Manihot esculenta*
manioc (sweet)	macaxeira	*bihirĩ*	*Manihot esculenta*
mbocayá palm	macaúba	*orokoyi’i*	*Acrocomia* sp.
monkey ladder vine	cipó-escada	*ihipa pepe*	*Bauhinia guianensis*
mumbaca palm	mumbaca	*yɨa̲ra’i*	*Astrocaryum mumbaca*
myrtle family	araçá	*aracï*	*Psidium* sp.
papaya	mamão	*mãmã’i*	*Carica papaya*
paricá	paricá	*payikã*	*Anadenanthera peregrina*
paxiúba palm	paxiúba	*pači’i*	*Socratea exorrhiza*
pineapple	abacaxi	*nanĩ*	*Ananas comosus*
sapote family	sapota, abiu, abiurana, frutão	*ara oho’i*	various *Sapotaceae*
sisal	carauá	*kɨrawã*	*Neoglaziovia variegata*
soapberry family	(?)	*čiñã*	*Cardiospermum halicacabum*
sweet potato	batata-doce	*đe’ti*	*Ipomœa batatas*
tauari (Brazil nut family)	tauari	*petĩ mi*	*Couratari oblongifolia*
tobacco	tabaco	*petĩ*	*Nicotiana tabacum*
yam	cará	*karã*	*Dioscorea trifida*
copal	copal	*ičiri’i*	*Trattinickia rhoifolia*

English	Portuguese	Araweté	Latin
		Mammals, reptiles	
agouti	cutia	*akocï*	*Dasyprocta agouti*
alligators	jacarétinga	*yičirečĩ*	*Caiman crocodilus*
	jacaré-coroa	*yičire hete*	*Paleosuchus* sp.

English	Portuguese	Araweté	Latin
Mammals, reptiles (*continued*)			
anaconda	sucuri	*moy oho*	*Eunectes murinus*
anteater (collared)	tamanduá-mirim;	*tãmãno̱ã*	*Tamandua tetradactyla*
anteater (silky)	tamanduá-í	*tamanoa̱'ï*	*Cyclope didactylus*
armadillo (nine-banded long-nosed)	tatu-etê	*tato hete (tato oho)*	*Dasypus novemcintus*
armadillo (seven-banded long-nosed)	tatuí	*tato'ï*	*Dasypus septemcintus*
armadillo (giant)	tatu-canastra	*tato ho̱wĩ'hã*	*Priodontes maximus*
brocket deer (red)	veado mateiro	*arapohã*	*Mazama americana*
brocket deer (gray)	veado-fobóca	*arapoha̱'ï*	*Mazama guazoubira*
bushmaster	surucucu	*ɨrɨkɨkɨ*	*Lachesis* sp.
capuchin monkeys	macaco-prego and others	*ka̱'ï*	*Cebus*
coatimundi	quati	*kacï*	*Nasua nasua*
collared peccary	caititu	*tatetɨ*	*Tayassu tajacu*
giant river otter	ariranha	*yatɨrã*	*Pteronura brasiliensis*
howler monkey	guariba	*ačiči*	*Alouatta* sp.
jaguar	onça (jaguar)	*ñã*	*Panthera onca*
kinkajou	jupará (macaco-da-meia-noite)	*yɨparã*	*Potos flavus*
night monkey	macaco-da-noite	*apoyiči*	*Aotus* sp.
opossum	gambás (mucuras)	*miko*	*Didelphys* spp.
paca	paca	*kararoho*	*Agouti paca*
saki monkey	cuxiú	*kocï oho*	*Chiropotes satanus*
sloths	preguiças	*a'i*	*Bradypodidœ*
tapir	anta (tapir)	*tapï'ï*	*Tapirus terrestris*
tortoise (red-footed)	jaboti vermelho	*yaacï katɨ*	*Geochelone carbonaria*
tortoise (yellow-footed)	jaboti-branco	*yaacï ete̱'ï*	*Geochelone denticulata*
turtle (river)	tracajá	*takayama*	*Podocnemis cayennensis*
white-lipped peccary	queixada	*tayaho*	*Tayassu pecari*

English	Portuguese	Araweté	Latin
Birds			
curassows	mutum	*mitɨ̃*	*Cracidœ (Crax; Mitu)*
curassow (Natterer's)	mutum-pinima	*mitɨ̃ ne̲we hã* (male) *mitɨ̃ parã* (female)	*Crax fasciolata*
curassow (razor-billed)	mutum-cavalo	*mitɨ̃ho*	*Mitu mitu*
cotingas	anambés	*moneme*	*Cotingidae*
	anambé-azul	*monemečï̃*	*Cotinga cayana*
	anambé-de-peito-roxo	*irirĩ me'e*	*Cotinga cotinga*
guans	jacus	*yakɨ*	*Cracidœ (Penelope; Pipile)*
	jacu-açu	*yakɨoho*	*Penelope obscura*
gypsy bird	cigana	*atonã*	*Ophistocomus hoazin*
harpy eagle	gavião-real (harpia)	*kanoho*	*Harpia harpyja*
heron	socó-boi	*haka*	*Tigrisoma lineatum*
juriti dove	juriti	*đorocï*	*Leptotila* sp.
laughing falcon	acauã	*hakõy*	*Herpetotheres cachinnans*
macaws	araras	*arã*	*Psittacidœ*
macaw (canindé) [blue-and-yellow macaw]	canindé	*kadï̃ne*	*Ara ararauna*
macaw (scarlet)	arara-canga (arara-piranga)	*arã hete (arađï)*	*Ara macao*
macaw (red-blue-and-green)	arara-vermelha-grande (arara-verde)	*araračĩ (tađïđahi)*	*Ara chloroptera*
macaw (blue)	arara-azul-grande (araruna)	*araročo oho (iwa̲dï)*	*Anodorhynchus hyacinthinus*
oropendola	japu	*yapi*	*Psarocolius decumanus*
parrots	papagaios, curicas	*ayiri*	*Amazona* spp.
parrot (blue-headed)	maitaca	*ara̲'ï*	*Pionus menstruus*
pygmy owl	caburé	*orokoro'ã*	*Glaucidium brasilianum*

English	Portuguese	Araweté	Latin
	Birds (*continued*)		
swallow-tailed kite	gavião-tesoura	*tapẽ*	*Elanoides forficatus*
tapir hawk	gavião-carrapateiro (?) gavião de anta (?)	*tamĩ*	*Milvago chimachima (?)* *Daptrius ater (?)*
tinamous	inhambu, jaó, macuco	*namo*	*Tinamidœ*
tinamou (great)	inhambu da cabeça vermelha	*namo ačĩ ayɨ*	*Tinamus major*
tinamou (banded)	jaó-verdadeiro, macucauá (?)	*namo oho*	*Crypturellus undulatus* (?)
toucan	tucano	*točĩ*	*Rhampastos*
trumpeter bird	jacamim	*yakamï̃*	*Psophia viridis*
vultures	urubus	*iriwo*	*Cathartidœ*
vulture (king)	urubu-rei (urubu-branco)	*iriwo čĩ*	*Sarcoramphus papa*
?)	tovacuçu	*ɨrɨwã*	*Grallaria varia*
	Fishes		
lectric eel	poraquê	*pɨreičey*	*Electrophorus electricus*
logfish	peixe-cachorra	*pïdã tïnã*	*Raphiodon vulpinus*
natrinxã	matrinxã	*amïđïcï*	*Brycon* sp.
iranhas	piranhas	*pako*	*Serrasalmus; Pygocentrus*
urubim	surubim	*čoro̲'ï*	*Pseudoplatystoma* sp.
eacock bass	tucunaré	*tekɨnere*	*Cichla* sp.
rairão	trairão	*pïda oho*	*Hoplias* sp.
	Insects		
ocandeira ant	tocandira	*tɨkãhãyi*	*Paraponera clavata*
ruchid beetles (fruit boring weevils)	bicho-de-coco	*natah̲o*	*Pachymerus nucleorum*
umblebee	mamangaba	*mãmãñã*	*Xylocopa* sp.

Appendix 4

Glossary of Araweté Terms

The following is a list of the most frequently used Araweté terms in the text. For botanical and zoological vocabulary, see Appendix 3.

amɨte: other (of a different kind); nonrelative
anĩ: same-sex sibling; relative
Ãñĩ: malevolent spirits of the forest
-a̲'o we: "spiritual agency," the active manifestation of an absent being (see *ta̲'o we*)
apĩhi: female friend (of a man)
apĩhi-pihã: same-sex friend
apĩno: male friend (of a woman)
Aranãmĩ: the divinity who raised up the firmament
aray: shaman's rattle
awacï mo-tiarã: "to make the maize ripen," the seasonal movement of dispersing to the forest
awacï ñã: "owner of the maize," the couple who sponsors a mild beer festival
Awĩ peye: "shamans of enemies," a class of divinities
awĩ: enemy, non-Araweté
Ayaraetã: a terrestrial spirit associated with honey
bïde: human beings, person, Araweté, "we" (inclusive)
čiye: fear-respect, shame
dɨ: other (of the same kind); sibling
ɗokã: "to serve," the rite of offering strong beer to gods and the dead
ha'iwã: mortal illness resulting from supernatural cause
hado'i (tado'i): brother-in-law
hẽñã mi re: "forsaken ones," one of the epithets for humans and animals
hiro: body, container, wrapping
howï'hã: great, large (also applied to supernatural correlates of certain animals)
ĩ: "soul," vital principle, image, representation, shadow
Iaracĩ: a cannibalistic celestial spirit, eater of assai with honey
Iaraɗï: a terrestrial spirit, owner of white-lipped peccaries
ɨha me'e pe: "those who left," one of the epithets for the *Ma̲ï*
ɨha me'e rĩ: "those who will go," one of the epithets for humans
ɨka hete me'e: "really existent (beings)," an expression referring to beings without culture or transcendence
Iraparaɗï: a celestial entity into which an Araweté killer is transformed; also "enemy" in the god's parlance
irapã: bow, firearm; metaphor for the penis and the labia of the vulva
Iwikatihã: "He-of-the-lower-side," Master of Water and of fish
kaakɨ hã: consciousness, memory
kamarã: non-Indians

kã'ɨ da: "sour beer," strong maize beer

kã'ɨ hẽ'ẽ: "sweet beer," mild maize beer

kã'ɨ ñã: "owner of the beer," the couple who sponsors a strong beer festival

kã'ɨ mo-ra: "to make the beer sour," the ceremonial hunt that precedes a strong beer festival

koako hã: abstinence

kɨyaha: diaphanous, transparent, exterior; also refers to a psychophysical state

Ma̲ï: Divinity, celestial divinities

Ma̲ï demï-đo: "food of the gods," a name applied to ceremonial foods and to humans

Ma̲ï đĩ: "future god," one of the epithets for human beings

Ma̲ï hete: "real gods," the principal class of divinities in the pantheon

mara: to put, posit, place, create

marakay: singer (of music during *pɨrahe* and strong beer festivals)

Me'e Ñã: "Jaguar-Thing," a divinity who eats tortoise

me'e a̲'ï: a category of deadly foods and actions

me'e hehi a re: "eaters of the roasted (meat)," one of the epithets for *Ãñĩ*

me'e wi a re: "eaters of the raw (meat)," one of the epithets for the *Ma̲ï*

mo-a̲'o: to cause nostalgia, to cause someone to become estranged from him- or herself due to sadness and longing

mo-a̲o we: "to disappear," to be transformed into a specter

-mone: "to carry"; also refers to the shamanic operation of redirecting a soul into the body

moropĩ'nã: killer

ñã: owner, master, representative

-ođɨ moMa̲ï: "to divinize"

ođïpïđa kã: the celestial skin-changing bath that the dead undergo

pepi kã: counterpart, payment, revenge

peye: shaman

peyo: "to stir the air up, to fan"; the shamanic operation of guiding gods and the dead to earth to eat certain foods

pɨrahẽ: a type of dance and musical genre

pɨrɨ o: cannibal

pɨro̲wĩ'hã: "ancients," "ancestors"

-reme: a suffix attached to the name of a person who is deceased or absent a long time

ta̲'o we: a human specter, the terrestrial portion of a dead person

tã ñã: "owner of the village," chief

te'õ me'e: corpse

teka katɨ we: "place of good existence," the heavens

tenotã mõ: leader

tiwã: potential affine, cross-cousin, nonrelative

Towa̲ho: an ancient enemy tribe

wewe: "lightweight"; also refers to a psychophysical state

Notes

CHAPTER 1

1. By this, I am not subscribing to the idea of an "elementary form" as the privileged means of access to the phenomenon. I am simply suggesting that the Araweté present with greater clarity certain metaphysical tensions that lie hidden beneath the cosmological bureaucratism typical of other groups who are linguistically and geographically close to the Araweté.

2. Cf. Fernandes (1963:353–54), who says, "The social organization of the Tupinamba is strictly subordinated to the tribal religious system," and speaks of "the predominance of the religious system over the organizational system."

3. P. Clastres (1987: chap. 9) has already pointed this out in the Guarani case.

4. In Brazil, the legal recognition of Indian lands as reservations requires four steps: interdiction, when a preliminary declaration announces that use of the area by outsiders is prohibited; delimitation, when boundaries are charted on a map and officially approved by FUNAI; demarcation, when actual boundary markers are placed on the land; and homologation, when the reservation is formally ratified by a decree issued by the president of the Republic and published in the Official Register. Powerful economic and political interests have prevented the overwhelming majority of indigenous lands from reaching the final stage.

5. Three weeks after I left, a group of Parakanã attacked the village and wounded the FUNAI agent, although most of the Araweté were gone at the time. One month later, the Parakanã attacked again, wounding two Araweté women and a boy. In retaliation, the Araweté killed a Parakanã man in April 1983.

6. "I have observed among them [the Tupinamba] that just as they love those who are gay, joyful, and liberal, on the contrary they so hate those who are taciturn, stingy, and melancholy" (Léry 1990 [1578]:99). In fact, one of the things that most surprised the Araweté about the behavior of white people was their inexplicable fluctuations in mood and spirit. Sadness and "seriousness" are negatively valued. "To not laugh" (*pɨkã ĩ*) is a euphemism for rancor, and the notion of "joyfulness" (*tori*) has profound philosophical resonances. In other Tupi-Guarani languages, the cognates of *tori* designate ritual activity.

7. Although the Araweté pay little attention to social formalities, they possess an extensive and subtle psychological vocabulary; this form of expres-

sion tends to supplant the sociological vocabulary as a means of explaining attitudes and behaviors.

8. Baldus observes (1976:456) that in 1935, the Tapirapé who survived contact explained their reasons for abandoning three villages to concentrate in one not by citing their demographic reduction, but by explaining that they had no more shamans left in them. This observation is especially interesting given that the Tapirapé developed a ceremonial organization with Central Brazilian features, which enjoins a population size larger than what is usual in Amazon societies (Wagley 1977:32, 39). Nevertheless, it was the lack of shamans, not of a certain number of people, that they cited as an explanation.

9. One night I watched a laughing group of women, who were pounding maize, throw themselves into reproducing the style of pounding (the force and angle of striking the pestle, the circular movement completing the sequence, the breathing) of various women who had died. Also, as children are growing up, they are jokingly nicknamed after dead people according to their peculiarities that recall the deceased. I probably fell into this case when they compared me to dead people and conferred on me various nicknames that evoked their memory.

10. Although they exhibit no "thanatomania" or "profoundly religious desire to die," as Schaden (1969:174) claimed the Guarani do, the Araweté's essential ambivalence in the face of death must be underscored.

11. The citation of direct discourse is characteristic of all Tupi-Guarani languages, and the verb "to say" is the most commonly used citation marker. What appears to be peculiar to the Araweté is their emphasis on specifying by name the person who "said" what is transmitted to someone else.

12. The Tupi-Guarani literature classically refers to a total "dependence" of the group on the words of the shaman. But in the Araweté case at least, certain factors complicate the matter: the coexistence of various shamans, as well as people's recollection of deceased shamans' words, can transform the formula "thus spoke such a shaman" into less of a guarantee than a relativizing of the authority of the information.

13. In 1987, the village received four more Araweté who, separated from the tribe twenty-five years earlier, were captured by the Kayapó-Xikrin of Catetê and released by FUNAI employees. See chap. 2, sect. 4, on the group's history.

14. These are used as occasional alternatives for their small clay pans, mortars, and rufflepalm roots, respectively.

15. The "canteen" system failed with the departure of the person then in charge at the Post. In 1988, the Araweté sporadically continued to deliver artisanry for sale, but this did not cover the cost of the goods they consumed. Finally, in August 1988, FUNAI obtained a substantial indemnification from a logging firm that had invaded Araweté lands and cut a great quantity of mahogany; this money, if indeed applied exclusively to the Araweté, would be capable of meeting their needs for a few years.

16. I once heard a FUNAI worker suggest that, "If we were to allow it, or if

they could, all these people would move to the city of Altamira and within one week no one would hear any more business about the Araweté."

17. I noted in my diary in September 1982, "This voracious exuberance, this 'predatory expansiveness' that makes them want everything of the whites all the time and which exasperates the Post employees so much (who naturally want the Araweté to become 'civilized,' but not so fast nor at their expense) makes me think that the Araweté have caught by the teeth a prey much bigger than they can swallow, but haven't yet realized this."

18. Iara Ferraz, my former wife, accompanied me on the first trip to the Ipixuna, where she stayed for a month, returning for another month in February 1982.

19. That is, other people's voices: those who would ask to sing into the recorder did not make much of an issue out of hearing themselves (except for the children).

20. This reaction at times seems to lead to a neoculturalism tempered by structural analysis from which it is difficult to escape when, as in my case here, it is a matter of discussing a particular sociocultural configuration. But postulating a priori a "cosmological" cause for the social order is not an adequate solution for South American ethnology, since this would result in maintaining (in an inverted form) the distinction between discourse and practice, ideology and organization. Rather, the solution lies in dissolving these dichotomies into a set of principles informing the various planes that can be analytically distinguished in social reality.

It should be noted that structuralism is not a method for describing particular societies. Lévi-Strauss's differential comparison became more productive precisely when it abandoned social totalities and moved on to subsystems (mythology), but it entailed the dissolution of the societies that had been compared, taking them as accidental moments of structures that were both more general and less total. As he remarked: "It is high time that anthropology freed itself from the illusion gratuitously invented by the functionalists, who mistake the practical limitations imposed upon them by the kind of studies they advocate for the absolute properties of the objects with which they are dealing. An anthropologist may confine himself for one or more years within a small social unit, group or village, and endeavor to grasp it as a totality, but this is no reason for imagining that the unit, at levels other than the one at which convenience or necessity has placed him, does not merge in varying degrees into larger entities, the existence of which remains, more often than not, unsuspected" (Lévi-Strauss 1981:609). If such is the case, then articulating the Araweté questions with their Tupi-Guarani transformations is more than a mere recourse for filling in gaps in my ethnography. But this does not mean that all attempts to characterize local problematics are invalid—in fact, this is precisely what I will be trying to do.

Chapter 2

1. The Pacajá River, which empties into the Amazon between the Xingu and the Tocantins, should not be confused with the Bacajá, tributary of the

Xingu and traditional territory of the Araweté. On the history of the Arara, see Menget 1977.

2. Métraux further proposes that the first migratory wave from the Tapajós had headed directly for the Amazon and the lower Xingu, resulting in the Juruna-Shipaya and Takunyapé, whose languages then followed an independent evolution. But he is mistaken in connecting the Takunyapé to the Juruna group—the former's language is Tupi-Guarani; the latter's, another branch of Tupi.

3. "*Língua Geral*" here refers to the lingua franca derived from Tupinamba used by the mestizo population, the missionaries, and the "reduced" (missionized) Indians of Amazonia from the seventeenth to the nineteenth centuries. See Rodrigues (1986: chap. 10) on the different Brazilian *Línguas Gerais* (all originating from Tupi-Guarani).

4. Itiriti (*Ischnosiphon obliquus, I. puberulus*) is a type of cane of the arrowroot family from which the outer part is stripped and spliced into strands used in basketry weaving.

5. On female clothing, see the works of Ribeiro (1981, 1983, 1985). Other Tupi-Guarani have female clothing, but only the Araweté use a head covering and an inner girdle. This small piece of thick canvas, which tightly encircles the thighs from the top of the pubis to about 30 cm. below it, is put on at the first menstruation. It restricts movement considerably, making women adopt a peculiar gait. Women never stand up straight, even among themselves when they are naked (i.e., without the girdle). They bathe in a squatting position with their legs together. This may be linked to the lengthening of the labia minora, a central part of their erotic arts. Prepubescent girls, although wearing the outer skirt since childhood, do not mind walking around nude. Between puberty and the birth of the first child, adherence to the norms of modesty is fluctuating; afterwards, imperative. The men, for their part, show extreme modesty in untying the string encircling the prepuce.

6. Genipap is a black, resistant tannin made from the bark of the genip tree (*Genipa americana*).

7. This is similar to the Guarani synedoche *jeguaka-va*, designating masculine humanity in Mbyá songs (Cadogan 1959:28ff.). The difference is that, in the Guarani case, the *jeguaka* (cf. Araweté *yɨakã*) is associated with religious dances and marks the function of the *pai* or shaman, not that of the warrior (Schaden 1969:29). This is consistent with the difference between the Araweté *pɨrahẽ* (profane or warrior dance/song) and the Guarani *porahei* (sacred song or prayer).

8. Many of the varieties of these plants were introduced by FUNAI employees or obtained from peasants; others were adopted from the Asuriní.

9. Balée (1989a:11) states that "the average surface of Araweté swiddens covered by maize alone is about 82%, according to my measurements."

10. Stone axes are frequently found in Araweté territory, but people claim they do not know, and have never known, how to make them. They say that stone axes were made by the celestial *Maï* spirits. Moreover, the Araweté claim to have "always" (that is, within the memory of the oldest people) used

iron axes, found in clearings abandoned by other groups and in sites occupied by Brazilian colonists. Nevertheless, all adult men know how to utilize stone axes and how to attach the heads to handles.

11. Tinamous: ground-dwelling birds of the *Tinamidae* family, similar to partridges, called in Portuguese "inhambu," "jaó," "macuco," consumed in that order of frequency by the Araweté. See Appendix 3.

12. The milk secreted for several days after childbirth.

13. The work of opening up water holes, excavated by hand in humid soil, is designated not by the verb *karã*, to dig, but by the verb *maya*, which is also applied to sexual deflowering and to the men's manipulation of the female genitalia (see chap. 7, sect. 1).

14. See the list of botanical and zoological terms in Appendix 3 for precise identification of each species.

15. Balée (1988:51) reports that the Araweté also raise bruchid beetle grubs (fruit-boring weevils) in rotting babassu fruits in their houses. Besides being eaten, their fat is rubbed on bows to make them more flexible.

16. I even saw men chewing maize for fermented beverages (when their wives were menstruating), or using a sling-blouse to carry children.

17. Compare this with the Trio assertion, "We can live without meat; without bread we die" (Rivière 1969:42). The Araweté speak of an enemy tribe, the *O'i woko* (Long Arrows), nomads who live solely off hunting and flour of babassu mesocarp. They are also called *ɗepe ã*, "eaters of flour [of babassu]," a practice that, for the Araweté, approaches savagery. Would they be the Guajá (Balée 1988)?

18. As among the Tapirapé (Wagley 1977:60) and the Wayãpi (Grenand 1980:42).

19. For the Kaapor, the pair is manioc-turtle (Huxley 1956:183–84). The proper Araweté term for "fat" is *čirã*. The notion of *čewe* more properly refers to the idea of substantiality or nutritive force, which in the case of animal meat depends on the layer of fat. Another food said to be *čewe* is honey. The vagina is *čewe*, and the sexual act is referred to as eating (*o*) the woman or the vagina. *Čewe* foods cause sleepiness and enervation, and are contraindicated for shaman initiates. Against this category of foodstuffs are counterposed the *hẽ'ẽ*, "sweet foods," such as banana, papaya, potato, pineapple, and mild maize beer; the *'da*, "sour foods," such as strong maize beer, assai, and sweet potato; the *hatĩ*, "hard foods," such as the several types of cornmeal, Brazil nuts, and babassu. It is worth noting that honey and sex are not in the category of sweet foods, but of fatty or substantial foods, contrary to the majority of human cultures; but they are still categorized together.

20. In conditions of some degree of security, this average was probably four years, judging by the age difference between people born in the same village. The Araweté would move when the gardens had to be opened at too great a distance from the village, which posed risks of enemy ambushes.

21. The Parintintin, Tapirapé, and Wayãpi move their villages after many deaths occurred (Kracke 1978:9; Wagley 1977:88; Grenand 1982:237). The Kaapor abandon a village when the chief dies (Huxley 1956:126), which is

consistent with the Tupi-Guarani conception, perhaps a pan-Amazonian one, of the leader as the "owner" of the local group. Compare with the Piaroa (Kaplan 1975:58), the Trio (Rivière 1969:37, 234) and the Maku (Silverwood-Cope 1980:124). Notice the general pattern of death then abandonment of the village, and its relation to concepts of territoriality and temporality dominant in the region.

22. Thus, for example, the name of the river *Kãñĩna̱dĩ-no nĩ* is derived from the village *Kãñĩna̱dĩ-no ɨpã*, named after a deceased, that lay in its vicinity. Three large waterfalls of the Ipixuna are named for events that happened nearby: *Iwikɨ̃ karã he*, "place where people dug" (referring to a hunt where there were so many mosquitos that the men slept in holes); *Arakɨrĩ o he*, "where chickens were eaten" (during the transference of the group by FUNAI employees after contact); *Yičirepa reñã he*, "where Yičirepa was abandoned" (by her mother, for being too sick to continue walking during the relocation of 1976). Notably, the rivers of their former territory in the Bacajá basin are *not* known by the names of the dead, but rather, by simple "proper" names (Electric Eel, Banana Tree, Straight Waters) or by names evoking enemies (River of the Kayapó; River of the *Towa̱ho*). The Ipixuna does not have a name—it is simply *paranĩ*, "the river"—just as the village at the Indian Post lacks one. Names are given to what is distant in time or in space.

23. This general percentage would certainly fall if all the deceased of recent generations were remembered. It is reasonable to suppose that the losses from warfare are more readily remembered than deaths by disease, especially those of small children.

24. The custom of decapitating dead enemies was common among the Arara, Juruna, Shipaya, and Curuaya (Nimuendaju 1948b:236). All these tribes wore long hair, including the Arara, who differed in this respect from the contemporary Arara.

25. An important distinction exists between *dɨ* and *amɨ̃te*, two terms that can be translated as "other." *Dɨ̃* signifies "similar other," "other of the same kind" (Tupi-Guarani cognates: *yrõ, irũ*, etc., for "friend," "companion"). *Amɨ̃te* is "different other," "other of a different kind." Both terms are central in the kinship terminology; the first connotes consanguinity, the second, potential affinity.

26. This is a situation common to various other Tupi-Guarani. The Tenetehara present a great variation in village composition in temporal terms, and the sentiment of belonging to a particular village "is not strong" (Wagley & Galvão 1949:16). The Parintintin do not take sides according to village affiliation in conflicts arising during ceremonies, despite the fact that "some rivalry between neighboring local groups seems to be endemic" (Kracke 1978:63). Finally, the Tapirapé, who in 1939 formed a single village composed of the survivors of four others and who maintain a strong memory of village affiliations (as well as a form of personal identification using the name of one's village), nevertheless do not use these affiliations as a foundation for its factional structure (Wagley 1977:83–85). It is noteworthy that these last two tribes have social structures that are intermediate between the extended

family and the tribe (exogamic moieties and ceremonial moieties, respectively). The village is not a fundamental conceptual unit, either as a structure capable of integrating domestic groups or as a source of territorial identity.

27. The principal source of information on the contact history are the manuscript diaries of the expeditionist J. E. Carvalho (1977), which Berta Ribeiro kindly allowed me to consult.

Chapter 3

1. This is the same concept written as *-ɨpã* in the description of the toponymy (see chap. 2). In many Tupi-Guarani words, initial *t-* and initial *h-* mark, respectively, the indeterminate (absolute) and determinate (relative) forms of the concept expressed in the root. These change to *r-* (postnasal: *n-*) in certain compound constructions. In Araweté, after a final *-ï*, the initial *r-* changes to *d-* or *đ*, although irregularities exist.

2. The nature of the insult (*ɨkɨrã*) that *Aranãmĩ*'s wife made to him is especially enigmatic. She "threw out his footprints" (*ipipa mara heti*), that is, undid the marks left by the divinity's feet on the rocks. I was not able to discover why this was offensive.

A conjugal conflict as the cause of the separation of human beings and gods or culture heroes is recurrent among the Tupi-Guarani, such as the Kaapor (Huxley 1956:220), Tenetehara (Wagley & Galvão 1949:34), and Guarani (Nimuendaju 1978 [1914]:68–69). The woman's original sin was either her disbelief in her husband's magical powers or her incestuous adultery.

3. *Hema* is a category that includes climbing plants and those that send out creeping vines or offshoots. *Tema ipi* are the buds on tuberculates. The Araweté conceive of the progression of the generations not in the form of a tree, as we do, but as genealogical "creepers" that spread over the earth.

4. I was also told that the stars (*yahi tatã*, "moon fire") are fires lit in the upper worlds. The association of stars with caterpillars is also made by the Kayabi (Grünberg n.d. [1970]:166) and Shipaya (Nimuendaju 1981 [1922]:16). To my surprise, the Araweté never seemed to understand my point when I tried to obtain the names of their constellations. In our long conversations about the sky, I was not even able to learn the names of the stars or the planets (except for Venus, "the moon's lover"). They related the change of seasons to the flowering or fruiting of plant species and the songs of birds or insects, never to the position of the stars. Although the problem was most likely due to my incompetence, I should point out that the Araweté showed more interest in what happened on the "inside" (*haipi ti*) of the sky, domain of the gods, than in the visible celestial bodies, located "below the sky" (*iwã nakape iro*).

5. Certain proverbial idioms express the singularity of the sun and the multiplicity of moons. To signify that one has not forgotten old offenses, one says, *e'e te karahi*, "it is the same sun" (that shines today and shone when the affront was committed). When a woman wants to refuse a man's sexual invitations, she puts off her acceptance to the indefinite "tomorrow," saying, *amĩte yahi*, "when there is another moon (I will do what you ask of me)."

6. The underworld is called *Ma̲ï đakape tĩ mõ*, "junction, barrier of the

Mai̲." *Hakape tĩ* means "to unite" or "to seal off." For instance, houses that are joined and share a wall are said to be *hakape tĩ mõ.* Accordingly, the lower world can be understood as either sealing the cosmic sphere or as being linked to the celestial worlds through the human tier, which would therefore be a kind of membrane separating the divine domains.

7. This is a weak version of the theme of the "burnt world," common to various American cultures (Lévi-Strauss 1969b:293), which is correlated with the theme of the universal deluge, a weak form of the "rotten world." The pygmy owl is called the Mother of Night by the Mbyá (Cadogan 1959:18), and the jealous Lady of Daylight by the Tapirapé (Wagley 1977:177).

8. See the similar Kayabi belief about the *menem'ɨ* lizard (Grünberg n.d. [1970]:163). It is notable that the name of the *tarayo* lizard, which lives by rivers and resembles a small iguana, is the same as the *Mai̲* of the lower world, *Tarayo,* who, as we saw, is associated with water. Nevertheless, the Araweté deny any sort of association between the animal and the homonymous spirit.

The Araweté say the *tamĩ* hawk has a celestial double that is the source of rain. They also call this bird a "tapir hawk" because it is always near the tapir, his "brother." I am not sure whether this bird is *Milvago chimachima* or *Daptrius ater*—both species eat vermin that plague tapir and deer. The Shipaya consider a "tapir hawk" to be the master of fire and associate it with the vulture (Nimuendaju 1981:19). The common Tupian theme of the theft of the vulture's fire by mankind is not found among the Araweté. On the other hand, the Shipaya substitution of the vulture by the tapir hawk clarifies the Araweté association between the latter bird (or one closely related to it) and the rain—an indirect proof of the "rotten world" seen in the myth of the universal deluge.

9. See below and chapter 7.

10. The Guarani express the same terror of the sky falling and humanity being annihilated. Schaden (1969:175) interprets this as an influence of the Christian apocalypse via the Jesuits. The Wayãpi say that the weight of the dead will cause the sky to collapse. They also conceive of an inexorable rotting of the earth (Gallois 1985:192; 1988:354–55), comparable to the notion in Apapokuva eschatology that the earth is old and weary (Nimuendaju 1978 [1914]:91, 149). Such concepts among the Tupi-Guarani articulate a sense of irreversible time, hence constituting the foundation of an entire theory of history.

11. Compare this to the Gê, who posit a fundamental difference *me/mbru,* human/animal, that is, Culture/Nature (Seeger 1981:22). Or compare it to the Piaroa, where the difference gods/humans/animals is produced by the intersecting of two philosophical categories, the "life of the senses" (animals and humans) and the "life of the spirit" (humans and gods) (Kaplan 1982:9–10, 23).

12. This is one of the few basic terms for which I could not obtain cognates in other Tupi-Guarani languages. It can serve a pronominal function as the

first person plural inclusive and appears to be supplanting the classical Tupi-Guarani form *ñãne.*

13. An important race of wild spirits, the *Ãñĩ* (discussed later) were characterized as *bïde* only in the context of questioning by the anthropologist, stupid enough to think that "*Ãñĩ*" signified "bat" (*ãñirã*). The *Ãñĩ* may be "*bïde,*" but before all else they are *awĩ,* enemies; this value predominates over the criteria of anthropomorphism.

14. A similar problem has been raised by Campbell (1982:236–59; 1989:104–13). To phrase it this way, however, forces somewhat the notion of *peye* (a cognate of the well-known "pajé"), which focuses on humans who actualize such a spiritual quality. In addition, the Araweté never defined a class of beings by the criteria *ɨpeye hã;* they merely pointed out such power in one or another species of being.

15. See chap. 2, note 25, on the difference between *đĩ,* "similar other," and *amɨ̃te,* "different other." This contrast will come up again in chapter 6, sect. 3, when categories of relatives and nonrelatives are discussed.

16. White-lipped peccaries and howler monkeys, no doubt because they live in bands, are a rich source of metaphors for social life, especially for war. Thus, the Araweté compared the Kayapó tactic of surrounding their enemies with their own technique used against herds of pigs. They enjoyed mimicking the panic of howler monkeys and peccaries when attacked by hunters: the animals would screech, "*Awĩ, awĩ!*"

These examples suggest that "enemy" is an active position, connoting the attacker more than the attacked. Humans do not consider the animals they hunt to be *awĩ,* but the latter conceive their hunters to be such. The exception is the jaguar, since it maintains reciprocal relations of predation with humans and is an *awĩ.* Thus, while *bïde* represents the concept of Subject and *awĩ* that of Other, the former does not hold the privilege of agency, nor is the latter conceived of as the object or recipient of an action. To the contrary, it is *bïde* that appears to occupy a passive position. Accordingly, the figure of the Araweté warrior-killer is paradoxical: being the masculine ideal-type of *bïde,* he defines himself as the *awĩ* of an *awĩ,* and so in a certain sense as an *awĩ* himself. Later I will argue that the position of *bïde* is identified with femininity when counterposed against the masculine character of exteriority (gods and enemies).

17. In this, I am inspired by Lienhardt (1961), whose characterization of the Dinka *Nhialic* would apply well to the Araweté *Ma̲ï* (omitting the formers' status as creator of mankind), involving separation, celestial location, oscillation between abstraction and concreteness, unity and multiplicity, principle and substance. I know that the term "god" is rarely, if ever, used by anthropologists in referring to superhuman beings of Amazonian cosmologies—perhaps because of an affected anti-ethnocentricism which ends up subscribing to the Western conception of Divinity. The Araweté *Ma̲ï* have nothing to do with a personalized, intangible, creator Absolute, of course. But as Hocart (1970 [1936]:49) remarked in a similar context, "Why not call them gods?"

This allows us to measure the distance separating humans from Divinity, in both our cosmology and the Araweté's, and goes a long way towards understanding what "paganism" is all about. *Maï* is a cognate of the Tupi-Guarani forms *Maíra, Mbahira,* etc.

18. *Maï oho* appears to designate those *Maï hete* who are mature males. But sometimes the term struck me as connoting a singular entity, as "the great *Maï.*" The divinity *Topĩ* (whose name is a cognate of *Tupã,* the classical Tupi-Guarani god) occupies a lesser place in the pantheon.

19. Accordingly, the *Maï hete* receive eloquent appellations: *teka pɨkɨ,* long lived; *ɨwerã me'e,* flashing; *kuča mi re,* covered with designs; *hewo me'e,* perfumed; *temimã ñã,* masters of pet birds; *marakã me'e,* musicians; *peye,* shamans; *odɨpïda kã ñã,* masters of the skin-changing bath (which rejuvenates). The skin of the gods is white and soft, since it is always being renewed. Against this white background, the black genipap paint is said to flash. The general notion of the Maï as celestial and shining beings is another argument in favor of the translation "god": the Indo-European form **deiwos* also has this double connotation. The complex shininess-whiteness-designs-spirituality typical of the *Maï* beings can be found among the Guarani (Schaden 1969:155; Cadogan 1959:26), the Aché (Cadogan 1968:66; P. Clastres 1972:302–3), and the Omágua and Cocama (Espinosa 1935:56, 90, 140; Métraux 1948:702).

20. *Odɨ̈* is a reflexive pronoun; *mo* is a causative that verbalizes names; *-owã* is a verb signifying "to transform"; *-mõ* is an instrumental dative.

21. The *Maï* can be called "grandparents" or by affinal terms. Humans address the *Ãñĩ* as "grandfathers," while animals address them by affinal terms.

22. That is, to the *Ãñĩ* we are peccaries, just as to peccaries, we are *awĩ* (cf. note 16). Compare this with what Grenand (1980:42) says of the Wayãpi concerning the vision that men have of animals, animals of men, and that held by the Sun and Moon of both.

23. Compare with the Parintintin cognate *pojý* (Kracke 1978:26).

24. The mythic-prophetic theme of a "Land without Evil" played a fundamental role in the Tupi and Guarani migrations in the sixteenth and seventeenth centuries, and possibly also before the European invasion. It continues to be present among the contemporary Guarani. It concerns a land or a state of the world in which there exists no death, hunger, work, or incest prohibition. See Nimuendaju 1978; Métraux 1979 [1928]; H. Clastres 1978; Shapiro 1987.

25. The jaguar is a cannibal (*pɨrɨ o*) and an eater of raw food, in opposition to humans, who are *tatã me'e,* "(beings) provided with fire." Characterizing animals and humans by their alimentary regime is common. The vulture, for instance, is defined as *'de we ã,* an eater of bad-smelling things. Certain especially despised enemies, such as the Parakanã, are called eaters of vultures or eaters of excrement. Gods without fire (*Maï datã-ĩ*) is a joking epithet given to whites, due to their habit of drying slabs of meat in the sun—as the gods once did.

26. Such a distinction between "good" and "bad" cannibalism can be

found in various cultures. The criteria of distinction vary: either by the mode of consumption, the part consumed, who consumes, or who is consumed. See, for example, Pouillon 1972:17; Guidieri 1972:104; Poole 1983:7; Clastres & Lizot 1978:125ff.

27. Compare this with the Apapokuva *oioú*, "to find," as meaning "to create" (Nimuendaju 1978:71).

28. The white-lipped peccaries were not created during this maize beer feast; they belong to *Iaraɨdï*, who causes them to be born from babassu buds. The theme of the transformation of wooden cultural objects into fish and alligators is found among the Parintintin (Kracke 1978:4) and in the Apapokuva cycle of the adventures of the twins (Nimuendaju 1978:79–80). The theme of the transformation of humans into animals at a beer festival is found among the Siriono (Holmberg 1969:118) and, beyond the Tupi-Guarani, among the Piaroa (Kaplan 1981a:14). For the Piaroa, the human origin of animals lies behind the need to perform a shamanic transformation of all meats into vegetables before being consumed, since eating meat would be a form of cannibalism (echoing certain Guarani beliefs) (cf. Kaplan 1981a: 7–9; 1982:10ff.).

29. Thus, the *Ãñĩ* as well as the *Maï* are characterized as savages: the first for not having houses, the second for "not having had" gardens or fire. The Araweté are aware that they too had no gardens or fire before the owl and *Piïpi* gave them to man and the gods. But the insistence with which they associate the *Maï* with this state of Nature is significant.

30. In the sky there are no peccaries, coatimundis, or armadillos. The first belong to the Master of Peccaries; coatimundis are associated with the *Ãñĩ*, being their favorite food. I do not know why there are no armadillos, but there is a celestial "armadillo god" (*Aiyirime* or *Tato-Maï*).

31. Cf. the same associations of yellow among the Mybá (Cadogan 1959: 33–41).

32. *Apa* is "thing." It may enter into genitive constructions as well as possessive ones. As a rule, *Maï apa* means simply "divine," attribute of the gods.

33. The notion of *ñã* (which should not be confused with its homonym *ñã*, jaguar) is a cognate of the Guarani *jara*, the Tenetehara *zara*, the Wayãpi *ijar*, etc. This notion calls to mind classical themes of Amazonian culture, such as the "Master of the Animals" and the "owners" of the forest and of the water. The term *ñã* connotes ideas such as leadership, control, representation, responsibility, and ownership of some resource or domain. The *ñã* is always a human or anthropomorphic being. But other ideas are involved as well. The *ñã* of something is someone who has this something in abundance. Above all, the *ñã* is defined by something of which it is the master. In this last connotation, he is at the same time "the representative of" and "represented by" this something. Such is the case, for example, with the synedoche *yɨakã ñã*, "masters of the diadem," designating the male community. The juridical notion of ownership is the least important aspect and not even always present. The Araweté do not have a general conception of the cosmos as a set of domains possessed by different *ñã* with whom man must come to

terms or fight—as do the Tenetehara (Wagley & Galvão 1949: 102–4 or the Wayãpi (Gallois 1984). At least this is not the emphasis of their cosmology; recall the previous analysis of the notion *ɨka hete me'e,* beings that do not have *ñã,* i.e., that are not pets of (or trees planted by) spirits. As we will see, however, there are numerous terrestrial spirits that are *ñã.*

34. The Masters of White-lipped Peccaries do not, of course, come to eat their pets. What characterizes the "owner" of a species is that he does not eat this species; he takes care of it (*ipa̲'ï*) and controls its reproduction. The *ñã* of collectively consumed foods, when they exist, are always spirits of our cosmic level.

35. The mystical dangers associated with foods belong to another system, one involving "arrows" or "shamanic stuff" of the products consumed, which must be neutralized by the shamans. See chapter 5.

36. During my visit in 1988, a dozen new names of *Ma̲ï* appeared.

37. As one informant suggested, "like an outboard motor on a canoe."

38. The *tapẽ* must not be killed, or else we will fall from trees and die. Among the Kaapor, it is the animal familiar of the shaman; among the Tembé, it is linked to sorcery (Huxley 1956: 192–93). For the Apapokuva, it is the bird of *Tupã* and is linked to the rain (Nimuendaju 1978: 75).

39. This theme parallels that of two groups of mythic beings who live on earth, the *Yičire pa* and the *Pa̲'ï,* the first associated with the Araweté, the second with whitemen. These two tribes ate each others' buttocks. The *Pa̲'ï* are conceived as being great technologists, masters of iron, machines, and other crafts.

40. More specifically, this bee is a mamangaba, a very ferocious species of solitary bee or wasp that makes its nest in rotten tree trunks. The "eternal bumblebee" lands on the old skins of the souls of the dead that lay stretched out in the sun while the *Ma̲ï hete* feast on their flesh.

41. *"Koropï," "Karo̲ã," "Yɨrɨpadɨ̈"* are cognates of the Brazilian terms of Tupi origin, "Curupira," "Caruara," and "Jurupari," respectively. Such words emerged in the writings of the chroniclers and missionaries of the sixteenth century about the Tupinamba, designating spirits of the forest, masters of game animals, and other supernatural beings or principles which became integrated into the cosmology of the rural Brazilian populations, especially in Amazonia. The "Jurupari" in particular was identified with the devil by the missionaries in Amazonia (while in the south of the country this function was preferentially occupied by the "Anhanga" spirits—cf. Tupinamba *Añang* and Araweté *Ãñĩ*). Recall that the ceremonial complex of sacred flutes of the Tukano and Arawak peoples of the Rio Negro is known as the "Jurupari cult" (S. Hugh-Jones 1979: 3–9). The word entered the *Língua Geral* and appears to have been adopted by peoples of non-Tupi languages to translate divers religious categories, mythical personages, and the like.

42. An identical belief for the same category of spirits, but threatening young women who are menstruating, can be found among the Mbyá (Schaden 1969: 112).

43. I do not know to what this role of the spirits of the *iwirã ñã* type should

be attributed. A possible hypothesis is that their participation in the couvade (as a threat) and in homicides (as helpers) defines the killer as the inverse of a father.

44. *Iwaho* is produced by black bees that lack stingers but have a relatively painful bite when they latch onto people's scalps and sweaty bodies. Their hives are very large, having the appearance of termite nests and an entrance in the form of a protuberance (the "penis" of the *iwaho*), and are located in tall trees such as courbaril or Brazil-nut trees.

45. The kinkajou (related to coatimundis and raccoons, see Appendix 3), is also a character of the Kaapor underworld, associated with the blue-boned monster *Ae* that reigns there (Huxley 1956:227, 231–33). He has an equivalent in Araweté cosmology who is associated with the terrestrial souls of the dead: the *apoiyiči*, the night monkey. In some regions of Amazonia, it is common to call the kinkajou (in Araweté: *yɨparã*) the "midnight monkey," which suggests some kind of similarity between these two animals, both nocturnal but of different genera.

46. Despite the terrestrial localization of the *Mbahira*, these beings, like the Araweté *Maï*, are associated with stone. The *Mbahira* people are less important than the celestial people and are identified with femininity (Kracke 1984b). Kracke points out elsewhere (1984a) the difficulty of establishing systematic oppositions among the different cosmic domains such that they would correspond to the division of Parintintin society into exogamic moieties. It is clear, however, that the opposition between the Harpy Eagle and Curassow moieties involves a contrast between "upper" and "lower."

47. The Tapirapé system is similar to that described by Carneiro da Cunha (1981:165) for the Krahó: (Forest:Village)::(Dead:Living)::(Dead Whites:Dead Krahó)::(West:East).

48. A similar difficulty was noted by Carneiro da Cunha (1981) for Krahó eschatology: the importance of "areas open to fabulation," where individual fantasy reigns, revolving about a restricted structural nucleus. In the Araweté case, it is not simply the eschatology that suffers (or benefits) from this fluidity; it characterizes the cosmological discourse as a whole. I would suggest that the difference between the Gê and the Tupi-Guarani lies in the position occupied by the enunciator of cosmological discourse. Among the former, shamans are relatively marginal figures, structurally speaking; among the latter, they are absolutely central. Araweté cosmological creation does not occur in the areas *left over* for invention, but occupies a preeminent position in social and religious life. The Tupi-Guarani parallels are many, ranging from the citations by chroniclers of "thus speak our shamans," "what our *caraibas* saw" (Thevet, *apud* Métraux 1979 [1928]:106–7, 110), to the luxuriant "theologies" elaborated by Guarani religious chiefs as documented by Schaden (1969, 1982) and Cadogan (1959, 1962, 1968).

49. The *Ãñĩ* are the *Anhanga* or *Aignan* of the Tupinamba and the missionaries, a word which was translated as "Devil." Métraux (1979:47–50) disagrees with the identification of the *Anhanga* with the wandering souls of the dead, as proposed by the chroniclers. Relying on myths of the Tupinamba,

Apapokuva, and Tenetehara, he asserts that the *Anhanga* are merely characters in mythology, harmful terrestrial spirits, and that the identification with the dead was due to a homonymy between *añanga* and the terms for the soul (*ang, anguera*). Although it is not possible here to resolve the question of the semantic relationship of these words, the fact is that the contemporary materials do associate the *Anhanga* with the specters of the dead—even in those groups whose languages reveal no similarity between the terms. In Tenetehara, moreover (one of Métraux's examples), *azang* are in fact the spirits of the dead (Wagley & Galvão 1949: 100). Nimuendaju (1978: 73–74, 62), who distinguishes the *Añãy*, mythological beings, from the *anguéry*, the terrestrial ghosts of the dead, suggests that the first are cast in the same mold as the Kaingang figure, i.e., the greatest enemy of the Apapokuva. What all this suggests is that the relation of the *Anhanga* with the dead is not linguistic, but logical: the dead (or rather, their terrestrial specters) are thought of as enemies. Hence, this spirit of death is a mixture of images of savagery, bellicosity, rottenness, and cadaverous appearance. That the concept of *añã* has come to connote, besides the spirit associated with the dead, notions such as the Wayãpi's concept of magical force (and even positive magical force), is simply an indication of the ambivalence of the Other in Tupi-Guarani cosmologies.

It would be overly fastidious to follow out the trajectories of other Araweté terms. Suffice it to comment on the path of the notion of *Karo̱ã*, the cannibal mountain spirits: the protoform **Karuguara* is transformed into the Tapirapé Thunder (*Kanawana*), the Kayabi Master of Water (*Karuat*), the Guarani Rainbow (*Karugua*), the general term for Supernaturals in Tenetehara (*Karowara*), and the concept of a *mana*-like force among the Akuáwa (*karowara*) and Kaapor (*karuwa*).

50. And, moreover, condensing traits of the various *Maíra* with those of the *Tupã* of other cosmologies—not just in the association of *Tupã* with thunder, but in his frequent relationship to the celestial souls of the dead. For instance, it is the god of thunder *Hyapú guasú* who receives the souls of the Kayová (Schaden 1969: 155).

51. Schaden (1959) mentions the most famous, and most unfounded, etymology of the Tupinamba *Mair*, suggested by Teodoro Sampaio: *mbae ira*, "that which is apart, solitary, lives distant."

CHAPTER 4

1. The equivalent among the Guarani is the *avati-mongarai*, "baptism of maize" (Nimuendaju 1978 [1914]:107–8), the only occasion when an entire Guarani group convenes down to the very last person. It also corresponds to the Tapirapé Thunder Ceremony and the Tenetehara Maize Festival (Wagley 1977: 195; Wagley & Galvão 1949: 125–27).

2. Approximately one-seventh of this stored maize is used for seeds.

3. One limitation on the length of these excursions is the quantity of toasted cornmeal brought along to the forest. *Mepi* is no longer edible after

one week. Since the Araweté do not like going without it, rarely do such trips last longer than this.

4. The shamanic rites of assai and honey in this season are performed in the village; those of fish can take place in the forest if the fishing site is distant from the village.

5. I do not know why. I never attended a *peyo* of howler monkey, nor that of honey or assai; the first was not performed from 1981 to 1983, and the second two occurred in October of 1982 while I was out of the area. The Araweté say that it is the smoke of the gardens that brings the rains, since it irritates the *Maï* by clouding their domains.

6. The Tenetehara who assign the planting of manioc to the men, while the women plant the rest of the cultigens (Wagley & Galvão 1949:47). The Maize Festival is one of two principal ceremonies of the Tenetehara, performed to protect the maize from the *azang*; it is opposed to the Honey Festival, which has the function of providing game. However, the Tenetehara festivals cannot be superimposed on those of the Araweté. Among the former, the Maize Festival is held at the height of the rains while the maize is maturing; it has a connotation of adolescent initiation and a strong association with shamanism. The Honey Festival takes place at the end of the dry season and is not linked to shamanic performances. Among the Araweté, the "Maize Festival" unfolds into two: the festivals of mild beer and of the strong. The first marks the end of the rains; the second takes place throughout the dry season. The shamanry of maize, although beginning at the height of the dry season, extends through the entire rainy season.

7. This form of house is called *a hete,* "true house." Ribeiro describes it thus: "A wooden framework is bound to three supports and a crossbeam. The roof and the side walls, forming an arch, are covered with babassu palm leaves. The front and back walls, like the door screen, are made of superimposed woven mats. This house, with its rectangular plan, has no separation between the roof and the side walls, and is characterized by the diminutive size of the door" (Ribeiro 1983:14).

8. Nor does the residential section of the current village leader face onto this medial area, but is turned towards another patio.

9. It contrasts radically with the Gê conception of the village as an entity that preexists and survives its components. This is well illustrated in the case of the Bororo village of Pobojari, composed of *one single man* who reconstructed the village circle and situated his house in the appropriate clan positioni (Crocker 1979:253).

10. Youths who are still single, even if they live in their own house and have hunted that day, are never invited nor invite others to eat in this ritualized form. In both cases, they depend on their parents. Children participate much less in these nocturnal alimentary rounds, eating principally from the family pot. To call (or be called to) a collective meal is a sign of social maturity and is something that recently married youths are embarrassed to do.

11. Compared to the moderation and solemnity of the Asuriní communal

meals, or to what the chroniclers said about the Tupinamba, who maintained a "marvellous silence" and composure during meals (in contrast to their unruliness during beer drinking parties [Léry 1990 [1578]:75), the Araweté manner stands out as frankly "savage." But this tumultuous and individualistic behavior regarding food offered by other patios does not seem to me to be pure informality; it is too regular to be simple disorder. It is, rather, a modality of joking relations, a ceremonial structure of hospitality. The *Maï*, descending to earth to eat, behave in the same manner: they shove the shaman and devour the food chaotically. It should also be noted that this behavior only characterizes meals that involve more than one patio or section, not the etiquette of domestic meals.

12. This estrangement of the hunter in relation to his catch is found among the Kaapor (Huxley 1956:78–79), and is an attenuated form of the widespread interdiction against eating what one has hunted (P. Clastres 1987:114–16, 120–22); Rivière 1969:214, note 2), the most significant expression being the Tupinamba rule: the executor of a war captive is the only one who does not eat the victim.

13. Apart from the most central group around the singer, everybody else chatters during the song, drifts from the melody, gets out of tune, hums more than sings, and the like. The overall impression is one of relative confusion, with the singer being the pole of attraction and organization around which the rest of the participants lie at varying distances in space and involvement. Such a system, as well as the lack of "climaticity," is reminiscent of Philips' analysis (1974) of Warm Springs "Indian time."

14. For example, it may also mark the introduction of a man into another village or residential section. In 1982, a youth who lived in his parents' section married the daughter of the village headman and moved into her section. For several nights after he had begun to build his house, the young people of both sections performed a *pïrahẽ* in the patio of the wife's section (granted, without much liveliness). The recently married youth was the singer. This was what people used to do long ago, I was told, when a man moved to the village of his wife.

15. In the daily dances of the dry season, the singer is chosen ad hoc every night from among those who enjoy the position, normally someone with the "killer" status. The singer for the strong beer festival is determined ahead of time: he is the one who led the collective hunting expedition preceding the feast.

16. On the question of collective action, see Wagley (1977:118–24), who discusses the problems the Tapirapé had in reaching a group decision, given their ethos of being "egalitarian to an extreme."

17. Such a mode of propagation of activities is not restricted to the economic sphere. While I was there, the village seemed to pass through cycles, concerning matters all the way from superficial fashions in songs or games up to sociological spheres. Thus, for example, if a youth got married, soon afterwards the whole village began to explore connections between boys and girls in the age bracket of ten to twelve years. A temporary exchange of spouses,

creating an *apĩhi-pihã* relation between two houses, would produce a paramatrimonial "hemorrhaging" of partners circulating rapidly from house to house.

18. The difference between cases of "contagion" and those requiring an initiating action is not all that clear-cut: some actions that, from the point of view of the village as a whole, are experienced as contagion depend on a *tenotã mõ* at the lower level, i.e., the residential sections.

19. I always had difficulty in conveying the idea of "chieftainship" to the Araweté; I know no word equivalent to "to give orders." The closest notion is *mo-kaakɨ̄* (literally, "to make someone think"), to convince, remind, suggest. When I wanted to explain the nature of the relation between the head of the FUNAI Post and the head of the FUNAI office in Altamira, I resorted to the word *tenotã mõ;* at that, the Araweté lit up: "Ah, yes, so he's the one who goes in front when the two of them go hunting." The word *moro̱wī̃'hã,* cognate of the Tupinamba *morubixaba,* "chief," simply means old, adult, or great (it struck me as a variant of *pɨro̱wī̃'hã,* old, ancient, ancestral); it has the connotation of authority and knowledge. One cannot, however, be the *moro̱wī̃'hã* "of" any group or person.

20. Arado-hi was the *tenotã mõ* of the women, while her husband was that of all the villagers. She had in fact a certain ascendence over the women, but since there was no context in which women act collectively, I never saw her exercise any initiatory functions. Having a somewhat volatile temperament and a sharp tongue, she was nevertheless capable of getting a number of "daughters" to help her in tasks such as weaving, husking maize, and so forth.

21. Maize is planted without separate plots. The titular couple of the garden does not control or limit the supplies of maize taken by each domestic unit; it is a shared plantation where each man cleared the forest and each woman planted. Sweet potatoes, yams, manioc, tobacco, and cotton are planted in sectors, each one under the care of a domestic unit.

22. Similarly, former Araweté villages apparently varied between a situation of maximal cohesiveness and minimal population, on the one hand, and the current situation of maximal population and minimal cohesiveness, on the other—in other words, between the uxorilocal extended family, simple or amplified (married children, unmarried siblings of the head couple), and the juxtaposition of equally powerful extended families. If it were possible to determine an ideal type of village, it would consist of a group of married siblings, with a few couples already constituting extended families of two generations and one of these extended families occupying the position of "owner of the village." The village on the eastern side of the Ipixuna, abandoned in 1981, was quite close to this model.

23. I refer to dispersal since all the activities requiring a *tenotã mõ* are ones facing *outside* the village (except for the *pɨrahẽ* dances). Even the founding of a new village is oriented this way, since it implies the abandoning of the old one and, as a rule, the fragmenting of its population. Although a focus of unification, the role of leader nonetheless functions as a coordinator of dispersal.

24. This does not mean that Yɨrĩñato-ro *had* to sing or be the last to sing for a collective hunt to be undertaken.

25. Yɨrĩñato-ro is the man with the greatest number of uxorilocally married daughters (three, plus a classificatory daughter who lives in the same patio, although belonging to another agricultural unit) and the greatest number of "sons-in-law" dispersed through the village.

26. The question of political chieftainship among the Tupi-Guarani is thorny, and I do not want to attack it here. The Araweté case has numerous Amazonian analogies. The idea of the headman as the founder and base of the local group is found among the Parintintin, the Kaapor, the Wayãpi, the Guiana groups, and the Tukano (Kracke 1978:33; Huxley 1956:66–67; Gallois 1988:22; Rivière 1984:72ff.; C. Hugh-Jones 1979:46). The "legitimating" and contagious value of the actions of the Kalapalo *anetaw*, "owners of the village," is analogous to the Araweté case, although more formalized (Basso 1973:132ff.). The few attributes of the Araweté "owner of the village" contrast with the redistributive and directive functions of the Parintintin *ruvihav*, who divides up plots of land among group members and distributes game brought to the village (Kracke 1978:42–44). The latter's first function is a weakened and generalized form of the Araweté situation of the extended family's communal garden, where the head determines *one* locale where *all* of the members of his family (but only them) will work. The distinction between *tã ñã* and *tenotã mõ* may correspond to the Kamayurá difference between the "representative of the land" and the "representative of the people" (Bastos 1978:61, note 19); it does not, however, reach the point of constituting a system of co-leadership of the Parintintin type (Kracke 1978:40). Nor does the distinction between *tã ñã* and *tã nɨpã nã hã* attain the rigidity of the distinction that Lévi-Strauss perceived among the Tupi-Kawahib (1958:334) between "chief," "bodyguard," and "lesser functionaries."

All this suggests that, as among so many Amazonian groups, the position of the Araweté headman results from the coalescence of certain attributes—father-in-law, shaman, warrior—and of a certain personality disposition. No factor alone is sufficient for determining the position, which thus appears to be a condensation point of various attributes, not a formal office fulfilled by mechanical criteria.

CHAPTER 5

1. If the maize is still very green, what is produced instead of *mepi* is meal, properly speaking: *awacï ko̱'ï*, made of maize that is first ground raw and then toasted.

2. They like to compare the long line of pots to a herd of peccaries: "*tayaho pɨkɨ!*"

3. The same holds while mild beer is being made, but it only lasts one night. Menstruating women may not chew the maize; if the female owner of the maize has her period while the *kã̱'ɨ'da* is being made, she asks a sister to substitute for her temporarily. In July 1981, a large amount of beer, ready to

drink, was all tossed out because the owner aborted. "Lots of blood in the beer," they said.

4. When the hunters separate into groups, each camp describes the other as *iwirã dɨ̄ ne hã*, "those who are in other trees," a metaphor that evokes the habit of howler monkeys whereby bands headed by different males occupy their own trees. This figure of speech (also used to indicate the difference between father and father's brother in relation to ego) assumes additional significance in the context of the hunting parties for beer feasts, in that the male howler monkey is the prototype of the *marakay*. If the band of hunters splits up into groups, one group should follow the leadership of the *marakay*, while the other should follow the *marakã memo'o hã*, the "song teacher."

5. They do so also to take advantage of the husbands' absence. During the *kã̱'ɨ̄ mo-ra*, the women attain a high state of erotic excitement; since the owner of the beer is under a sexual interdiction, they descend upon any remaining men. The theme of women's jokes during this period always revolves around metaphors associating beer and semen. Once when two men and I stayed behind in the village, the girls knocked on our doors, bringing bowls and asking to have them filled with semen.

6. It is possible, although improper, to hold a feast of mild beer without performing a *peyo*; the same is true for tortoises and other foods. The collective consumption of honey and assai requires a *peyo*, although these two products can be consumed privately, something that does not happen with strong beer, which is always drunk collectively—and therefore always prelibated by the gods.

7. It is here, I suspect, that postcontact changes most affected Araweté ritual organization. The multivillage character of the beer festivals and the association of the singer-warrior with the guests (in opposition to the sponsor of the drink, who occupies a "feminine" position as nourisher) must have had symbolic resonances that I could not make out. The Araweté beer festival clearly belongs to the family of Amazonian intervillage ceremonies that deal with potential affinity, such as the *javari* of the Upper Xingu, the *reahu* of the Yanomami, the *shodewika* of the Waiwai, etc.

8. Léry (1990 [1578]:75), Cardim (1906 [1584]:421), and Abbeville (1975 [1614]:239) all contrasted the moderation and silence of the Tupinamba while eating with the excesses and singing while drinking (beer), and were surprised at the mutual exclusion of beer and food (for Europeans belonging to the civilization of table wines, this must have caught their attention). What is worth emphasizing here is the oral opposition: drink + word (song) *versus* food + silence.

9. During the *caxiri* feast of the Wayãpi, quite similar to the beer festival of the Araweté, the "master of the feast" (the analogue of the singer) is as a rule a brother of the "hostess owner of the *caxiri*" and therefore a brother-in-law of the male sponsor of the drink (Gallois 1988: 154). We have here a stronger version of the Araweté structure: the drink is directly identified with a woman, and the "logical affinity" (residential or village exteriority) between singer and sponsor in the Araweté ritual changes into real affinity.

10. Following out his analogy, it could be said that the dances performed to "make the beer heat up" during its production and fermentation correspond to the role of *dɨ̃ mõ*, "those who help to complete" the fetus, performed by men other than the main genitor. See chapter 7, sect. 1.

11. The beer has ears. During the phase of its preparation, no one in the village should pronounce the verb *ɨwa*, "to explode, split," or else the drink may get the idea of doing this to people. The drink is ferocious (*ñarã hetĩ*) and thus related to other beings with sharp and vengeful ears. For instance, one should not speak about the shamanry of tapir or deer near the smoked carcasses of these animals, or else their spirits will avenge themselves by burning the guilty party. We could say that the fermented (beer) degenerates into the rotten and "rots" anyone who drinks it, making the belly swell up and explode like a putrified cadaver; the smoked degenerates into an emitter of fire, a carbonizer (tapir and deer need a *peyo* only when they are smoked).

The miscarriage of the beer hostess in 1981 was attributed to the fermentation of the drink. Pregnant women must not prepare beer, at least during the first months of gestation, when a great deal of semen is needed to consolidate the fetus, which is immature (*dači*, green) and sensitive to cold. Suspending sexual relations during the phase of fermentation would make the fetus die of cold; inversely, the gestation within the woman would remove the fermentive power of the beer in the pots.

12. There is no term specifically for "to ferment." The root *'da* can be translated as "sour," "bitter," "fermented," and "alcoholic." Fermentation is a "boiling" or "bubbling": *i-pipo* is the form used to construct the verb *mo-pipo*, "to boil" (to cook in water). Because of its peculiarity of boiling without fire, the fermentation of beer approaches another kind of magical water: the "basin of souls" in the celestial world. These are circular depressions of stone (similar to those where fish are trapped during the dry season and killed with fish poison) filled with effervescent, bubbling water, where the dead are put to revive and change their skin (discussed at length in chap. 7, sect. 4).

"To digest" is also a general verb, *mo-yawẽ*, "to make pass" (as a cloud in the sky passes, as a headache passes, and so forth). This verb can be used in the sense of "coming to," reviving, as a synonym of *ɨperãy*; the Master of the Vultures blows in the face of the souls who have recently arrived in the sky, "*to mo-yawẽ*," to awaken them.

13. As in so many cultures, the sexual act is conceived as an "eating" (*o*) of the woman by the man.

14. This accords with the traditional form of designating the female gender by its sexual organ: *hamã*, vagina. Thus, if I asked why any two men were fighting, the answer was, "*hamã ne*," "because of a vagina." The Araweté, with their Rabelaisian penchant, will resort to other metaphors for vaginas of the village, but the names of types of honey are the most frequently used.

15. The opposition honey/tobacco, in the context of extracting xupé, assimilates (and consequently separates) the hive full of bees (with one end spewing smoke like a cigar) to the men at the foot of the tree (as if by smoking they would get stuffed with ferocious bees).

16. Every time a shaman dreams of this divinity or the other celestial jaguars (*Ñã yari* or *Ñã nowĩ 'hã*), he must warn the village in the morning, especially the parents of small children, so that they can put feathers on them. Harpy eagle feathers repel the jaguars who must certainly be circling the village. If I understood correctly, this decoration is associated with *kanoho ra'o we*, the spirit of the harpy eagle, which beats its wings and frightens the jaguars. While jaguars seem to have a preference for children, the harpy eagle is an animal with a different relationship to fecundity: women who eat its meat will no longer menstruate and will become sterile.

17. Compare this placement with that prevailing in the case of honey. When honey is shamanized in the village, people are supposed to stay securely inside their houses; in the forest, people should look for a site that is lower than the campsite and wait for the arrows of the honey to be dispersed, passing above their heads—a schema that seems to replicate the "higher" situation of honey in relation to men.

18. This effect is similar to that produced by the spirit of a dead enemy, who makes the killer's bangs fall out, exposing his forehead. The theme of hair loss associated with deer meat can be found among the Kaapor (Huxley 1956:84), where one must not sing or speak while consuming it.

19. The Araweté do not share the widespread Amazonian belief in the "recycling" of the dead into game animals, and of dead animals into human souls or humanlike agents, although they have the notion of spirits of tapir, deer, etc. Never having seen the shamanry for these animals, I do not know their degree of "anthropomorphism" or interaction with the shaman. What is certain is that there is no relationship between the *Maï* and the spirits and/or Masters of animals. The spirits of shamanized animals (those of deer and tapir, which we eat, as well as those of snakes or scorpions, which bite us) must be *killed* by the shaman, not placated or gratified, as happens, for example, in the Mundurucu ceremonies in honor of the "Mothers of the Game" (Murphy 1958:58–61). Nor is there any notion of the theft of human souls by game animals, as among the Mundurucu (Murphy 1958:25) and the Pakaa-Nova (Vilaça 1989). The Araweté system can be usefully compared with the Bororo case, where the *bari* shaman offers meat to the *bope* (celestial and cannibal spirits, but different from the *Maï*, who synthesize the *bope* and *aroe* aspects of Bororo cosmology) so that they will consume and "spoil" them, i.e., make them comestible for humans (see Viertler 1976; Crocker 1985).

20. The sexual nature of honey is clear in the food taboos of the Parintintin, who say it is the only food with malignant effects that can be passed through sexual relations (Kracke 1981:117). Lévi-Strauss points out the association honey = menstrual blood in American mythology (1973), but Kracke's data (1981:121–22) and mine show that honey is equally associated with sperm.

Chapter 6

1. *Pihã* may be analyzed as *pi-hã*, "that which is together [with X]."
2. Although the expression *"he pihã"* ("my companion") can be used to

refer to the spouse irrespective of sex, men rarely use it. Women are never designated teknonymically as the *pihã* of their husbands.

3. A son, however, never calls his genitor the "partner of [mother's name]"; he always uses the vocative *papãy* and the term of reference *he ro,* or names him by the form "father of X." He can refer to his mother's husband (not his F) by the first term, even if this man is ego's FB. But even here the tendency is to use kin terms as vocatives, not personal names. One's father and mother are the people least often designated by personal names.

4. *Heray he re,* a term also applied to the firstborn.

5. With the arrival of the "new" Araweté in 1987, one of the girls of the village had her name changed, since she carried the childhood name of one of the newcomers, in whose memory it had been chosen (and whom everyone thought had died long ago). Some people gave me the usual explanation, that the homonym was painful to the ears of the adult woman; others told me that the child would not grow if she kept that name (as if two people could not occupy the same "onomastic space" at the same time).

6. If a child, while growing up, reminds others of a deceased person, the latter is not necessarily his eponym. Resemblances with the dead, frequently pointed out, serve as a basis for joking nicknames (often the teknonym of the child's deceased look-alike), but these have nothing to do with his or her true name and eponym.

7. The relationship between personal names and terms from the enemy or divine series is always recognized. The situation is different for the rest of the classes. When I tried to confirm that a name really was the same as, shall we say, a tree, they told me, "No, it is different." That is, it was a *personal* name, conferred in memory of a deceased; the tree was irrelevant. Nevertheless, jokes were frequently made that designated an animal or object by the teknonym of the adult who carried the "homonymic" childhood name. An *aray* rattle was called "*Iriwɨpay-ro,*" since Aray was the childhood name of this man; the wind was sometimes called "grandson of Madïpay-hi," since the childhood name of this woman was Iwito-iari, "Grandmother Wind" (the name of a divinity). No restriction is imposed on the use of one's own "name" when it designates an object; Iriwipay-ro used the word "*aray*" like everybody else. The restriction applies to uttering the name, not the word. That one's own name can be stated in cited discourse suggests that the Araweté "problem" is to avoid the coincidence between the subject in the utterance and the subject who does the uttering.

8. Here I am referring to tendencies, since there are firstborns with names given according to the other criteria, and vice versa (as is indicated by the quantitative distribution). I did not undertake a detailed statistical study of the matter. Nor did it ever occur to me to discuss these tendencies with the Araweté, who never talked about them as rules.

9. The use of mythical personages who are *tema ipi* ("origin of the creeping vines," cf. chap. 3, sect. 1), such as Mɨrɨakã and Moikato, is the only instance when the expression *pɨr̲owĩ'hã ne* could be translated as "after an

ancestor," and the only one that can mean that one of these personages is being evoked, not a deceased eponym. Such names are frequently used, but they are few in number, and it is not always clear whether they concern a mythical ancestor, an enemy, or a being who became a divinity.

10. Although about 50 percent of childhood names are given after enemies or gods, only about 10 percent of adult teknonyms have roots that were chosen according to these criteria.

11. Thus Lévi-Strauss (1977b: 73) contrasted systems in which names and identities come from within and systems "of traditional headhunters," in which their fundamental motive is the capture of souls and names from outside society.

12. The classic explanation by Métraux of the change of name after the execution—a protection against revenge by the dead—is in my opinion precarious. The question was less a change of name than an accumulation of names; and these were taken to inspire fear (Staden 1928: 146), not out of fear.

13. Such an inversion is consistent with another: Yanomami spiritual exocannibalism is correlated with a funerary osteophagy. Those who consume the ashes of the dead assert their right to exercise vengeance (Albert 1985). Among the Tupinamba, those who ate the war prisoner out of revenge did so to assert themselves as potential objects of revenge by the enemy group (Carneiro da Cunha & Viveiros de Castro 1985).

14. *Anĩ* is clearly a cognate of the Tupinamba *anama,* "relative," but *tiwã* is more difficult to analyze. Although it recalls the Tupinamba complex of the brother-in-law/enemy (*tovaja*), it is more likely a cognate of the form *atuasaba* (*tuasap, atour-assap*) and the Guarani *tyvasa,* which have been translated as "ally," "partner," or "compadre." Léry (1990 [1578]: 184–85) states that it is a vocative used between a certain kind of formal friends linked by relations of mutuality (with belongings in common), but between whom matrimonial exchange is prohibited. Evreux (1929 [1615]) speaks of *tuasap* as a *guest;* this was what the Tupinamba called the resident French interpreters who enjoyed sexual access to their hosts' daughters or sisters. Among the Apapokuva, *tyvasa* are compadres linked by name-giving (Nimuendaju 1978: 109). Finally, *tiwã* resembles the Kamayura term for "cross-cousin": *yatuhap* (Oberg 1953: 112) or *yatiwahap* (Bastos 1992). Lévi-Strauss (1943) has pointed out the connection between the complex of ritual affinity and such "*tiwã*" positions.

15. One of the innumerable joking forms for speaking about any female cross-cousin or *tiwã* is to designate her parents by the kinship term that links them to her, followed by the *expression đo pi rĩ ĩ,* "whom I haven't yet eaten [but am going to]." Among the Kayabi, the standard term for cross-cousins of both sexes has been translated as "thing-eat-(future)-(perfective)" (Weiss 1985: 116).

16. Once while I was discussing a marriage between classificatory siblings, I asked someone if this was not incorrect. The interlocutor, who had an indi-

rect interest in the affair, argued with scholastic shrewdness that the couple was in an "ex-sibling" relation: everybody knows that siblings do not marry, ergo they were not siblings. An unassailable syllogism . . .

17. This is exactly like the Parintintin case, where, although oblique unions are not permitted, bilateral symmetrical exchange is conceived of as a short cycle, of the type associated by Lévi-Strauss with patrilateral and avuncular marriages: in ceding a sister to someone else, a man acquires a right over her children as spouses for his own children (Kracke 1984a: 113, 119, 124).

The Araweté matrimonial ideology has clear parallels with the Guianese social landscape. Their emphasis on the B/Z bond to the detriment of that between WB and ZH (which makes the Araweté conform more to Yalman's [1962, 1967] and Rivière's [1969] view than to that of Dumont [1983] and Kaplan [1975], but cf. Dumont 1983: 153), seems to me to be derived from the symbolic unmarkedness of affinity in favor of the system of sexual friendship, and is consistent with the uxorilocal bias of the Araweté.

18. There are three different types of "Hawaiianization" of Dravidian terminologies in Lowland South America. In some cases, this neutralization affects the *entire* terminology, but it is not thereby anything more than a contextual encompassment of distinctions internal to the cognatic field, as in the Kalapalo case (Basso 1970). In other cases (such as the Pemon and Waiwai: Rivière 1984: 67–69), such neutralization seems to have the purpose of resolving contradictions in the system of attitudes; the Hawaiian equations are unambiguated by reference to the bifurcation of G+1, and the ideal of marriages that are close and specified as "cross" relations is maintained. Finally, in other cases (Tapirapé, some Jivaro, Kulina, Upper Xingu—see Shapiro 1968, Taylor 1990, Pollock, 1985, Viveiros de Castro 1977), neutralization may or may not accompany a "matrimonial Hawaiianization," that is, a *positive* concept of genealogical distance as a condition of marriageability.

19. The suffix *hete*, "true," attached to a term can denote, for example, actual siblingship, but also close classificatory siblingship (FBS versus FFBSS or the son of father's *apĩhi-pihã*), or it can emphasize that a person so designated behaves in a manner compatible with his kinship position. The suffix *-pe*, meaning "ex-," can be employed to stigmatize a bad relative. Also, it is always possible to specify a genealogical relation covered by the category term through descriptive circumlocutions: "made by a *to dɨ̄*," "coming from the belly of a *hi amɨ̄*," etc.

20. To the 45 houses in the village in 1982, there corresponded 23 gardens, 13 of them opened by more than one conjugal family. Of these 13, 8 involved 11 affinal relations of the type WF+WM/DH. Of these 11 relationships, 6 were conceived as being based on the WM/DH relation (in which cases the WMH, although an owner of the garden, was not a WF), and 2 on the WF/DH relation. The associations based on other criteria occurred in 6 gardens: 6 F+M/S relations, of which only 1 was conceived as being based on the F/S tie; 4 on the M/S tie (where MH was not the F); and 1 on the double tie F+M/S. Only 2 agricultural associations were based on B/B ties, and 1 on the MB/ZS

tie. The situation thus attests to the tendency towards "agricultural uxorilocality," confirmed in 11 cases, against 6 where the married sons remained working in the garden of their fathers (or mothers); and of these 6, 4 involved virilocalized wives who were orphans without mothers. Of the 10 remaining gardens, all were adjacent to others (collective or conjugal ones); this proximity was based on ties of siblingship or horizontal affinity and only in 2 cases on relations of vertical affinity (WM/DH). See above (sect. 3), on the relation between types of residential sections and types of connections among gardens.

21. Compare this to the Parintintin term for incest: *oji'u*, "to eat oneself" (Kracke 1984a: 123, note 4), which is also how the Maku define it (Silverwood-Cope 1980: 152).

22. Note that the type of sharing called by the same name, *oyo pepi*, results in women going to the house of their *apĩno* for a few days. In such cases, it is the men, in effect, who "exchange" wives, but in the case of a definitive exchange, it is the men who will change their residence, ideally speaking (given uxorilocality).

23. ". . . a new marriage renews all marriages concluded at other times, and at different points in the social structure, so that each connexion rests upon all the others and gives them, on its establishment, a recrudescence of activity" (Lévi-Strauss 1969a: 65).

24. Thus, for example, the terminological relations among three men, as one of the (#1) justified it, was as follows:

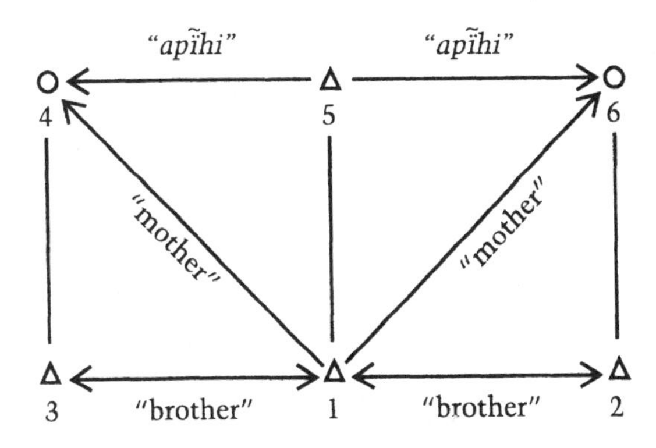

This would explain the presence of #2 (physically handicapped and unmarried) in the section headed by #1. In turn, #3 is at the same time a "brother" to #1 and a "son" to the latter's wife. Note that #2 and #3 do *not* call each other "brother." The terminology of kinship and friendship is not transitive.

25. *Translator's note:* see Lévi-Strauss 1969a [1949]:497, where the original French "vivre entre soi" was misleadingly translated as "[to] keep to oneself," giving the phrase an individualistic connotation.

CHAPTER 7

1. *Ta'i*, the male term for "son," is also the generic form for children, offspring of animals, buds of plants; *-re* is one of the marks of the nominal preterit that are affixed to all terms for parts of the body thought of "in themselves" or separated from the body.

2. *Hopï* is a spatiotemporal marker with a linear-durative aspect: *pe ropï*, "along the path, walking"; *ɨwahẽ nopï we*, "from the moment of arrival, upon arriving [and for a while afterwards]."

3. The coexistence of patrilateral notions of conception with the bilateral recognition of a community of abstinence (I prefer to not speak here of "substance") can be found among other Amazonian groups—Yawalapíti and Suya, for example (Viveiros de Castro 1977:206; Seeger 1981:150)—and perhaps even among the hyperpatrilateral Tupinamba (Monteiro 1949 [1610]:413).

4. The mixture of human seed with that of spirits, as indicated earlier, causes the mother to miscarry and die. Among the Tapirapé, the excessive mixture of seeds leads to infanticide (Wagley 1977:134); among the Kamayurá, to twinship, which also entails the death of the children (Bastos 1978:35). The Araweté, who do not accept multiple births either, attribute them to the fact that the mother, as an adolescent, had eaten too many eggs of tortoise, turtle, and alligator. The Tenetehara attribute twinship to unnatural coitus with the "evil forest demon, Marana ýwa" (Wagley & Galvão 1949:70). The notion of *oyo pitiwã*, "to work cooperatively" in a sexual sense, is also found among the Aché, where *japetyva* refers to the secondary husband, the marginal contributor to the child's substance (P. Clastres 1972:22–23).

5. The practice of raising a spouse is mentioned for the Tenetehara (Wagley & Galvão 1949:78, 90), the Tapirapé (Wagley 1977:157), and the Wayãpi (Grenand 1982:117), but only in the last case is it associated with marriage to FZ or MB. Among the Tupinamba, where the "raising" of wives was a privilege of powerful men (Soares de Souza 1971 [1587]:305), the role of the cutter of the navel cord fell to the F in the case of sons, and to the MB in the case of daughters, within the context of ZD marriage (Fernandes 1963 [1949]:174–76, 218–19). The marital right of the cutter of the navel cord is found in an inverse form among the Aché: both the "one who lifted up" (*upiaregi*) the child and the "one who cut the navel cord" (*jware*) are types of godfathers, sexually forbidden to their *chave*, whom they must nevertheless feed (P. Clastres 1972:45–47). The intervention of the Parintintin MB occurs on the occasion of naming the child, when he secures his right over the child, but on behalf of one of his children (Kracke 1984a:112–13).

6. This does not mean that right after ingesting the *iwirara'i* tea, the parents start eating this animal; it is forbidden until the navel cord of the child dries up. The Asuriní and the Kaapor also do not eat red-footed tortoise, *Geochelone carbonaria*, during the couvade; the Guajá prohibit this species and another, the yellow-footed tortoise, *G. denticulata*; the Tembé do not prohibit either one; and the Kaapor prescribe the meat of *G. denticulata* as the only edible meat for menstruating women, parents of newborns, and pubes-

cent girls (Balée 1985 and personal communication, 1989). The Araweté, who proscribe the *yaacï katɨ* (*G. carbonaria*), do not appear to prescribe the consumption of the other species; however, since parents in seclusion usually eat tortoises they have in stock, and since they must follow numerous other alimentary prohibitions, the tendency would be towards the preferential consumption of *yaacï ete'ï* (*G. denticulata*). There appears to be a Tupi-Guarani system of "tortoise transformations" at work, which should be further explored. I thank W. Balée for having called my attention to this point.

7. This affinity between a child and the burnt can also be found in cases of convulsions caused by the Master of the Mumbaca Palm (see chap. 3, sect. 3). Four children who were thus afflicted fell into the fire and died of burns.

8. The dangerous capacity of the fathers of newborns to attract snakes, however, does form part of a system. Among the Kaapor, if a pregnant woman sees someone bitten by a snake, "she loses her hair, her flesh also falls away, and she dies" (Huxley 1956:206). The husband of a pregnant woman, in the Wayãpi case, may not kill snakes, otherwise the fetus "loses its skin" and dies; in turn, the seclusion of the parturient is due to fear of *moyo*, the anaconda Master of Water, who abhors the smell of blood and kidnaps the child's soul (Campbell 1982:273–74; 1989:129, 135). Among the Ñandeva and the Kayová, *odjepotá*, transformation into an animal (the punishment for those who venture out into the forest during the couvade and menstruation), is mainly attributed to *karuguá*, the Rainbow, which, among the Araweté, Wayãpi, and Aché, is a snake with great olfactory sensitivity. Then again, among the Munduruсu, a woman who bathes during her first menstruation or shortly after childbirth will have her soul stolen by a pit viper (probably *Bothrops*, possibly *Lachesis* [Murphy 1958:26]).

Two themes are interwoven here: the relationship between sexuality and odor (of blood and sex), which attract snakes, and the theme of skin loss, which brings to mind *a contrario* the capacity for skin renewal that snakes have (the classic Amerindian symbol of immortality). The falling away of the fetus' skin, or of the hair and flesh of a pregnant woman, is a deadly foreshadowing of the process of the celestial resurrection of the dead through a change of skin—a theme encountered among the Wayãpi and Kaapor. Among the Tapirapé, the theme is inverted and lacks the snakes: it is only after the "postnatal skin" falls away (the layer adhering to the annatto with which the neonate is coated) that the parents leave the couvade (Wagley 1977:140).

Among the Aché, the capacity to attract wild animals marks the *bayja* state of the father of a newborn; he takes advantage of this to go out to the forest to hunt. But he also attracts jaguars as well as the Rainbow snake, who falls into a cannibalistic rage. Childbirth and menstruation lead to *bayja* (P. Clastres 1972:26–28, 37–38, 179).

For the Araweté, there is no direct relationship between menstruation and snakes. But the Master of Water, who elsewhere is a snake (anaconda), represents a threat to menstruating women and babies. The Rainbow snake, in turn, detests the smell of sex, attacking shamans who venture into the sky bearing this blemish. Two other ideas appear to be linked to this complex: if someone points his finger at the rainbow, his mother will die; also, the rainbow becomes "furious" when there are pregnant women in the village. Finally, one more transformation is noteworthy: shamans who have been bitten by a bushmaster are attributed with the power, not at all appreciated, to cause torrential rains every time a *peyo* is held. Thus, it is just as much aquatic snakes (anacondas) as terrestrial and venomous ones (bushmasters, pit vipers) that connect water, sex, blood, and odor. Also, compare the Araweté term *peye,* shaman, with its cognate among the Aché, who have no shamans: for the latter, *paje* are men who are immune to snake venom (P. Clastres 1972:268).

9. The key word of this "milk nostalgia" is *mo-a̱'o.* It can be glossed as "to become estranged from oneself because of the absence of something desired."

10. Howard (personal communication 1990) was also told by the Waiwai that they practice this technique.

11. The practice of handing over young girls to elders in this manner does not reflect any gerontocratic privilege, but is, rather, a form of pairing people who are before and beyond their full reproductive capacity. The elderly and the handicapped thus form conjugal units with prepubescent girls and remain integrated into the ideal system where each adult must live with a spouse in a conjugal house. Reference to "raising" the spouse is also made of the less frequent unions between young men and elderly women.

12. The Suya and Kayapó, who use male lip plugs, are also the only peoples in the region among whom the stretching of the labia of the vulva has been recorded (Seeger 1981:83; Lea 1986:238), but there it does not seem to have the same symbolic weight as among the Araweté. At any rate, considering the extreme modesty of Araweté women in exposing the labia—the equivalent of exposing the glans, also a cause of great shame—it might be possible to see in the complex of labia majora/girdle a device of emphasis and control over female sexuality, like its Kayapó masculine analogue, the penis sheath (see Turner 1969, 1980).

13. I observed that such independence of husband and wife was contradicted several times. During the influenza epidemic of 1982, many people, whose spouses were fevered, had their own heads shaven (in order to cool down their bodies). This may suggest the widespread idea that spouses, after a long period of living together, end up creating bonds of substance (Da Matta 1982:56).

14. A probable cognate of *ha'iwã* is the Aché concept of *baivwã,* a mortal illness caused by the direct handling of a skeleton or by the consumption of coatimundi flesh (a funereal animal), undiluted honey, or pure human flesh prepared and served without vegetable foods (P. Clastres 1972:163, 300, 328). Another cognate may be the Mbyá *ã'yvõ,* which Cadogan (1959:66) translates as "to foretell misfortune," and analyzes as "to wound [the soul] with an arrow."

15. Two days before I left Ipixuna in 1983, Arado-hi succumbed to a malaria pre-coma. "Why?" "She just wanted to leave"; "She wanted to be the

wife of a *Maï*"; "She wanted to make us nostalgic"; "Someone has been stirring up the bones of Awara-hi, spreading *me'e rahi* and *hahi we.*" Finally someone declared he had seen fire in the sky, so everyone concluded that "*iwã na'iwã hã,*" the sky had stricken Arado-hi (who escaped by a miracle, and a little bit of quinine with adrenaline).

16. It should be noted that a paradigm seems to be operating: *ha'iwã,* disease; *ho'irã,* sadness; *ha'irã,* desire; to which *ho'imã,* hunger, could be added. I will not risk tracing their etymologies beyond pointing out that *ho'irã* and *ha'irã* appear to contain the root of the verb for "becoming enraged," *mo'irã* (the nominal form *ñarã* can be derived from the reflexive form). The verb that describes the state of angry covetousness or envy, with a clear sexual connotation, belongs to this family: *oyi mirã.* The translation of *ñarã* as "anger" is imperfect, since *ñarã* also refers to the positive impetus to incorporate something. Two different case markings clarify this: one may be *ñarã* with someone (*ñarã X-rehe*) or *ñarã* because of, as a function of, someone (*ñarã X-re*). A man expresses his sexual desire by saying he is *ñarã namã ne,* "angry because of a vagina." The presence of the concept of an aggressive impulse in the word "sadness," *ho'irã,* suggests the idea that sadness is an active passion, not completely distinct from rancor. The similar verb *hero-irã (hero-* being a causative-comitative), which signifies "to scorn," "to abandon" (a wife, an offer), signifies the rancor provoked by the object of scorn.

17. The Aché posthomicide rite involves coating the killer with the white down of vultures to make him lightweight, but the concern here is not the loss of the soul, but the invasion of the killer's body by the cannibal soul of the victim (P. Clastres 1972:259).

18. It is worthwhile to contrast this "burial under grills" with the well-known Tupinamba burials in "urns," i.e., pots for beer. We can also see in this funerary form a transformation of the Gê theme of the *four-de-terre* earth oven (a cooking pit where heated stones are placed beneath and atop the food and covered with earth and leaves), where Lévi-Strauss (1981:612–17) elaborates in the context of a Tupi/Gê opposition: against the exo-cannibalism and the ceramics of the Tupi are contrasted the Gê earth oven with its funerary symbolism and their myths of MB/ZS solidarity. Here, elaborating on a previous deduction (1969b:143), Lévi-Strauss shows how the Gê and the Tupi classify culinary values differently: for the former, the rotten and the raw connote nature, in opposition to the culturally cooked; for the latter, only the rotten belongs to nature, while the cooked *and* the raw signify culture. The system is confirmed in the first instance among the Araweté, given that the "grill of the *Ãñĩ*"—roasted, a more "natural" mode of preparing meat—is associated with the rotten (the natural transformation of the raw), while the "eaters of the raw" are in fact eaters of the boiled (the cultural transformation of the raw). Undoubtedly, relative to the *Ãñĩ,* the *Maï* are "culture" in opposition to "nature."

19. The idea that rain, passing between the poles of the rack, accelerated the decomposition of the body suggests that this method of burial is a com-

promise between the system of exposing the corpse on wooden racks, found among the Siriono (Holmberg 1969:232), and the system of accelerating the process of rotting through irrigation, of the Bororo type.

20. In contrast to the majority of other Tupi-Guarani, the Araweté never buried their dead inside the house, but always in the forest, even when the village was definitively abandoned (the exception being the death of children). On the other hand, I believe that they are the only ones who name a village after someone who died there.

21. The semantic domain of Araweté eschatology makes heavy use of nominal markers of time: *-pe* or *-we,* for the past, and *-rĩ* (*-nĩ*), for the future. All Tupi-Guarani languages exhibit this conceptual form of construction, which underscores the difference between the pure state, in itself or in the present, of the lexemic concept, and its temporal realization, that is, the non-present. The past suffixes frequently indicate states of separation (actual or logical: terms for parts of the body, for example, are affixed with these markers when thought of as separate from their whole); the future suffix indicates intentionality and potentiality.

22. This does not signify any insubstantiality or "symbolism" of these spiritual meals. When the Araweté say that something is eaten *ɨpeye hã iwe,* "by shamanic means," they are expressing the idea that the *ĩ* of things are converted into essences: it is a sacramental operation, not a trope.

23. As Vernant (1983:308–9) states, "A double is not at all the same thing as an image. It is not a 'natural' object, but nor is it simply a product of the mind. It is not an imitation of a real object or an illusion of the mind or a creation of thought. The double is something separate from the person who sees it, something whose peculiar character sets it in opposition, even in appearance, to familiar objects in life's ordinary setting. It exists on two contrasting planes at the same time: at the very moment that it shows itself to be present it also reveals itself to be not of this world and as belonging to some inaccessible, other, sphere."

24. The theme of exposing the forehead is recurrent. The *Ãñĩ* have such a characteristic, as do the Kayapó and killers of enemies (whose bangs fall out). It is ugly to expose the forehead: whites, enemies, and the god *Aranãmĩ* are called "big face" (see Cardim's reference to the Tupinamba's hairstyle à la Saint Thomas [1906 (1584):423]).

25. Thus, a series of animals are linked to the specters of the dead: coatimundis, opossums, and night monkeys. The association of coatimundis with the dead is found among the Aché, who say they are the ones responsible for leading the *ove* soul to the sky, being themselves *ove* (P. Clastres 1972:163). Meliá et al. (1973:91) attribute this function to the anteater. For the Suruí, the coatimundi is a funereal animal (Laraia, personal communication, 1984). The "coatimundi tooth" is a magical instrument of the Akuáwa shaman and is endowed with *karowara* power (Andrade 1984). Earlier (chap. 3, note 45), the role of the kinkajou among the Kaapor was mentioned. Huxley (1956: 227ff.) refers to myths in which this animal appears linked to moonlight and the eating of flowers; the Araweté also say that night monkeys "eat flowers"

(actually they feed on flower nectar, among other things). The Kaapor link the kinkajou to jaguars of the underworld, and oppose jaguars to opossums (according to the mythological pair *Mair*'s Son/Opposum's Son—*Mair* being the Master of Jaguars). The Wayãpi associate the kinkajou and the sloth with the dead and the underworld. The Aché take jaguars to be cannibal incarnations of the dead.

This system appears to be organized around two central oppositions: raw versus rotten and jaguar versus opossum. The latter animal has several combinatory variants: the coatimundi, the kinkajou, the night monkey, and the two edentates, the anteater and the sloth. The terrestrial specter of the Araweté belongs to the world of opossums, coatimundis, etc. We can thus expect the jaguar-function to belong to the sky—to the cannibalism of the *Maï*—if the reader will permit such a "transcendental deduction."

The Araweté eat coatimundis, but not kinkajous, opossums, or night monkeys.

26. With this in mind, I believe that the idea of the definitive abandonment of a village after any death should be qualified. None of the villages bear names of children, while the dead whose names identify villages are always remembered by the group, even when they had not been "owners of the village," shamans, or killers; many are women. See Gallois (1984) on the Wayãpi, who move from a village whenever several people died there, or when a "prominent individual" passes away.

27. The notion of "the living," "alive," is expressed by the word *hekawe* (cf. Tupinamba *ikobe*), the participial form of the verb "to exist." The living are "those that exist," those who are present. The celestial souls belong to this category, the terrestrial specters do not.

28. Besides deer, tapirs, howler monkeys, trairão fish, and poisonous creatures (see chap. 5, sect. 3), other animals have *ha'o we* that can be dangerous in certain contexts. The spirit of the trumpeter bird takes revenge on anyone who does not eat the bird roasted, causing *ha'iwã*; the word "egg" (*hopïnã*) should not be pronounced near the flesh of coatimundi or fish with sharp teeth, or else these animals will bite one's belly; the euphemism "thing" (*apa*) should be used instead. This pertains to the complex of verbal taboos, which apply to maize beer, the Master of Water, *Iaracĩ*, tapir and deer, and certain songs.

29. Briefly, I will mention the Aché *ian-ve* and *o-ve*, principles liberated after death; the Wayãpi *iã*, the soul of a living person, which bifurcates into *te-an-wer* and *t-ai-we* in death; *mo-au*, "to dream," in the same language; the Parintintin concept of *ra'uva* and the verbal form *-ra'uv*, which refer to actions in dreams and to the specter of the dead, in contrast to the "shadow," *'ang*; in Tenetehara, the verbal suffix *-'u* for "dreaming" or "conjecturing," the noun *me'e ra'u* for "something ominous," and *t-a'u-wer* for "phantasm," and again, *ang*, for "soul-shadow"; in Akuáwa, *i-unga* and *o-wera*, soul of the living and of the dead; the Tapirapé *i-ynga* and *in-vuera* for "soul" and "soul of the dead"; in Guarani, the concept of *juru t-au-gue*, "ghostly mouth," the telluric part of the soul; and the Mbyá verb *ra'u*, "to dream." See: P. Clastres

1972: 303; Cadogan 1962: 60, 62, 69; 1978: 42–4; Gallois 1984; Campbell 1982: 270–72; 1989: 127; Grenand 1982: 222; Kracke 1983; Boudin 1978; Andrade 1984; Wagley 1977: 168, 181; Baldus 1970: 351–52; Dooley 1982: 310.

30. Note the significant ambiguity of the expression *bïde rĩ*, used for paternal semen and the celestial soul: semen is to the living what the living are to the soul. The living are thus potential divinities. This supports the idea that humans are to the gods as children are to adults (see chap. 3, sect. 1), and this is why only death fully actualizes the potential contained in *bïde*.

31. I would speculate that the localization of the *ĩ* in the trachea (where the larynx is inserted into the chest) is linked to two notions: this is an open site, a sort of fontanel that never closes, and it might have something to do with the melodious quality of souls.

32. This place evokes the *ka'aorowapy*, "the surface of the trees of the jungle," the secondary paradise of the Guarani of Amambái (Cadogan 1962: 70).

33. The name of the bath where the skin is changed is derived from *pïɨda*, to peel. This is a classic theme of South American mythology. The association of the *Maï̲* with stone and the change of skin belongs to the theme of immortality and the briefness of life (Lévi-Strauss 1969b: 149–63). The rejuvenating bath in effervescent water is found in a Kayabi myth (Grünberg n.d. [1970]:186–87). Among the Tapirapé, it is a pot of truly boiling water that makes the mythical twins grow (Wagley 1977: 179–80). The bath in *Mair's* "magic water" confers immortality through a change of skin in a Kaapor myth (Huxley 1956: 200–201), where another Araweté motif is found: the "lengthening" of the dead, an operation that *Mair* makes them undergo. The Araweté *ha̲'o we*, upon leaving the body, is as small as a rat; the Master of the Vultures "stretches" it (*ipiha*). The gods are much taller than humans; the magic bath makes them grow—recall that "we are children." Among the Wayãpi, we have a modernization of the theme of boiling without fire: upon arriving in the sky, the dead "are dirty and rotten, but there they take a bath with soap and become just like people" (Gallois 1985: 183, citing an Indian).

34. "If, after burying the deceased, they hear some distant peals of thunder, they say it is some phantoms who feed upon dead bodies and who thus have gathered to eat this one" (Montoya 1951: 274). Also see the Aché *pichua*, meteorological signs of the souls of the dead (P. Clastres 1972: 231).

35. The shamanic act of bringing the deceased is described as *mo-pirã* (*yɨpe iwi ɨhe*), "to cause to step (again on earth)." This can be compared with the Guarani *mo-pyrõ*, the incarnation of a divine word-soul in a child (Cadogan 1950: 244).

Chapter 8

1. This corrects what was said in the Brazilian edition (Viveiros de Castro 1986: 519), that the dead-turned-divinities eat the souls who have just arrived. Everyone with whom I took up the question again in 1988 was insistent that the celestial *ha̲'o we* are not cannibals. It is necessary to distinguish between the dead who exist as the dead (those who appear in songs) and those

who blend into that undifferentiated mass of the divine population and who are not exactly *ha'o we,* since they no longer exist in the group memory. The celestial dead who *interest* the living are the recent dead—hence, the dead are not cannibals.

2. I know very little about Araweté dreams. "To dream" is *ɨče yu, ɨče kɨyaha yu, ɨče ra̲'o yu: ɨče* is the verb for "to sleep," *-yu* is the suffix for "eternal" or "transcendent" (see chap. 3, sect. 2), *kɨyaha* is the state of "translucence" (to be discussed later in this section,) and *ra̲'o* is the verb aspect that indicates immateriality or unrealized potentiality, and appears to contain the root *-a̲'o* (see chap. 7, sect. 3).

3. See Wagley (1977: 191–92, 198–210) on identical collective sessions of intoxication intended to induce dreams in Tapirapé shamanic candidates, and on how shamans are resuscitated after being knocked down by Thunder: "We die and tobacco brings back life. Without tobacco Thunder would kill us" (1977: 208). The first thing the *Ma̲ï* ask for from the shaman is a puff from his cigar.

4. This does not mean that the *Ma̲ï* do not reveal themselves as real beings, *hiro,* during shamanic sessions. But for beginners, the gods are always *hiro,* that is, completely *exterior.*

5. Cigar butts should never be thrown away, or else one will become lost in the forest. See the same belief among the Shipaya (Nimuendaju 1981: 12). Perhaps this implies that tobacco is something that guides us to divinity.

6. Even though women are the ones who weave the rattle's inner structure, they must not shake it once it is completed; it rouses the gods, who might kill the imprudent woman.

7. The bow/rattle opposition is pertinent. The bow is fabricated entirely by men and presupposes the sexual disjunction within the couple: during the carving and the bending of the piece, sex is interdicted, lest the vagina break the weapon literally and metonymically. The rattle requires the technical collaboration of the couple, but subsequent sexual activity is a metaphorical breaking of the *aray:* what is broken is communication with the gods.

The bow is obtained through the separation of a piece of wood from a massive matrix, the trunk of a *Tabebuia* tree, felled by the man; the rattle is produced through the composition of a dispersed matrix (itiriti cane), usually collected by women. The bow is the support (*hɨpã*) of the arrows, which are designated by the double synecdoche *kano pepa,* "harpy eagle feathers," applied even to those using curassow feathers. The rattle is the support of macaw feathers: its name is probably derived from *arã,* "macaw." The harpy eagle is a masculine bird; killed or captured, it is owned by men, and its feathers are used only in the fabrication of arrows; women who eat harpy eagle will cease to menstruate. Tame macaws, the source of the feathers for rattles, are always female property, and their feathers serve as adornments for both sexes. Also, whereas macaws are the most striking symbol of the village, a feminine world, harpy eagles are symbols of the celestial and masculine world of the gods.

8. Concerning the ethnographic singularity of the Araweté *aray,* I have re-

cently run across information on a very similar object belonging to another Tupi-Guarani group. Such an object can be seen in a watercolor of Hercule Florence (an artist accompanying the Expedição Langsdorff of 1821–1829), which shows a "Village of the Apiaká," a Central Tupi-Guarani tribe living on the Rio Arinos, Mato Grosso. One of the men depicted in the watercolor is carrying in his hand something that Nimuendaju (1948c:314) characterizes as "a kind of scepter made of six macaw tail feathers with their bases covered with down." Since "scepters" are objects that are not especially common among the Tupi-Guarani, and since no other information corroborates such an interpretation, I would suggest, given the notable resemblances between the two, that this object is a shaman's rattle of the same type as the *aray* (see Expedição Langsdorff 1988:76–79).

9. I attended several killings of the *ha̲'o we* of spiders and stingrays, accomplished without shamanic songs, and the capture and killing of four *Ãñĩ* that penetrated the village one night. The *Ãñĩ* sang through the shaman's mouth (who alternated this song with another that brought the *Ma̲ï*) about how they had run all night long through the forest and had killed three anteaters. A neighbor shot the *Ãñĩ* as they took refuge in a clump of sisal.

10. This is not always easy to distinguish. Thus, for example, the *opiwani* movement, the forceful stamping of the shaman's right foot while he dances bent over and huffing, is a sign of the gods' presence. One time when a shaman brought a deceased daughter, marked by a resounding *opiwani*, someone commented that "Iwane is making her father stamp his foot forcefully." The verb prefix that was employed suggested that the action was caused through participating in it, not that Iwane had "possessed" her father. The notion of possession is foreign to Araweté thought; souls may exit but they do not enter other people's bodies.

11. There were some who disagreed with this interpretation, suggesting instead that the girl was addressing not the soul of her FB, but the man himself, sleeping in a nearby house. Likewise, at least one person speculated that the girl who sang was not Kãñĩpaye, but a classificatory daughter of the shaman who had died more recently. "Only Kãñĩpaye-ro and his wife know who it was." This does not mean that the main enunciator cannot be named.

12. Notably, none of the dead named in the song are designated as "deceased" or as "X-*ra̲'o we*," but as existing in the present. The only one who is "deceased" is the shaman.

13. Or this may refer to the shininess of the harpy eagle feathers. One of the shamanic names of this bird is *ia'i ɨwã nehã*, "that which resides next to the face (leaves) of the Brazil-nut tree," an expression that also serves as a synecdoche for "arrows" and alludes to warfare.

14. *Imone* songs may have a content that is entirely foreign (in superficial terms) to the problematic of the operation. Songs for alimentary *peyo* always bring the divinities associated with the relevant food. An *imone* is undertaken at the shaman's initiative, not the patient's.

15. It may be objected that *peyo* rituals for food, involving the arrival of specific gods, exhibit an external constraint. This may be so, but it applies to

the gods, not to the dead who occasionally descend with them. Besides, several times *peyo* were not performed because no shaman managed to become inspired on the preceding night: "The gods didn't come." At any rate, I do not know the exact relationship between dreams and songs; what is certain is that the shaman does not dream the song; rather, he sings the dream, that is, interprets it, in both senses of the term. Also, I know that shamans can sometimes sing without having dreamed, by inducing visions and speech through the massive ingestion of tobacco.

16. The importance of the conjugal unit in shamanism is found among other Tupi-Guarani, such as the Tapirapé (Wagley 1977:195, 201, 203, 208) and Guarani (Nimuendaju 1978:51, 105). There is also a clear relationship between shamanism and leadership of an extended family among these peoples. The association of shamanism and conjugality also appears among the Bororo (Crocker 1985:210).

17. This term refers only to the Araweté slayer. Cognates with the same signification are found in Aché (*brupiare*) and in Parakanã (*moropiarera*) (P. Clastres 1972:248; C. Fausto, personal communication, 1989). In the *Língua Geral, marupiara* designates a good hunter who does not miss his mark. This term is complex; it should be compared to the form *rupia* given by Montoya (1876 [1640], glossed as "adversary (contrary), enemy, harmful thing," and nominalized as *rupiara*. See also Boudin 1978, Vol. 2.

18. Women, who do not sing while they dance, may freely repeat war songs, doing so in the same falsetto register they use when repeating *Maï marakã*. Dance songs do not make use of vibratto; they play with the duration of syllables and a system of cuts or intervals that "break" the words in half, and use an almost hypnotic repetition.

19. These include (1) *Ačiči reiyi pe* ("Howler Monkey Entrails"): associated with the Monstrous Howler Monkey, it cannot be sung during the phase when maize is ripening (when, besides, no *pɨrahẽ* is performed, since everyone is in the forest), or else it will not grow; (2) *Ñã nemĩ-nã nĩ* ("Future Victim of a Jaguar"): this is the song of jaguar killers; it also prejudices maize while it is sprouting, and cannot be sung by boys; (3) *Yato wĩ* ("Yato's People"): a group of enemies who dispersed; it has deleterious effects on maize; and (4) the "Centipede," "Monstrous Spider Monkey," and "Gigantic Tortoise" songs, and those of the mythical enemies Itakaɗï, Ta'akati, Maɗapi: all these are lethal, *ha'iwã hã*, and singing them is quasi-suicidal. I never heard any of them.

Also, the *original* enunciation of a song commemorating the death of an enemy may not be accompanied by prepubescent boys, much less by women.

20. Notice that there is an incongruence: the Parakanã wear very short hair, hence the image of "long hair" is somewhat improper. This suggests that the song must have appropriated some traditional figure of speech, probably from some song referring to the *Towaho*, a tribe described as "long-haired people."

21. Compare this with the cannibalism of the Yanomami killer, who vomits his victim's fat and hair, a sign that he has eaten his soul; also com-

pare how the Yanomami killer is possessed by his victim's "vital principle," which torments him and drives him crazy, in a manner analogous to the "arrival" of the *awĩ na̲'o we* in the Araweté case (Lizot 1985:5, 176).

22. The Maku also think of the young as "green" and "raw" (as opposed to those who are older, "mature," as we also say) (Silverwood-Cope 1980:140). The Shipaya offer an attenuated and humorous variant of the warrior's invulnerability in the Beyond: only the souls who arrive wearing a necklace of human teeth are spared a beating (a "cooking"?) administered by the spirit who greets them (Nimuendaju 1981:30). The Araweté theme, in turn, is a weak variant of the Tupinamba dogma that only killers gained acess to immortality (discussed later).

23. However, while enemies were eaten, jaguars were not. A jaguar, as a symbol of cannibalism, was treated as if he were a human: his head was smashed. An enemy, on the other hand, was treated as if his captors were jaguars: he was eaten.

Among all the Tupi-Guarani groups, I believe that only the Aché eat jaguars, which might be linked to two ideas: the *ove*-soul of an "important man" is transformed into a cannibal jaguar, and the dead are eaten so that their souls do not eat the living, penetrating their bodies. The killer is also cannibalized by the victim, who penetrates him through the anus and eats his entrails; this *ianve*-soul must be vomited. The Aché method of avenging a natural death by executing another person of their own group (a child) produces a *sui generis* torsion in the game of identification between the deceased and the killer: the assassin of the child was adopted by the latter's mother (P. Clastres 1972:242–43, 250–51, 259–60, 275, 302, 332–33).

24. Compare this with the role of trophy skulls for the Shipaya and with the spirits of Kayapó killed by the Tapirapé, who become the shamans' "familiars" and warn them of attacks by living Kayapó (Nimuendaju 1981:23–24; Wagley 1977:184–85).

25. One time when I asked whom the gods were speaking about in a *peyo*—concerning an *Iraparadï* who smoked a lot—they told me, "about you." The term can also be used as an accusation, as in the case of a song in which a dead woman asked for "her *Iraparadï*": everyone understood that she was speaking about her husband, who let her be captured by the Parakanã as he fled in cowardice. By means of this ironic sketch, the husband was defined as his wife's "killer."

Chapter 9

1. As Kant's argument goes (1958 [1787]:192): "In the analytic judgment we keep to the given concept, and seek to extract something from it. If it is to be affirmative, I ascribe to it only what is already thought in it. If it is to be negative, I exclude from it only its opposite. But in synthetic judgments I have to advance beyond the given concept, viewing as in relation with the concept something altogether different from what was thought in it. This relation is consequently never a relation either of identity or of contradiction;

and from the judgment, taken in and by itself, the truth or falsity of the relation can never be discovered."

2. This helps us understand the Kaapor idea (where shamanism is a value subordinated to war) that the opossum is a shaman (Huxley 1956:221). The fact that the specters of the Araweté shamans sing, thus displaying a greater "animation" than common specters, may be an inversion of the "anti-opossum" status, that is, jaguar-like and imputrescible, of the celestial souls of slayers.

3. Earlier I mentioned in passing the Guarani "cult of bones" (H. Clastres 1978 [1975]:20–21) and the theme of *kandire,* the nondecay of the skeleton, linked to that of *aguyje,* maturation-perfection, the transcendence of "raw" human matter on the way towards the divine. The association between specter and flesh is also seen in the Kaapor *Anyang,* which has green skin (rotten) and does not have bones (Huxley 1956:180). This can be compared with the Timbira *mekarõ,* which has only skin and bones; in contrast to the Araweté case, this indicates its lack of vitality. Permanence for the Timbira is located in the actual skeleton and in names (Carneiro da Cunha 1978:145). The Bororo, among whom these oppositions are highly developed, present an interesting transformation of the theme of the skin of the dead. The hide of a jaguar killed by an *aroe maiwu,* a substitute of the deceased that avenges him, must be offered to the clan relatives of the defunct. He is a kind of final *perigraphé* or circumscription of the person of the deceased (Novaes 1981). Among the Araweté, it is the "jaguar" gods who keep the skins of devoured souls as trophies.

4. In this version, the common dead inhabit abandoned villages, mechanically repeating their lives; their souls suffer a regressive transmigration into smaller and smaller animals (see also Murphy 1958:26 on the Mundurucu) until they are extinguished.

5. Shamans have sexual relations with female white-lipped peccaries, thereby spawning the pigs. This belief inverts the Guarani complex of *odjepotá,* transformation into an animal through sexual contagion after eating raw meat. It also suggests an "animalization" of the Tapirapé shaman, his extrasocial position. The death of a shaman makes the celestial Jaguar send jaguars to earth (Wagley 1977:185): instead of being linked to opossums, as in the Kaapor case, the shaman here is a "jaguar-function."

6. This holds also for the Siriono: the souls of "good" men do not return to haunt the living, but those of "bad" men do (Holmberg 1969:243). Holmberg declares emphatically that there is not posthumous Beyond, but he mentions two types of spirits of the forest, the *kurúkwa* and the *abačikwaia,* both identified with the specter of the deceased.

7. This term has many cognates in Tupi-Guarani languages: the Tenetehara *piwara,* Wayãpi *ompiwan,* Kayabi *ngarupiwat,* designating animal spirits or spiritual powers of shamans. It is the same as the Guarani *tupichua,* which Montoya (1876) derives from *rupi* + *guara,* and which translates as "(spirit) familiar of sorcerer." *-Guara* is an agent-marker; the form *rup* or

rupia could be the same that enters into the Araweté *moropï'nã*, killer, and would mean "enemy." See chapter 8, note 16.

8. Another name for this specter is *takykuéri gua* (Cadogan 1959:104), which can be analyzed as "that which stays behind," that which remains (cf. Dooley 1982:29, *akykue*). This literally repeats the Araweté notion that the specters "stay behind us" (see chap. 7, sect. 4).

9. It is, in other words, "a meaning which transcends the distinction between the real and the imaginary: a complete meaning of which we can now hardly do more than evoke the ghost in the reduced setting of figurative language. What looks to us like being embedded in *praxis* is the mark of thought which quite genuinely takes the words it uses seriously, whereas in comparable circumstances we only 'play' on words" (Lévi-Strauss 1966:265).

Chapter 10

1. As Sahlins (1983:83) remarked, "In the global system of sacrifice [in Fiji], raw women and cooked men have the same finality. Both are reproductive, 'life-giving': the woman directly, the sacrificial victim as means of the exchange of *mana* between men and gods. Here, then, is another expression of their equivalence: a barren wife is not strangled to accompany the soul of her husband to the afterworld (*Bulu*), ancestral source of human and natural reproduction; and as for the deceased warrior who had never killed, never brought home a human sacrifice, he is condemned to endlessly pound a pile of shit with his warclub, through all eternity . . . It is, as the Maori say, 'the battlefield with men; childbirth with women' . . . The Aztecs formed and acted on the same representation of social reproduction." Indeed, see Sahagún (1969 [1577]:167) regarding the Aztecs: "And when the baby had arrived on earth, then the midwife shouted; she gave war cries, which meant that the little woman had fought a good battle, had become a brave warrior, had taken a captive, had captured a baby." From Classical Greece to the Anggor of New Guinea, through the Jivaro and the Yanomami, this same correlation can be seen between feminine states or attributes—menstruation, birth, or marriage—and aggressive masculine actions (Vernant 1988:34; Huber 1980:48; Taylor 1985:161; Albert 1985).

2. I do not believe it necessary to discuss either the "discoveries" of Arens (1979), who reveals a profound ignorance about the Tupinamba (see Forsyth 1983, 1985), nor the ethnocentric lucubrations of Girard (1977:274–79); Florestan is more substantial about (and as) the scapegoat. A useful summary of Tupinamba sources and interpretations is found in Métraux 1967.

3. In postulating a "cult of the dead" as the basis of the war complex, Florestan repeats a theory of Steinmetz (and E. Rhode). It derives the juridical penalty from blood revenge, and this in turn from fear of the dead, the basis of their cult. Mauss (1969 [1896]:681), in a meticulous critique, observes that the cases of revenge demanded by the spirits of ancestors are empirically rare, therefore incapable of supporting the universality required by Steinmetz's theory; he also notes that they emerge "where the patriarchal family is per-

fectly organized, where the ancestor is a god and acts as such." But this is exactly what Florestan intended to demonstrate by examining Tupinamba sacrifice, thus committing a *petitio principii.*

Nothing is intrinsically wrong with linking "ancestralization" and human sacrifice. It is valid, for example, for the Melanesian Fataleka (Guidieri 1980) or the Amazonian Yagua (Chaumeil 1985: 153). But nothing is intrinsically necessary about this link either, and the Tupinamba materials do not lead in this direction.

4. This is also encountered among the Jivaro: in the absence of human heads to make the *tsantsa,* those of sloths are used (Harner 1973: 148). Each people, one might say, has its oxen and cucumbers.

5. This seems to indicate that even those who died at home must be avenged (see also Leite 1956–58, 1: 307)—a very liberal interpretation of "blood revenge" and *lex talionis.*

6. Léry describes a form of communication between the dead and the living that involves a reference to war, but I do not believe that this passage authorizes the idea that the dead impose an "imperative of revenge" or require a sacrificial offering of captives. His remarks concern beliefs about a particular kind of bird: "But the mystery that I want to mention is this: his [the bird's] voice is so penetrating . . . that our poor Tupinamba, who hear him cry more often in the night than in daytime, have the fantasy imprinted in their brain that their deceased relatives and friends are sending them these birds as a sign of good luck, and especially to encourage them to bear themselves valiantly in war against their enemies. They believe firmly that if they observe what is signified to them by these augurs, not only will they vanquish their enemies in this world, but what is more, when they die their souls will not fail to rejoin their ancestors behind the mountains and dance with them" (Léry 1990: 91).

7. A few enemy women were spared and taken as concubines; after their death, however, their skulls were ritually split open. Their captors thus took advantage of them twice over.

8. Thevet (1953: 193–94) relates that the captive was feathered and the women showered him with parrot feathers as he entered the village "as a sign of his death." The executor, for his part, imitated a bird of prey approaching its quarry (Cardim 1906: 436).

9. Since I have just mentioned the Bororo, it is interesting to note that the famous *aroe* concept, which means, among many other things, "personal name," was analyzed by the Salesian encyclopedists as originally signifying "feathers" (Albisetti & Venturelli 1962: 100–108). I thank Terence Turner for directing my attention to this reference.

10. Father Antonio Blázquez was delighted with the signs of Christianization among the Tupi of Bahia: "They also sold all of their featherwork used to clothe themselves and their women, an occurrence which most certainly is a sign of the Holy Spirit having touched their hearts. Because these feathers of theirs are the finest adornments that they have, and they wore them when

they killed their opponents and ate them." (Blázquez [1559] in Leite 1956–58, 3:137). Staden is concise: "Their treasures are the feathers of birds" (1928:147).

11. The custom of killing and eating the children of captives borne by women of the group scandalized the Europeans. The child could be eaten by its mother and grandparents (Soares de Souza 1971:325). Thevet explains this by the patrilateral theory of conception: children of enemies were enemies; they were killed "so they would not turn into enemies" (1953:139–40).

12. *Translator's note:* the terms used here allude to theological debates in the Christian church about the nature of the Eucharist and transubstantiation of the host. According to the O.E.D., "manducation" refers to the action of eating (e.g., carnal, literal, spiritual manducation) the host, which may be understood as "according to the flesh" or "according to the spirit."

13. Note that "contrary" was the word for "enemy" in sixteenth-century Portuguese, as well as in Tupinamba (*tovaja:* "brother-in-law," "enemy," "something opposite from oneself," "something facing oneself").

14. Thevet (1953:283–84) even implies that the captive took the name of the deceased whom he "substituted" in relation to the widow.

15. As we have seen, Florestan says that ritual death "put the integrity of the 'person' at risk," requiring a sacrifice in reparation (Fernandes 1970:320). This is based on an obscure observation by Magalhães de Gandavo (1922:85) that "their dead will go through a future life wounded or cut in pieces or in the condition in which he left this life." Besides sounding strange when compared to all the other texts that affirm how "handsome" ritual death is and how horrible it is not to be eaten, this passage leads down a false path by confounding individual destiny and collective response.

16. Léry (1990:124–25) reports the following typical dialogue between slayer and victim: "'Are you not of the nation . . . which is our enemy? And have you not yourself killed and eaten of our kinsmen and friends?' The prisoner, more fearless than ever, replies . . . "*Pa, che tan tan, ajouca atoupave:* that is, 'Yes, I am very strong, and have slain and eaten a great many . . . O, I have never hesitated: how bold I have been in attacking and seizing your people, of whom I have eaten time and time again,' and so he goes on. 'And for that reason,' says he who is standing there ready to slaughter him, 'since you are now here in our power, you will presently be killed by me, then roasted on the *boucan* and eaten by all the rest of us.' 'Very well,' replies the prisoner . . . 'my kinsmen will avenge me in turn.'"

17. He thereby anticipated, Lestringant continues, the symbolic reading of modern anthropology, which only reappeared after a long hiatus of naturalization. The naturalizing tendency was already represented in Montaigne's time by Cardan, a sort of truculent and proteinic forebear of Marvin Harris.

18. Thevet narrates the story of a widow who, outraged by the cowardice of her husband's kin, goes to war and brings back enemies so that her children can avenge their father. Becoming accustomed to this role, she ends up assuming the appearance of a man and becomes celibate. In the absence of prisoners, women would turn into men: this seems to be the moral of the story.

19. It is interesting to compare this system with the logic of naming among the Gê-Timbira peoples: there, the sister's husband settles part of his debt by producing an alter-ego of his wife's brother—his son will be named for (and by) the latter (Ladeira 1982:81). The Tupinamba gave a daughter in exchange for a wife, or a captive in exchange for themselves—a captive who would bring names to the wife's brother when the latter killed him and, moreover, enable him to obtain a wife. If the Timbira sister's son is a double of his mother's brother, the Tupinamba captive is an equivalent of the sister's daughter, or of the sister's husband himself (his comestible version, so to speak) for the wife's brother. Names, enemies, children, and women circulate through the same channels.

20. The relationship between avuncular marriage and political power can still be seen today among the Kaapor (Balée 1984:183).

21. Rivière (1969:272–75), in discussing the Trio, questions Kirchoff's interpretation of avuncular marriage as a way of avoiding brideservice. This may also be a valid point for the Tupinamba, but my point concerns uxorilocality. Among the Tupi-Guarani, as in the Guianas, avuncular marriage is part of a general strategy of endogamy, which creates residential solutions a posteriori, always starting from an "uxorilocal attractor" at base from which one wants and one may (if one can) escape.

Here, I wish to take the opportunity to diverge from Laraia's hypothesis (1971; 1972:34–36) of a patrilinear and patrilocal horizon for the Tupi, with matrilocality supposedly being the fruit of historical changes. The immense majority of Amazonian peoples (including the Tupi-Guarani) present complex systems of residence; Gê uxorilocality and Tukano virilocality, with their normative and (quasi-)universal functioning, are more exceptions than the rules. The Amazonian rule, if it is possible to speak of one, is this: within a general tendency towards uxorilocality, the powerful and their sons do *not* live according to this residential solution. This applies to the Parintintin (Kracke 1978:35ff.), Kayabi (Grünberg n.d. [1970]:113, 120), Guarani (Schaden 1969:95), Wayãpi (Grenand 1982:136; Gallois 1980:40), Tenetehara (Wagley & Galvão 1949:25–29), Tapirapé (Wagley 1977:93–96), Siriono (Holmberg 1969:128, 148), and Kaapor (Balée 1984:162ff., 176). Besides the Tupi, witness the Upper Xinguanos, with their difference between the "elite" and "commoners" residentially significant (Bastos 1978:34, 61); the Pareci, where only the sons of chiefs stay at home (Costa 1985:99—this would be "Arawakan" in general; cf. Schmidt n.d. [1917]:48ff.); the Munducuru (Ramos 1978); the Jivaro (Descola 1982:311); the Yanomami (Ramos & Albert 1977:7–8, 21); and naturally the Guianas (Rivière 1984). Even the uxorilocal Suya and Shavante allow exceptions for chiefs. In the Tupinamba case, prowess in warfare was seemingly the sociological *clinamen* that favored escape from the uxorilocal drift; in other societies, it is more stable forms of hierarchy.

22. I must add here a retrospective cautionary note in light of some recent discussions concerning Amerindian warfare. I do not think that the Tupinamba data support in any way whatsoever the pseudo-Darwinian speculations (embellished by a doubtful statistical apparatus) of Chagnon (1988,

1990) about Yanomami blood revenge, the differential reproductive success of killers, and so forth. As regards the Yanomami, my position is wholly on the side of Albert (1985, 1989, 1990) and Lizot (1989). What I have been analyzing here is Tupinamba *cosmology* (such as it can be apprehended from the chroniclers' accounts) and its probable influences on *social organization considered as an ideological order.* The data do not allow us to make any estimates about actual rates of "violent" deaths, ritual or otherwise; the available documents suggest that they were not exceptionally high. Tupinamba battles, as described by the chronicles, involved a great deal of shouting, boasting, and gesticulating. War parties would sometimes travel up to two hundred miles to assault an enemy village and then return with just one captive, leaving no victims behind. The capture of this prisoner, who could live for years among his captors before being put to death, benefited many different people (the captors, the women, the executioner). When ritually killed, the body of a single enemy was eaten down to the last bit by hundreds of people (the enemies' flesh was thus symbolically, if not actually, scarce). As regards the polygamy of chiefs and famous warriors and the ideal status of the chief as a renowned warrior, it is hard to distinguish what may be an idealized view from a faithful representation of reality, bearing in mind what can be seen in contemporary Amerindian societies. I think the Tupinamba situation fits well into the general picture of "brideservice societies" given by Collier and Rosaldo, especially concerning their suggestion that the correlation between polygamy and war prowess may have been more ideological than objective (1981:294, 312). This said, one cannot ignore the numerous data that point to the high *value* attributed to martial proficiency, vengeance, the qualifying nature of ritual killing, as well as to the connection between warfare and marriage. Be that as it may, although the Tupinamba were doubtless extremely bellicose, they do not impress me as having been particularly "violent" (a word we should be wary of when speaking about alien social forms). The chroniclers and missionaries portray their communal life as remarkably joyous and urbane. And, as I have already argued, their hatred of enemies and the entire complex of captivity, execution, and cannibalism were predicated on a thorough acknowledgement of the *humanness* of the Other—which had nothing to do, of course, with any "humanism." In sum, instead of putting society and its ideological products to the service of death, as Western cultures have done all too often, the Tupinamba have put death to the service of society.

Works Cited

Abbeville, Claude d'. 1975 [1614]. *História da missão dos padres capuchinhos na ilha do Maranhão e terras circunvizinhas.* Trans. S. Milliet. São Paulo: Itatiaia/Editôra da Universidade de São Paulo. (Originally published as *Histoire de la mission des Pères Capucins en l'Isle de Maragnan et terres circonvoisines.*)

Adalbert, *Prince of Prussia.* 1849 [1847]. *Travels of His Royal Highness Prince Adalbert of Prussia in the south of Europe and in Brazil, with a voyage up the Amazon and Xingú.* Trans. R. H. Schomburgk and J. E. Taylor. London: D. Bogue.

Albert, Bruce. 1985. "Temps du sang, temps des cendres: Représentation de la maladie, système rituel et espace politique chez les Yanomami du sud-est (Amazonie brésilienne)." Doctoral dissertation, Université de Paris-X, Nanterre.

———. 1989. "Yanomami 'violence': Inclusive fitness or ethnographer's representation?" *Current Anthropology* 30 (5):637–40.

———. 1990. "Yanomami warfare: Rejoinder." *Current Anthropology* 31 (5):558–63.

Albisetti, César and Venturelli, Ângelo Jayme. 1962. *Enciclopédia Bororo,* vol. 1. Campo Grande: Museu Regional Dom Bosco.

Anchieta, José de. 1933 [1554–94]. *Cartas, informações, fragmentos históricos e sermões (1554–1594).* Vol. 3, *Cartas Jesuítas.* Rio de Janeiro: Civilização Brasileira.

Andrade, Lúcia M. M. de. 1984. "*Karowara:* Um conceito para se compreender o xamanismo e a cosmologia asuriní." Paper presented at the symposium "Cosmologia tupi," XIV Reunião Brasileira de Antropologia, Brasília.

Arens, William. 1979. *The man-eating myth: Anthropology and anthropophagy.* New York: Oxford University Press.

Arnaud, Expedito. 1978. "Notícia sobre os índios Araweté, Rio Xingu, Pará." *Boletim do Museu Paraense Emílio Goeldi* Antropologia n.s. 71:1–20.

Baldus, Herbert. 1970 [1949]. *Os Tapirapé: Tribo tupi no Brasil Central.* São Paulo: Companhia Editôra Nacional/Editôra da Universidade de São Paulo.

———. 1976 [1964]. "O xamanismo na aculturação de uma tribo tupi do

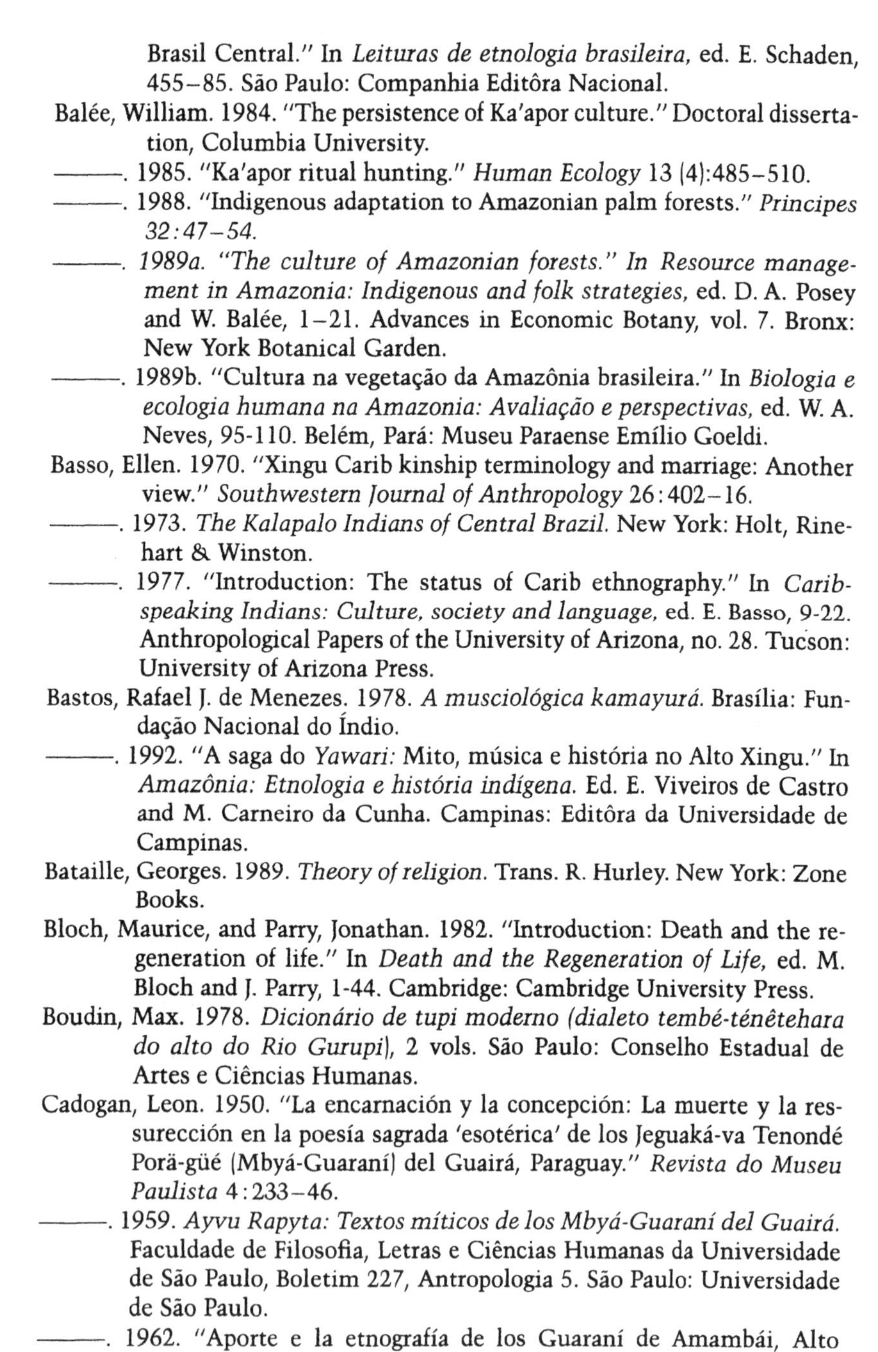

Brasil Central." In *Leituras de etnologia brasileira*, ed. E. Schaden, 455–85. São Paulo: Companhia Editôra Nacional.

Balée, William. 1984. "The persistence of Ka'apor culture." Doctoral dissertation, Columbia University.

———. 1985. "Ka'apor ritual hunting." *Human Ecology* 13 (4):485–510.

———. 1988. "Indigenous adaptation to Amazonian palm forests." *Principes 32:47–54.*

———. *1989a. "The culture of Amazonian forests." In Resource management in Amazonia: Indigenous and folk strategies*, ed. D. A. Posey and W. Balée, 1–21. Advances in Economic Botany, vol. 7. Bronx: New York Botanical Garden.

———. 1989b. "Cultura na vegetação da Amazônia brasileira." In *Biologia e ecologia humana na Amazonia: Avaliação e perspectivas*, ed. W. A. Neves, 95-110. Belém, Pará: Museu Paraense Emílio Goeldi.

Basso, Ellen. 1970. "Xingu Carib kinship terminology and marriage: Another view." *Southwestern Journal of Anthropology* 26:402–16.

———. 1973. *The Kalapalo Indians of Central Brazil*. New York: Holt, Rinehart & Winston.

———. 1977. "Introduction: The status of Carib ethnography." In *Carib-speaking Indians: Culture, society and language*, ed. E. Basso, 9-22. Anthropological Papers of the University of Arizona, no. 28. Tucson: University of Arizona Press.

Bastos, Rafael J. de Menezes. 1978. *A musciológica kamayurá*. Brasília: Fundação Nacional do Índio.

———. 1992. "A saga do *Yawari:* Mito, música e história no Alto Xingu." In *Amazônia: Etnologia e história indígena*. Ed. E. Viveiros de Castro and M. Carneiro da Cunha. Campinas: Editôra da Universidade de Campinas.

Bataille, Georges. 1989. *Theory of religion*. Trans. R. Hurley. New York: Zone Books.

Bloch, Maurice, and Parry, Jonathan. 1982. "Introduction: Death and the regeneration of life." In *Death and the Regeneration of Life*, ed. M. Bloch and J. Parry, 1-44. Cambridge: Cambridge University Press.

Boudin, Max. 1978. *Dicionário de tupi moderno (dialeto tembé-ténêtehara do alto do Rio Gurupi)*, 2 vols. São Paulo: Conselho Estadual de Artes e Ciências Humanas.

Cadogan, Leon. 1950. "La encarnación y la concepción: La muerte y la ressurección en la poesía sagrada 'esotérica' de los Jeguaká-va Tenondé Porä-güé (Mbyá-Guaraní) del Guairá, Paraguay." *Revista do Museu Paulista* 4:233–46.

———. 1959. *Ayvu Rapyta: Textos míticos de los Mbyá-Guaraní del Guairá*. Faculdade de Filosofia, Letras e Ciências Humanas da Universidade de São Paulo, Boletim 227, Antropologia 5. São Paulo: Universidade de São Paulo.

———. 1962. "Aporte e la etnografía de los Guaraní de Amambái, Alto Ypané." *Revista de Antropologia* 10 (1,2):43–91.

———. 1968. "Chono Kybwyrá: Aporte al conocimiento de la mitología guaraní." In *Las culturas condenadas,* ed. A. Roa Bastos, 43-60. Mexico City: Siglo XXI.

Campbell, Allan T. 1982. "Themes for translating: An account of the Wayãpi Indians of Amapá, Northern Brazil." Doctoral dissertation, Oxford University.

———. 1989. *To square with genesis: Causal statements and shamanic ideas in Wayãpi.* Iowa City: Iowa University Press.

Canetti, Elias. 1981. *Crowds and power.* Trans. C. Stewart. London: Penguin.

Cardim, Fernão. 1906 [1584]. "A treatise of Brasil." In *Hakluytus posthumus or Purchas his pilgrimes,* vol. 16, ed. S. Purchas, 417–503. Republication of 1625 translation. Glasgow: James MacLehose & Sons.

Carneiro da Cunha, Manuela. 1978. *Os mortos e os outros: Uma análise do sistema funerário e da noção de pessoa entre os índios Krahó.* São Paulo: Hucitec.

———. 1981. "Eschatology among the Krahó: Reflection upon society, free field of fabulation." In *Mortality and immortality: The anthropology and archaeology of death,* ed. S. Humphreys and H. King, 161–74. London: Academic Press.

Carneiro da Cunha, Manuela, and Viveiros de Castro, Eduardo. 1985. "Vingança e temporalidade: Os Tupinambás." *Journal de la Société des Américanistes* 71:191–208.

Carvalho, João E. 1977. "Diário da frente de atração do Ipixuna (27/05/76 a 17/11/77)." Manuscript in personal collection of B. Ribeiro.

Carvalho, Sílvia M. S. 1983. "A cerâmica e os rituais antropofágicos." *Revista de Antropologia* 26:39–52.

Castello Branco, José M. B. 1956. "Nos vales do Xingu e do Tapajós: Aspectos de sua revelação e de sua conquista." *Revista do Instituto Histórico e Geográfico Brasileiro* 231:3–137.

Chagnon, Napoleon. 1988. "Life histories, blood revenge, and warfare in a tribal population." *Science* 239:985–92.

———. 1990. "Reproductive and somatic conflicts of interest in the genesis of violence and warfare among tribesmen." In *The anthropology of war,* ed. J. Haas, 77–104. Cambridge: Cambridge University Press.

Chaumeil, Jean-Pierre. 1985. "Echange d'énergie: Guerre, identité et reproduction sociale chez les Yagua de l'Amazonie péruvienne." *Journal de la Société des Américanistes* 71:143–158.

Clastres, Hélène. 1968. "Rites funéraires guayakí." *Journal de la Société des Américanistes* 57:63–72.

———. 1972. "Les beux-frères ennemis: A propos du cannibalisme tupinamba." *Nouvelle Revue de Psychanalyse* 6 ("Destins du cannibalisme"): 71–82.

———. 1978 [1975]. *Terra sem mal: O profetismo tupi-guarani.* Trans. R. Janine Ribeiro. São Paulo: Brasiliense. (Originally published as *La terre sans mal: Le prophétisme Tupi-Guarani.*)

Clastres, Hélène, and Lizot, Jacques. 1978. "La part du feu: Rites et discours de la mort chez les Yanomami." *Libre* 3:103–33.
Clastres, Pierre. 1972. *Chronique des indiens Guayakí*. Paris: Plon.
———. 1987. *Society against the state: Essays in political anthropology.* Trans R. Hurley in collaboration with A. Stein. New York: Zone Books.
Collier, Jane, and Rosaldo, Michelle. 1981. "Politics and gender in simple societies." In *Sexual meanings: The cultural construction of gender and sexuality,* ed. S. Ortner and H. Whitehead, 275–329. Cambridge: Cambridge University Press.
Combès, Isabelle. 1986. "'Ceste tant estrange tragedie': Approche ethnohistorique du cannibalisme tupi-guarani." Master's thesis, Université Paul Valéry, Montpellier.
———. 1987. "'Dicen que por ser ligero': Cannibales, guerriers et prophètes chez les anciens Tupi-Guarani." *Journal de la Société des Américanistes* 73:93–106.
Coppet, Daniel de. 1981. "The life-giving death." In *Mortality and immortality: The anthropology and archaeology of death,* ed S. Humphreys and H. King, 175–204. London: Academic Press.
Costa, Romana. 1985. "Cultura e contato: Um estudo da sociedade paresí no contexto das relações interétnicas." Master's thesis, Programa de Pós-Graduação em Antropologia Social, Museu Nacional do Rio de Janeiro.
Coudreau, Henri. 1977 [1897]. *Viagem ao Xingu.* Trans. E. Amado. São Paulo: Itatiaia/Editôra da Universidade de São Paulo. (Originally published as *Voyage au Xingu.*)
Crocker, Jon C. 1977. "My brother the parrot." In *The social use of metaphor: Essays on the anthropology of rhetoric,* ed. J. D. Sapir and J. C. Crocker, 164–92. Philadelphia: University of Pennsylvania Press.
———. 1979. "Selves and alters among the Eastern Bororo." In *Dialectical Societies: The Gê and Bororo of Central Brazil,* ed. D. Maybury-Lewis, 249–300. Cambridge, Mass.: Harvard University Press.
———. 1985. *Vital souls: Bororo cosmology, natural symbolism and shamanism.* Tucson: University of Arizona Press.
Da Matta, Roberto. 1982. *A divided world: Apinayé social structure.* Trans. A. Campbell. Cambridge, Mass.: Harvard University Press.
Daniel, João. 1976 [1757–76]. *Tesouro descoberto no rio Amazonas,* tomo 1. Separata dos Anais da Biblioteca Nacional, vol. 95. Rio de Janeiro: Biblioteca Nacional.
Deleuze, Gilles. 1990. *The logic of sense.* Ed. C. V. Boundas, trans. M. Lester and C. Stivale. New York: Columbia University Press.
Deleuze, Gilles, and Guattari, Félix. 1983. *Anti-Oedipus: Capitalism and schizophrenia.* Trans. R. Hurley, M. Seem, and H. R. Lane. Minneapolis: University of Minnesota Press.
Descola, Philippe. 1982. "Territorial adjustments among the Achuar of Ecuador." *Social Science Information* 21:301–20.

Detienne, Marcel. 1972. "Entre bêtes et dieux." *Nouvelle Revue de Psychanalyse* 6 ("Destins du cannibalisme"):231–46.

———. 1977. *The gardens of Adonis: Spices in Greek mythology.* Trans. J. Lloyd. Atlantic Highlands, N.J.: Humanities Press.

———. 1979. *Dionysos slain.* Trans. M. Muellner and L. Muellner. Baltimore: Johns Hopkins University Press.

———. 1989. "Culinary practices and the spirit of sacrifice." In *The cuisine of sacrifice among the Greeks,* ed. M. Detienne and J. P. Vernant, trans. P. Wissing, 1–20. Chicago: The University of Chicago Press.

Dole, Gertrude. 1969. "Generation kinship nomenclature as an adaptation to endogamy." *Southwestern Journal of Anthropology* 25:105–23.

Dooley, Robert. 1982. *Vocabulário do guarani (dialeto mbüa do Brasil).* Brasília: Summer Institute of Linguistics.

Dumont, Louis. 1980. "Towards a theory of hierarchy." In *Homo hierarchicus,* trans. M. Sainsbury, L. Dumont, and B. Gulati. Chicago: The University of Chicago Press.

———. 1983. "Stocktaking 1981: Affinity as value." In *Affinity as value: Marriage alliance in South India, with comparative essays on Australia,* 145–71. Chicago: The University of Chicago Press.

Erikson, Philippe. 1986. "Alterité, tatouage et anthropophagie chez les Pano: La belliqueuse quête de soi." *Journal de la Société des Américanistes* 72:185–210.

———. 1990. "Les Matis d'Amazonie: parure du corps, identité et organisation sociale." Doctoral dissertation, Université de Paris-X (Nanterre).

———. 1992. "A onomástica matis é amazônica?" in *Amazônia: Etnologia e história indígena.* Ed. E. Viveiros de Castro and M. Carneiro da Cunha. Campinas: Editôra da Universidade de Campinas.

Espinosa, Lucas. 1935. *Los Tupí del Oriente Peruano.* Madrid: Publicaciones de la Expedición Iglesias al Amazonas.

Evreux, Yves d'. 1929 [1615]. *Viagem ao norte do Brasil feita nos anos de 1613 a 1614 pelo Padre Ivo d'Evreux, religioso capuchinho.* Trans. C. A. Marques. Rio de Janeiro: Freitas Bastos. (Originally published as *Voyage dans le nord du Brésil fait durant les années 1613 et 1614.*)

Expedição Langsdorff. 1988. *Expedição Langsdorff ao Brasil 1821–1829.* Vol. 3, *Florence.* Rio de Janeiro: Edições Alumbramento.

Fausto, Carlos. 1989. "Xingu sob fogo cerrado." *Boletim da Associação Brasileira de Antropologia* 6:39–40.

Fernandes, Florestan. 1963 [1949]. *Organização social dos Tupinambá,* 2d ed. São Paulo: Difusão Européia do Livro.

———. 1970 [1952]. *A função social da guerra na sociedade Tupinambá,* 2d ed. São Paulo: Pioneira/Editôra da Universidade de São Paulo.

Forsyth, Donald. 1983. "The beginnings of Brazilian anthropology: Jesuits and Tupinamba cannibalism." *Journal of Anthropological Research* 39:147–78.

———. 1985. "Three cheers for Hans Staden: The case for Brazilian cannibalism." *Ethnohistory* 32 (1):17–36.

Gallois, Dominique. 1980. "Contribuição ao estudo do povoamento indígena da guiana brasileira: Un caso específico—os Wayãpi." Master's thesis, Departamento de Ciências Sociais, Universidade de São Paulo.

———. 1984. "Identificando *Añã:* Notas sobre o xamanismo wayãpi." Paper presented at the symposium "Cosmologia tupi," XIV Reunião Brasileira de Antropologia, Brasília.

———. 1985. "O pajé wayãpi e seus 'espelhos.'" *Revista de Antropologia* 27/28:179–95.

———. 1988. "O movimento na cosmologia wayãpi: criação, expansão e transformação do universo." Doctoral dissertation, Departamento de Ciências Sociais, Universidade de São Paulo.

Girard, René. 1977. *Violence and the sacred.* Trans. P. Gregory. Baltimore: Johns Hopkins University Press.

Goodenough, Ward. 1970. *Description and comparison in cultural anthropology.* Cambridge: Cambridge University Press.

Green, André. 1972. "Le cannibalisme: Realité ou fantasme agi?" *Nouvelle Revue de Psychanalyse* 6 ("Destins du Cannibalisme"):27–52.

Grenand, Pierre. 1980. *Introduction à l'étude de l'univers wayãpi: Ethnoécologie des indiens du Haut-Oyapock (Guiane Française).* Paris: SELAF/CNRS-ORSTOM.

———. 1982. *Ainsi parlaient nos ancêtres: Essai d'ethno-histoire wayãpi.* Paris: ORSTOM.

Grünberg, Georg. n.d. [1970]. "Contribuições para a etnologia dos Kayabi do Brasil Central." Trans. E. Wenzel. Manuscript, Centro Ecumênico de Documentação e Informação, São Paulo. (Originally published as "Beiträge zur ethnographie der Kayabí zentralbrasiliens," *Archiv für Völkerkunde* 24:21–186).

Guidieri, Remo. 1972. "Pères et fils." *Nouvelle Revue de Psychanalyse* 6 ("Destins du Cannibalisme"):85–109.

———. 1980. *La route des morts.* Paris: Seuil.

Harner, Michael. 1962. "Jívaro souls." *American Anthropologist* 64:258–72.

———. 1973. *The Jívaro: People of the sacred waterfalls.* Garden City, N.J.: Anchor/Doubleday.

Héritier, Françoise. 1982. "The symbolics of incest and its prohibition." In *Between belief and transgression: Structuralist essays in religion, history, and myth,* ed. M. Izard and P. Smith, trans. J. Leavitt, 152–79. Chicago: The University of Chicago Press.

Hertz, Robert. 1960 [1907]. "A contribution to the study of the collective representation of death." In *Death and the right hand,* trans. R. Needham and C. Needham, 29–86. Aberdeen: Cohen & West.

Hocart, Arthur. 1970 [1936]. *Kings and councillors: An essay in the comparative anatomy of human society.* Chicago: The University of Chicago Press.

Holmberg, Allan. 1969 [1950]. *Nomads of the long bow: The Siriono of eastern Bolivia.* Garden City, N.J.: Natural History Press.

Howard, Catherine V. 1992. "*Pawana:* A farsa dos 'visitantes' entre os Waiwai da Amazônia setentrional" in *Amazônia: Etnologia e história indígena.* Ed. E. Viveiros de Castro and M. Carneiro da Cunha. Campinas: Editôra da Universidade de Campinas.

Huber, Peter. 1980. "The Anggor bowman: Ritual and society in Melanesia." *American Ethnologist* 7:43–57.

Hubert, Henri, and Mauss, Marcel. 1964 [1898]. *Sacrifice: Its nature and function.* Trans. W. D. Halls. Chicago: The University of Chicago Press.

Hugh-Jones, Christine. 1979. *From the Milk River: Spatial and temporal processes in Northwest Amazonia.* Cambridge: Cambridge University Press.

Hugh-Jones, Stephen. 1979. *The palm and the pleiades: Initiation and cosmology in Northwest Amazonia.* Cambridge: Cambridge University Press.

Humphreys, Sally. 1981. "Death and time." In *Mortality and immortality: The anthropology and archaeology of death,* ed. S. Humphreys and H. King, 261–83. London: Academic Press.

Huxley, Francis. 1956. *Affable savages.* London: Rupert Hart-Davis.

Kant, Immanuel. 1958 [1787]. *Critique of pure reason.* Trans. N. K. Smith. New York: St. Martin's Press.

Kaplan, Joanna Overing. 1975. *The Piaroa: A people of the Orinoco Basin.* Oxford: Clarendon.

———. 1981a. "Masters of land and masters of water: Cosmology and social structure among the Piaroa." Manuscript, London School of Economics.

———. 1981b. "Review article: Amazonian anthropology." *Journal of Latin American Studies* 13:151–65.

———. 1982. "The path of sacred words: Shamanism and the domestication of the asocial in Piaroa society." Paper presented at the symposium "Shamanism in lowland South American societies: A problem of definition." 44th International Congress of Americanists, Manchester, England.

———. 1984. "Dualism as an expression of difference and danger: Marriage exchange and reciprocity among the Piaroa of Venezuela." In *Marriage practices in lowland South America,* ed. K. Kensinger, 127–55. Urbana: University of Illinois Press.

Kaplan, Joanna Overing, ed. 1977. "Social time and social space in lowland South American societies." In *Acts of the 42nd International Congress of Americanists (1976),* vol. 2, 7–394. Paris: Société des Américanistes/CNRS.

Kracke, Waud. 1978. *Force and persuasion: Leadership in an Amazonian society.* Chicago: The University of Chicago Press.

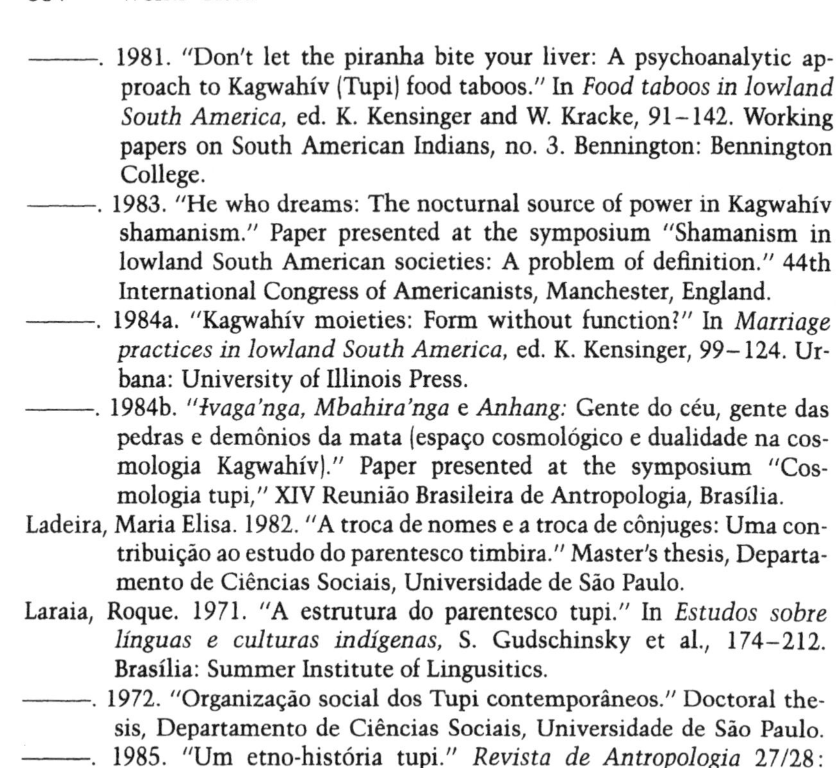

———. 1981. "Don't let the piranha bite your liver: A psychoanalytic approach to Kagwahív (Tupi) food taboos." In *Food taboos in lowland South America,* ed. K. Kensinger and W. Kracke, 91–142. Working papers on South American Indians, no. 3. Bennington: Bennington College.

———. 1983. "He who dreams: The nocturnal source of power in Kagwahív shamanism." Paper presented at the symposium "Shamanism in lowland South American societies: A problem of definition." 44th International Congress of Americanists, Manchester, England.

———. 1984a. "Kagwahív moieties: Form without function?" In *Marriage practices in lowland South America,* ed. K. Kensinger, 99–124. Urbana: University of Illinois Press.

———. 1984b. "*Ɨvaga'nga, Mbahira'nga* e *Anhang:* Gente do céu, gente das pedras e demônios da mata (espaço cosmológico e dualidade na cosmologia Kagwahív)." Paper presented at the symposium "Cosmologia tupi," XIV Reunião Brasileira de Antropologia, Brasília.

Ladeira, Maria Elisa. 1982. "A troca de nomes e a troca de cônjuges: Uma contribuição ao estudo do parentesco timbira." Master's thesis, Departamento de Ciências Sociais, Universidade de São Paulo.

Laraia, Roque. 1971. "A estrutura do parentesco tupi." In *Estudos sobre línguas e culturas indígenas,* S. Gudschinsky et al., 174–212. Brasília: Summer Institute of Lingusitics.

———. 1972. "Organização social dos Tupi contemporâneos." Doctoral thesis, Departamento de Ciências Sociais, Universidade de São Paulo.

———. 1985. "Um etno-história tupi." *Revista de Antropologia* 27/28: 25–32.

Laraia, Roque, and Da Matta, Roberto. 1967. *Índios e castanheiros: A empresa extrativa e os índios no Médio Tocantins.* São Paulo: Difusão Européia do Livro.

Lave, Jean. 1979. "Cycles and trends in Krikatí naming practices." In *Dialectical societies: The Gê and Bororo of Central Brazil,* ed. D. Maybury-Lewis, 16–44. Cambridge, Mass.: Harvard University Press.

Lea, Vanessa. 1986. "Nomes e *nekrets* kayapó: Uma concepção de riqueza." Doctoral dissertation, Programa de Pós-Graduação em Antropologia Social, Museu Nacional do Rio de Janeiro.

Leiris, Michel. 1981 [1934]. *L'Afrique fantôme.* Paris: Gallimard.

Leite, Serafim, ed. 1956–58. *Cartas dos primeiros Jesuitas do Brasil (1538–1563).* 3 vols. São Paulo: Comissão do IV Centenário da Cidade de São Paulo.

Lemle, Miriam. 1971. "Internal classification of the Tupi-Guarani linguistic family." In *Tupi studies,* vol. 1, ed. D. Bendor-Samuel, 107-30. Norman: Summer Institute of Linguistics.

Léry, Jean de. 1990 [1578]. *History of a voyage to the land of Brazil, otherwise called America.* Trans. J. Whatley. Berkeley: University of California Press.

Lestringant, Frank. 1982. "Le cannibalisme des 'cannibales' (1. Montaigne et la tradition)." *Bulletin de la Société des Amis de Montaigne* 9/10: 27-40.

Lévi-Strauss, Claude. 1943. "The social use of kinship terms among Brazilian Indians." *American Anthropologist* 45:398–409.

———. 1958. "Documents Tupi-Kawahib." In *Miscellanea Paul Rivet Octogenaria Dicata,* vol. 2, 323–38. Mexico City: Universidad Autonoma Nacional.

———. 1963a. "The concept of archaism in anthropology." In *Structural Anthropology,* vol. 1, trans. C. Jacobson and B. G. Schoepf, 101–19. New York: Basic Books.

———. 1963b. *Totemism.* Trans. R. Needham. Boston: Beacon Press.

———. 1966. *The savage mind.* Chicago: The University of Chicago Press.

———. 1969a. *The elementary structures of kinship.* Trans. J. H. Bell, J. R. von Sturmer, and R. Needham. Boston: Beacon Press.

———. 1969b. *The raw and the cooked: Introduction to a science of mythology,* vol. 1. Trans. J. Weightman and D. Weightman. New York: Harper & Row. (Paperback reprint, Chicago: University of Chicago Press.)

———. 1973. *From honey to ashes: Introduction to a science of mythology,* vol. 2. Trans. J. Weightman and D. Weightman. New York: Harper & Row. (Paperback reprint, Chicago: University of Chicago Press.)

———. 1974. *Tristes tropiques.* Trans. J. Weightman and D. Weightman. New York: Atheneum.

———. 1977a. "Comparative religions of nonliterate peoples." In *Structural anthropology,* vol. 2, trans. M. Layton, 60–67. New York: Basic Books.

———. 1977b. "Discussion" on presentations by F. Héritier and J. C. Crocker. In *L'identité,* ed. C. Lévi-Strauss, 72–80, 180–84. Paris: Grasset.

———. 1978. *The origin of table manners: Introduction to a science of mythology,* vol. 3. Trans. J. Weightman and D. Weightman. New York: Harper & Row.

———. 1981. *The naked man: Introduction to a science of mythology,* vol. 4. Trans. J. Weightman and D. Weightman. New York: Harper & Row.

———. 1987. *Anthropology and myth: Lectures 1951–1982.* Trans. R. Willis. Oxford: Blackwell.

Lienhardt, Godfrey. 1961. *Divinity and experience: The religion of the Dinka.* Oxford: Clarendon.

Lins, Elizabeth. 1985. "Música e xamanismo entre os Kayabi do Parque do Xingu." *Revista de Antropologia* 27/28:127–38.

Lizot, Jacques. 1973. "Onomastique yanõmami." *L'Homme* 13:60–71.

———. 1985. *Tales of the Yanomami: Daily life in the Venezuelan forest.* Trans. E. Simon. Cambridge: Cambridge University Press.

———. 1989. "A propos de la guerre: Une réponse à Chagnon." *Journal de la Société des Américanistes* 75:91–113.

Lopes da Silva, Maria Aracy. 1980. "Nomes e amigos: Da prática xavante a uma reflexão sobre os Jê." Doctoral dissertation, Departamento de Ciências Sociais, Universidade de São Paulo.

Magalhães de Gandavo, Pedro de. 1922 [1575]. "History of the Province of Santa Cruz" and "Treatise on the land of Brazil." In *Documents and narratives concerning the discovery and conquest of Latin America: The histories of Brazil,* no. 5, vol. 2. Trans. J. B. Stetson, Jr. New York: The Cortes Society.

Mauss, Marcel. 1969 [1896]. "La religion et les origines du droit pénal d'après un livre récent." In *Oeuvres,* vol. 2, 651–98. Paris: Minuit.

Maybury-Lewis, David. 1974. *Akwẽ-Shavante society.* New York: Oxford University Press.

Maybury-Lewis, David, ed. 1979. *Dialectical societies: The Gê and Bororo of Central Brazil.* Cambridge, Mass.: Harvard University Press.

McCallum, Cecilia. 1989. "Gender, personhood and social organization amongst the Cashinahua of Western Amazonia" Doctoral dissertation, London School of Economics.

Melatti, Julio César. 1979. "The relationship system of the Krahó." In *Dialectical societies: The Gê and Bororo of Central Brazil,* ed. D. Maybury-Lewis, 46–79. Cambridge, Mass.: Harvard University Press.

Meliá, Bartomé. 1978. "El que hace escuchar la palabra." In *Las culturas condenadas,* ed. A. Roa Bastos, 56–61. Mexico City: Siglo XXI.

Meliá, Bartomé; Grünberg, Georg; and Grünberg, Friedl. 1976. *Los Pãi-Tavyterã: Etnografía guaraní del Paraguay contemporáneo.* Asunción: Centro de Estudios Antropológicos de la Universidad Católica.

Meliá, Bartomé et al. 1973. *La agonia de los Aché-Guayakí: Historia y cantos.* Asunción: Centro de Estudios Antropológicos de la Universidad Católica.

Menget, Patrick. 1977. "Au nom des autres: Classification des relations sociales chez les Txicão du Haut-Xingu." Doctoral dissertation, Université de Paris-X, Nanterre.

Métraux, Alfred. 1928. *La civilisation matérielle des tribus Tupi-Guarani.* Paris: Paul Geuthner.

———. 1948. "The Guarani." In *Handbook of South American Indians.* Vol. 3, *The tropical forest tribes,* ed. J. Steward, 69–94. Bureau of American Ethnology, Bulletin 143. Washington, D.C.: Smithsonian Institution.

———. 1967. *Réligions et magies indiennes d'Amérique du Sud.* Paris: Gallimard.

———. 1979 [1928]. *A religião dos Tupinambás e suas relações com a das demais tribos Tupi-Guaranis,* 2d ed. Trans. E. Pinto. São Paulo: Companhia Editôra Nacional/Editôra da Universidade de São Paulo. (Originally published as *La religion des Tupinamba et ses rapports avec celle des autres tribus Tupi-Guarani.*)

Montaigne, Michel de. 1943 [1580]. "Of cannibals." In *Selected essays,* trans. D. M. Frame, 73–92. New York: Walter J. Black.

Monteiro, Jácome. 1949 [1610]. "Relação da província do Brasil, 1610." In *História da Companhia de Jesus no Brasil,* vol. 8, ed. S. Leite, 393–425. Rio de Janeiro: Instituto Nacional do Livro.

Montoya, Antonio Ruiz de. 1876 [1640]. *Gramática y diccionarios (arte, vocabulario y tesoro) de la lengua tupi ó guarani.* Vienna, Paris: Faesy & Frick, Maisonneuve.

———. 1951 [1628]. "Carta ânua do Padre Antonio Ruiz, Superior da Missão do Guairá, dirigida em 1628 ao Padre Nicolau Duran, Provincial da Companhia de Jesus." In *Jesuítas e bandeirantes no Guairá 1549–1640,* ed. J. Cortesão, 259–98. Manuscritos da Coleção De Angelis, vol. 1. Rio de Janeiro: Biblioteca Nacional.

Müller, Regina. 1987. "Os Asuriní do Xingu (de como cinquenta e duas pessoas reproduzem uma sociedade indígena)." Doctoral dissertation, Departamento de Ciências Sociais, Universidade de São Paulo.

Müller, Regina et al. 1979. "Eleição das áreas indígenas Koatinemo-Ipixuna-Bacajá (grupos indígenas Asuriní-Araweté-Xikrin)." Report submitted to Fundação Nacional do Índio, Brasília.

Murphy, Robert. 1958. *Mundurucú religion.* Berkeley: University of California Press.

Nimuendaju, Curt. 1932. "Idiomas indígenas del Brasil." *Revista del Instituto Étnológico de la Universidad Nacional de Tucumán* 2: 543–618.

———. 1948a. "Little-known tribes of the lower Tocantins River region." In *Handbook of South American Indians.* Vol. 3, *The tropical forest tribes,* ed. J. Steward, 203-8. Bureau of American Ethnology, Bulletin 143. Washington, D.C.: Smithsonian Institution.

———. 1948b. "Tribes of the lower and middle Xingu River." In *Handbook of South American Indians.* Vol. 3, *The tropical forest tribes,* ed. J. Steward, 213–43. Bureau of American Ethnology, Bulletin 143. Washington, D.C.: Smithsonian Institution.

———. 1948c. "The Cayabi, Tapayuna, and Apiaca." In *Handbook of South American Indians.* Vol. 3, *The tropical forest tribes,* ed. J. Steward, 307–20. Bureau of American Ethnology, Bulletin 143. Washington, D.C.: Smithsonian Institution.

———. 1978 [1914]. *Los mitos de creación y de destrucción del mundo como fundamentos de la religión de los Apapokúva-Guaraní.* Trans. J. Barnadas. Lima: Centro Amazonico de Antropologia y Aplicación Pratica. (Originally published as "Die Sagen von der Erschaffung und Vernichtung der Welt als Grundlagen der Religion der Apapocúva-Guaraní." *Zeitschrift für Ethnologie* 46: 284–403.)

———. 1981 [1922]. "Fragmentos de religião e tradição dos índios Šipáia." *Religião e Sociedade* 7: 3–47. Trans. C. Emmerich and E. Viveiros de Castro. (Originally published as "Bruchstücke aus Religion und Überlieferung der Šipáia-Indianer." *Anthropos* 14–15 [1919–20]: 1002–39; 16–17 [1921–22]:367–406.)

Novaes, Sylvia C. 1981. "Tranças, cabaças e couros no funeral bororo (a

propósito de um processo de constituição de identidade)." *Revista de Antropologia* 24:25–40.
Oberg, Kalervo. 1953. *Indian tribes of northern Mato Grosso, Brazil.* Institute of Social Anthropology, publication no. 15. Washington, D.C.: Smithsonian Institution.
Panofsky, Erwin. 1970. "Introduction: The history of art as a humanistic discipline." In *Meaning in the visual arts,* ed. E. Panofsky, 23–50. London: Penguin.
Philips, Susan. 1974. "Warm Springs 'Indian time': How the regulation of participation affects the progression of events." In *Explorations in the ethnography of speaking,* ed. R. Bauman and J. Sherzer, 92–109. Cambridge: Cambridge University Press.
Pires, J. Murça, and Prance, Ghilean. 1985. "The vegetation types of the Brazilian Amazon." In *Key environments: Amazonia,* ed. G. T. Prance and T. Lovejoy, 109–45. New York: Pergamon Press.
Pollock, Donald. 1985. "Looking for a sister: Culina siblingship and affinity." In *The sibling relationship in lowland South America,* ed. J. Shapiro and K. Kensinger, 8–15. Working Papers on South American Indians, no. 7. Bennington: Bennington College.
Poole, Fitz John P. 1983. "Cannibals, tricksters, and witches: Anthropophagic images among the Bimin-Kuskusmin." In *The ethnography of cannibalism,* ed. P. Brown and D. Tuzin, 6–32. Washington, D.C.: Society of Psychological Anthropology.
Pouillon, Jean. 1972. "Manières de table, manières de lit, manières de langage." *Nouvelle Revue de Psychanalyse* 6 ("Destins du Cannibalisme"):9–25.
Ramirez, Luiz. 1852 [1528]. "Carta de Luiz Ramirez do Rio da Prata a 10 de julho de 1528." *Revista do Instituto Histórico e Geográphico Brasileiro,* vol. 15, tomo 15:14–41.
Ramos, Alcida. 1978. "Mundurucu: Social change or false problem?" *American Ethnology* 5 (4):675–89.
Ramos, Alcida, and Albert, Bruce. 1977. "Descendência e afinidade: O contraste entre duas sociedades Yanoama." *Trabalhos em Ciências Sociais,* série antropologia 18. Brasília: Universidade de Brasília.
Ramos, Alcida, and Peirano, Mariza. 1973. "O simbolismo da caça em dois rituais de nominação." *Trabalhos em Ciências Sociais,* série antropologia 4. Brasília: Universidade de Brasília.
Ribeiro, Berta G. 1981. "Histórico do contato do povo Araweté." *Porantim* 34:14–15.
———. 1983. "Araweté: A índia vestida." *Revista de Antropologia* 26:1–38.
———. 1985. "Tecelãs tupi do Xingu." *Revista de Antropologia* 27/28: 355–402.
Rivière, Peter. 1969. *Marriage among the Trio: A principle of social organization.* Oxford: Clarendon.
———. 1984. *Individual and society in Guiana: A comparative study of*

Amerindian social organization. Cambridge: Cambridge University Press.

Rodrigues, Aryon. 1985. "Relações internas na família lingüística Tupi-Guarani." *Revista de Antropologia* 27/28:33–53.

———. 1986. *Línguas brasileiras: Para o conhecimento das línguas indígenas*. São Paulo: Loyola.

Roe, Peter. 1982. *The cosmic zygote: Cosmology in the Amazon Basin*. New Brunswick: Rutgers University Press.

Sahagún, Fray Bernardino de. 1969 [1577]. *Florentine Codex: General history of the things of the New Spain*, part 7, book 6. Trans. C. E. Dibble and A. J. O. Anderson. Santa Fe: University of Utah and School of American Research.

Sahlins, Marshall. 1983. "Raw women, cooked men, and other 'great things' of the Fiji Islands." In *The ethnography of cannibalism*, ed. P. Brown and D. Tuzin, 72–93. Washington, D.C.: Society of Psychological Anthropology.

Schaden, Egon. 1959. *A mitologia heróica de tribos indígenas no Brasil*. Rio de Janeiro: Ministério da Educação e Cultura.

———. 1969. *Fundamental aspects of Guarani culture*. Trans. L.-P. Lewinsõhn. New Haven: Human Relations Area Files, Inc.

———. 1982. "A religião guarani e o cristianismo: Contribuição ao estudo de um processo histórico de comunicação inter-cultural." *Revista de Antropologia* 25:1–24.

Schmidt, Max. n.d. [1917]. "Os Aruaques: Uma contribuição ao estudo do problema da difusão cultural." Trans. E. Sommer. Manuscript. Rio de Janeiro: Museu Nacional. (Originally published as *Die Arauaken: ein Beitrag zum problem der Kulturverbreitung*.)

Seeger, Anthony. 1975. "The meaning of body ornaments: A Suya example." *Ethnology* 14:211–24.

———. 1979. "What can we learn when they sing? Vocal genres of the Suya Indians of Central Brazil." *Ethnomusicology* 23:373–94.

———. 1981. *Nature and society in Central Brazil: The Suya Indians of Mato Grosso*. Cambridge, Mass.: Harvard University Press.

Seeger, Anthony; Da Matta, Roberto; and Viveiros de Castro, Eduardo. 1979. "A construção da pessoa nas sociedades indígenas brasileiras." *Boletim do Museu Nacional* 32:2–19.

Seeger, Anthony, and Viveiros de Castro, Eduardo. 1979. "Terras e territórios indígenas no Brasil." *Revista Civilização Brasileira* 12:101–9.

Shapiro, Judith. 1968. "Tapirapé kinship." *Boletim do Museu Paraense Emílio Goeldi* Antropologia n.s. 37:1–37.

———. 1987. "From Tupã to the Land without Evil: The Christianization of Tupi-Guarani cosmology." *American Ethnologist* 14 (1):126–39.

Silverwood-Cope, Peter. 1980. "Os Maku: Povo caçador do noroeste da Amazônia." *Trabalhos em Ciências Sociais*, série antropologia 27. Brasília: Universidade de Brasília.

Soares de Souza, Gabriel. 1971 [1587]. *Tratado descritivo do Brasil em 1587,* 4th ed. São Paulo: Companhia Editôra Nacional/Editôra da Universidade de São Paulo.

Sperber, Dan. 1985. *On anthropological knowledge.* Cambridge: Cambridge University Press.

Staden, Hans. 1928 [1557]. *Hans Staden: The true history of his captivity, 1557.* Trans. and ed. M. Letts. London: George Routledge & Sons.

Taylor, Anne-Christine. 1985. "L'art de la réduction: La guerre et les mécanismes de la différenciation tribale dans la culture jivaro." *Journal de la Société des Américanistes* 71 : 159–73.

———. 1990. *La parenté jivaro.* Unpublished manuscript. Paris.

Thevet, André. 1953 [1575]. *Le Brésil et les brésiliens. Le français en Amérique pendant la deuxième moitié du XVIe. siècle.* Ed. S. Lusagnet. Paris: Presses Universitaires de France.

———. 1978 [1557]. *As singularidades da França Antártica.* Trans. E. Amado. São Paulo: Itatiaia/Editôra da Universidade de São Paulo. (Originally published as *Les singularitez de la France Antarctique, autrement nommé Amerique.*)

Turner, Terence. 1969. "Tchikrin: A Central Brazilian tribe and its symbolic language of bodily adornment." *Natural History* 78:50–59.

———. 1979. "The Gê and Bororo societies as dialectical systems: A general model." In *Dialectical societies: The Gê and Bororo of Central Brazil,* ed. D. Maybury-Lewis, 147–78. Cambridge, Mass.: Harvard University Press.

———. 1980. "The social skin." In *Not work alone,* ed. J. Cherfas and R. Lewin, 112–40. Beverly Hills: Sage.

———. 1984. "Dual opposition, hierarchy, and value: Moiety structure and symbolic polarity in Central Brazil and elsewhere." In *Différences, valeurs, hiérarchie: Textes offerts à Louis Dumont,* ed. J.-C. Galey, 335–70. Paris: Ecole des Hautes Etudes en Sciences Sociales.

Vernant, Jean-Pierre. 1983. *Myth and thought among the Greeks.* London: Routledge & Kegan Paul.

———. 1984. "La belle mort et le cadavre outragé." *Bulletin de la Société de Thanatologie* 58/59:4–18.

———. 1988. *Myth and society in ancient Greece.* Trans. J. Lloyd. New York: Zone Books.

———. 1989. "At man's table: Hesiod's foundation myth of sacrifice." In *The cuisine of sacrifice among the Greeks,* ed. M. Detienne and J. P. Vernant, trans. P. Wissing, 21–86. Chicago: The University of Chicago Press.

Verswijver, Gustaf. 1983–84. "Ciclos nas práticas de nominação kayapó." *Revista do Museu Paulista* 29:97–124.

Vidal, Lux. 1977. *Morte e vida de uma sociedade indígena brasileira.* São Paulo: Editôra Hucitec/Editôra da Universidade de São Paulo.

Viertler, Renate. 1976. *As aldeias bororo: Alguns aspectos de sua organização social.* Série de etnologia 2. São Paulo: Museu Paulista.

Vilaça, Aparecida. 1989. "Comendo como gente: Formas do canibalismo wari (Pakaa Nova)." Master's thesis, Programa de Pós-Graduação em Antropologia Social, Museu Nacional do Rio de Janeiro.

Viveiros de Castro, Eduardo. 1977. Indivíduo e sociedade no Alto Xingu: Os Yawalapíti. Master's thesis, Programa de Pós-Graduação em Antropologia Social, Museu Nacional do Rio de Janeiro.

———. 1982. "O território araweté." Report submitted to Fundação Nacional do Índio, Brasília.

———. 1986. *Araweté: Os deuses canibais.* Rio de Janeiro: J. Zahar/ANPOCS.

Wagley, Charles. 1940. "World view of the Tapirapé Indians." *Journal of American Folklore* 53:252–60.

———. 1977. *Welcome of tears: The Tapirapé Indians of Central Brazil.* New York: Oxford University Press.

Wagley, Charles, and Galvão, Eduardo. 1949. *The Tenetehara Indians of Brazil: A culture in transition.* New York: Columbia University Press.

Weiss, Helga. 1985. "Kayabi (Tupian) kinship terminology." In *South American kinship: Eight kinship systems from Brazil and Colombia,* ed. W. Merrifield, 113–22. Dallas: International Museum of Cultures/ Summer Institute of Linguistics.

Wittgenstein, Ludwig. 1979 [1931]. *Remarks on Frazer's "Golden Bough."* Ed. R. Rhees, trans. A. C. Miles. Atlantic Highlands, N.J.: Humanities Press.

Yalman, Nur. 1962. "The structure of the Sinhalese kindred: a re-examination of the Dravidian terminology." *American Anthropologist* 64: 548–75.

———. 1967. *Under the Bo tree.* Berkeley: University of California Press.

Index